PAIDEIA: THE IDEALS OF GREEK CULTURE

Paideia: the Ideals of Greek Culture

By WERNER JAEGER

Translated from the German Manuscript
By GILBERT HIGHET

VOLUME II

IN SEARCH OF THE DIVINE CENTRE

New York
OXFORD UNIVERSITY PRESS

ΛΙΜΗΝ ΠΕΦΥΚΕ ΠΑΣΙ ΠΑΙΔΕΙΑ ΒΡΟΤΟΙΣ

CONTENTS

PREFACE

TEN YEARS after the writing of the first volume of this work, the second is now published. A third volume will follow it immediately. This preface introduces them both, especially since they constitute together a separate unit within the entire work: for both deal with the intellectual history of ancient Greece in the fourth century B.C., the age of Plato, and therefore supplement each other. These two volumes bring the history of the classical period of Hellas to a close. It is tempting to plan a continuation of the work through the later centuries of antiquity, since the ideals of paideia established by the classical age played such a dominant part in the further development and expansion of Greco-Roman civilization. I shall give a brief outline of this enlarged plan below. But, whether I shall be able to realize that ideal or not, I am grateful to fate for giving me the opportunity of bringing to completion my work on the greatest period of the life of Greece, which, after losing everything that is of this world—state, power, liberty, and civic life in the classical sense of the word—was still able to say with its last great poet, Menander: 'The possession which no one can take away from man is paideia'. It was the same poet who wrote the words chosen for the title-page of this volume: 'Paideia is a haven for all mankind' (*Monost.* 2 and 312).

If we believe that the essence of history is the organic life of individual nations, we must consider the fourth century as a more advanced stage in the decline, not only of Greek political power, but of the internal structure of Greek society. From that point of view we should find it impossible to understand why the period should be so important as to justify a treatment of such length as this. But, in the history of culture, it is an age of unique importance. Through the increasing gloom of political disaster, there now appear, as if called into existence by the needs of the age, the great geniuses of education, with their classical systems of philosophy and political rhetoric. Their cultural ideals, which outlived the independent political existence of their nation, were transmitted to the other peoples of antiquity and their successors as the highest possible expression of humanity. It is customary to study them in that supra-temporal light, free from the thwarted and bitter struggles of their age to attain political and spiritual self-preservation—the struggles which the Greeks characteristically interpreted as the effort to determine the nature of true education and true culture.

However, I have endeavoured, from the beginning of this work, to do something quite different: to explain the social structure and function of Greek ideals of culture against their historical background. It is in that spirit that I have treated the age of Plato in these two volumes; and if they have any worth, they will be particularly valuable for the understanding of Plato's philosophy. For he himself knew so well that his philosophy arose in a particular climate of thought and held a particular historical position in the whole development of the Greek mind, that he always made his dialectic take the dramatic form of a dialogue, and begin with an argument between representatives of various types of contemporary opinion. On the other hand, no great writer more clearly reveals the truth that the only lasting element in history is the spirit, not merely because his own thought survived for millennia, but because early Greece survives in him. His philosophy is a reintegration of the preceding stages of Hellenic culture. For Plato takes up, deliberately and systematically, the various problems of the pre-Platonic period, and works them out on a higher philosophical level. In this sense the entire first volume (not only those sections dealing with the pre-Socratic thinkers, but, even more, those on the lawgivers and poets) should be taken as an introduction to the study of Plato. Throughout this and the succeeding volume it is assumed that their predecessor has already been read.

Again, an indirect light is cast on Plato (who must be the culmination of any history of Greek paideia) by the contrast between his work and character and those of other great figures of the same era, usually studied as though they had no connexion with philosophy. I have attempted to interpret the rivalry of philosophical and anti-philosophical forces for the primacy of culture in the fourth century as a single historical drama, which cannot be broken up without impairing our understanding of the whole and obscuring the position of this antithesis, which is fundamental in the history of humanism down to the present day.

I have not taken the phrase 'fourth century' in the strictly chronological sense. Historically, Socrates belongs to the century before; but I have treated him here as the intellectual turning-point at the beginning of the age of Plato. His real influence began posthumously when the men of the fourth century started disputing about his character and importance; and everything we know of him (apart from Aristophanes' caricature) is a literary reflex of this influence on his younger contemporaries who rose to fame after his death. I was led to discuss medicine as a theory of the nature of man, in Volume III, by considering its strong influence upon the structure of Socrates' and Plato's paideia. It was my original intention to carry my second volume down to the period when Greek culture achieved world domination (see the Preface to Volume I). This plan has now been abandoned, in favour of a more complete analysis of the two chief representatives of paideia in the fourth century: philosophy and rhetoric, from which the two main forms of humanism in later ages were to derive. The Hellenistic age will therefore be treated in a separate book. Aristotle will be discussed with Theophrastus, Menander, and Epicurus, at the beginning of the Hellenistic period, an era whose living roots go deep into the fourth century. Like Socrates, he is a figure who marks the transition between two epochs. And yet, with Aristotle, the Master of those who know, the conception of paideia undergoes a remarkable decrease in intensity, which makes it difficult to set him beside Plato, the true philosopher of paideia. The problems involved in the relation between culture and science, which are characteristic of Hellenistic Alexandria, first come out clearly in the school of Aristotle.

Along with the cultural disputes of the fourth century described in these two volumes, and the impact of humane civilization upon Rome, the transformation of Hellenistic Greek paideia into Christian paideia is the greatest historical theme of this work. If it depended wholly on the will of the writer, his studies would end with a description of the vast historical process by which Christianity was Hellenized and Hellenic civilization became Christianized. It was Greek paideia which laid the groundwork for the ardent, centuries-long competition between the Greek spirit and the Christian religion, each trying to master or assimilate the other, and for their final synthesis. As well as treating their own separate period of history, the second and third volumes of this work are intended to bridge the gap between classical Greek civilization and the Christian culture of late antiquity.

The method of treatment was logically dictated by the nature of my material, which cannot be fully understood unless all the various forms, contrasts, strata, and levels in which Greek paideia appears, both in its individual and in its typical aspects, are carefully differentiated, described, and analysed. What is needed is a morphology of culture in the true historical sense. The 'ideals of Greek culture' are not to be set up separately in the empty space of sociological abstraction, and treated as universal types. Every form of areté, every new moral standard produced by the Greek spirit must be studied in the time and place where it originated—surrounded by the historical forces which called it forth and conflicted with it, and embodied in the work of the great creative writer who gave it its representative artistic form. No less objectively than the historian reports external actions and portrays characters, he must, when concerned with intellectual aspects of reality, record every phenomenon of importance that enters into the field of vision: it may be the ideal of character expressed in Homer's princes, or the aristocratic society reflected in the heroic young athletes of Pindar's poetry, or the democracy of the Periclean age with its ideal of free citizenship. Every phase made its own lasting contribution to the development of Greek civilization, before being supplanted, one and all, by the ideal of the philosophical citizen of the world and the new nobility of 'spiritual' man, which characterize the age of the huge Hellenistic empires, and form a transition to the Christian conception of life. Essential elements in each of these phases survived to later periods. This book frequently points out that Greek culture developed, not by destroying its previous selves, but always by transforming them. The coin which had been current was not thrown away as worthless. It was given a fresh stamp. Philo's rule μεταχάραττε τὸ θεῖον νόμισμα dominated Greek culture, from Homer to Neo-Platonism and the Christian fathers of late antiquity. The Greek spirit works by transcending heights previously reached; but the form in which it works is always ruled by the law of strict continuity.

Every part of this historical process is a stage; but no part is merely a stage and nothing more. For, as a great historian has said, every period is 'directly in touch with God'. Every age has the right to be appraised for its own sake; its value does not merely lie in the fact that it is a tool for making some other period. Its ultimate position in the general panorama of history depends on its power to give spiritual and intellectual form to its own supreme achievement. For it is through that form that it influences later generations more or less strongly and permanently. The function of the historian is to use his imagination to plunge deeply into the life, emotion, and colour of another, more vivid world, entirely forgetting himself and his own culture and society, and thus to think himself into strange lives and unfamiliar ways of feeling, in the same way as the poet fills his characters with the breath of life. This applies not only to the men and women but also to the ideals of the past. Plato has warned us against confusing the poet with his heroes, and his ideals with theirs, or using their contradictory ideas to construct a system which we ascribe to the poet himself. Similarly, the historian must not attempt to reconcile the conflicting ideas which come to the fore in the battle of great minds, or to sit in judgment over them. His task is not to improve the world, but to understand it. The persons with whom he deals may well be in conflict, and thereby limit one another. He must leave it to the philosopher to resolve their antinomy. Nevertheless, this does not make the history of the mind a matter of pure relativism. The historian should not, indeed, undertake to decide who possesses absolute truth. But he is able to use the criterion of Thucydidean objectivity on a large scale to mark out the main lines of a historical pattern, a true cosmogony of values, an ideal world which will survive the birth and death of states and nations. Thereby his work becomes a philosophical drama born of the spirit of historical contemplation.

In writing a history of paideia in the fourth century, the historian's choice of material is largely determined by the type of evidence which has survived. The documents were chosen for preservation in later antiquity entirely because of their relevance to the ideal of paideia; and practically every book which seemed from that point of view to lack representative importance was allowed to perish. The history of Greek paideia merges directly into the history of the transmission and manuscript survival of

classical texts. That is why the actual character and quantity of
the literature preserved from the fourth century are important
for our purpose. Every book surviving from that era is discussed
in this work, in order to show how the idea of paideia is consciously alive in them all, and dominates their form. The only
exception to this is forensic oratory. Although a great quantity
of it has survived, it is not separately treated here. That is not
because it has nothing to do with paideia: Isocrates and Plato
often say that Lysias and his colleagues claimed to be representatives of higher education. It is because political oratory soon
overshadowed the work done by the teachers of juridical rhetoric.
It would be impractical and undesirable to treat both branches
of oratory at length, since the material is so copious; and really
Isocrates and Demosthenes are more impressive oratorical
figures than the men who wrote court-speeches.

The study of Plato forms a book of its own within the two
present volumes. He has been at the centre of my interest for
many years, and naturally my work on him played a decisive part
in my conception of the book. It was principally of Plato that I
was thinking nearly twenty years ago, when I tried to draw the
attention of scholars to that aspect of Greek history which the
Greeks called paideia. I then stated the point of view from which
I have here studied him, in a series of lectures entitled *Platos
Stellung im Aufbau der griechischen Bildung* (Berlin 1928);
and indeed earlier than that, in my essay *Platos Staatsethik*
(Berlin 1924), which is referred to in the text. My ideas have
been diffused by a large number of articles, monographs, and
dissertations on Plato published by my pupils, and have had
some influence beyond that immediate circle; but I have never
before set them down as a connected whole. Surveying the book
now that it is finished, I could wish there had been a chapter on
Plato's *Timaeus,* to examine the relation between his conception
of the cosmos and the fundamental paideutic tendency of his
philosophy. Instead of describing the Academy a second time,
it will be enough to direct my readers to the chapter on it in my
Aristotle; and for Greek philosophical theology I have ventured
to refer to a book which is to be published in the near future.
My preliminary studies for the chapter on Greek medicine out-
grew the limits of this work, and were published as a separate
book (*Diokles von Karystos*). Similarly, my discussions of Isoc-

rates and Demosthenes are based on monographs I have previously published.

The notes are here much more extensive than in the first volume of *Paideia*. It has been necessary to group them all together at the end, which I regret for the sake of scholars who may use the book. However, I have agreed, hoping that a larger public will be encouraged to read it, and appreciating the risk which my publishers have taken by producing a work of such dimensions at this time. I must also thank them sincerely for the care they have given to the format and printing of my book.

I am particularly grateful to my translator, Professor Gilbert Highet of Columbia University, New York, who, although occupied with more urgent duties in war service, has finished translating my German manuscript under considerable difficulties, and has made it, not a translation, but a real English book. Moreover, he has contributed to it by checking and discussing every disputable passage, as well as by helping to settle all sorts of editorial problems. I wish to thank him publicly for his untiring interest in this book throughout its three successive volumes, to which he gave up several years of his own working life, and for the inestimable service which he has rendered to the reception of my work in the English-speaking world.

I also wish to thank my assistant, Dr. Helen A. Brown, for helping me in making the index to Volume II.

WERNER JAEGER

Harvard University
Cambridge, Massachusetts
July 1943.

TRANSLATOR'S NOTE

THIS translation was made from Professor Jaeger's manuscript, since the second and third volumes of his work have not yet been published in Germany. It has been discussed in detail with the author.

Excerpts from Greek books are occasionally expanded or compressed, to correspond with the scale of the quotation in the German manuscript. Where there are several possible interpretations of a passage, I have of course followed that chosen by Professor Jaeger. However, I am responsible for such small variations from custom as calling the φύλακες of the Republic 'guards' rather than 'guardians', which sounds more legal than military.

References are usually to the Oxford Classical Texts.

GILBERT HIGHET

Columbia University, New York

BOOK THREE

IN SEARCH OF THE DIVINE CENTRE

THE FOURTH CENTURY

In 404 B.C., after almost thirty years of war between the Greek states, Athens fell. The most glorious century of Greek achievement ended in the darkest tragedy known to history. The Periclean empire had been the greatest political structure ever built on Hellenic soil; indeed, it had for a time seemed to be the destined home for Greek culture throughout all ages to come. In the funeral speech over the dead Athenian soldiers, which Thucydides wrote soon after the end of the war and put in Pericles' mouth, he still saw Athens as lit by the last beams of that radiance. Through his words there still glows something of the ardour of that brief but brilliant dream, well worthy of the Athenian genius—the dream of building a state so skilfully that it might keep strength and spirit in perpetual equipoise. When he composed that speech, he already knew the paradoxical truth which all his generation had to learn: that even the most solid of earthly powers must vanish into air, and that only the seemingly brittle splendour of the spirit can long endure. It seemed as if the development of Athens had been suddenly reversed. She was thrown back a hundred years, to the epoch of isolated city-states. The victory over Persia, in which she had been the leader and the champion of the Greeks, had allowed her to aspire to hegemony over them. Now, just before she could secure it, it was snatched from her grasp.

The Greek world was convulsed by her disastrous fall. It left a great gap among the Hellenic states, which it proved impossible to fill. The moral and political repercussions of the defeat were felt as long as the state, as such, continued to have any real existence and meaning for the Greeks. From the very first, Greek civilization had been inseparably connected with the life of the city-state; and the connexion was closest of all in Athens. Therefore the effects of the catastrophe were, inevitably, far more than merely political. It shook all moral laws; it struck at the roots of religion. If the disaster was to be repaired, the process must start with religion and ethics. This realization entered both the theorizing of philosophers and the day-to-day life of the average man; because of it, the fourth century was an age of constant endeavours at internal and external reconstruction. But the blow had struck so deep that, from this distance, it seems doubtful from the very start whether the innate Greek belief in the value of this world, their confidence that they could bring 'the best state', 'the best life', into being here and now, could ever have survived such an experience to be re-created in its original purity and vigour. It was in that time of suffering that the Greek spirit first began to turn inwards upon itself—as it was to do more and more throughout the succeeding centuries. But the men of that age, even Plato, still believed that their task was a practical one. They had to change the world, *this* world—even although they might not manage to do it completely at the moment. And (although in a rather different sense) that is how even the practical statesmen now envisaged their mission.

The speed of the external recovery made by the Athenian state, and the vast amount of material and spiritual resources which it called into play, were truly astounding. This supreme crisis showed, more clearly than any other occasion in the history of Athens, that her true strength—even as a state—was the strength of the spirit. It was her spiritual culture which guided her upwards on the path to recovery, which in the time of her gravest need won back the hearts of the Greeks who had turned away from her, and which proved to all Hellas that she had a right to survive, even when she lacked the power to assert it. Therefore the intellectual movement which took place in Athens during the first decades of the fourth century must occupy the centre of our interest, even from the political point of view. When Thucydides looked back to the greatest era of Athenian power, under Pericles, and saw that the heart and soul of that power was the spirit of man, he saw truly. Now, as ever—indeed much more than ever—Athens was the cultural centre of Greece, its *paideusis*. But all its energies were concentrated upon the heavy task set by history to the new generation: the reconstruction of the state and of all life, upon a firm and lasting basis.

During the war, and even before its outbreak, changes in the structure of life had initiated this process, by which all the energies of the higher intellect were focused upon the state. It was not only the new educational theories and experiments of the sophists which pointed in that direction. Poets, orators, and historians too were drawn, ever more irresistibly, into the general current. At the end of the great war, the younger generation had been schooled by the frightful experiences of its last decade to throw all their strength into the task of the moment. If the existing state gave them no worthy social or political work to do, it was inevitable for their energies to seek some intellectual outlet. We have already traced the growth in educational emphasis throughout the art and thought of the fifth century, as far as the great History of Thucydides, which drew the appropriate moral from the political developments of the entire century. The same current of ideas now flows into the great stream of reconstruction. The immediate political and social crisis, with all the suffering it entailed, vastly increased the stress on education, strengthened its importance, enriched its meaning. Thus, the concept of paideia became the real expression of the rising generation's spiritual purpose. The fourth century is the classical epoch in the history of paideia, if we take that to mean the development of *a conscious ideal of education and culture*. There was good reason for it to fall in that critical century. It is that very awareness of its problems that distinguishes the Greek spirit most clearly from other nations. It was simply because the Greeks were fully alive to every problem, every difficulty confronting them in the general intellectual and moral collapse of the brilliant fifth century, that they were able to understand the meaning of their own education and culture so clearly as to become the teachers of all succeeding nations. Greece is the school of the western world.

From an intellectual point of view, the fourth century is the fulfilment of the promise, potential or half-realized, of the fifth and earlier centuries. But under another aspect, it is an age of tremendous revolution. The previous century had been dedicated to the task of bringing democracy to perfection, of attaining the ideal of self-government extended to all free citizens. Even although the ideal was never fully realized, even although many serious objections to its possibility in the world of practical poli-

tics have been raised, still, the world has it to thank for creating
the concept of a personality fully self-conscious and responsible
to itself. Even the reconstructed Athens of the fourth century
could be built on only one possible foundation, equality under
law—*isonomia*. Although Athens had lost the spiritual nobility
of the age of Aeschylus, when it seemed not too bold for an
entire community to aspire to the first rank of culture, that
ideal of equality had by now become classical. The Athenian
state appeared to pay no attention to the fact that, despite huge
material superiority, her defeat had revealed weak spots in her
political structure. The real impression of the Spartan victory is
to be found not in Athenian politics, but in Athenian philosophy
and paideia. The intellectual conflict with the Spartan point of
view exercised Athens all through the fourth century, down to
her death as an independent democratic city-state. The problem
was not so much whether she should accept the fact of Sparta's
victory, and change her laws and institutions to suit. Of course,
that was the reaction immediately after the defeat; but a year
after the war's end, the 'Thirty Tyrants' were expelled, and the
reaction swiftly stopped. But even when the democratic constitution was 'restored' and a general amnesty proclaimed, the problem was neither solved nor forgotten. It was simply shifted to
another sphere: away from that of practical politics to that of
intellectual effort for inward regeneration. People came to believe that Sparta was not so much a certain kind of constitution
as a certain type of educational system carried out with relentlessly consistent logic. Her strength lay in rigid discipline. But
democracy too, by its optimistic belief that men were capable of
ruling themselves, assumed that they should all be highly educated. This naturally suggested that education should be made
the fulcrum upon which (as in Archimedes' epigram) the world,
the political world, could be moved. This was not an ideal calculated to enthrall the masses; but that made it captivate the
imagination of the spiritual leaders all the more deeply. The
literature of the fourth century displays it in every possible
nuance: from ingenuous and uncritical admiration of the Spartan
principle of collective education, to complete rejection of that
principle, and its replacement by a newer and loftier ideal of
culture and of the relation between individual and community.
And there are others who preach neither the foreign ideals of

the victorious foe, nor a philosophical Utopia of their own creation, but the past glories of their own Athens. Looking back-
ward, they strive to unmake history; yet often the splendid historical past they admire and try to revive is merely the reflection
of their own political principles. Much of that is romantic antiquarian dreaming. But it undeniably contains a note of stern
realism—for it always starts from a trenchant criticism of the
present day and its inadequate ideals. And all these preachments
take the form of educational effort: that is, of paideia.

The men of the fourth century thought hard about the relation of state and individual, because they were trying to remake
the state, starting from a moral reformation in the individual
soul. But there was another reason too. It was that they had
come to understand how much the individual citizen's life is
affected by social and political factors—as was inevitable in
Greece, which had always been a land of city-states. The attempt
to create a new type of education in order to make the state
stronger and better was inevitably bound to make them conscious of the reciprocal influence of individual and community
upon each other. They naturally came to think that Athenian
education, hitherto run on an entirely private system, was fundamentally wrong and ineffective, and should be replaced by communal education. The state itself took no steps to answer this
claim; the philosophers took it up, and managed to get it universally accepted. Even the collapse of the city-state's political
independence only illuminated its importance and its meaning
more clearly. Here, as so often in history, the knowledge which
might have saved came too late. Not till after the catastrophe
at Chaeronea did the Athenians gradually realize that their state
should be penetrated with the ideal of paideia, of a culture which
suited the Athenian spirit. The sole extant speech of the orator
and legislator Lycurgus (*Against Leocrates*) is a document of
that patriotic regeneration. He took up Demosthenes' efforts
to re-educate the Athenian people, and tried to make them something more than mere improvisation, by proposing legal enact-
ments to systematize them. But this does not change the fact that
the great systems of paideia created during the fourth century,
although they grew up under the protection of freedom of
thought, were not intellectually rooted in contemporary Athenian
democracy. The catastrophe of defeat and the spiritual difficulties

---

of democracy did indeed give the initial impulse to those trains of reasoning; but after they were set in motion, they could not be confined within the limits set by tradition, and did not restrict themselves to defending tradition either. They went their own way, and worked out their new ideal systems with perfect liberty. Not only in religion and ethics, but in politics and education too, the Greek mind soared high above the here-and-now, and created an independent spiritual world for itself. Its journey towards a new paideia started with its realization that a newer and higher ideal of state and society was necessary, but it ended with the search for a new God. The paideia of the fourth century, after it saw the kingdom of earth blown into dust, fixed its home in the kingdom of heaven.

Even in the external development of literature we can see an end, and a new beginning. The great poetic forms—tragedy and comedy—moulded by the fifth century were indeed still utilized, because they had the prestige of tradition: an astonishing number of respectable poets continued to write in them. But the mighty inspiration of tragedy had vanished. Poetry now lost its spiritual leadership. More and more, the public called for regular revivals of the masterpieces of last century, and finally they were ordered by law. Partly, the great plays had become cultural classics—they were learnt at school, and quoted as authorities in speeches and treatises, like Homer and the early poets; and partly —since it was acting which had come to dominate the stage— they were used as valuable vehicles for modern actors to experiment with, heedless of their form and content, and interested only in the possibilities of histrionic effect. Comedy went stale. Politics was no longer its main interest. It is too easy to forget that even in the fourth century an enormous amount of poetry (particularly comic poetry) was still being written. But all those thousands of plays have disappeared. All the literature that has been preserved is the work of the great prosaists—Plato, Xenophon, Isocrates, Demosthenes, Aristotle, and a number of lesser spirits. And yet this apparently arbitrary choice is just: for the real creative work of the fourth century was done in prose. Its intellectual superiority to poetry was so overpowering that it finally blotted all trace of its rival out of history. It was only New Comedy, beginning in the second half of the fourth century with Menander and his fellow-artists, that had much influence on men of that and later ages. That was the last type of Greek poetry which was really addressed to a wide public—not indeed to the polis, like its predecessors (Old Comedy and Tragedy of the great age), but to 'cultured' society, whose life and ideas are mirrored in it. Yet the real struggles of the age appear, not in the sensitive and humane speeches, the civilized converse of this decorous art, but in those far deeper explorations of truth, the dialogues of the new philosophical prose-poetry, in which Plato and his associates revealed to the outer world the innermost meaning of Socrates' search for the aim of life. And the orations of Isocrates and Demosthenes allow us to take part in the problems and sufferings of the Greek city-state, in this, the final phase of its existence.

These new types of prose literature are more than reflections of their authors' personalities. They are the expression of great and influential schools of philosophy and rhetoric, of violent political and ethical movements, the movements in which all the energies of thinking men were concentrated. Even the form in which these efforts find their outlet distinguishes the intellectual life of the fourth century from that of the fifth. Thinkers now make systems, announce programmes, work for stated ends. Contemporary literature embodies the conflicts of all these schools and doctrines. They are all still in their passionate youth: and their general interest is vastly enhanced by the fact that their problems grow directly out of the life of their time. The centre of the entire struggle is paideia. In it all the various expressions of contemporary thought—philosophy, rhetoric, and science—find a higher unity. And they are joined by the practical subjects —politics, economics, law, strategy, hunting, agriculture, travel, and adventure—the special sciences like mathematics and medicine, and the arts of sculpture, painting, and music. They all offer their contribution to the problem which exercised all Greece at that time. They are forces which claim to mould character, to impart culture: and they profess to explain the principles on which their claim is based. This vital inner unity in the epoch with which we are dealing cannot be grasped and explained in a purely literary history of the type so common in recent years, concerned with mere form, with the stylistic *eidos* or pattern. It is in the bitter but magnificently enthusiastic struggle to determine the nature of true paideia that the real life of the period finds its characteristic expression; and the literature of that time is real only in so far as it shares in that struggle. Prose won its victory over poetry through the alliance between the strong educational forces that had been increasingly important in early Greek poetry, and the rational thought of this age, which was now more and more concerned with the real problems of human life. And at last the philosophic or protreptic element in literature cast off its poetic form entirely. It made itself a new form, more suited to its needs, and able to compete with poetry on its own ground—indeed, a new and higher type of poetry in itself.

The spiritual life of Greece was being concentrated within limited schools or narrow intellectual societies. Thence, such schools and societies gained a new cultural energy, and a richer, fuller life of their own. But compare this with earlier ages. Then, higher culture was the preserve of one class (e.g. the ruling aristocracy), or was imparted to the entire nation in the form of great poetry, through words and music, dance and gesture. In this new era, the spirit was dangerously separated from society, and suffered the fatal loss of its function as a constructive force within the community. That loss always occurs when poetry ceases to be the medium for intellectual creative work, and for the definitive utterances of life; and when it gives way to more strictly rational forms. Easy as it is to observe this after it has happened, the process of change appears to be subject to fixed laws, and, once it is complete, cannot be reversed at will. Consequently, the power of moulding the nation as a whole, so richly possessed by poets in early times, did not increase as awareness of the educational problem and the earnestness of educational experiments increased. On the contrary, we feel that as the more binding forces of life—religion, morality, and 'music', which for the Greeks always included poetry—lost their power, so the masses escaped from the formative influence of the spirit. Instead of drawing from the pure spring, they contented themselves with cheap and flashy substitutes. The standards and ideals to which every class in the nation once paid allegiance were still announced, and that too with increased rhetorical embellishment; but less and less real attention was paid to them. People enjoyed hearing about them, and could be enthralled for the moment; but few were moved from the heart by them, and for most people they were useless at the critical moment. It is easy to say that the cultured classes ought to have tried to bridge the gulf. The greatest man of his age, the thinker who saw the difficulty involved in building up society and the state more clearly than any other, was Plato; and Plato in his old age took up that challenge. He explained why he was unable to give a universal gospel. Despite all the conflicts between the philosophical culture he represented and the ideal of education through politics maintained by his great opponent Isocrates, there was in this respect no difference between them. Nevertheless the will to make the highest powers of the spirit contribute to building up a new society was never more serious and more conscious than in this age. But it was chiefly directed to solving the problem of educating leaders and rulers of the people; and only after that to discovering the method to be used by the leaders in moulding the community.

The point of attack has shifted. This shift, which (in principle) began with the sophists, distinguished the new century from its predecessor; and at the same time it marked the beginning of a historical epoch. The new colleges and schools took their origin from that new attitude to the problem. They were closed societies, and that fact can be understood only from their origin, which rendered it inevitable. Of course it is hard to say what influence they could have exercised on the social and political life of Greece, if history had granted them a longer time to make their endeavour. Their true effect turned out to be quite different from that which they at first envisaged; for after the final collapse of the independent Greek city-state, they created western science and philosophy, and paved the way for the universal religion, Christianity. That is the real significance of the fourth century for the world. Philosophy, science, and their constant enemy, the formal power of rhetoric—these are the vehicles through which the spiritual legacy of the Greeks was transmitted to their contemporaries and successors in the East and West, and to which, above all else, we owe its preservation. They handed on that inheritance in the form and with the principles which it got from the fourth-century effort to determine the nature of paideia—that is, it was the epitome of Greek culture and education, and Greece made its spiritual conquest of the world under that motto. From the point of view of the Greek nation, it might appear that the price they paid for this title to universal glory was too great. And yet we must remember that the Greek state did not die of its culture; philosophy, science, and rhetoric were only the form in which what was immortal in the Greek achievement could be handed on. Thus, over all the development of the fourth century there lies the tragic shadow of collapse; and yet there falls on it the radiance of a providential wisdom, before whose face the earthly destiny of the most gifted nation is only one day within the long life of its historical achievement.

THE MEMORY OF SOCRATES

ὁ ἀνεξέταστος βίος οὐ βιωτὸς ἀνθρώπῳ

SOCRATES is one of the imperishable figures who have become symbolic. The real man, the citizen of Athens who was born about 469 and executed in 399 B.C., shed most of his personality as he entered history and became for all eternity a 'representative man'. It was not really his life or his doctrine (so far as he had any doctrine) which raised him to such eminence, so much as the death he suffered for the conviction on which his life was founded. In the later Christian era he was given the crown of a pre-Christian martyr; and the great humanist of the Reformation period, Erasmus of Rotterdam, boldly numbered him among his saints, and invoked him with 'Sancte Socrates, ora pro nobis!' But that very prayer, although there clings to it a reminiscence of the Church and the Middle Ages, breathes the spirit of that new epoch which opened with the Renaissance. In medieval times Socrates was scarcely more than an illustrious name mentioned by Aristotle and Cicero. But with the Renaissance his side of the balance suddenly rose, while that of Aristotle, the prince of scholasticism, sank down. Socrates became the leader of all modern enlightenment and modern philosophy, the apostle of moral liberty, bound by no dogma, fettered by no tradition, standing free on his own feet, listening only to the inner voice of conscience—preaching the new religion of this world, and a heaven to be found in this life by our own spiritual strength, not through grace but through tireless striving to perfect our own nature. Yet these phrases are inadequate to express all that he has meant to the centuries since the close of the Middle Ages. No new ethical or religious idea could be born, no spiritual movement could develop, without appealing to him. The rebirth of Socrates was brought about not simply by a revival of scholarly interest, but by a genuine enthusiasm for his mind and character as they were described in Greek writings now rediscovered, especially in the books of Xenophon.[1]

However, nothing could be further from the truth than the idea that, whereas the Middle Ages had made Aristotle the basis of all Christian philosophy, all the efforts which were made to found a new 'religion of humanity' under Socrates' leadership were in opposition to Christianity. On the contrary: the pagan philosopher now helped to create a modern culture in which the indestructible content of Jesus' teaching was blended with certain essential features taken from the Greek ideal of humanity. This was brought about by the revolutionary new view of life which now thrust its way to mastery—a view made up of increasing confidence in human reason and increasing awe of the newly discovered law of nature. Reason and Nature had been the foundations of classical civilization. When Christianity deliberately sought to take over these principles and make them part of itself, it was doing exactly what it had been doing since the first centuries of its expansion. Every new epoch of Christian development had, in its own way, challenged and conquered the classical conceptions of man and God. In this unending process, it was the role of Greek philosophy (with its vast power of refined abstract reasoning) to offer an intellectual defence of 'Reason' and 'Nature' and their rights—in other words, to function as 'rational theology' or 'natural theology'. After the Reformation had made the first serious attempt to return to the 'pure' form of the Gospel, there followed, as an inevitable reaction and compensation, the Socrates-cult of the age of enlightenment. This cult did not attempt to displace Christianity, but to give it additional forces which seemed to the men of that age indispensable. Even pietism—the revolt of pure Christian feeling against a rational theology which had hardened into lifelessness—appealed to Socrates' name and believed him to be a spiritual ally. Socrates was often compared to Christ. To-day, we can see the real importance of a possible reconciliation, brought about by Greek philosophy, between Christian religion and 'the natural man', and we can judge how greatly such a reconciliation would be helped by a picture of classical culture that centred on the figure of Socrates.

Since the beginning of the modern era, he has had an enormous influence as the pattern of an *anima naturaliter Christiana*. But he paid dearly for his fame when Nietzsche renounced Christianity and proclaimed the advent of the Superman. Soc-

rates appeared to be so long and closely linked to the dualistic
Christian ideal, by which each person was split into two separate
parts, body and soul, that he was bound to fall along with it.
At the same time, Nietzsche's hatred for him revived, in a new
guise, the old hatred of Erasmus' humanism for the scholastic
notion that life and humanity could be reduced to a number of
abstract concepts. He held not Aristotle but Socrates to be the
real embodiment of the rigidly intellectual academic philosophy
which had kept the European mind in chains for more than half
a thousand years, and which he (a true pupil of Schopenhauer)
saw still at work in the theological type of thought represented
by the German Idealistic school.[2] He owed much of this conception of Socrates to the picture of the philosopher drawn by
Zeller, in his then epoch-making *History of Greek Philosophy;*
and that in its turn was influenced by Hegel's reconstruction of
the dialectic process in which the mind of western Europe had
developed by reconciling the conflict between classical and Christian ideals. Now a new humanism was proclaimed, which turned
to combat the prestige of this mighty tradition. It discovered
and canonized what it called 'pre-Socratic' Greek thought. *Pre-
Socratic* really meant *pre-philosophical.* For Nietzsche and his
followers, the thinkers of that archaic age blended with the great
poets and musicians of their time into a composite portrait entitled 'The Tragic Age of Greece'.[3] In the tragic age and its
works, the Apollinian and Dionysian elements which Nietzsche
strove to unite were still miraculously conjoined. Body and soul
were still one. In that springtime, the glorious Hellenic harmony
(so weakly and poorly realized by the men of the afterworld)
was still a calm mirror-surface, hiding dangerous and unplumbed
depths beneath. But when Socrates brought about the victory
of the reasoning, the Apollinian element, he destroyed the tension in which it had counterweighed the irrational Dionysian
element, and thereby broke the harmony. He (declared
Nietzsche) took the tragic view of life held by archaic Greece
and made it ethical, made it intellectual, made it an academic
corpse.[4] All the idealizing, moralizing, and spiritualizing vapour
into which the energies of the later Greeks dissipated themselves
was spun out of Socrates' brain. He had been considered by
Christian thought to be the utmost possible limit of 'Nature'

which could be tolerated; and now Nietzsche asserted that he had really driven Nature out of Greek life and put the Unnatural in its place. Thus Socrates was deprived of the secure, if not supreme, place which the nineteenth-century idealists had assigned him in their historical picture, and was once more drawn into the intellectual battles of the present. Once again he became a symbol, as he had so often been in the seventeenth and eighteenth centuries; but now he was a negative symbol, a sign of corruption and defeat.

To be singled out for this great attack was, in a way, an honour to Socrates; and it increased the intensity of the dispute about his real importance. Whether Nietzsche's violently icono-clastic judgment were true or not, it was still the first sign in many years that Socrates had not lost his strength and his challenge. Superman felt him to be a dangerous threat to the security of his own existence! We can hardly say that Nietzsche drew a new picture of Socrates. In this age of acute historical consciousness, drawing a new picture of a historical character means something directly opposite to what Nietzsche did, in detaching Socrates almost entirely from his age and his concrete surroundings. But surely Socrates, far more than most great figures, deserves to be judged within his own historical context—Socrates, who was so absorbed in the task set him by his own age that he did not deign to leave a single line of writing to posterity. In his relentless war against the excessive rationaliza-tion of modern life, Nietzsche had neither interest in nor sympa-thy for the spiritual difficulties of Socrates' time. Still, that crisis (which we have described as 'the crisis of the Athenian soul') was the moment in which history chose to place Socrates: des-tiny made it the background of his life. But even if Socrates is judged predominantly in relation to his place and time, there are still many possibilities of misunderstanding him—as is clear from the large number of portraits of Socrates which have recently been given to the world. Uncertainty and eccentricity of thought are commoner in dealing with him than in any other question in the whole history of classical thought. We must therefore begin our discussion with the elementary facts.

THE SOCRATIC PROBLEM

The most elementary fact we can grasp is not Socrates himself, because he wrote nothing, but a number of works by his pupils, all written about the same time. It is impossible to say definitely whether some of these were published during his lifetime, but it is highly probable that they were not.[5] There are obvious parallels, often pointed out, between the origins of the Socratic literature and those of the earliest Christian tradition about the life and teachings of Jesus. As with Jesus, it was only after Socrates' death that his influence on his pupils grew into a definite picture of him. That overwhelming experience made a deep and violent break in their lives. Apparently it was under the impact of the catastrophe that they began to write down what they knew of their master.[6] And then the portrait of Socrates, which had hitherto been fluid and mutable, began to grow rigid, and its features to be fixed for his contemporaries and for posterity. Plato even makes him tell the jury, speaking in his own defence, that his followers and friends will not leave the Athenians in peace after his death, but will carry on his work as a relentless questioner and adviser.[7] The programme of the Socratic movement is contained in these words, and its influence was multiplied by the rapidly growing Socratic literature.[8] His pupils determined that the unforgettable personality of the man, whom earthly justice had killed in order to obliterate him and his words from the memory of the Athenian people, should be so immortalized that neither then nor thereafter could his warnings ever grow faint in men's ears. The moral disquietude which had until then been confined to the small circle of his adherents now spread until it affected the public at large. His thought became the focal point of all the literature and philosophy of the new century, and the movement arising from it was, after Athens' temporal power collapsed, the mainstay of its worldwide spiritual dominion.

From the remains of that literature which have come down to us—Plato's dialogues, Xenophon's dialogues, Xenophon's *Memoirs of Socrates,* and the fragments of the dialogues written by Antisthenes and Aeschines of Sphettus—different as they are in many respects, one thing is clear: the chief aim of his pupils was to re-create the incomparable personality of the master who had transformed their lives. The dialogue and the biographical memoir are new literary forms invented by the Socratic circle to serve that purpose.[9] Both owe their existence to the conviction of his pupils that Socrates' intellectual and spiritual power as a teacher could not be dissociated from his character as a man. Difficult as it was to give a clear impression of his personality to men who had never seen or met him, it was imperative that the attempt be made. We can hardly overemphasize the revolutionary daring of such an enterprise, from the Greek point of view. The Greek's way of looking at men and human character was just as much governed by convention as his own private and public life. We can see how Socrates might have been eulogized in the manner dominant in the classical period, if we look at another literary genre which was invented in the first half of the fourth century—the encomium. This genre too was created in order to express admiration for an outstanding individual; but its only method of doing so was to assert that its object possessed all the virtues appropriate to the ideal citizen or the ideal ruler. The truth about Socrates could never have been told in that way. And so, from the study of his character, there arose for the first time the art of psychological description, whose greatest master in antiquity was Plato. The literary portrait of Socrates is the only truly lifelike description of a great and original personality created in classical Greece. Those who created it meant neither to explore the recesses of the human soul nor to engage in fine-drawn ethical investigations, but to reproduce the impression of what we call *personality*—although they had neither the concept of personality nor words to express it. Socrates' example had changed the meaning of areté; and that change is reflected in the inexhaustible interest that attaches, then as now, to his character.

But his character was chiefly expressed in his influence over others. It worked through the spoken word. He himself never wrote anything down, since he held that the only important thing was the relation between the word and the living man to whom it was, at one particular moment, addressed. This was an almost insuperable difficulty for anyone who wished to describe him, especially since he used to converse in questions and answers—a form which would not fit any of the traditional literary patterns. That is true, even if we assume that some of his conversations had been recorded and could therefore be reconstructed with some accuracy, as is shown by the example of Plato's *Phaedo*. It was that difficulty which moved Plato to create the dialogue-form, the form that was copied by the other pupils of Socrates.[10] But although we can come very close to the personal character of Socrates, particularly through the writings of Plato, his pupils differed so radically from one another about the content of his conversations that they soon came to open dispute and lasting enmity. In his early essays Isocrates shows how this exhibition delighted malicious observers from outside the charmed circle, and how much easier it made the task of the 'opposition' in turning the unenlightened against the Socratics. A few years after Socrates died, the group of his adherents broke up. Each of his disciples clung passionately to his own idea of the master's teaching, and there actually arose a number of different Socratic schools. Hence the paradox that, although we have far more historical tradition about Socrates than about any other ancient philosopher, we still cannot agree about his real significance. It is true that to-day, with increased skill in historical understanding and psychological interpretation, we seem to have firmer ground to stand on. But the pupils of Socrates whose descriptions we read have so closely fused their own characters with his (simply because they could not separate themselves from his effect on them) that it is doubtful whether, after thousands of years, we can ever distil out of that compound the pure Socratic essence.

The form of the Platonic dialogue was quite certainly created by a historical fact—the fact that Socrates taught by question and answer. He held that form of dialogue to be the original pattern of philosophic thought, and the only way for two people to reach an understanding on any subject. And the aim of his life was to reach understanding with the people he talked to. Plato, a born dramatist, had written tragedies before he met Socrates. According to tradition, he burnt them after he felt the impact of the great questioner's personality. But when, after Socrates' death, Plato determined to keep his master alive, he found that, in imitating the conversations of Socrates, he could enlist his dramatic genius in the service of philosophy. Not only the dialogue-form, however, owes its origin to Socrates. The fact that certain highly characteristic paradoxical utterances occur again and again in the conversations of Plato's Socrates, and reappear in the Socratic writings of Xenophon, makes it certain that the content of Plato's dialogues does to some extent stem from Socrates' thought. The problem is how far they are really Socratic. Xenophon's records agree with Plato only to a small extent, and then leave us with the feeling that Xenophon says too little, and Plato too much. Even Aristotle expressed the view that most of the philosophy attributed by Plato to Socrates was not his, but Plato's doctrine. On that judgment he based several assumptions whose value we shall examine later (p. 23). He holds Plato's dialogues to be a new artistic form, midway between poetry and prose.[11] That doubtless refers first of all to the form, which is really that of an intellectual drama in prose. But, considering Aristotle's view of the freedom with which Plato handled the historical Socrates, we must infer that he considered the dialogues to be a mixture of poetry and prose in content as well as in form: they blend *Wahrheit und Dichtung,* Truth and Imagination.[12]

Naturally, any attempt to use the dialogues of Xenophon and the other pupils of Socrates as historical sources is subject to the same doubts and difficulties. The *Apology* of Xenophon (often dismissed as spurious, but lately accepted as genuine once more) is immediately suspect because of its obvious intention to whitewash Socrates.[13] But his *Memoirs of Socrates* (the *Memorabilia*) were long held to be historically reliable. If they were, we should be immediately freed from all the uncertainty which attends every step we make in discussing the dialogues. But recent research has shown that the *Memoirs* too are heavy with subjective colouring.[14] Xenophon knew and admired Socrates as a young man, but was never one of his regular pupils. He soon left him, to serve as a soldier of fortune in the campaign undertaken by the rebellious Persian prince Cyrus against his brother Artaxerxes. He never saw him again. His books about him were mostly composed some decades later. The only apparently early one is the *Defence*—a vindication of Socrates against a certain 'indictment'.[15] This 'indictment' was obviously a literary fiction, and has been identified with a pamphlet published between 400 and 390 by the sophist Polycrates. Lysias and Isocrates certainly wrote replies to it, but we learn from Xenophon's *Memoirs* that he took up the cudgels at the same time.[16] It was evidently this *Defence* that first brought Xenophon (already half-forgotten as a friend of Socrates) into the circle of Socratic writers, although he was silent for many years after writing it. He later attached it to the beginning of the *Memoirs;* but its structural unity, its completeness, and its definite purpose are enough to show that it was once a separate work.[17]

Its purpose, like that of the *Memoirs* themselves, is admittedly to show that Socrates was in the highest degree a patriotic, pious, and righteous citizen of the Athenian state, who sacrificed to the gods, consulted soothsayers, helped his friends in trouble, and always did his duty in public life. The only objection to this is that, if Socrates had been simply a Babbitt, he would never have aroused the suspicion of his fellow-citizens, far less have been condemned to death as dangerous to the state. Recently, Xenophon's appraisal of Socrates has been made even more difficult to accept, by scholars who have undertaken to prove that he was writing so long after the events recorded, and that he had so little talent for philosophical thought, that he had to base his work on other books, particularly those of Antisthenes. If true, this would be interesting: it would allow us to reconstruct the work of a pupil of Socrates and opponent of Plato who is as good as lost to us. But it would reduce Xenophon's Socrates to a mere mouthpiece for Antisthenes' moral disquisitions. No doubt the hypothesis has been pushed too far; but such investigations keep us alive to the possibility that Xenophon, despite, or even because of, his philosophical *naïveté,* created a picture of Socrates which is in many features quite as subjective as we believe Plato's to have been.[18]

Such being the character of the evidence, is it possible to escape the horns of this dilemma? Schleiermacher was the first to express the full complexity of this historical problem in a single condensed question. He too had reached the conviction that we can trust neither Xenophon nor Plato exclusively, but must, like skilful diplomats, play one party off against the other. So he asked: 'What *can* Socrates have been, in addition to all Xenophon says he was, without contradicting the characteristic qualities and rules of life that Xenophon definitely declares to have been Socratic—and what *must* he have been, to give Plato the impulse and the justification to portray him as he does in the dialogues?'[19] Of course these words are not an *Open Sesame* to the whole question. They merely define as accurately as possible the doubtful sphere within which we must use as much critical finesse as we can. They would certainly let us fall helplessly back on our own subjective impressions, if there were not another criterion to tell us how far we should follow each source of evidence.

That criterion was long held to be provided by the remarks of Aristotle on the subject. He appeared to be a disinterested scholar and thinker, who had not such passionate personal interest in proving who Socrates was and what he meant as had Socrates' immediate pupils, and who was still near enough him in time to know more about him than was possible for any modern.[20] Aristotle's historical statements about Socrates are all the more valuable to us because they are confined to one problem: the relation between Socrates and Plato's doctrine of Ideas. That was a central problem, much debated in Plato's Academy; and besides, in the twenty years that Aristotle spent there, he must often have heard the question of the origin of that doctrine discussed. Now, Plato's dialogues present Socrates as the philosopher who puts forward the doctrine of Ideas, and who definitely assumes that it is known to his pupils. Is Plato's portrayal of Socrates historically accurate in this matter, or is it not? The question is fundamentally important if we hope to reconstruct the intellectual process which led from Socrates' teaching to the creation of Plato's philosophy. Aristotle, who does not accept the doctrine of Ideas—that universal concepts have an objective existence distinct from the existence of the individual things perceived by the senses—makes three important statements about Plato's relation to Socrates on this point.

(1) As a young student, Plato attended the lectures of the Heraclitean Cratylus, who taught that everything flows and nothing has a permanent existence. Then, when he met Socrates, a new world opened up to him. Socrates confined himself entirely to questions of morality, and tried to discover the eternal essence of the Just, the Good, the Beautiful, etc. At first glance, the idea that everything changes and the assumption that there is a permanent truth seem to be mutually exclusive. But Cratylus had so entirely convinced Plato that everything changes, that his conviction could not be shaken even by the powerful impres-

sion he received from Socrates' determined search for a fixed point in the ethical world. Plato therefore concluded that Cratylus and Socrates were both right, because they were speaking of two different worlds. Cratylus' statement that everything flows referred to the only world that he knew—the world of sensible phenomena; and Plato continued even later to maintain that the doctrine of eternal change was true for the world of sense. But Socrates, in the search for the conceptual essence of those predicates like 'good', 'just', 'beautiful', on which our existence as moral beings is based, was looking towards a different reality, which does not flow but truly 'is'—because it remains immutably and eternally the same.

(2) The universal concepts, to which Socrates had introduced him, Plato now considered to compose the world of true Being, which is remote from the world of eternal change. He named these essences, which we can grasp only in thought, and in which the world of true Being consists, the Ideas. In this he went beyond Socrates—who had neither spoken of Ideas nor assumed that they were separate from the world of sense.

(3) According to Aristotle, Socrates can be justly and indisputably credited with two things: he defined the general concepts, and he used the inductive method to discover them.[21]

If this account is correct, it makes it very much easier to distinguish the Socratic and the Platonic elements in the figure of Socrates presented to us in Plato's dialogues. Schleiermacher's research-formula need not remain an unattainable ideal, but can in some degree be put into practice. In those dialogues which the research of the last century has shown to be Plato's earliest works, Socrates is really always asking about universals: what is courage? what is piety? what is self-control? And even Xenophon, in passing, expressly says that Socrates constantly carried out enquiries of that nature and tried to define such concepts.[22] There is then, it seems, a way of escape from our dilemma: *Plato or Xenophon?* Socrates is the founder of the philosophy of abstract concepts. That is how Zeller, carrying out Schleiermacher's method of investigation in his *History of Greek Philosophy,* presents him.[23] According to this conception, Socrates was, so to speak, a modest preparatory stage before Plato's philosophy. He avoided Plato's daring metaphysical adventures, and, by turning away from nature and confining himself to ethical questions, showed that his real interest was in finding a theoretical basis for a new practical rule of life.

For many years this was accepted as the final solution of the problem. It was based on the great authority of Aristotle, and buttressed by sound scientific method. But it could not be permanently satisfactory, because it made Socrates into a thin and unconvincing figure, and his conceptual philosophy into a mere triviality. That was the abstract academic figure whom Nietzsche so savagely attacked. There were many whose belief that Socrates was a figure of world-shaking importance could not be destroyed by Nietzsche; and they simply lost their faith in Aristotle's reliability. Was he really perfectly disinterested about the origin of the doctrine of Ideas which he so violently opposed? Was he himself not mistaken in his account of the historical facts? Was he not governed, especially in his ideas about the history of philosophy, by his own philosophical preconceptions? Surely it was quite understandable that he should pass by Plato and go back to Socrates, and make Socrates more moderate—i.e. more Aristotelian? But did he really know any more about him than what he thought he could discover from Plato's dialogues? With these and similar questions modern research into the teaching of Socrates began.[24] Once more scholars had to abandon the firm ground on which they had built; and nothing proves the uncertainty of the question to-day more clearly than the polar differences between the various portraits of Socrates which have been worked out since. A good example is provided by the two most impressive and most scholarly modern attempts to find the historical Socrates—the great book on him by the Berlin philosopher, Heinrich Maier, and the work done by the Scottish school which is represented by the philologist J. Burnet and the philosopher A. E. Taylor.[25]

Both parties begin by dismissing Aristotle's evidence. Both consider Socrates to be one of the greatest men who ever lived. The dispute between them can be reduced to one question—was Socrates really a philosopher, or was he not? They agree that he was not, if the earlier view of him was right in describing him as merely a subsidiary figure standing at the entrance to Plato's mighty philosophical edifice. But they differ widely in their reasoning beyond this. According to Maier, the greatness of Socrates cannot possibly be measured by judging him simply as a theoretical philosopher. What he did was to create a new attitude towards life, which formed the climax of a long and painful ascent towards human freedom, and which can never be transcended by any other. The gospel he preached was the self-mastery and self-sufficiency of the moral character. Thus he was the antitype of Christ, and of the oriental religion of redemption. The struggle between these two principles, these two gospels, is even now only beginning. Not Socrates, but Plato, founded philosophical idealism, created logic, discovered the abstract universal. Plato was a wholly different and independent person, not to be compared with Socrates: he was a systematic thinker, a constructor of theories. In his dialogues he used the freedom of the artist to attribute his theories to Socrates. It is only in his early works that he gives a picture of Socrates as he actually was.[26]

The Scottish scholars also hold that Plato is the only pupil of Socrates who could really give a sympathetic picture of his master—but they think that he did so in *all* his Socratic dialogues. Xenophon, for them, is the Philistine *par excellence,* who does not understand anything of Socrates' real significance. But he realized his own limitations, and therefore undertook merely to write supplements to other men's books about Socrates. Wherever he touches a real philosophical problem, he turns away, and contents himself with a brief hint to show the reader that Socrates was much greater than he can depict him. According to this view, the great mistake in current thought about Socrates is to believe that Plato did not intend to describe him as he really was, but meant to show him to be the creator of Plato's own Ideas, although he had nothing to do with them. Plato was not a man who could thus palter in a double sense. Some have made an artificial distinction between the early Plato and the later Plato, and have assumed that only the 'early Plato' wanted to depict Socrates' self, while the 'later Plato' used his master as a mask for his own gradually developing philosophy. This, according to the Scottish school, is inherently improbable. Besides, Plato's early dialogues presuppose the doctrine of his later and more constructive works (e.g. *Phaedo* and *The Republic*). The real truth is that, as soon as Plato stopped setting forth Socrates' teaching and began to expound his own doctrines instead, he stopped using Socrates as the leading figure in his dialogues, and, with perfect consistency, used other persons, sometimes anonymous, to express them. Socrates was just what Plato says he was—the man who created the doctrine of Ideas, the theory of pre-existence and reminiscence, the creed of immortality, and the ideal state. In a word, he was the father of European metaphysics.[27]

These are the two extreme views of the question. In one, Socrates is not a philosopher at all, but an ethical inspiration, a hero of the moral life. In the other, he is the creator of speculative philosophy, which Plato personifies in him. The meaning of this dichotomy is simply that the old division which, apparently immediately after Socrates' death, split his disciples into opposing schools, has reappeared, and once again each school is creating its own Socrates. There are, as before, two main parties. Antisthenes denied that it was possible to know anything, and the centre of his doctrine was 'Socratic strength', the inflexible moral will. Plato on the other hand held that Socrates' pretence of knowing nothing was merely a stage on the way to discovering a deeper, more unshakable knowledge of values already latent in the soul. Each of these two interpreters once more steps forward to claim that his own Socrates is the true Socrates, with all his thought brought to completion. It cannot be merely a coincidence that the same two contradicting views should have appeared after Socrates' death and reappeared in our own day. Nor can we explain its reappearance by the fact that our evidence stems from one or the other of these parties. No: Socrates' own personality must have contained the duality which makes him intelligible to both of them at once. It is from that point of view that we must attempt to transcend the inadequacy of both views—for they are inadequate, although in a sense each of them is factually and historically justified. Although both Maier on the one hand and Burnet and Taylor on the other approach the problem on historical principles, their own ways of thinking have coloured their interpretation of the facts. Each party has felt it impossible to accept a Socrates who had reached no decision about problems which they themselves felt to be decisive. The historian must therefore infer that Socrates' own personality united the contradictions which even then or soon after his death fell apart. That makes him more interesting, and more complex, from our point of view, but also harder to understand. He was a very great man, and his greatness was felt by the wisest of his contemporaries. How can he have been both great and inconclusive? Was he the last embodiment of a harmony which, even in his lifetime, was in process of dissolution? Whatever the truth may be, he seems to stand on the frontier between the early Greek way of life and a new, unknown realm, which he had approached more nearly than any other, but was not fated to enter.

SOCRATES THE TEACHER

The lines on which Socrates is now to be described have been set by the whole trend of our investigation. He is the central point in the making of the Greek soul. He is the greatest teacher in European history. If we attempt to find his greatness in the field of theory and systematic philosophy, we shall either concede him too much and Plato too little, or else end in disbelieving in it altogether. Aristotle is correct in holding that the theoretical structure of the philosophy which Plato puts in Socrates' mouth was essentially the work of Plato himself. But Socrates is much more than the collection of stimulating ideas which is left when we subtract the theory of Ideas and the rest of the dogmatic doctrine from Plato's picture of him. His importance lies in another dimension. He is neither the continuator of a scientific tradition nor the inheritor of an assortment of philosophic doctrines. Literally, he is the man of his time. He breathes the air of history, and is lit up by its rays. He climbed to intellectual independence and self-mastery out of the Athenian middle class, that unchanging, God-fearing, conscience-heeding stock to whose staunch loyalty its great aristocratic leaders, Solon and Aeschylus, had appealed long before. And now that stock found a voice and spoke, through the mouth of its own son, the child of the stonemason and the midwife, from the deme Alopeké. Solon and Aeschylus had once appeared just at the right moment to take over and incorporate in their own thought the germinal revolutionary ideas imported from abroad. They had so profoundly mastered and fertilized those ideas that, instead of smashing the Athenian character, they had evoked its strongest forces. And now Socrates appeared, in the same kind of spiritual crisis. Periclean Athens, mistress of a mighty empire, was flooded with influences of many different kinds and origins; and, despite her brilliant expertness in every sphere of art and practical life, she was about to lose her spiritual foothold. Intoxicated by the exuberance of her own verbosity, she had in the briefest of moments talked all traditional values out of existence. And then Socrates came forward, to be the Solon of the moral world. For it was from the moral world that state and society were being undermined, and through it they must be saved. For the second time in Greek history it was the Attic spirit which summoned the centripetal forces of the Greek soul to combat the centrifugal—by setting up a firm moral order to counterbalance that creation of Ionian thought, the philosophical cosmos of warring natural forces. Solon had discovered the natural laws of the social and political community. Socrates now explored the moral cosmos in the human soul.

His youth fell into the era of rapid expansion after the great victory over Persia, an era marked abroad by the creation of the Periclean empire and at home by the introduction of complete democracy. The statement of Pericles in the funeral speech, that in Athens no merit or talent was refused an opportunity to display itself,[28] is proved by the example of Socrates. Neither his descent, nor his rank, nor even his appearance, predestined him to gather around him many of the sons of the Athenian aristocracy who looked forward to careers as statesmen, or to belong, as he did, to the cream of Attic society, the *kaloi kagathoi*. The earliest traditions speak of him, about the age of thirty, as an adherent of Anaxagoras' pupil Archelaus. The tragic poet Ion of Chios, in his travel-diary, recorded meeting Socrates in his company on the island of Samos.[29] Ion, who knew Athens well and was a friend of Sophocles and Cimon, adds that Archelaus belonged to Cimon's circle. He must, then, have introduced Socrates as a young man to Cimon.[30] We cannot tell whether his political views were affected by this contact with the great nobleman who had conquered Persia and headed the pro-Spartan conservative party in Athens.

In the prime of his life, he saw Athenian power rise to its height, and the greatest glories of classical Attic poetry and art created; he was received in the home of Pericles and Aspasia; among his pupils were politicians of brilliant and doubtful reputation, such as Alcibiades and Critias. At that time, the Athenian state was straining every nerve to maintain the dominance it had won in Greece, and it demanded great sacrifices of its citizens. Socrates was several times distinguished for gallantry in battle. At his trial, this was emphasized in order to offset his political deficiencies.[31] Although a great lover of the common people,[31a] he was admittedly a poor democrat. He could not admire the zealous political activity of the Athenians in the assembly and the law-courts.[32] He made only one political appearance in his lifetime. He was serving as chairman of the assembly at which the admirals who had won the victory of Arginusae were (without legal precedent) condemned to death en bloc, because they had been prevented by bad weather from picking up the survivors of wrecked Athenian ships. Socrates, alone among the prytaneis, refused to put the proposal to the vote, because it was against the law.[33] Later, that might be interpreted as a patriotic act; but it was undeniable that Socrates held the democratic principle of majority-rule to be fundamentally wrong, and held, instead, that the state should be governed by the wisest and ablest men.[34] It is an easy inference that he came to this conclusion during the Peloponnesian war, when the Athenian democracy was growing more degenerate every year. He had grown up surrounded by the spirit of the Persian victory, and he had seen the rise of the Athenian empire. The contrast must have been too sharp not to create all kinds of critical doubts in his mind.[35] These views brought him the sympathy of many of his fellow-citizens who had oligarchic leanings, and later, at his trial, their friendship was cast up to him. The masses did not understand that Socrates' independent attitude was absolutely different from that of ambitious conspirators like Alcibiades and Critias, and that it had an intellectual basis which was far broader than the sphere of politics. But it is important to understand that in Athens at that time even the man who stood apart from political action was thereby taking up a political attitude, and that state problems decisively influenced the thought and action of every single citizen, without exception.

Socrates grew up in the period which saw the first philosophers and the first philosophical activities in Athens. Even without the tradition about his relation to Archelaus, we should have to assume that, as a contemporary of Euripides and Pericles, he made an early acquaintance with the natural philosophy of Anaxagoras and Diogenes of Apollonia. We need not doubt that the account of his own development he gives in Plato's *Phaedo* is historically accurate [36]—at least when he speaks of his early interest in the physics of Anaxagoras. In Plato's *Apology*, he expressly denies having any special knowledge in that field; [37] but, like every cultured Athenian, he had read Anaxagoras' book, which (as he says in the same passage) could be bought for a drachma from the book-pedlars in the orchestra at the theatre.[38] Xenophon reports that, even later, he used to go through the works of 'the sages of old'—i.e. the poets and philosophers—with his young friends in his own house, in order to extract important passages from them.[39] So far, then, Aristophanes, when he describes Socrates as expounding Diogenes' physical theories about a Vortex creating the cosmos and Air being the basic principle of all existence, is perhaps not so wide of the truth as most people think. But how far did he incorporate these scientific doctrines into his own thought?

In the *Phaedo* he says that he expected great things when he took up Anaxagoras' book.[40] Somebody had given it to him, and had led him to expect he would find in it what he was looking for. That means that, even beforehand, he had been sceptical about the physicists' scientific explanations of the universe. Anaxagoras too disappointed him, although the beginning of the book had excited his hopes. There, Anaxagoras said something to the effect that Mind was the principle which built up the cosmos; yet as the book went on he made no further use of this explanation, but, like all the other physicists, referred everything to mechanical causes. Socrates had expected him to explain how things happened, and to show that they happened in that way 'because that was best'. That is, he thought that the rule of nature must be directed to a useful end. According to the account in *Phaedo* Socrates moved on from this criticism of the natural philosophers to reach the doctrine of Ideas; and yet, according to Aristotle's very convincing statement, the doctrine of Ideas cannot be attributed to the real Socrates at all. Doubtless Plato felt he was justified in making Socrates expound the doctrine that the Ideas are the ultimate causes of all phenomena, because he himself had gradually reached it through Socrates' investigations into the nature of the Good which is in all things.

Socrates also investigated nature in order to find an answer to his question. In Xenophon's *Memoirs* he holds conversations about the purpose which governs the structure of the universe, and tries to discover all that is good and purposeful in nature, so as to prove the existence of a constructive spiritual principle in the world.[41] What he says about the technical perfection of the organs of the human body seems to come from a work on natural philosophy by Diogenes of Apollonia.[42] Socrates could scarcely claim that the separate proofs he adduces were original: so that is no objection to our considering this conversation to be historically genuine in all essentials. If it contains borrowings, they are particularly characteristic of Socrates' way of thinking. In Diogenes' book he found what, in Plato's *Phædo,* he says he was looking for [43]—namely, the principle of Anaxagoras applied to the myriads of individual phenomena in nature. But still this conversation does not make him a natural philosopher: it only shows the point of view from which he approached cosmology. It was natural for a Greek to try to find in the cosmos the principle which he held to be the basis of order in human life, and to derive it from the cosmos. We have already pointed that out several times, and now find it proved once more in the case of Socrates.[44] Thus, his criticism of the natural philosophers indirectly proves that, from the very beginning, his interest was directed to problems of morality and religion. There was really no period in his life devoted to natural philosophy, for science could not answer the question which was in his heart, and on which everything else depended. Therefore, he left it alone. The unerring directness with which he always moved towards his goal is the sign of his greatness.

His lack of interest in natural philosophy has often been emphasized by Plato, by Aristotle, and many others since. But there is another aspect of that fact which is easily overlooked. Xenophon's description of his attempts to trace a purpose in the universe shows that his approach to nature was the very reverse of that followed by the early scientists. It was anthropocentric. His deductions all started with man and the structure of the human body. If the facts he cited were really taken from Diogenes' book, then that helps to confirm the point—for Diogenes was not only a natural philosopher, but a famous doctor; and therefore in his system (as in those of some others of the later physicists, for instance Empedocles) human physiology occupied a far greater place than in any of the older, pre-Socratic natural systems. This was bound to stimulate Socrates' interest and to suggest novel problems to him. And now we can see that, as well as his obvious negative attitude towards contemporary natural science, he had a positive attitude, which is often overlooked. We should not forget that natural science then included not only cosmology and 'meteorology', which we usually think covered the whole field, but also the art of medicine, which was just then entering (both in theory and in practice) upon the great expansion described in the next volume. Even a doctor like the author of the contemporary work *On ancient medicine* held medical science to be the *only* part of natural science that was based on real experience and exact knowledge. He believed that the natural philosophers and their hypotheses could teach him nothing, but had much to learn from him.[45] This anthropocentric attitude was characteristic of the age of later Attic tragedy and of the sophists. It was connected—as Herodotus and Thucydides show—with the empirical approach manifested in the emancipation of medicine from the cosmological hypotheses of the natural philosophers.

Medical science, then, is the most striking parallel to Socrates' rejection of the high-flown speculations of the cosmologists. It shows the same sober determination to examine the *facts* of human life.[46] Like it, Socrates found that human nature, which is the part of the world best known to us, was the firmest basis for his analysis of reality and his clue to understanding it. As Cicero says, he brought philosophy down from heaven into the cities and homes of men.[47] That means, as we now see, not only that he changed its interest and the objects of its study, but also that he worked out a more rigid conception of knowledge (if indeed there is such a thing as knowledge). What the old philosophers had called knowledge was really philosophical hypotheses about the universe—which, for Socrates, means cloud-capped fantasy, gorgeous nonsense.[48] Whenever he expresses respect for its lofty wisdom, unattainable to him, he is speaking ironically.[49] He himself (as Aristotle correctly observed) always proceeded by induction;[50] and his method is akin to that of the matter-of-fact empiricist in medicine. His ideal of knowledge

was τέχνη, which was best exemplified in the art of healing, especially because that art had a practical aim in view.[51] At that time
there was no such thing as exact science. Contemporary natural
philosophy was all that was inexact. Therefore there was no
philosophical empiricism either. In the ancient world, the principle that experience is the basis of all exact knowledge of reality
was insisted upon by medicine, and by medicine alone. That is
why medical science held a higher, more philosophical rank in
the intellectual world then than it does now. Also, it was medical
science which passed that idea on to the philosophy of our own
age. Modern philosophical empiricism is the child, not of Greek
philosophy, but of Greek medicine.

We must always remember Socrates' respect for medicine,
which was one of the greatest intellectual forces of his day, if
we are to understand his place in ancient philosophy and his
anthropocentric attitude. His use of medical examples is notably
frequent. And he did not use them at random: he used them because they fitted the pattern of his thinking; in fact they suited
his view of his own personality, his ethos, his whole life. He
was really a doctor. Xenophon actually says he thought quite
as much about his friends' physical health as their spiritual welfare.[52] But he was mainly a doctor of the soul. The way in which
he reasons about the physical structure of man, in his proof
that the universe has a purpose, shows plainly that his teleology
is closely connected with his empirical, quasi-medical outlook.
It is only to be understood in connexion with the teleological
conception of man and nature which was being openly acknowledged, for the first time, in medical science, and thenceforward
grew more and more definite until it found final philosophical
expression in Aristotle's biological view of the universe. Socrates' search for the nature of the Good, of course, was the manifestation of an interest which was entirely his own, and which
he had learnt from no one else. An earnest natural philosopher
of his time must have judged it to be the enquiry of a mere
dilettante, to which the pure physicist's heroic scepticism could
find no answer. But that dilettante's question was a creative one;
and it is important for us to realize, by comparison with the
medical books of 'Hippocrates' and Diogenes, that it formulated
the most profound doubts of all that epoch.

We do not know how old Socrates was when he began, in Athens, the work in which his pupils' dialogues show him as engaged. Plato places some of his conversations in the first years of the Peloponnesian war—in *Charmides*, for example, Socrates has just returned from the hard campaign of Potidaea. At that time he was nearly forty; but doubtless he had begun to teach some time before that. Plato believed that the living context of his conversations was extremely important—so much so that he described it again and again with the most delightful detail. Socrates did not talk in the timeless abstract world of the lecture-hall. He belonged to the busy life of the Athenian athletic school, the gymnasium, where he was soon a regular and indispensable visitor like the trainer and the doctor.[52a] Of course those who took part in those conversations of his which were famous throughout Athens did not necessarily stand about in the athlete's usual Spartan nakedness, although they may often have done so. But it was not by mere chance that the dramatic duels of thought on which Socrates spent his life took place in the gymnasium. There was a profound symbolic resemblance between Socrates' conversations and the act of stripping to be examined by the doctor or trainer before entering the ring for a contest. Plato makes Socrates himself draw this parallel several times.[53] The Athenian of those days was more at home in the gymnasium than between the narrow four walls of the house where he slept and ate. There, in the clear light of the Greek sky, young and old daily assembled to keep their bodies fit.[54] The intervals of rest were taken up with conversation. No doubt it was often mere gossip; and yet the most famous philosophical schools in the world—the Academy and the Lyceum—bear the names of well-known Athenian athletic grounds. Anyone who had something of general interest to say which could not properly be said in the assembly or the law-court went and said it to his friends and acquaintances in the gymnasium. It was always exciting to see whom one would meet there. For a change, one could visit any one of many such institutions, private or public.[55] An *habitué* like Socrates, who was interested in people as such, knew everyone on the ground; and no new face (especially among the young men) could appear without his noting it and asking whose it was. As a keen observer of the young, he was unequalled. He was the great authority on human nature.

His sharp questioning was the touchstone by which every talent and every latent power could be tested; and the most distinguished citizens asked his advice on the upbringing of their sons.

Only the symposium, with the weight of tradition behind it, could equal the intellectual vitality of the gymnasium. Therefore Plato and Xenophon depict Socrates' conversations as taking place in both these milieux.[56] All the other situations they mention are more or less casual—Aspasia's salon, for instance, or the shops in the marketplace where people gathered to chat, or the home of a rich patron of philosophy during a famous sophist's visit. The gymnasia were the most important meeting-place of all, because people attended them regularly. They were not simply training-grounds for the body: by encouraging the contact of mind with mind they generated an intellectual heat which made them the most receptive soil for any new thought or enthusiasm. They were the place of leisure and relaxation: no special interest could survive very long there, and business could not be carried on in such surroundings. Therefore their frequenters were all the more ready to discuss the general problems of life. And they were not interested in the subject alone, but also in the intellectual subtlety and elasticity with which it was discussed. There came into being a sort of intellectual gymnastics, which was soon quite as elaborate and quite as much admired as the training of the body. It was early recognized to be what physical training had long been considered, a form of paideia. The 'dialectic' of Socrates was a perfectly individual and native type of exercise, the extreme opposite to the sophistic educational method which grew up at the same time. The sophists were wandering teachers of foreign origin, haloed with the bright light of fame, adored by a circle of devoted pupils. They taught for money. They gave instruction in special arts or branches of knowledge, and addressed a chosen public—the culture-hungry sons of the propertied class. Their long and showy lectures were delivered in private houses or improvised lecture-halls. Socrates, on the other hand, was a simple Athenian, whom everyone knew. His effects were hardly perceptible: he would start a conversation, spontaneously and apparently purposelessly, on any question which happened to come up. He did not teach, and had no pupils—at least so he said. He had only friends, or companions. Young men were fascinated by the sharpness of his edged mind which nothing could withstand. He was for them an ever new and truly Attic drama: they listened with minds enraptured, they enthusiastically applauded his triumphs, and they tried to imitate him by examining human nature in the same way in their own homes and among their own friends. The best young minds of Athens were drawn to Socrates, and, once they had approached, his magnetic personal charm never let them free again. Anyone who tried to treat him with haughty indifference or cold reserve, anyone who took exception to the pedantic form of his questions or the deliberate triviality of his examples, soon had to get off his high horse and stand humbly on the ground.

It is not easy to find a single description which will explain this strange and complex person. With loving care and elaborate detail, Plato depicts all his characteristic ways; but seems, by doing so, to hint that Socrates could not be defined—he must be known. On the other hand, it is easy to understand why the severe historians of philosophy dismiss all these features in Plato's picture of Socrates as mere poetic decoration. It all seems to lie beneath the high level of abstract thought on which philosophers ought to move and have their being. It is only an indirect way of describing Socrates' intellectual power, by dramatically showing its more than intellectual effect upon living men. Yet, unless we realize to the full Socrates' concern for the welfare of the actual individual to whom he is speaking, we cannot understand *what* he is saying. Although the philosopher may consider that relationship unessential in the abstract, academic sense, Plato shows that for Socrates it was essential. And that is enough to make us suspect that we are always in danger of seeing him through the medium which *we* call philosophy. True, Socrates himself describes his 'activity' (πρᾶγμα—characteristic word) as 'philosophy' and 'philosophizing'. In Plato's *Apology* he assures the jury that he will never give it up as long as he lives and breathes.[57] But we must not think that he means what philosophy became in later centuries after a long process of development—a method of abstract thought, or a body of doctrine consisting of theoretical statements, which can easily be considered in detachment from the man who created it. The whole of Socratic literature, with one voice, denies that Socrates' doctrine can be detached from his individual self.

What then is that 'philosophy' of which Plato holds Socrates to be the model, and to which Socrates professes his adherence in his own defence-speech? Plato explains its nature in many dialogues. He comes to lay more and more emphasis on the *results* of the enquiries undertaken by Socrates and his interlocutors; but he must have felt that, in doing so, he was still true to the essence of the Socratic spirit. He meant each dialogue to prove its fertility anew. But, since it is hard for us to fix the point at which his Socrates becomes more Plato than Socrates, we must try to define 'philosophy' on the basis of his most precise and simple statements. There are quite a number of them. In the *Apology,* still horrified at the colossal wrong done to Socrates and hoping to win other disciples for his master, he described the essence and the meaning of his work in the shortest and plainest form. The speech is too artfully constructed to be merely a revised version of the actual speech which Socrates made, extempore, in court;[58] still, it is amazingly true to Socrates' real life and character. It begins by correcting and disavowing the caricature of Socrates which had been created by the comic poets and by public opinion; and then there follows a thrilling profession of faith in philosophy, which Plato meant to be a parallel and companion-piece to Euripides' famous profession of loyalty to the Muses.[59] But Socrates makes his avowal in the face of imminent death. The power which he serves can not only beautify our life and alleviate our sufferings, it can conquer the world. Immediately after this protest, 'I shall never give up philosophy', there follows a typical example of his method of speaking and teaching. To understand its content, we must begin with its form—as exemplified in this and many other passages of Plato's work.

He reduces the true Socratic method to two main devices: exhortation (*protreptikos*) and examination (*elenchos*). Both are couched in the form of questions. The question-form is a descendant of the oldest type of *parainesis,* or encouragement, which we can trace back through tragedy to the epic. In the introductory conversation of Plato's *Protagoras* we can see both these Socratic devices in juxtaposition once more.[60] That dia-

logue, which contrasts Socrates with the great Protagoras, pa-
rades before us every variety of the set forms in which the
sophists used to teach: myth, proof by argument, explanation
of a poem, enquiry by question-and-answer. But Socrates' own
peculiar methods of speech are depicted just as humorously and
vividly, in all their bizarre pedantry and ironic modesty. Both
in the *Apology* and in *Protagoras* Plato shows us that the two
basic devices of Socrates' talk—exhortation and examination—
are fundamentally akin to each other. Actually, they are just
different stages of one spiritual process. This can be proved by
the *Apology,* where Socrates describes his method as follows: [61]

'I shall never give up philosophizing and urging you and
making my point clear to everyone I meet, saying what I always
say: "My good sir, you are an Athenian, a citizen of the city
which is greatest and most noted for its wisdom and power;
are you not then ashamed to be worrying about your money
and how to increase it, and about your reputation, and about
your honour, instead of worrying about the knowledge of good
and truth and how to improve your soul?" And if anyone contradicts me and says that he does worry about his soul, I shall
not let him off at once and go away, but question him and examine him and refute him; and, if I think that he does not possess
virtue, but simply says he does, I shall reproach him for under-
estimating what is most valuable, and prizing what is unimportant. I shall do this to everyone I meet, young and old,
stranger and citizen—but particularly to you citizens of Athens,
because you are nearer me in blood. For this, you must realize,
is God's command to me; and I think that no greater good has
ever happened to you than this my service to God. For all that
I do is go round and persuade young and old among you not
to give so much of your attention to your bodies and your
money as to the perfection of your souls.'

Socrates says that he 'philosophizes'. Obviously, he does not
mean by this that he engages in abstract thought, but that he
exhorts and teaches. One of the methods he uses is Socratic
examination and refutation of all sham knowledge and artificial
excellence (areté). That examination is only one part of the
whole process as he describes it, although it usually seems to be

the most original aspect of it. But before we investigate the character of this dialectical 'examination of men'—which is generally considered the essence of Socratic philosophy, because it contains more of the theoretic element than the rest—we must look a little more closely at Socrates' introductory speech of admonition. When he compares the existence of the business man, always panting to make money, with his own higher ideal, his comparison turns on the care or attention which men give to the goods they prize most highly. Instead of care for money-making, Socrates advises care for one's soul (ψυχῆς θεραπεία). This idea appears at the beginning of his speech, and recurs at the end.[62] But there is nothing to prove that the soul is more important than the body or external goods. That is assumed to be obvious, although in practice men do not behave as if it were. For us, there is nothing remarkable in that, at least in theory; in fact, it seems rather a commonplace. But was it so obvious for the Greeks of that age as it is for us, who are the heirs of two thousand years of Christian tradition? Socrates makes the same point in his discussion with the young man in *Protagoras*. There too he begins by saying that his young friend's soul is in danger.[63] The theme of the soul's danger in this connexion is typical of Socrates, and always leads to his summons to take care of the soul. He speaks like a doctor—only his patient is not the physical man but the spiritual being. There is an extraordinarily large number of passages in the writings of his pupils where the care of the soul is described by Socrates as the highest interest of man. Here we can penetrate to the very heart of his view of his own duty and mission: he felt that it was educational, and that the work of education was the service of God.[64] It can be properly described as a religious duty, because it is the duty of 'caring for the soul'.[65] For, in Socrates' view, the soul is the divine in man. Socrates defines the care of the soul more closely as the care of the knowledge of values and of truth, *phronésis* and *alétheia*.[66] The soul is no less sharply distinguished from the body than it is from external goods. This implies a Socratic hierarchy of values, and with it a new, clearly graduated theory of goods, which places spiritual goods highest, physical goods below them, and external goods like property and power in the lowest place.

There is a huge gulf between this scale of values, set forth by Socrates with such confidence in its obviousness, and the popular Greek one, well expressed in the fine old drinking-song: [67]

> *Health is best for mortal men,*
> *Next best is being fair to see,*
> *Blameless wealth is next again,*
> *Last, youth and friends and revelry.*

Socrates' thought has added something new—the inner world. The areté of which he speaks is the excellence of the soul.

But what is the soul, which he calls *psyché*? If we approach the question from the philological side first, it is striking that, both in Plato and in the other Socratics, Socrates always uses the word *soul* with exceptional emphasis, a passionate, a beseeching urgency. No Greek before him ever said it in that tone. We can feel that this is the first appearance in the Western world of what we now, in certain connexions, call the soul—although modern psychologists do not consider it to be a 'real substance'. Because of the intellectual contexts in which the meaning of the word has developed, we always hear ethical or religious overtones in the word *soul*. Like his 'service of God' and 'care of the soul', it sounds Christian. But it first acquired that lofty meaning in the protreptic preaching of Socrates. Let us not ask meanwhile how far the Socratic conception of the soul influenced Christianity in its various phases, either directly or through the medium of later philosophies, and how closely it coincides with the Christian idea of soul. What we must do here is to realize what an epoch-making conception it was, in the spiritual history of Greece.

If we consult Rohde's great book *Psyche,* we shall find that Socrates appears to have no importance in the development of the Greek spirit. Rohde passes over him altogether.[68] That was partly due to the prejudice against Socrates as a 'rationalist' which he shared with Nietzsche from his youth up, but even more to the special way in which he approached his subject. Despite himself, his attitude was still Christian, so that he treated the cult of the dead and the belief in immortality as the focal point of his vast and comprehensive history of the soul in all its aspects. We can admit at once that Socrates made no essential contribution to either of these realms of thought. But it is remarkable that Rohde never notices where, and when, and through whom the word *psyché,* soul, acquired the particular character which made it truly representative of all the values implicit in the intellectual and moral personality of Western man. As soon as it is clearly stated that this first happened in Socrates' educational speeches of exhortation, it is impossible for it to be doubted. The scholars of the Scottish school have already emphasized this point. Their work was entirely uninfluenced by Rohde's book. Burnet has a fine essay in which he traces the development of the conception of soul through the whole spiritual history of Greece. He shows that neither the Homeric and epic *eidolon,* the shade in Hades, nor the air-soul of the Ionic philosophers, nor the soul-daemon of Orphic belief, nor the *psyché* of Attic tragedy can explain the new meaning given to the word by Socrates.[69] I myself early reached the same conclusion by analysing the form of Socrates' speeches, as I have done above. It is hardly possible to understand the pattern of the Socratic exhortation without feeling the peculiar spiritual emotion which attends Socrates' use of the word *soul.* His protreptic speeches are the germ out of which grew the diatribe (the stump-sermon delivered by the travelling Cynic and Stoic preachers of the Hellenistic age), and in its turn the diatribe influenced the structure of the Christian sermon.[70] But the point is not only that a literary form was continuously handed on through various ages and uses. Scholars have often worked out the details of its transmission from that point of view, by tracing how separate themes from the protreptic speech were taken over and adapted by its successors. But the basis of all these three types of speech is this creed: 'What shall it profit a man, if he gain the whole world, and lose his own soul?' In his *Wesen des Christentums* Harnack rightly described this belief in the infinite value of the individual soul as one of the pillars of the religion of Jesus.[71] But before that it had been a pillar of Socrates' 'philosophy' and Socrates' educational thought. Socrates preaches and proselytizes. He comes 'to save the soul'.[72]

We must pause for a little here, before we can go any further in explaining, as clearly and simply as possible, the fundamentals of Socrates' conception of his mission. We must reach some critical estimate of the facts, because they directly affect our

own lives. Was Socrates' teaching a Greek forerunner of Christianity? Or did he, rather, introduce a strange Oriental spirit
into Greek thought, which, through the mighty educational
power of Greek philosophy, worked enormous changes in the
history of the world, and moved towards a union of the West
with the East? Is there not another example of the same trend
in the Orphic movement, which can be traced in many different
ways, in Greek religion from the sixth century on? That creed
separated the soul from the body: it held that the human spirit
was a fallen daemon housed in the prison of the body, whence,
after death, it would wander through a long series of incarna-
tions until it returned at last to its home in heaven. And yet,
though many consider Orphism to be Oriental or 'Mediter-
ranean', its origin is obscure; and none of its eschatological and
demonological beliefs appear in Socrates' conception of the
soul. It was Plato who introduced them into his mythical embel-
lishments of the Socratic soul and its destiny. The doctrine of
immortality set forth in Plato's *Phaedo* and the doctrine of pre-
existence which appears in *Meno* have both been attributed to
Socrates,[73] but these two complementary ideas are clearly Platonic in origin. Probably Socrates' real opinion about the immortality of the soul is correctly set forth in the *Apology*—
where, confronting imminent death, he leaves it doubtful what
happens to the soul afterwards.[74] That suits his dry, critical,
undogmatic mentality better than the arguments for immortality
advanced in *Phaedo*; although it is natural that a man who
thought so nobly of the soul should have pondered much on the
problem even if he could not solve it.[75] In any case, he did not
believe that the solution was all-important. For the same reason,
he never made any assertions about the exact kind of reality to
be attributed to the soul. He did not think (as Plato did) that
it was an independent 'substance', because he did not state clearly
whether it could be separated from the body or not. To serve
it was to serve God, since he held that it was the mind and the
moral reason. That was why it was the holiest thing in the
world—not because it was a guilt-laden daemon-visitor from
a far-off heavenly region.

Therefore there is no escape from the conclusion. All the remarkable traits in Socrates' teaching which seem to have the
charm of Christian feeling are actually Hellenic in origin. They

stem from Greek philosophy; and only those who completely misconceive its character can refuse to believe that they do. The Greek spirit reached its highest religious development, not in the cults of the gods around which the history of Greek religion is usually written, but chiefly in philosophy, assisted by the Greek gift for constructing systematic theories of the universe. Philosophy is indeed a relatively late stage of consciousness, and it is preceded by the myth. But no one who has grasped the structural connexions of human thought can believe that Socrates was any exception to the law of organic development that governed the history of Greek philosophy. Analogies and preliminary stages to his teaching can be pointed out in the Dionysian and Orphic cults; but that is not because his characteristic ideas and remarks were copied from sects which can be coolly dismissed as unGreek or warmly admired as Oriental. Socrates was a hard, plain thinker: it would have been ruinous for him to admit the influence of orgiastic cults which appealed to the irrational elements in the soul. The truth rather is that these sects or cults are the only forms of old popular religion among the Greeks which really look like the beginning of an individual type of faith or seem to have a correspondingly individual way of life and form of propaganda.[76] In philosophy, the realm of the thinking mind, parallel forms either arise independently out of analogous spiritual situations, or else are due to the borrowing of words and phrases from current religious clichés, which are used as metaphors in the language of philosophy, and are thereby debased.[77]

An exceptionally large number of these religious-sounding expressions in Socrates' talk arose from the analogy of his work with that of a doctor. That is what gives its specifically Greek colouring to his view of the soul. His attitude that man's spiritual existence was part of his 'nature' was produced partly by habits of thought centuries old and partly by the fundamental structure of the Greek mind. And here at last we meet the real difference between the Socratic philosophy and the Christian soul. The only way to understand the soul of which Socrates speaks is to take it together with the body as two different sides of *one* human nature. In his thought, there is no opposition between psychical and physical man; the old conception of *physis* which stems from natural philosophy now takes in the spirit too, and thereby is essentially changed. Socrates cannot believe that man has a monopoly of spirit.[78] If there is a place for spirit anywhere in nature, as the existence of man's phronésis shows that there is, then nature must in principle be capable of spiritual powers. But just as, because of the coexistence of body and soul as different parts of the same human nature, man's physical nature is spiritualized, so the soul in its turn assumes a surprising new reality: it becomes a *physis* in its own right. In the eyes of Socrates, the soul seems no less plastic than the body, and therefore capable of receiving form and order. Like the body, it is part of the cosmos. In fact, it *is* a cosmos in itself; although no Greek could doubt that the principle manifested in the order of these different realms was essentially one and the same. Therefore the analogy of soul and body must extend to what the Greek calls areté. The qualities which usually came under the name of aretai, 'excellences' or 'virtues', in the Greek polis— courage, prudence, justice, piety—are excellences of the soul just as health, strength, and beauty are excellences of the body. That is, they are the appropriate powers of particular parts of the soul or their co-operation cultivated to the highest pitch of which man's nature is capable. The cosmic nature of physical and spiritual virtue is simply the 'symmetry of the parts' on whose co-operation both soul and body depend. With this in mind, we can see how Socrates' conception of 'the good' differs from the corresponding conception in modern ethics. Most untranslatable of all concepts, it very readily produces misunderstandings. We can grasp its Greek meaning as soon as we think of it not as 'good' but as 'good *for* one' *: for that makes plain its relation to the man who possesses it, and for whom it is good. The Good is, in Socrates' eyes, that which we ought to will or do for its own sake. No doubt. But it is likewise the Useful, the Beneficent, and hence also the Enjoyable and Happiness-bringing—because it helps man's nature to fulfil itself.

Once we accept this, it becomes obvious that morality is the expression of human nature rightly understood and trained by knowledge. It is differentiated from simple animal existence by the fact that man has a mind and soul, without which he could not have an ethical code. But to train the soul in obedience to

* 'Goods', which in English means valuable property, has the same sense of value and utility.

that code is simply to follow the path natural for man, by doing which he reaches harmony with the nature of the universe —or, in Greek terms, attains perfect happiness, *eudaimonia*. Socrates was profoundly convinced that man's moral existence harmonizes with the natural order of the world, and in that conviction he was in full and unqualified agreement with the Greek feeling of every epoch. What is new in his thought is his belief that man cannot reach this harmony with Being through the cultivation and satisfaction of his own senses and his bodily nature (however confined it may be by social prohibitions and duties), but only through complete mastery over himself in accordance with the law he finds by searching his own soul. By thus asserting that man must strive to master the realm which is most wholly his own—the soul—Socrates added to his characteristic Greek eudaemonism a new power to resist external nature and destiny in their increasingly dangerous threats against human liberty. Goethe asked what would be the purpose of all the wondrous show of suns and planets in the cosmos, if it did not make possible the happiness of one human being. And Socrates would, on his own assumptions, certainly not have called that question 'wicked'—as it has been called by modern critics, in this age when reality and morality are no longer at one. The 'rationalist' Socrates found no difficulty in harmonizing his ethical *eudaimonia* with the facts of reality, although we are now crushed by their impact, since we are morally discordant with them. Nothing shows that better than the cheerfulness with which, on that last day, he drained the cup of poison.

Socrates declared the soul to be the source of the highest values in human life. Thereby he produced that emphasis on the inner life which characterizes the later stages of Greek civilization. Virtue and happiness now became qualities of the spirit. In making this change, Socrates was fully aware of its implications. He even claimed that the art of painting should be dominated by the spirit. Painters, he said, should not only imitate the beauty of the body but also express the character of the soul (ἀπομιμεῖσθαι τὸ τῆς ψυχῆς ἦθος). In his conversation with the great painter Parrhasius, recorded by Xenophon,[78a] this idea is put forward as quite new; and Parrhasius says he is doubtful whether painting can ever enter the world of the invisible and unsymmetrical. Xenophon describes the interview as if Socrates'

insistence on the soul's importance had revealed the whole un-
guessed and unexplored spiritual world to the artists of his day.
Socrates asserts that the body, and the face in particular, is
merely a reflection of the soul and its qualities, while the painter
approaches this great thought with wonder and hesitation. That
story is symbolic. Whatever the relation of philosophy to art at
that period may have been, Xenophon certainly believed that
philosophy, and philosophy alone, had led the way into the new-
found land of the soul. It is difficult for us to measure the
gigantic effects of this change. Its immediate result was that a
new order of values came into being and was dialectically
worked out in the philosophical systems of Plato and Aristotle.
In that form it became the foundation for all the later cultures
which have received the torch from Greek philosophy. We cannot but admire these philosophers for their amazing power of
planning the structures of abstract thought in which the truth
realized by Socrates could be more clearly seen and understood
—so that it formed, as it were, the centre of a systematic picture of the universe, to which all else was referred. But still, 'in
the beginning was the Deed'. It was Socrates' summons to men
to 'care for their souls' that really turned the mind of Greece
towards a new way of life. From that time onwards, a dominant
part in philosophy and ethics was played by the concept of life,
bios—human existence regarded not as the mere lapse of time
but as a clear and comprehensible unity, a deliberately shaped
life-pattern. This innovation was caused by the way Socrates
lived; he played the part of a model for the new *bios*, the life
based on spiritual values. And his pupils realized that the
greatest strength of his paideia came from the change he had
introduced into the old educational concept of the heroic
Example which is a pattern for other lives to follow. He made
himself the embodiment of the ideal of life which he preached.

We must now try to give a more detailed description of his
teaching. Although Plato in the *Apology* makes him describe the
care of the soul as 'the service of God',[79] that phrase really has
no supernatural implications. On the contrary, a Christian would
think his system very simple and worldly. To begin with, he does
not think that the care of the soul implies the neglect of the
body. How could he, when he had learnt from doctors of the

body that the soul likewise needs special 'treatment' both in sickness and in health? His discovery of the soul does not mean its separation from the body, as is so often mistakenly averred, but its domination over the body. However, one cannot take care of one's soul properly unless one's body itself is healthy. Juvenal's prayer, *mens sana in corpore sano,* is spoken in the true Socratic spirit. Socrates himself neither neglected his own body nor praised those who neglected theirs.[80] He taught his friends to keep their bodies fit by hardening them, and held elaborate discussions with them about proper diet. He opposed overeating because it hindered the care of the soul. His own life was run on a regimen of Spartan simplicity. Later we must discuss the moral rule of physical *askésis,* and study the meaning to be attached to that Socratic idea.

Both Plato and Xenophon give the most probable explanation of Socrates' effectiveness as a teacher—that it was due to his complete unlikeness to the sophists. They were the recognized virtuosi, something quite new in the art of teaching. Socrates always seems to be watching them and rivalling them, correcting what he judges to be their mistakes. Although he has a higher aim in view, he starts from their level. Their paideia was a mixed product, made up of elements of very various origins. Its purpose was the training of the mind; but they could not agree what was the knowledge that trained the mind best. Each of them had his own specialty, and naturally believed it to be the best suited for mental training. Socrates did not deny that the things they taught were valuable. But his summons to care for the soul implied a standard by which to judge their subjects, and certain limitations to them.[81] Some of the sophists held that the doctrines of natural philosophy were good educational material. The old natural philosophers themselves had never suggested this, although they felt that, in a higher sense of the word, they were really teachers. It was a new problem to decide whether the young could be educated by scientific study. As we have seen, it was not because Socrates did not understand the physicists' problems that his interest in natural philosophy was small, but rather because the questions he asked were not the same as theirs. If he dissuaded others from elaborate research into cosmological problems, it was because he believed their intellectual energies would be better employed on thinking about 'human things'.[82] Besides, the ordinary Greeks held cosmic matters to be daemonic, beyond the powers of mortals to understand. Socrates shared this feeling, which even appears at the beginning of Aristotle's *Metaphysics*.[83] He had similar reservations about the mathematical and astronomical studies practised by the more realistically minded sophists like Hippias of Elis. He himself had been a very keen student of these subjects, and held that a certain knowledge of them was indispensable; but he believed very firmly that it should not go too far.[84] This information we get from Xenophon, who has been accused of utilitarianism and a one-sided devotion to practical subjects. Unflattering contrasts have been drawn between his Socrates and the Socrates of Plato, who says in *The Republic* that mathematics is the only real way to philosophy.[85] But the latter view was influenced by Plato's own intellectual development, which made him a dialectician, interested in the theory of knowledge; whereas, in the work of his old age—*The Laws*—where he is discussing not higher but elementary education, he takes the same attitude as Xenophon's Socrates.[86] Thus Socrates' special interest in 'human things' provides a standard of choice among the subjects which had hitherto been held to constitute culture. The question 'How far should we study X?' implies greater questions: 'What is the good of X?' and 'What is the purpose of life?' Until those questions are answered, education is impossible.

So, once again, the ethical factor returns to the focus of interest, from which it had been thrust by the sophistic educational movement. That movement had arisen from the ruling classes' need for higher education and from the new importance attached to intellectual ability.[87] The sophists had a clear practical aim in view—to train statesmen and political leaders; and, in an age which worshipped success, the clarity of their aim had assisted that shift in emphasis from ethics to intellect. Now Socrates had re-established the necessary connexion between moral and intellectual culture. But he did not try to counter the sophists' political education with an *un*political ideal, consisting of pure character-building. The aim of education could not be altered: in a Greek city-state it was bound to be always the same. Plato and Xenophon agree in stating that Socrates taught politics.[88] If he had not, how could he have clashed with

the state? Why was he condemned? The culmination of the
'human things' on which he concentrated was, for Greek feeling,
the welfare of the community, on which the life of the individual depended.[89] A Socrates whose teaching was not 'political'
would have found no pupils in the Athens of his day. What was
new in him was that he held the heart of human life, of communal life too, to be the moral character. But that was not what
made Alcibiades and Critias go to him and become his pupils.
Driven by the ambition to play a leading role in the state, they
hoped that he would show them how to satisfy it.[90] That was
exactly what Socrates was accused of doing; and Xenophon tries
to excuse him by pleading that the use they later made of their
political training ran counter to Socrates' purposes in teaching
them.[91] In any case, they were astounded when they came to
know him better and found him to be a great man, who strove
with the whole passion of his soul to find and possess 'the
good'.[92]

But what kind of political education did he give? We cannot
really ascribe to him the Utopian state-theory he expounds in
Plato's *Republic,* for it is entirely dependent on the Platonic
doctrine of Ideas. Nor is it probable that, when he was teaching, he did as he does in Plato's *Gorgias:* where he claims to be
the only real statesman of his time, and says that, compared
with his work, the efforts of all the professional politicians, aiming as they do at mere external power, are empty nonsense.[93]
These emotional overtones were added afterwards by Plato, in
his attack on the whole political tendency which had led to Socrates' condemnation. But the crux of the problem is this: why
did Socrates himself take no part in political life, but give others
a political education? [93a] Xenophon gives us a fine survey of the
large number of subjects he covered in his political discussions—
although we must utilize Plato's Socratic dialogues on the nature
of areté in order to understand their deeper significance. Xenophon informs us that Socrates went into all sorts of problems
of political technique with his pupils: the differences between
various types of constitution,[94] the origin of laws and political
institutions,[95] the aim of the statesman's activity, the best preparation for the statesman's career,[96] the value of political concord,[97] the ideal of obedience to law as the highest civic virtue.[98]

He discussed not only the administration of the polis but that of the home, the οἰκία. Politics and 'economics' (oikonomika = housekeeping) were always closely connected in Greek minds. Like the sophists (who often treated these topics) he frequently started with passages from the poets, particularly Homer, using them as texts on which to develop examples, or by which to illustrate political ideas. In those days, a man who knew and taught Homer well was called Ὁμήρου ἐπαινέτης, because he taught by picking out certain passages of the poet for praise.[98a] Socrates was accused of anti-democratic tendencies in his choice.[99] We have already mentioned his criticism of the system of election by lot which mechanized the selection of officials, and of the democratic principle that the majority is always right.[100] However, his criticism was not a party affair. The best proof of this is the unforgettable scene at the beginning of the *Memorabilia*. During the rule of the Thirty, Socrates is summoned to the government offices by his former pupil Critias, now the supreme ruler of Athens, and is ordered to stop teaching, with a concealed threat of death if he disobeys: and this although his particular activity did not fall under the general interdict on rhetorical teaching which was cited as a pretext.[101] The rulers of the city obviously knew that he would tell the truth about their misdoings just as ruthlessly as he had about the extravagances of mob-rule.

Our authorities agree that Socrates talked freely about military matters, so far as they touched questions of politics and ethics. We cannot really determine how far their evidence corresponds to the historical facts; but it is not at all unlike the historical Socrates to give detailed explanations of the best laws of war and the best military training for citizens, as Plato makes him do in *The Republic*.[102] In Plato's *Laches* two influential Athenians ask him for advice whether they should have their sons trained in the newest combat technique, and two famous Athenian generals, Nicias and Laches, are anxious to hear his opinion. The conversation soon rises to a higher plane, and changes to a philosophical discussion of the nature of courage. Xenophon gives a number of his discourses on the education of the future general.[103] That branch of political education was specially important in Athens, because there was no official military school, and the citizens elected to the generalship were often very badly trained for their duties. Private tutors appeared (obviously as a product of the long war) and professed to teach strategy. Socrates' standard of technical competence was pitched too high to let him give instruction on matters in which he had no special knowledge. In such cases we often see him trying to discover the right teacher for prospective pupils who have come to him. For instance, he sent a student to Dionysodorus, a wandering professor of military affairs who had just arrived in Athens.[104] Subsequently, he criticized Dionysodorus severely when he heard that he had only given the young man instruction in tactics, without explaining how he was to use his skill, and that he had explained how to post the good and bad soldiers, without explaining who was good and who was bad. Another time, he picked up Homer's formal description of Agamemnon, 'shepherd of the people', and based on it a discourse about the true virtues of a leader. In this too he attacked the idea that generalship was a purely external skill, a mere matter of professional technique. For instance, he asked a newly posted cavalry officer whether he thought it was part of his duty to improve the horses of his troop; and if so, whether he should improve the men too; and if so, whether he should improve himself also—because the soldiers would follow the best man most willingly.[105] Significantly enough, being an Athenian, he attached great importance to the general's powers of oratory— and in that the generals' speeches in Thucydides and Xenophon support him.[106] By comparing the good general to the good economist and administrator, he is enabled to reduce both excellences to one principle, and call them qualities necessary to the good leader.[107]

One of these conversations leaves general themes behind and passes over to discuss more topical matters. This is his talk with the younger Pericles, on whose military skill he placed high hopes during the later years of the Peloponnesian war.[108] That was a period of incessant decline for the power of Athens; and Socrates, whose youth had been passed in the Athenian expansion after the Persian wars, now looked nostalgically back on the years of vanished greatness. He drew an ideal picture of the old virtue (ἀρχαία ἀρετή), as fair and ominous as any of those by Isocrates and Demosthenes.[108a] Is that picture nothing more than a reflex of the historical philosophy so often expounded in their speeches (after all, the work in which Xenophon inserts it was written late in his life), or do its comparisons between the degenerate present and the victories of the past really go back to ideas expressed by Socrates towards the end of his life? We must admit that Xenophon's description of the historical background is strongly reminiscent of the period when he was writing the *Memoirs*. Socrates' conversation with the younger Pericles is full of topical significance for Xenophon. Still, that does not prove that Socrates never expressed such ideas. A considerable time before Isocrates wrote his idealizations of the past, Plato's *Menexenus* made Socrates eulogize the areté and paideia of earlier generations, in a speech on the dead Athenian warriors which he claims to have heard from Aspasia, and which contains many of these same ideas.[109] To counter the hopeless pessimism expressed, not unnaturally, by Pericles' son, Xenophon's Socrates calls on the Spartan element in Athenian national spirit.[110] He does not believe that his country, torn by discord though it is, can be sick to death. He points out that Athenians are capable of accepting severe discipline in choirs, in gymnastic contests, and in the navy; and suggests that the authority still possessed by the Areopagus is a sign of hope for the future, although the discipline of the army is corrupt and its generalship vague and aimless. One generation later, the restoration of the authority of the Areopagus is an essential point in Isocrates' plan for regenerating the dangerously radical democracy; and Socrates' remark that the discipline of the chorus should be a pattern for the discipline of the army recurs in the first of Demosthenes' *Philippics*.[111] If Socrates really expressed these or similar ideas, then the opposition to the progressive degeneration of liberalism in the state might well have one of its roots in the Socratic circle.[112]

The problem of educating leaders for the state (which Xenophon puts in the foreground) is the subject of a long discussion between Socrates and Aristippus of Cyrene—who was later to become the chief advocate of hedonism.[113] It is an amusing glimpse of the intellectual opposition between Socrates and his pupil, which must have been very early apparent. The basic assumption made by Socrates is that all education must be political. It must train men to be either rulers or subjects. The distinction between the two kinds of training extends even to food and regimen. The infant prince must learn to ignore physical needs and desires in order to fulfil urgent duties; must be master of his own hunger and thirst; must be used to short sleep, late to bed and early to rise; must not be afraid of hard work; must not be lured by the bait of sense; must be hardened to resist heat and cold; must not grumble at sleeping out in the open. Anyone who cannot do all that is a subject, not a ruler. Socrates gives this education in self-control and abstinence the Greek name for 'training', *askésis*.[114] This 'training' (like 'the care of the soul') is an essentially Greek educational ideal, which, blended with later additions from Oriental religions, has had a vast influence on the culture of succeeding ages. But Socrates' askésis, or asceticism, was not the virtue of the monk, but the virtue of the ruler. Of course it meant nothing at all to Aristippus. He wanted to be neither master nor slave, but simply free; and his only aim was to live as pleasant a life as possible.[115] That, he held, was impossible for the citizen of a state: only a permanent alien, a *metic,* who was not a part of the citizen body and had no civic obligations, could enjoy such a life.[116] In opposition to his new and subtle type of individualism, Socrates represents the classical ideal of permanent citizenship, and holds that his political mission is to educate his pupils to be rulers, through voluntary askésis.[117] For the gods grant men no real good without difficulty and earnest work. He gives, like Pindar, a mythical example of this kind of paideia: the sophist Prodicus' famous fable of Heracles at the cross-roads, telling how Heracles was educated by Lady Areté.[118]

It was through Socrates that self-control became a central conception in our moral code. Whereas the popular ideal of law-abidingness had demanded only that we should pay external obedience to law, the ideal of self-mastery claims that moral action originates in the soul of the individual. But since Greek ethical thought started with society and the political idea of government, the Greeks realized the meaning of self-mastery by comparing the soul to a well-governed polis. The best way for us to understand the real significance of this transference of political ideals to the soul is to recollect how, in the age of the sophists, the external authority of law broke down. The result was that the inner law became supreme.[119] At the very time when Socrates was striving to solve the problem of morality, there appeared a new word in the Attic dialect: ἐγκράτεια, which means moral self-control, moderation, and steadfastness. Socrates' pupils Xenophon and Plato began to use it about the same period, and they used it frequently. In addition, Isocrates, who is strongly influenced by Socratic thought, had it now and then. The conclusion is inevitable, that this new concept originated in the ethical thinking of Socrates.[120] The word derives from the adjective ἐγκρατής, used of anyone having power or authority over anything. But the noun is found only in the meaning of moral self-mastery, and does not appear before this period; therefore it was obviously created to express the new concept, and did not exist beforehand as a purely legal term. *Enkrateia* is not any particular virtue, but (in Xenophon's words [121]) 'the foundation of all virtues': for it means the emancipation of reason from the tyranny of man's animal nature, and the establishment of the legitimate mastery of the spirit over the passions.[122] Since Socrates held the spiritual element in man to be the real self, we can translate the word *enkrateia,* without reading more into it than is actually there, by 'self-control', which is its direct descendant in our own language. The word contains the germ of Plato's *Republic* and of the idea on which *The Republic* is founded—the idea that justice is man's harmonious agreement with the law within his own soul.[123]

The Socratic principle of self-control implies a new freedom. It is noteworthy that the ideal of freedom, which has dominated modern thought since the French Revolution, was far less important in classical Greece, although of course the Greeks were well acquainted with it. The chief thing Greek democracy tried to secure was civic and legal equality, τὸ ἴσον. 'Freedom' was a concept with too many meanings to be useful in securing equality. It could mean the independence of an individual, or the whole state, or the nation. Of course they spoke of a free polity, or called the citizens of such a state free, to show that they were not slaves. But the primary meaning of 'free' (ἐλεύθερος) is 'not a slave' (δοῦλος). It does not have the all-embracing, indefinite ethical and metaphysical content of the modern idea of freedom, which has been penetrated and enriched by all the art, poetry, and philosophy of the nineteenth century.[124] Our ideal of freedom originated in the philosophy of natural rights. It led everywhere to the abolition of slavery. The classical Greek ideal of freedom was a positive concept from the realm of political rights. It was based on the existence of slavery as a permanent institution, in fact as the foundation of the liberty of the citizen body. The kindred word ἐλευθέριος ('liberal') describes the conduct appropriate to a free citizen, whether in generous spending, or in frank speaking (which would be improper in a slave), or in a gentlemanly way of life. The 'liberal' arts are those which belong to 'liberal' education—and that is the paideia of the free citizen, as opposed to the uncultured vulgarity of the unfree, of the slave.

It was Socrates who first regarded freedom as a moral problem; after him it was debated with varying degrees of interest in the Socratic schools. So far, there was no fundamental criticism of the social system that divided the inhabitants of one polis into freemen and slaves. That division remained. But it lost its deepest meaning when Socrates transferred the contrast between slavery and freedom into the inner moral world. A new idea of spiritual freedom now arose, to correspond to that development of 'self-control' as the rule of reason over the desires.[125] He who possessed it was the opposite of a man who was the slave of his own lusts.[126] The only importance of this for political freedom is its implication that a free citizen or a ruler can still be a slave, in the Socratic sense of the word. But that led to the conclusion that such a man was not really free, not really a ruler. It is interesting to see that although the idea of autonomy (which is used in this connexion by modern philosophers) was very important in Greek political thought to signify that a polis was independent of the authority of other states, it was not carried over into the moral sphere like those other notions. The thing that mattered, in Socrates' eyes, was evidently not that a man should simply be independent of some external norm, but that he should really be master of himself. So moral autonomy would mean, for him, to be independent of the animal side of one's nature: it would not contradict the existence of a higher cosmic law of which this moral phenomenon, self-control, would be an example. Closely connected with this moral independence is Socrates' ideal of frugality and independence of external things, *autarkeia*. It is mainly Xenophon (perhaps influenced by Antisthenes' books) who emphasizes this; [127] Plato does not make so much of it; but it is impossible to doubt that Socrates actually preached it. The Cynic school of moralists developed it after Socrates' death, and made abstemiousness the distinguishing mark of the true philosopher. But Plato and Aristotle bring it in too, in their description of the philosopher's perfect happiness.[128] The wise man, in his independence of the external world, re-creates, on the spiritual plane, a quality of the mythical heroes of old. The greatest of them, in Greek eyes, was the warrior Heracles with his labours (πόνοι), and the heroic quality was self-help. It began with the hero's power to 'make his hands keep his head' against enemies, monsters, and dangers of all kinds, and to come out victorious.[129] Now this quality becomes a spiritual one. It can be attained only by a man who conforms his wishes and endeavours to those things which are within his power to obtain. Only the wise man, who has tamed the wild desires in his own heart, is truly self-sufficient. He is nearest to God: for God needs nothing.

Socrates expounds this 'Cynic' ideal with full knowledge of its implications, in his conversations with the sophist Antiphon—who was trying to shake the loyalty of Socrates' pupils by joking about his poverty.[130] But Socrates does not seem to have carried it to the same individualistic extremes as the Cynics did after him. His autarky does not, like theirs, imply non-citizenship, the severance of all human ties, and indifference to *all* external things. Socrates still belongs to the polis. Therefore, he includes under 'political life' every kind of community: he thinks of man as part of a family, with his place in a circle of relatives and friends—the natural smaller societies without which man could not exist. Thereby he extends the ideal of harmony from the realm of political life (for which it was first worked out) to that of the family, and proves the necessity of co-operation in family and state by the analogy of the organs of the body—the hand, the foot, and others, none of which could exist in isolation.[131] And yet he was accused of undermining the authority of the family by his teaching. The charge shows that his influence on young people could sometimes be a great danger to old-fashioned family life.[132] He was in quest of a firm standard for human conduct, which could not be supplied even by rigid adherence to parental authority at a time when all traditions were collapsing. In his discussions, current prejudices were coolly dissected. On the other hand, we must not forget how many fathers asked his advice on the education of their sons. His conversation with his own adolescent son Lamprocles, who had complained of his mother Xanthippe's bad temper, shows how far he was from condemning anyone out of hand or from rebelling against all usage in his impatience with the natural ways, and even the weaknesses, of parents.[133] He explains to Chaerecrates, who cannot get on with his brother Chaerephon, that the relation between brothers is a sort of friendship, and that, as even the animals show, we are naturally disposed to it.[134] In order to develop it into something valuable, we need knowledge and understanding, just as we do to make the proper use of a horse. This knowledge is nothing new or complicated. Anyone who wants to be well treated by others must begin by treating them well. The principle is the same in friendship as in enmity.[135]

At this point we must examine Socrates' idea of friendship. It is not merely a theory, but has its roots in the Socratic way of life: for in that, philosophy and intellectual effort are indissolubly connected to friendly association with one's fellow-men. Our sources unanimously emphasize that point and attribute to Socrates a great number of new and profound ideas about the relation of man to man. In Plato, the Socratic concept of *philia*, affection, is raised to the metaphysical plane in *Lysis, Phaedrus,* and *The Symposium.* Later we must examine the theories Plato builds on it; meanwhile we must set against it Xenophon's evidence, which gives the problem of friendship just as much importance in another way.

A good friend is a possession of great value throughout one's life. But the worth of friends varies as much as the worth of slaves. Anyone who understands that will ask himself how much he means to his friends, and do his best to raise his value to them.[136] This new estimate of the value of friendship is symptomatic of the war-years. It rose throughout the war, and produced a whole literature of friendship in the post-Socratic schools of philosophy. We can find the praise of friendship in early Greek poetry too, of course. In Homer it is comradeship in war; in Theognis' aristocratic educational code it is mutual protection in the dangers of public life and during political upheavals.[137] This point is stressed by Socrates too. He advises

Crito to find a friend who will be like a watchdog to guard
him.[138] The lonely man was frightfully insecure in that time when
increasing political disharmony and sycophancy were undermining the firm basis of society and of all human relationships, even
the family. But what gave Socrates mastery of the new art of
friendship was his realization that all true friendships are
founded, not on external usefulness, but on spiritual value. True,
experience shows that there is often no friendship or good will
between good men with high ideals, but oppositions much more
violent than those which divide worthless people.[139] It is thoroughly disheartening to realize that fact. Men are naturally
predisposed to friendship as much as to enmity. They need one
another, and co-operate for mutual benefit; they have the gift
of sympathy; they do kindnesses and feel gratitude. But also
they strive to attain the same ends, and therefore compete with
one another, whether their aims are noble things or simply
pleasures; they are separated by differences of opinion; strife
and anger lead to war; desire for greater possessions makes
them hostile to each other; envy breeds hate. And yet friendship slips through all these hindrances and binds good men together—so that they prefer its spiritual worth to gold or honour,
and ungrudgingly allow their friends to dispose of their property
and their services, just as they enjoy the possessions and services
of their friends. Why should a man's efforts to attain lofty
political ends, honour in his own city, or distinction in its service,
keep him from being friendly instead of inimical to another
man who thinks in the same way?

The first necessity in friendship is to perfect one's own character. Then, one must have the gift of the 'lover' (which Socrates
ironically says he possesses)—of the man who needs others and
seeks them out, who has received from nature and developed
to an art the ability of pleasing those who please him.[140] Such
a man is not like Homer's Scylla, who grasps at men at once, so
that even far away they take flight. He is like the Sirens, who
lured men from a distance with their magical singing. Socrates
puts his own genius for friendship at the service of his friends,
in case they need his mediation in winning friends. He holds
friendship to be not only the chain that binds every political
association, but the real form of every productive connexion
between men. That is why he does not speak of his 'pupils' (as

the sophists do) but of his 'friends'.[141] This Socratic expression later entered the regular language of the great philosophical schools, the Academy and the Lyceum, and survived as an academic cliché.[142] But for Socrates it was no cliché. He always saw his associates, not as pupils, but as complete personalities; and the task of improving the young, which the sophists professed to perform, was for him (although he despised the sophists' self-exaltation) the deeper meaning of all his friendly association with others.

It is an amazing paradox that this supremely great teacher avoided calling his own work paideia, although everyone regarded him as its most perfect embodiment. Of course the word could not be permanently shelved: Plato and Xenophon use it incessantly to describe Socrates' activities and his philosophy. But he himself thought that contemporary educational theory and practice had made the word too heavy for him to use.[143] It either claimed too much or meant too little. Therefore, when he was accused of corrupting the young, he explained that he had never claimed to be trying to teach them [144]—meaning, to subject them to the professional training given by the sophists. Socrates was not a 'teacher', but he was constantly 'in quest' of a true teacher without ever finding one. What he always found was a capable specialist, who could be recommended in this or that field; [145] but he could not find a *teacher*, in the full sense of the word. A real teacher is a rare bird. True, everyone claims to be assisting in great works of paideia: poetry, the sciences, the arts, the law, the state, the sophists, rhetors, and philosophers, and even every honest Athenian citizen who helps to maintain law and order in the city imagines he is doing his best to improve the young.[146] Socrates does not believe that he himself understands that art. He is only surprised that he is the only man who is corrupting the young. He measures the great pretensions of others by a new conception of paideia, which makes him doubt their validity; but he feels himself that he too is beneath his own ideal. And so it becomes apparent, behind all this genuine Socratic irony, that Socrates has a far higher idea of the real teacher's task and its difficulty than any of his contemporaries.

His ironic attitude to his own teaching helps to explain the apparent paradox that he both maintains the necessity of paideia and rejects the most earnest efforts of others to produce it.[147] Socrates' educational love, his *erôs*, falls chiefly on exceptional young men, who are fit for the highest intellectual and moral culture, for areté. Their quick intelligence, their good memory, and their eagerness to learn call for paideia. Socrates is convinced that such men cannot attain all they want to and at the same time make others happy unless they are properly educated.[148] There are some who despise knowledge and rely on their own talents. To these, he explains that they are exactly the ones who most need schooling—just as the best horses and dogs, who naturally have the finest breed and temper, must be sternly controlled and disciplined, while, if untrained and undisciplined, they become worse than all others. Gifted natures need insight and critical judgment more than ordinary ones, if they are to achieve something suited to their abilities.[149] As for the rich man who thinks he can look down on culture, Socrates opens his eyes too, and shows him how useless is wealth employed without judgment, and for bad ends.[150]

But he is just as cutting about the cultural snobbery of those who proudly believe they are elevated above their contemporaries by their literary knowledge and intellectual interests, and are already certain of winning the greatest successes in political life. Euthydemus, that blasé youth, is a rather charming representative of this type.[151] Socrates' criticisms of his general culture find a chink in his highly polished armour: for, although he seems to have books on every possible special field, from poetry to medicine, mathematics to architecture, still he has one gap in his shelves. There is no guide to political virtue there. And for a young Athenian political virtue is the natural goal of any general intellectual education. Is it, then, the only art in which a self-taught man can speak with authority,[152] though in medicine he would be called a quack? Can a man get confidence from everyone in the art of statesmanship, not by pointing to his teacher and his previous performances, but by proving that he knows nothing? Socrates convinces Euthydemus that the calling he is preparing for is a kingly one,[153] and that no one can succeed in it without being just. In the same way as he inspires uncultured people to do something to improve themselves, so now he awakens the culture-snob to the fact that he lacks the one essential—knowledge. Euthydemus is drawn into a cross-examination about the nature of justice and injustice, which shows him that he really understands neither of them. And now, instead of book-learning, he is shown another way to reach political virtue, which begins with the recognition of his own ignorance, and with self-knowledge—namely, with the knowledge of his own powers.

Our evidence puts it beyond a doubt that this was the genuine Socratic procedure, and that the aim of his educational passion was this same political virtue. The meaning of political virtue is shown most clearly in Plato's early Socratic dialogues. To-day these works are usually called by the name Aristotle gives them —he calls them the *ethical* dialogues.[154] But nowadays that name easily leads to misunderstandings. We do not think that 'ethical' implies sharing in the life of the community—which was its natural meaning for Aristotle;[155] in fact we often think that the essence of ethics is its separation from politics. This separation of the inner life of each individual from the community is not merely an abstraction made by modern philosophers. It is deeply rooted in our thought and ways of life. It is created by the centuries-old double standard of the modern 'Christian' world— which recognizes the severe claims of the Gospel on the individual's moral life, but judges the actions of the state by other, 'natural' standards. Not only does this dissociate two elements which were unified in the life of the Greek polis, but it changes the very meaning of ethics and of politics. This fact, more than anything else, renders it difficult for us to understand Greece: for it makes us just as liable to misapprehension when we say that the virtues Socrates discusses are 'political', as when we speak of 'ethical' dialogues. When we say that the Greek's whole life and morality was 'political' in the sense meant by Socrates and Aristotle, we mean something very different from the modern technical conception of politics and the state. We can realize that, if we only think of the difference between the abstract-sounding modern term 'state' (from the late Latin *status*) and the concrete Greek word 'polis', which vividly calls up before our minds the living whole of the human community and the individual lives organically connected with it and with each other. Now, it is in that classical sense that Plato's Socratic dialogues on piety, justice, courage, and prudence are investigations of the nature of 'political' virtue. As we have already shown, the typical number *four,* in the fourfold canon of what are usually called the Platonic cardinal virtues, shows that the canon is a survival of the ideals of civic virtue current in the early Greek polis, because we find it mentioned as early as Aeschylus.[156]

Plato's dialogues reveal an aspect of Socrates' work which in Xenophon is almost entirely hidden by his activity in encouraging and admonishing others. That is the *elenchos,* his cross-examination and refutation of his interlocutor. However, as Plato's description of the regular patterns of Socrates' speech shows (p. 38), this examination is the necessary complement to the exhortation: it loosens the ground in preparation for the seed, by showing the examinee that his knowledge is only imaginary.

These cross-examinations always run along the same lines. They are repeated attempts to find the general concept underlying a particular name descriptive of a moral standard, such as 'courage' or 'justice'. The form of the question (What is 'courage'?) seems to show that the aim of the investigation is to find a definition. Aristotle expressly says that the definition of concepts was an achievement of Socrates,[157] and so does Xenophon.[158] If true, this would add an important new feature to the picture we have so far worked out: it would make Socrates the inventor of logic. On this was based the old view that he was the founder of the philosophy of concepts. But recently, Maier, contesting the evidence of Aristotle and Xenophon, has endeavoured to prove that it was simply derived from Plato's dialogues, and that Plato was simply expounding his own doctrine.[159] According to this thesis, Plato found the outlines of a new conception of knowledge in Socrates, and from them developed logic and the abstract concept; Socrates was only an exhorter, a prophet of moral independence. However, there are quite as many difficulties in the way of accepting this view as in believing its opposite, that Socrates taught the theory of Ideas.[160] That Aristotle's and Xenophon's evidence is only taken from Plato's dialogues cannot be proved and is not probable.[161] Our evidence is unanimous in presenting Socrates as the invincible master of the art of dialectic—conversation in question-and-answer form—although Xenophon makes less of that art than of his protreptic activity. What the purpose and the meaning of these attempts to define concepts might be is another question; but there can be no doubt that Socrates made them. We must grant that if we took the traditional view that he was simply a philosopher of abstractions, we could not understand why his pupil Antisthenes devoted himself entirely to ethics and moral exhortation. But, on the other hand, if we limit his teaching to the 'gospel of the moral will', we cannot understand the origin of Plato's theory of Ideas, and the fact that Plato connects it closely with Socrates' 'philosophizing'. There is only one escape from this dilemma. We must acknowledge that the form in which Socrates attacks the ethical problem was not simply a prophetic message, an overwhelming moral preachment; but that some of the energy of his adjurations to 'take care of the soul' went into an endeavour to discover the nature of morality by the power of the logos.

The purpose of the Socratic dialogue is, by discussion with other men on a subject which is of incomparable interest to all concerned—namely, the highest values in human life—to reach an agreement which must be recognized as valid by everyone. In order to reach this result, Socrates always starts with what is admitted, either by his interlocutor, or by people in general. This admission is used as the 'hypothesis', the foundation. Then the discussion works out what follows from the hypothesis, and tests those findings by other facts which we know to be established. Therefore an essential factor in the dialectic advance is the discovery of the contradictions which confront us when we base arguments on certain definite statements. These contradictions compel us to re-examine the correctness of the judgments we had laid down as true, and sometimes to revise them or abandon them. The aim of all this process is to bring separate phenomena in the realm of moral standards under one supreme general standard. But in his investigations Socrates does not start by looking for this 'Good in itself'. He starts with some 'virtue' denoted by the name of a particular moral quality—for instance, the quality we call bravery or justice. Thus, in *Laches*, there are a number of attempts to find out what 'courage' is; but the statements made about it must be dropped, one after another, because each of them describes the nature of courage too narrowly or too broadly. Socrates' discussion of justice with Euthydemus in Xenophon's *Memoirs* follows the same lines.[162]

This, then, is really the method of the historical Socrates. The word 'method' is not adequate to express the ethical meaning of the procedure. But it is a Socratic word, and is an appropriate description of the great cross-examiner's approach, which was natural enough to him but had been polished into an art. Externally it might easily be confused with a very dangerous cultural skill which was developed to the rank of an art about the same time—skill in winning disputations. And there are in Socrates' conversations many triumphs of argument, which remind us of the catch-arguments so beloved by the 'eristics'. We must not underestimate the pure love of verbal competition in his dialectic. Plato has given a lifelike representation of it, and we can see why rivals or contemporaries (like Isocrates) who did not belong to the Socratic school could simply call the Socratics professional arguers.[163] That shows how strongly others were conscious of the argumentative side in Socrates' method. But still, with all their enjoyment of the fun of this new intellectual gymnastics, with all their sporting enthusiasm for Socrates' sure and supple grasp, Plato's dialogues are dominated by a deep seriousness and a whole-hearted concentration on the real object which is at stake in the game.

The Socratic dialogue is not the practice of some new art of logical definition on ethical problems. It is only the μέθοδος, the 'way' taken by the logos to reach right action. None of Plato's Socratic dialogues results in the discovery of a real definition for the moral concept it has been examining—in fact, it was long believed that they ended without any result at all. But they did reach a result, although we cannot detect it until we take several dialogues together and so work out what is typical in them all. All these attempts to define the nature of a specific virtue end in the conclusion that it must be a kind of *knowledge*. Socrates does not care so much for the distinction between the several virtues —namely, the definition of each one—as for the common element they all share, namely, 'virtue in itself'. From the beginning of each talk, the tacit expectation or presumption that this will be a sort of knowledge seems to haunt the discussion: for what would be the use of expending all this mental energy on solving an ethical problem unless the questioner hoped to get nearer in practice to his goal, the attainment of good? Nevertheless, this belief held by Socrates is opposed to the opinion which has been current throughout the history of morals. Most people have always thought that, too often, a man sees perfectly well what he ought to do, and yet decides to do what is wrong.[164] That we call moral weakness.[165] The more compellingly Socrates' arguments seem to show that areté must ultimately be knowledge, and the more eagerly his dialectic investigations are pursued with that fair prize in view, the more paradoxical this way of reaching results must seem to the dubious onlooker.

In these conversations we see the Greek faith in and love for knowledge, raised to its highest power. After the mind has compelled the various parts of the external world to arrange themselves in an ordered structure, it attempts the even bolder task of bringing the dislocated life of man under the rule of reason. Aristotle, who still held this bold faith in the architectonic powers of the mind, thought as he looked backwards that Socrates' 'virtue is knowledge' was an intellectual exaggeration; and he tried to bring it into the proper proportion by emphasizing the importance of taming the passions in moral education.[166] But Socrates' assertion was not meant to be the revelation of a psychological truth. Anyone who tries to extract from his paradox the positive meaning that we are working out will easily recognize that he disliked what had until then been called knowledge, and had been proved to be devoid of moral force. The knowledge of good which he reaches, starting from all the separate human virtues, is not an intellectual operation, but (as Plato recognized) the now conscious expression of something existing in the spirit of man. It is rooted in the depths of the soul, at a level where to be penetrated by knowledge and to possess the object known are not two different states but essentially one and the same. Plato's philosophy is an effort to descend to those new depths in the Socratic conception of knowledge and to draw out all that is in them.[167] For Socrates, it is no contradiction of the statement 'virtue is knowledge' to say that in the experience of most men knowing good is not the same as doing it. That experience merely shows that real knowledge is rare. Socrates does not boast of possessing it himself. But by proving that men who think they have knowledge really know nothing, he prepares the way for a conception of knowledge which corresponds to his postulate and really is the profoundest force in the human soul. For him, that truth (the existence of that knowl-

edge) is unconditionally established, because as soon as we analyse it by our assumptions we find that it lies at the basis of all
ethical thought and action. But for his pupils 'virtue is knowledge' is not simply a paradox, as at first it seemed; it is the
description of one of the highest potentialities in human nature,
which was once realized in Socrates, and which therefore exists.

The knowledge of good, to which the discussion of the separate virtues always leads, is something more comprehensive than
courage or justice or any single areté. It is 'virtue in itself', vari-
ously manifested in each separate virtue. But here we run into
a new psychological paradox. If courage, for example, is the
knowledge of good with special reference to those things which
are really to be feared or not to be feared, then the single
virtue of courage obviously assumes the knowledge of virtue as a
whole.[168] Therefore it must be indissolubly connected with the
other virtues, justice, prudence, and piety; and it is either identical or extremely similar to them. But in our moral experience
there is no commoner observation than that an individual can
be distinguished by the greatest personal courage, and yet be
extremely unjust, intemperate, or godless; while another man
can be thoroughly temperate and just without being brave.[169]
So, even if we go so far as to admit that the several virtues
are 'parts' of one comprehensive Virtue, we can hardly concede
to Socrates that this Virtue is wholly effective and present in
each of its parts. At most, we might think of the virtues as parts
of a face, which has, let us say, fine eyes and an ugly nose.
Nevertheless, on this point Socrates is quite as unyielding as in
his conviction that virtue is knowledge. True virtue is one and
indivisible.[170] A man cannot have one part of it without the
others. The brave man who is intemperate, imprudent, or unjust may be a good soldier in the field, but he is not brave against
himself and his real enemies, his own tyrannous desires. The
pious man who faithfully performs his duties to the gods, but
is unjust to his fellow-men and intemperate in his hatred and
fanaticism, cannot possess true piety.[171] The generals Nicias and
Laches are surprised when Socrates expounds the nature of true
courage to them, and see that they have never really thought
it out, realized it in its full greatness, far less embodied it in
themselves. And the severe pietist Euthyphro finds himself
stripped and naked in all the humiliation of his self-righteous

and vindictive piety. What people call virtue in the traditional sense is revealed as a mere aggregate of the products of various one-sided types of training—one whose elements stand in irreconcilable ethical contradiction to one another. Socrates is pious *and* brave, just *and* temperate, all in one person. His life is both a battle and the service of God. He does not neglect his ritual duties to the gods: and that is why he can show the man who is pious in that external way alone that there is a higher kind of piety than his. He has fought with distinction in all his country's campaigns: and that is why he can argue against the highest commanders of the Athenian armed forces that there are other victories than those won sword in hand. So then, Plato distinguishes between the vulgar man-in-the-street virtue and higher philosophical perfection.[172] He sees Socrates as a moral superman. But he would express that by saying that Socrates alone possesses 'true' virtue.

If we examine Socratic paideia in Xenophon's description, which we used to get a first general survey of its rich content,[173] we shall find that it seems to consist of a string of separate practical questions about human life. If we examine it as presented by Plato, the underlying unity of these questions at once becomes evident—in fact, we finally recognize that Socrates' knowledge, or phronésis, has only one object: it is knowledge of the good. But if all wisdom culminates in one knowledge, to which we are inevitably brought back by every attempt at closely defining any single human good, there must be an essential kinship between the object of that knowledge and the inmost nature of human effort and will. As soon as we recognize that kinship, we can realize how deeply Socrates' assertion that virtue is knowledge is rooted in his whole view of life and humanity. He himself of course did not establish a complete philosophical system of human nature. It was Plato who did that; but Plato believed it was already present in the thought of Socrates. All that was needed to prove that was to work out what followed from one of Socrates' favourite statements. A complete metaphysical system was latent, not only in his 'virtue is knowledge' and 'virtue is indivisible', but in his three words 'nobody errs willingly'.[174]

That sentence is the sharpest and boldest expression of the paradox of Socrates' educational wisdom. At the same time it explains the direction in which all his energy is expended. The experience of individuals and of society, recorded in legal codes and the philosophy of jurisprudence, makes a ready distinction between voluntary and involuntary acts or misdeeds; thereby it appears to prove that the opposite of Socrates' statement is correct.[175] That distinction too is based on the element of knowledge in human activity: it passes quite a different judgment on wrongs done knowingly and wrongs done unknowingly. But the Socratic idea implies that there can be no wrongdoing with knowledge, for if there were, there would be voluntary wrongdoing. The only way to resolve the contradiction between this view and the long prevalent conception of guilt and error is to do as we did with the Socratic paradox of knowledge—to infer that he is using a different conception of *will* from the usual juristic and moral one. The two views lie on two different levels. Why can Socrates not accept any distinction between wrongdoing with and without knowledge? Because wrongdoing is an evil and justice a good, and it lies in the nature of good that it should be willed by everyone who recognizes it to be good. Now the human will becomes the centre of dispute. All the catastrophes caused by infatuated will and desire in Greek myth and tragedy seem to argue conclusively against Socrates' statement. All the more firmly does he emphasize it, and thereby at the same time he exposes the tragic view of life, and shows that it is a superficial view. He holds it to be a contradiction in itself to say that the will can knowingly will what is bad. This assumes that human will has a purpose: not to annihilate and injure itself, but to preserve itself and build itself up. It is reasonable in itself, because it is directed towards the good. This is not refuted by the countless examples of infatuated misdoing which cause human misery. Plato makes Socrates distinguish sharply between desire and will. Real will exists only when based on true knowledge of the good at which it is directed. Mere desire is an effort aimed towards apparent goods.[176] Where the will is conceived of as having this deep positive purpose, it is naturally based on knowledge; and to obtain this knowledge, if it is possible to do so, means human perfection.

Ever since Socrates framed the concept, we have been talking of men's *decisions,* and of the *aim* of human life and action.[177] The aim of life is what the will naturally wills—good. The metaphor *aim* assumes the pre-existence of another, the *way*, which is much older in Greek thought and has a separate history.[178] But there were many different 'ways', before the way could be found which led to the Socratic end. The good was imaged, now as the End on which all the ways of human effort converged (the *telos* or *teleuté*),[179] now as the Aim (*skopos*) [180] on which the shooter directed his arrow, and which he might hit or miss. In these images, life took on another appearance. It became movement towards a consciously willed stopping-place or climax, or the act of aiming at an object. It became inner unity, it took on form, it set up a tension. Man now began to live in constant watchfulness, 'looking towards the target', as Plato often says. It was Plato who worked out in abstract theory and concrete image all these consequences of the Socratic conception of life, and embodied them in his portrait of Socrates, so that it is hard to draw an exact line of demarcation between him and Socrates. However, the thesis that nobody errs willingly presupposes that the will is directed to the Good as its *telos,* and since not only Plato but the other Socratics too have that idea, it is clearly Socrates' own. What Plato did was to objectify in philosophy and art the new attitude to life created by Socrates. He classified men, according to the telos each strove to attain, under various types of life, and extended this idea to take in all realms of existence. In Plato Socrates began a rich development which attained its climax in Aristotle's 'biological' philosophy of life.

However important these consequences may be for the history of philosophy, it is Socrates' idea of the *aim of life* which marks the decisive point in the history of paideia. It threw a new light on the purpose and duty of all education. Education is not the cultivation of certain abilities; it is not the communication of certain branches of knowledge—at least all that is significant only as a means and a stage in the process of education. The real essence of education is that it enables men to reach the true aim of their lives. It is thus identical with the Socratic effort to attain *phronésis,* knowledge of the good. This effort cannot be restricted to the few years of what is called higher education. Either it takes a whole lifetime to reach its aim, or its aim can never be reached. Therefore the concept of paideia is essentially altered; and education, in the Socratic sense, becomes the effort to form one's life along lines which are philosophically understood, and to direct it so as to fulfil the intellectual and moral definition of man. In this sense, man was born for paideia. It is his only real possession. All the Socratics agree on this point. Therefore it must have come into the world through Socrates, though he himself said he did not know how to teach. Numerous judgments could be quoted to prove that through the changes initiated by Socrates the concept and the meaning of paideia took on a broader and deeper spiritual significance and that its value for man was raised to the highest point. It will be enough to cite a remark made by the philosopher Stilpo, a prominent member of the Socratic school founded in Megara by Euclid. After the sack of Megara, Demetrius Poliorcetes wished to show Stilpo special favour by compensating him for the loot of his house: so he commanded him to render an account of all the property he had lost.[181] Stilpo wittily replied, 'No one carried off my paideia.' This epigram was a new version, revised to fit the time, of a famous maxim by one of the seven wise men, Bias of Priene, which is still current in its Latin form: *omnia mea mecum porto*, 'all that is mine I carry with me'. For the follower of Socrates, paideia became the sum-total of 'all that was his'—his inner life, his spiritual being, his culture. In the struggle of man to retain his soul's liberty in a world full of threatening elemental forces, paideia became the unshakable nucleus of resistance.

But Socrates did not take his stand outside the wreckage of his homeland, as did the philosophers of the early Hellenistic age. He remained within an intelligent and (until shortly before his death) a powerful state. The harder it fought against a world of foes for its existence, during the last decades of Socrates' life, the more important his educational work became to it. He wished to guide his fellow-citizens to 'political virtue', and to show them a new way to recognize its true nature. Although, outwardly, he lived in a period when the state was breaking up, he lived spiritually in the traditional era of earlier Greece, when the polis was the springhead of all the highest goods and values in life—Plato's *Crito*, very movingly, makes that clear.[182] But while he still believed in the political purpose of human life, he could not, because the spiritual authority of the state's law had been so gravely impaired, share the faith of any of the great old believers in Law, Solon, for instance, or Aeschylus. The sort of political education he wanted to give presupposed, as its first condition, the re-establishment of the inward moral authority of the polis. True, he does not seem, like Plato, to have believed in principle that the contemporary state was too ill to be cured. He was not, in spirit, a citizen of an ideal state made by himself, but through and through a citizen of Athens. And yet it was from him above all that Plato received the conviction that the recovery of the state could not be effected simply by the re-establishment of its outer authority, but must begin in the conscience of each man (as we should put it) or (the Greek phrase) in the soul itself. It is only from that inner source of truth that, purified by the examination of the logos, the real standard which is incontestably binding for all can be derived.

Therefore it was in Socrates' eyes entirely unimportant whether or not the man who helped others to know this standard was Socrates or not. Often and often he drives this point home. 'It is not I, Socrates, but the logos that says this. You can contradict me, but you cannot contradict it.' Still, philosophy was potentially at war with the state as soon as it turned away from the study of nature to look at 'human things', namely the problems of the state and of areté, and professed to set up standards for them. That was the moment when it gave up the heritage of Thales, and became the heir of Solon. Plato realized the necessity of this conflict between the state which has the authority and the philosopher without office who is searching for the norm of conduct; and he tried to abolish it by making the philosophers the rulers in his ideal state. But Socrates was not living in an ideal state. All his life he remained a plain citizen in a democracy, where everyone else had just as much right as he had to talk about the highest problems of public welfare. Therefore he explained that he himself was obeying a special command from God.[183] But the guardians of the state felt that this eccentric Athenian's self-chosen role merely disguised the rebellion of an intellectually superior person against the things that seemed right and good to the majority: therefore it was a threat to the state's security. The state wishes to be, alone and unchanged, the foundation of everything else. It seems to need no other basis to support it. It cannot bear

to have a moral standard set up with the claim to be absolute,
and it sees in such a standard nothing but the attempt of a pre-
sumptuous individual to make himself judge of the community's
actions. No less a one than Hegel denied that subjective reason
had the right to criticize the morality of the state, which (he declared) is itself the fountainhead and the concrete reason for
the existence of all morality on earth. That is a thoroughly
classical idea, and teaches us how to understand the opposition
of the Athenian state to Socrates. From that point of view Socrates was simply a revolutionary fanatic. But no less classical is
the attitude of Socrates himself—who prefers the state as it
should be (or rather, as it was) to the state as it is, and says
so in order to bring it back to harmony with itself and its true
nature. From this side, it is the decadent state which is the real
renegade, and Socrates is not just the voice of 'subjective reason'
but the servant of God,[184] the only man who stands on firm
ground while all others totter and fall.

His pupils took various attitudes to his conflict with the state,
which is best known to us from Plato's *Apology*. The least satisfactory to us is Xenophon, because he does not see the principles
at stake. Himself banished from his country for aristocratic tendencies, he strove to show that Socrates was condemned and
executed only because his views on preserving the state were
quite misunderstood. In other words, the whole thing was just
an unfortunate accident.[185] Among those who did recognize the
profound historical necessity of Socrates' death, many took the
view we have already seen represented by Aristippus in his discussion with Socrates of the nature of true paideia.[186] He held
that it was the inevitable conflict between the spiritually free
individual and the community with its inevitable tyranny. There
is no escape from that conflict so long as one lives as the citizen
of a political community, he said; and men of his type withdrew
from life, because they did not feel the call to martyrdom, but
wanted only to remain unobserved and ensure themselves some
enjoyment of life or intellectual leisure. They lived in foreign
countries as resident aliens, so as to be free of all civic duties,
and built themselves an ivory tower on this unsteady foundation.[187] It is easier to understand that behaviour if one realizes
that historical conditions were not the same for them as for

Socrates. In the *Apology* Socrates himself, exhorting his fellow-citizens to areté, begins his address with 'You, citizens of the city which is greatest and most famous for its wisdom'; and that is an important guide to his motives in making the exhortation.[188] By inserting it, Plato intends to characterize Socrates' own position indirectly. But could Aristippus have felt the same emotion when he thought of his own birthplace, the rich African colonial city of Cyrene?

Only Plato had enough Athenian feeling and enough 'political' feeling to understand Socrates fully. In *Gorgias* he shows the preliminary stages of the tragedy. There we see how it came about that it was not the conscienceless rhetors and sophists from abroad, training their pupils to exploit the state and to have profitable careers as cavaliers of fortune, but the Athenian burgher, filled with deep anxiety for his state and with the sense of responsibility for its future, who suffered the fate of being put away as intolerable to his own country.[189] His criticism of the degenerate state was bound to look like opposition to it, although his purpose was to reconstruct it. The representative leaders of the miserable Athens of his day felt themselves to be under indictment—although Socrates found excuses for the embarrassment in which he placed them, and declared that the desperate state of his city was only the crisis of a long wasting disease.[190] He preferred to look for the germ of the infection back in the era which the prevalent historical view presented as days of splendour and power. But that harsh judgment only strengthened the impact of his negative criticism.[191] We cannot hope to separate the fine gradations in which Socrates' part of this view passes into Plato's, and no subjective judgment can carry conviction. But, whether Socrates held it or not, this at least is undeniable—Plato's will to rebuild the state (which produced his greatest works) was formed by his experience of the tragic conflict with the contemporary state into which Socrates was drawn by his educational mission to reform the world. Plato never says that Socrates should have behaved in any other way. He never says that the jury could have been wiser or better. It was inevitable for both sides to be what they were, and fate took its unalterable course. The conclusion Plato drew was that the state must be reformed so that the real man could live in it. The historian can only judge that the time had come when the state was no longer strong enough to incorporate the realms of morality and religion, as it had done in early Greece when the state was all in all. Plato shows what the state ought to have been if it were to fulfil its original purpose at the time when Socrates proclaimed the new aim of human life. But the state was not what it ought to have been, and it could not be altered. It was too much of this world. And so Plato was led, by his discovery of the inner world and its values, not to reform the existing state, but to create a new ideal republic in which man could have his eternal home.

That is the timeless significance of the tragedy of Socrates, as revealed most clearly in Plato's philosophical struggles to solve the problem. Socrates himself was far from thinking of the conclusions that Plato drew from his death. He was still further from judging and interpreting his conflict and death as part of the history of the human spirit. If historical understanding had existed in his time, it would have destroyed the tragic element in his destiny. The doom which he suffered with the passionate emotion of a unique unconditioned experience would have been reduced to a natural process of development. To see one's own time or even one's own life as history is a doubtful privilege. The conflict could only have been met and suffered with the simplicity with which Socrates stood up and died for his truth. Even Plato could not follow him along that way. Ideally, he asserted that man must be part of his state; but for that very reason he retreated from political reality, or attempted to realize his ideal somewhere else, where conditions were better. Socrates was heart and soul bound to Athens. Except as a soldier going to fight for her, he never left her once.[192] He did not travel far away, like Plato; he did not even go beyond the suburbs, because he could not talk to the trees.[193] He says that he exhorted both foreigners and citizens to take care of their souls, but he adds 'particularly citizens of Athens, who are nearer me in blood'.[194] His service of God was dedicated not to 'humanity' but to his polis. That is why he did not write books: he only talked to men who were actually present. That is why he did not lecture on abstract theories, but argued his way to an agreement with his fellow-citizens about a common idea, presupposed in every such conversation, and rooted in common origin and a common home, common history and tradition, common laws and constitution. This sharing in a common knowledge or belief gave concrete content to the universals he was always seeking. His comparative neglect of science and learning, his enjoyment of dialectic and argument about questions of value are Athenian; his feeling for the state, for morality, and for the fear of God is Athenian; and not least Athenian is the intellectual charm which plays round his whole life. He was not attracted by the idea of escaping from prison, through gates unlocked by his friends' gold, and crossing the frontier into Boeotia.[195] In the moment of temptation, he said, he saw the laws of his city, which his judges had misused, appear before him and remind him [196] of all he had received from them since childhood, of his ties to his parents, of his birth and education, and of the benefits he had shared with other citizens in his later life. He did not leave Athens before, although he could have done so if he objected to anything in her laws; he had felt well contented there for seventy years. Thereby he acknowledged the laws, and now he could not withdraw his acknowledgment. Plato probably was not in Athens when he wrote these words. He fled to Megara with the other disciples of Socrates after his master's execution,[197] and wrote his earliest Socratic works either there or while travelling. He may not have known whether he would ever return to Athens. That casts a strange sidelight on his description of Socrates' endurance, even to his fulfilment of his last civic duty, which was to drink the poison cup.

Socrates was one of the last citizens of the type which flourished in the earlier Greek polis. At the same time, he was the embodiment and the finest example of the new form of moral and intellectual individualism. Both these characters were united in him, without impairment of either. The former pointed back to a mighty past; the latter looked forward to the future. Thus, he was a unique event in the history of the Greek spirit.[198] By the attraction and repulsion of the two poles of his nature, his ethical and political ideal of education was created. That gave it its profound internal tension—the realism of its starting-point and the idealism of its aim. This is the first appearance in the West of the problem which was to live through many centuries, the problem of state and church. For, as Socrates shows, that is not a problem peculiar to Christianity. It is not necessarily con-

nected with either an established church or a faith in revealed
religion; but appears at a similar stage in the development of the
Greek 'natural man' and his culture. Here, it is not the conflict
of two forms of society, each conscious of its power, but the
tension between the individual's citizenship in an earthly community and his immediate spiritual subjection to God. The God
in whose service Socrates performs his educational work is different from 'the gods in whom the polis believes'. The charge
against Socrates was chiefly based on that point:[199] and it was
well directed. It was of course wrong to think of the notorious
daemon whose inner voice held Socrates back from many
actions.[200] At most, his possession of a daemon can only mean
that, as well as the power of knowledge for which he cared
more than others, he possessed a very great deal of the quality
of instinct which blind rationalism so often lacks. Instinct, not
the voice of knowledge, was the meaning of the *daimonion*—as
is shown by the occasions of its intervention which he refers
to. But the knowledge of the nature and the power of good,
which had with overwhelming power taken possession of his
soul, became for him a new way to find God. Socrates' intellectual character made it impossible for him to give his allegiance
to any dogma. But any man who lives and dies as he did is
wholly the servant of God. His creed, that we must obey God
more than men,[201] is as surely a new religion as his faith in the
all-surpassing importance of the soul.[202] From this faith in God
there grows up, in Socrates, a new form of the heroic spirit,
stamped from the very beginning by the Greek ideal of areté.
In the *Apology* Plato presents him as the incarnation of the
highest courage and greatness of spirit, and in *Phaedo* he tells
of his death as a heroic triumph over life.[203] This Greek areté,
even in its highest incarnation, remains true to its origin. No less
than the deeds of Homer's heroes, the struggles of Socrates
made a new and splendid example to form the characters of
those who looked on it—an example which was to find, in Plato,
its poet and its prophet.

3

PLATO AND POSTERITY

MORE than two thousand years have passed away since Plato stepped to the forefront of the intellectual life of Greece, and turned all eyes towards his new Academy; and still, to this day, the character of any philosophy is determined by the relation it bears to Plato. After him, every epoch of classical culture was marked by Platonic characteristics, however strangely altered they might be; and finally, at the close of antiquity, the Greco-Roman world was dominated by the intellectual religion of Neo-Platonism. The classical civilization which put on Christianity, and, blended with it, passed into the Middle Ages, was a civilization whose thought ran wholly along Platonic lines. That is the only possible way to understand such a man as Augustine, who created the philosophy of history which the Middle Ages were to adopt, by taking Plato's *Republic* and Christianizing it into his *City of God*. Aristotle's philosophy itself was only another form of Plato's; and it was through assimilating Aristotle's philosophy that mediaeval civilization, both of the east and of the west, was able at its highest development to take over the conception of the universe established by classical thought.

In the Renaissance, the age of humanism, when classical culture was reborn, Plato too returned to life. His books, which had been practically unknown to the mediaeval western world, were rediscovered. Yet the Platonic undercurrents of mediaeval scholasticism had been fed by Augustine's Christian Neo-Platonism and the books of the mystic who goes under the name of Dionysius the Areopagite; and similarly, when Plato was rediscovered in the Renaissance, men first of all learnt to understand him through the still-living tradition of Christian Neo-Platonic teaching which was brought over to Italy with the manuscripts from Constantinople by refugees from the Turkish invasion. As introduced to the Italians of the Quattrocento by the Byzantine theologian and mystic Gemistos Plethon, and as taught in Florence by Marsilius Ficinus at the Platonic Academy of Lorenzo

77

dei Medici, Plato was seen through the eyes of Plotinus; and the same is true of the succeeding eras, until the end of the eighteenth century. Plato was thought of chiefly as a religious prophet and mystic; and, in the same degree as this aspect of the world was neglected by the new rationalist, scientific, and mathematical thinkers, his influence on contemporary thought was, with some notable exceptions, restricted to the theological and aesthetic movements of the period.

The change came at the end of the eighteenth century. The true Plato was discovered; and it was Schleiermacher—himself a theologian, but in active contact with the newly awakened spirit of German philosophy and poetry—who initiated the movement that led to his discovery. Even then, Plato was treated chiefly as the metaphysician who wrote of the Ideas. Students and thinkers turned again to his philosophy as the deathless prototype of that kind of speculative theorizing about the ontological structure of the universe which was losing ground fast, and which had been gravely impugned by Kant's criticism of the foundations of knowledge. Even in the age that followed (the age which saw the growth of the great idealistic systems of German philosophy) Plato was still thought to be the fountainhead of the new metaphysical energy which had inspired their creators. It looked like a new renaissance of the Greek spirit. Plato was not simply a philosopher. He was the philosopher *par excellence*. Meanwhile our knowledge of classical antiquity was increasing; a new type of classical scholarship developed on a broad historical basis (Wolf, Boeckh); and Plato's books began to be studied from a new point of view. The trend of this approach was towards seeing Plato, who had become a mighty figure detached from time and history, within his own social background, and making him a real, solid, historical character.

Since he was more difficult to understand than any other Greek or Roman writer, scholars tried to reconstruct his philosophy in the characteristic eighteenth-century manner, by abstracting any dogmatic content that could be found in his separate dialogues. From scattered utterances, they endeavoured to build up metaphysical, physical, and ethical theories for him comparable to those of later philosophers, and to fit them all into a system—for they could not conceive of a philosopher without a system. But Schleiermacher had the romanticist's keen perception that form is the expression of intellectual and spiritual individuality; and it was he who recognized the special property of Plato's philosophy—that it was intended not to take the form of a closed and orderly system, but to look like a continuous philosophical discussion aimed at discovering the truth. Of course, Schleiermacher did not fail to see that some of Plato's dialogues have much more constructive content than others. He distinguished those which contained a good deal of creative philosophy from those which were merely formal and introductory. But even though he assumed that they were all inwardly connected with one another, and with an ideal whole outlined more or less completely by the individual dialogues, he still held that the essential characteristic of Plato was to set forth philosophy in the life and movement of dialectic rather than in the form of a finished system of dogma. At the same time he pointed out Plato's polemic allusions to his contemporaries and opponents in various dialogues, and showed how his thinking was in many ways bound up with the philosophical life of his age. And thus Plato's books, which set scholars a difficult task, full of hard hypotheses, helped to create a new concept of scholarly interpretation, far higher than the customary patterns of purely grammatical and antiquarian scholarship. We may en say that, just as Alexandrian philology worked out its hods by research on Homer, the philosophical historians of ie nineteenth century found their best and most searching discipline in discussing the problem of Plato.

This is not the place for a detailed history of that much-vexed question. The work done on it has not always been on the same level as Schleiermacher's first great endeavour to apprehend the miracle of Plato's philosophical achievement, both through the philologist's attention to detail and through the aesthete's sympathetic perception of the organic whole. There are almost no limits to the detailed study which has been devoted to research on the text and on the authenticity of separate dialogues attributed to Plato. In fact, the whole Platonic question seemed to be losing itself in these shallows, after C. F. Hermann started the fashion of regarding Plato's books as stages in the gradual *development* of his philosophy. For this brought into the centre of interest a problem which had hitherto been little considered,

and gave it much greater importance. This was the problem of
the dates at which the several dialogues had been written. Since
there was virtually no absolute criterion to use in dating them,
scholars had previously tried to arrange them in chronological
succession according to their contents—and chiefly by using any
available signs of a single developing didactic plan underlying
them. It was a natural enough way to approach the problem,
and had been chiefly upheld by Schleiermacher. But it seemed to
be proved false by the suggestion that the dialogues could be
recognized as the successive stages of an *involuntary development* of Plato's thought. By analysing their content, scholars had
reached contradictory conclusions about their sequence. Therefore they now attempted to discover their relative chronology
by observing minute variations in their language and establishing particular characteristics of style which were common to certain groups of dialogues and to them alone. This method, in its
turn, was at first successful; but it was later discredited by its
own exaggerations. It actually undertook, by the purely mechanical application of language-tables, to determine the exact date
of every dialogue. But we must not forget that the greatest
revolution in the understanding of Plato since Schleiermacher is
due to a purely philological discovery. It was the Scottish scholar,
Lewis Campbell, who observed that a number of Plato's longer
dialogues are connected by common characteristics of style that
appear in the unfinished work of his old age, *The Laws*. He concluded, rightly, that these characteristics were peculiar to the
style of Plato's old age. Even if it is impossible to establish the
chronological sequence of *all* his dialogues in this way, we can
divide his books into three principal groups, and with a good
deal of probability assign most of the dialogues to one or another
of them.

This philological discovery naturally gave the *coup de grâce*
to Schleiermacher's widely accepted view: for it proved that a
number of the dialogues on problems of method, which he had
considered early and preliminary works, were really works of
Plato's ripe maturity. The general conception of Plato's philosophy, after remaining virtually unchanged for half a century,
was revolutionized. The focus of interest now shifted to the
'dialectical' dialogues like *Parmenides, The Sophist,* and *The*

Statesman, in which Plato, towards the end of his life, seems to be criticizing or reinterpreting his own theory of Ideas. At the time of Campbell's discovery, the great German idealistic systems of the nineteenth century had collapsed, and philosophers were beginning to turn back, with a new critical outlook, to the problem of knowledge and its methods. A certain number of them tried to find a fresh answer to Kant's critique of the problem. These neo-Kantians were naturally surprised and fascinated by the reflection of their own difficulties in the philosophy of Plato's old age, which had been hitherto unsuspected but was now revealed by the new chronology of his dialogues. Some held that the works of his old age meant his abandonment of his own early metaphysics (Jackson, Lutoslawski), others took the Neo-Kantian view that his Ideas originally were and always remained *methods* (so the school of Marburg). In any case, the new philosophical attitude to Plato overemphasized his interest in method just as much as the metaphysical approach of the previous fifty years had overpraised Platonic and Aristotelian metaphysical dogmatism in opposition to Kant.

Despite this contrast, the new conception of Plato, which treated the problem of method as the core of all his thought, had one point in common with the earlier metaphysical interpretation. Both held the *theory of Ideas* to be the real substance of his philosophy. Aristotle, after all, had done that: for his criticisms of Plato's teaching centred on the Ideas. The new interpretation of Plato culminated by maintaining that Aristotle's objections to the Ideas were misunderstandings; but in putting the emphasis entirely on this logical aspect of Plato, it indirectly proved that it derived from Aristotle's view of Plato, though it differed from his final conclusions. While Plato was still alive, and reaching the end of his career, criticism of his teaching within the Academy had (as the dialectical dialogues show) concentrated for some time on the ontological problem of method. That was where Aristotle's criticism of the theory of Ideas started. And yet, that leaves out a great deal of Plato's thought—as we can see by reading the dialogues that come between *Crito* and *The Republic.* Even in Plato's old age, the discussion of the Ideas is counterbalanced by *The Laws,* where the theory plays no part whatever, although the book is more than one-fifth of all Plato wrote. Still, it was not unnatural for the idealistic philosophers of the nineteenth century to take a renewed interest in Plato's theory of Ideas, and for their interest to be strengthened by the increasing concentration of contemporary philosophy upon logical problems. This tendency was encouraged by the constantly recurrent attempt of academic philosophers to extract all the positive teaching that Plato's dialogues contained—namely, all that the nineteenth century held to be philosophy, and therefore to be essential in Plato's work.

The next important step forward in the understanding of Plato's work was also an entirely philological discovery, although again it broke down a narrow philosophical conception of his meaning. This time the discovery did not concern the chronological sequence of his books, but their authenticity. Although even the ancients knew that there were some bogus works in the Platonic corpus, it was not until the nineteenth century that criticism of suspected books became really intensive. Of course it went too far in its scepticism, and finally stopped. Fortunately, although it left many difficult points obscure and undecided, it seemed not to have affected the traditional view of Plato's philosophy. His principal works were, for any competent judge, above suspicion; those which were impugned were almost all books of secondary importance. But his Letters also were held to be spurious. A number of those preserved under his name are quite certainly forged—and that fact had caused them all to be rejected. Thus, although some of them contain admittedly valuable historical information about Plato's life and his journeys to the court of Dionysius, the despot of Syracuse, scholars took refuge in the explanation that the forger of the Letters in question had incorporated much genuinely useful material in his forgeries. But historians like Eduard Meyer, struck by the real importance of the Letters as historical documents, came out for their authenticity, and were followed by philologists. In his great biography of Plato, Wilamowitz declared the most important of them—the sixth, seventh, and eighth—to be genuine. The assertion is now almost universally believed. Since then, scholars have been engaged in drawing the implied conclusions, and fitting them into the general picture of Plato's life and character. These

conclusions are considerably more important than appeared at
the time of the discovery.

Wilamowitz himself was trying to describe not Plato's philosophy, but his life. Accordingly, he took Plato's own statements in the seventh Letter about how he went to Sicily to
attempt to convert the tyrant of Syracuse, and about his own
political development, principally as autobiographical data.
Plato's moving description of his own repeated endeavours to
play an active part in politics not only made effective scenes for
his biographer to describe, in contrast to the cloistered quiet of
the Academy, but revealed the troubled psychological background of his career. It was now apparent that his contemplative life was not a gentle retirement, but was imposed by the
tragic opposition of destiny to a natural ruler born out of his
time. His various attempts to become an active statesman were,
it appeared, unhappy episodes in a life of pure reasoning, in
which he tried again and again to achieve political fulfilment for
certain ethical ideals of his philosophy. But once we realize that
the man who, in the seventh Letter, speaks of his own spiritual
development and the aims of his life, and whose attitude to his
own philosophy is determined by his career, is the true Plato,
we are bound to revise our whole conception of the significance
of his philosophy. It is impossible to separate his life from his
work. If it is true of any thinker, it is true of Plato that his
entire philosophy is the expression of his life, and that his life
is his philosophy. His two greatest books are *The Republic* and
The Laws. That means that he did not think of politics as the
occupation of a few periods in his career when he was trying to
turn thought into action; he thought of it as the framework of
his entire spiritual life, the principal and comprehensive object
of his whole thought. After long years of constant endeavour
to understand the true nature of his philosophy, I had finally
reached this view of it, without having given the Letters any
real consideration—because I had always shared the current
prejudice against their authenticity. It was not only Wilamowitz's brilliant personality, and the powerful reasons he adduced,
that converted me to believe the autobiographical data in the
seventh Letter were genuine, but, even more, the fact that the
description of his own character and career which Plato himself
gives in that Letter corresponded in every particular to the in-

terpretation of them which I myself had independently reached
by the detailed analysis of all his dialogues.

It is of course impossible for us here to analyse every one of
his books in such detail. Still, it is necessary to describe how his
teaching about the true character of areté and paideia was philosophically built up, stage by stage, in one dialogue after another.
The reader himself must understand what a dominating position
Plato himself assigned to that problem in his intellectual world,
what kind of roots it grew from, and what form it took upon
the soil of his philosophy. Therefore it is necessary to follow the
progress of his thought from its origin to its culmination in his
two main works, *The Republic* and *The Laws*. We may take the
smaller dialogues together as a group; but the greater works,
Protagoras, Gorgias, Meno, The Symposium, and *Phaedrus,*
which contain Plato's essential ideas about education, must be
treated independently from this point of view. Naturally *The
Republic* and *The Laws* will be the real core of our exposition.
Throughout, our aim is to take the picture of Plato which
emerges from these books, and set it in its right place in the
history of Greek thought. We are to consider his philosophy as
one of the triumphs of a culture (a paideia) which by his time
had become historically and philosophically conscious. We shall
therefore not treat it as a detached system of philosophical concepts, but try to show (more completely than is usually done)
the organic function it has within the general movement of
Greek thought and the development of Greek tradition. The
details of its technical equipment will therefore concern us less
than the formative outlines of the problems with which history
itself challenged Plato's thought, and on which his works took
shape. If this means that the real emphasis will be placed on the
'political' character of his philosophy, then the meaning of
'politics' in this connection is determined by the entire history
of paideia—and particularly by what we have said in the previous chapter about Socrates and his influence as a 'statesman'.
The history of paideia, considered as the genetic morphology of
the ideal relation between the individual and the polis, is the
indispensable philosophical background for the understanding of
Plato. All human effort to reach the truth is ultimately justified
for Plato, not (as for the great natural philosophers of the era

before Socrates) by the urge to solve the riddle of the world, but by the necessity of knowledge in maintaining and shaping human life. His aim was to bring the true society into being as the proper milieu for the achievement of the highest virtue possible to man. He was a reformer inspired by the educational spirit of Socrates, whose aim was not only to see the true nature of things, but to do good. His entire work as a writer culminated in two great educational systems—*The Republic* and *The Laws;* and similarly his thought always centred on the problem of the philosophical assumptions underlying all education, and was aware of its own lofty claim to be the highest power in moulding the human soul.

Thus Plato put on the mantle of Socrates. He inherited his master's leadership in the great debate in which philosophy criticized the educational forces of his age and the historical tradition of his nation: sophistic and rhetoric, legislation and the state, mathematics and astronomy, gymnastics and medicine, poetry and music. Socrates had said that knowledge of the good was man's goal and his standard. Plato now sought to find the way to this goal, by asking what was the nature of knowledge. Having passed through the purifying fire of Socratic 'ignorance', he felt capable of pressing on to that knowledge of absolute values to which Socrates had aspired, and thereby restoring the lost unity of knowledge and life. Plato's 'philosophy' sprang from Socrates' φιλοσοφεῖν. Its position in the history of Greek *thought* is defined by the fact that it is paideia, and that it is aimed at finding a large-scale solution to the problem of educating human beings. From another point of view, its position in the history of Greek *paideia* is defined by the fact that it points to philosophy and knowledge as the highest form of education and culture. It takes the traditional problem, how a better type of man is to be educated, and sets out to answer it by building up a new pattern of reality and value. This new code takes the place of the former foundation of all culture—religion. Or rather it is itself a new religion. That is its essential difference from a scientific system like that of Democritus, which is the complete antithesis, in the history of knowledge, to Plato's philosophy, and which historians of philosophy rightly compare with it as being one of the truly original creations of the Greek mind. And yet Greek natural philosophy—whose originators in

the sixth century we have already described as the creators of
true rational thought and true pioneers in the history of paideia
(see vol. I, p. 150 f.)—was in the age of Anaxagoras and
Democritus becoming more and more a professional concern of
scholars and specialists. It was Socrates and Plato who first
created a form of philosophy that could play its own powerful
part in the dispute started by the sophists about the nature of
true education, and could even claim to settle it. Although, starting with Aristotle, the scientific tendency in philosophy grew
stronger and stronger after Plato, he nevertheless infused something of his own educational spirit into all later philosophical
systems, and thereby raised philosophy in general to be the
highest cultural force of the later classical world. The man who
founded the Academy is rightly considered as a classic wherever
philosophy and science are respected and taught as formative
forces on the soul of man.

PLATO'S SMALLER SOCRATIC DIALOGUES
THE PROBLEM OF ARETE

In the long series of Plato's books there are some which resemble one another so closely as to form a unified group. They are usually called the 'Socratic dialogues' in the strict sense, although they are not the only ones built around the personality of Socrates. They represent the Socratic dialogue in its original form, simplest and closest to reality. They are short enough to seem like a casual conversation. The point from which they start, the end towards which they move, the inductive method they follow, and the examples they use, are all so much alike as to fall into a typical pattern, obviously that of the original which they are intended to represent. They are all in the easy colloquial Attic of conversation; throughout Greek literature there is nothing to equal the unaffected charm, genuineness, and freedom of their light idiomatic speech. Even without their contrast to the richer language and more complicated structure of works like *The Symposium, Phaedo,* and *Phaedrus,* the freshness and bloom of this group would be enough to mark it off as the work of Plato's youth. It was inevitable that the art of the dialogue, under the hands of the craftsman who created it, should develop a greater elaboration in the course of years, and end by incorporating tortuous arguments, complicated proofs, contests of eloquence, and dramatic changes of scene. There can be no doubt that one of Plato's chief purposes in creating these little pictures was to show his master practising his famous dialectic art.[1] He was a born dramatist, and the rapid vicissitudes and *peripeteiai* through which the argument pursued its logical course were bound to challenge him to imitate them. *Euthyphro* implies and alludes to the trial of Socrates; and since *Crito* and the *Apology,* both dealing with his death, form part of the same group, it is most probable that all the books composing it were written after he was executed. The fact that they do not all mention his death is not against the assumption that these exquisite miniatures were not created simply by a childish urge to imitate, but by the agony of the beloved master's death and the yearning to immortalize his memory.

Lately it has been suggested that when Plato began to write his dialogues his purpose was not profound and philosophical, but merely poetic and imaginative—which in this case means childish.[2] That too is why scholars have tried to place what they have called his first 'dramatic essays' before Socrates' death.[3] Of course that makes them into amusements of Plato's youth— impressionist sketches, as it were, in which he tried to capture the spiritual activity, the grace, and the irony of Socrates' talk. Accordingly, they have been subdivided into two groups: one referring to Socrates' trial and death (*Crito,* the *Apology, Euthyphro,* and *Gorgias*), and another which contains no such tragic allusions, and whose careless gaiety proves that it was composed before his execution.[4] This latter group has been supposed to be purely dramatic in purpose, and to have no philosophical import whatever; and it has been broadened so as to include even the prolific ideas and difficult reasoning of *Protagoras.*[5] It is thought to be valuable evidence for Plato's development—not so much for the growth of his philosophical thought, as for that of his literary powers before the birth of his philosophy. If this were true, we should have to think that, in this transitional period and in the works which belong to it, Plato as a young poet and dramatist was enthralled by the philosophical drama of Socrates' conversations, and impelled to imitate it, but was really more concerned with the drama than with its serious meaning.

To look at Plato's first dialogues in this purely aesthetic way is to impose ideas proper to the modern impressionistic age upon classical literature; and that is not safe. But even if it were, the theory makes too much of the poet in Plato at the expense of the philosopher in him. No doubt his philosophical readers have always been apt to neglect the form for the sake of the content, although he obviously attached very high importance to it. Only a great poet could give style the lofty place it occupies in his work, where it is the real and immediate revelation of the nature of things. Still, no critic has ever discovered a passage in Plato's works where poetic form and philosophical content do not completely interpenetrate. From the very first we see that his artistic powers are inseparably attached to one subject, to which he remains true even in his old age.[6] It is scarcely possible that in his first essays this subject—Socrates and his soul-transforming influence—should have had *none* of the deeper meaning which it has in all his later books. On the contrary: we should expect to find them full of the great realization which he gained through associating with Socrates and sharing in his search, and which unfolded itself in every possible way in his later books. Before he met Socrates (in very early youth, therefore) he had been a pupil of the Heraclitean philosopher Cratylus; and, according to Aristotle's not improbable account, by moving away from Cratylus' theories of eternal flux to Socrates' search for an eternal moral truth, he had been thrown upon a dilemma which he could not escape until he had made his fundamental distinction between the sensible and the intelligible world—namely, the theory of Ideas.[7] While still engaged in that conflict, Plato cannot possibly have wanted to depict Socrates merely as an artist might, with no philosophical intention. His first dialogues were not written while he was still in doubt. Not only in each separate dialogue, but throughout the entire group, his thought always moves with marvellous assurance straight towards the end he has in view. For in each of them is a different treatment of the same fundamental problem, which appears more and more clearly behind them all, the more we read them. The central problem round which they all move, with such awareness as to exclude any possibility of chance in their composition, is the nature of areté.

At first glance, Plato's early dialogues seem to be separate investigations of moral concepts such as courage, piety, and self-control. Socrates and his interlocutors try to define what each of these virtues really is. Socrates always proceeds in the same way. He gets the other man to make a statement which turns out to be an amusing proof of the speaker's awkwardness and inexperience in this kind of enquiry. All the usual mistakes are made, and patiently corrected by Socrates. Every new definition is partly true, and corresponds to some real experience, which goes to explain the nature of the virtue under discussion. But none of the answers is satisfactory, because none of them fully covers the subject. It is rather like a practice course in elementary logic, conducted by a first-rate mind: all the more so because the constant repetition of analogous mistakes and tricks of method shows that there is particular emphasis on the methodical side of these conversations. Plato does not portray a random dialogue of wandering questions and answers. He knows the rules of the game. And he is obviously trying to direct the reader's attention to them and to give practical examples of their use. The author of these dialogues is not a man who has just realized that a proper definition of courage cannot begin 'Courage is when you . . .' Even without being able to prove it, we feel at once that every step, right or wrong, which he makes his speakers take, has been planned with full consciousness of its meaning. One would need to be very naïve to believe that, just because none of the dialogues ends in a methodical definition of the subject under discussion, they are the first fumbling ventures of a beginner in a still unexplored field. What is called the 'negative result' of these cross-examinations, these *elenctic* dialogues, means something quite different. We end our conversation with Socrates by discovering that we do not really know what we thought we knew—namely, the nature of courage or self-control. But this barren harvest of all our efforts is not discouraging, as it would be if we merely realized our own helplessness, but rather stimulating. It inspires us to grapple with the problem again. Several times Socrates says in so many words that the question will be taken up again later: as the real Socrates may well have said on many such occasions. When we observe in reading them that not one of the little dialogues concludes with the expected result, but all turn into a question-mark at the end, we feel a philosophical excitement which has a profound educational influence.

Listening and watching at his master's conversations, Plato had often felt his power to guide men's souls. He must have known that as an author his own greatest and hardest task in re-creating Socrates' teaching was to make his readers feel the same influence he had once felt himself. He could not do it simply by writing down Socrates' questions and the answers he had received. Indeed, that might have been extremely boring to read, if it lacked the real dramatic drive. His great literary discovery was that there is enormous dramatic charm and excitement in the powerful advance of a purely philosophical or scientific research, striving towards its goal in a succession of new and startling evolutions. No form of communicating thought can awake the interest and sympathy of the reader so surely as a well-planned conversation aimed at discovering the truth. The repeated attempts of the Socratic dialogues to reach the truth by pooling the intelligence of the speakers show Plato's full mastery in the pedagogic art of making his readers wish to co-operate. As we read, our thoughts outstrip the discussion and try to reach its end; so that when Plato brings us, not once only but every time, to what seems to be an impasse, he makes us wish to think beyond it and go on with the train of reasoning started in the discussion. If these were real conversations at which we happened to be present, it might be pure chance that they came to a negative conclusion. But a philosophical writer and teacher who brings us again and again to a confession of ignorance must mean to do more than give a lifelike picture of the proverbial 'ignorance' of Socrates. He is setting us a riddle, and he believes the solution lies within our grasp.

These conversations are all attempts to find out the nature of one virtue; and they all lead to the admission that this virtue, whichever it is, must be some kind of knowledge. If we ask 'knowledge of what?' we discover that it is knowledge of the good. We recognize this for Socrates' well-known paradox: Virtue is Knowledge. But at the same time we feel that a new force is at work in Plato's Socratic dialogues, not merely to re-create the master himself, but also to take up his problem and go further with it. The attentive reader will see the workings of this force in the fact that Plato's Socrates is exclusively concerned with the problem of virtue. From the *Apology* we know that the real Socrates tried above everything else to exhort his fellow-men to practise 'virtue' and 'the care of the soul'; and that the cross-examination which went along with his exhortation and convinced his interlocutor of his own ignorance was just as much a part of that protreptic mission. Its aim was to disquiet men and move them to do something for themselves. But in Plato's other books of this early period, the protreptic preaching is far less important than the elenctic cross-examination. Clearly Plato wants to push his readers forward to the knowledge of virtue, without letting them stop at the consciousness of their own ignorance. The helplessness (*aporia*) which was Socrates'

perpetual state was for Plato a challenge to solve the problem
and escape. He tries to find a positive answer to the question:
what is virtue? It is clear that he is following a well-planned
course: for in these dialogues he takes up first one virtue, and
then another. Apparently he does not go beyond Socrates' confession of ignorance; but only apparently. For each of these
attempts to define this or that special virtue culminates in the
acknowledgment that it must be knowledge of the good. This
concentrated advance shows clearly that the strategy of its guide
is directed wholly towards one problem: what is the nature of
that knowledge which Socrates vainly sought among men—
which must nevertheless lie buried somewhere in the soul, because without it man cannot reach true perfection? and what is
the nature of its object, the 'good'?

To begin with, neither question is answered. But we are not
simply left in darkness: a firm hand guides us through it. With
astonishing flair for the essential, Plato seems to have reduced
that Protean thing, the Socratic spirit, to a few clear outlines.
By drawing them with a firm hand, he made the picture of
Socrates which was to be permanent. But though these features
were characteristic of the real Socrates, they have here hardened
into concentration on one problem alone. Plato's attention, like
that of his master, was centred on that problem because it was
essential to our life here that it should be solved. But the clarity
with which all its theoretical sequelae are worked out in these
early dialogues proves also that it was deeply rooted in a world
of ideas which Plato knew well, although it was still kept in the
background of his thought. It is not revealed until we reach
Protagoras and *Gorgias* and look forward to *The Republic*.
Thus, in his earliest works, there appears the problem with
which all his interpreters since Schleiermacher have been concerned: can his books be explained separately, or must each of
them be interpreted through all the rest? Schleiermacher thought
the latter answer was certainly the right one. He believed it was
obvious that Plato's books, although instead of developing his
thought into a well-planned system they took the pedagogical
form of the dialogue, were nevertheless meant from the first to
form one intellectual whole which was dialectically unfolded,
step by step, through them all. But his antagonists believe
that these steps were *temporal* stages in the 'development'

of Plato's thought, and that, of the various groups into which Plato's works fall, each represents the opinion he held at a certain period of his life. They think it quite impossible to take one of Plato's books in which he deals with some problem for the first time, and to explain it by those of his later works which seem to cast a brighter and more spacious light on the problem and his approach to it.[8]

The problem becomes acute when we discuss the dialogues of his youth. Those who believe them to be merely little dramatic character-sketches naturally keep them apart from all his other works.[9] But even scholars who believe they have some philosophical meaning usually treat them as relics from a purely 'Socratic' period of Plato's life, and assume that they contain little or nothing of Plato's own thought.[10] They take *Gorgias* to be the first work which contains the outlines of his doctrine. Also, *Gorgias* seems to be the first dialogue envisaging the political problem which was to be fully worked out between 380 and 370 in that masterpiece, *The Republic*. Accordingly, these little Socratic dialogues are merely ethical enquiries of the type regularly pursued by Socrates. Those who hold this view generally assume (and of course the assumption would add a great deal of weight to their theory) that when Plato was writing his first dialogues he had not yet formulated the theory of Ideas. There are, it is said, no direct allusions to it in them, and it was not created till later in his life, when he was interested in logic and the problem of knowledge, as he is beginning to be in *Meno*. Therefore, apart from the literary charm and grace of these early dialogues, their chief value is historical, and we should treat them simply as evidence for the character and teaching of the real Socrates.

This method of approaching Plato's works has certainly brought out a large number of important facts which have never had as much attention as they deserved. If it had not, it could never have held the field for so many years against all other interpretations. Plato wrote dialogues all his life; but the language, the style, and the structure of the dialogue-form underwent an enormous change in his hands between *Laches* and *Euthyphro* and *The Laws*—a change which was not wholly due to the difference between the subjects he was treating. With deeper knowledge of his work we have come to see that con-

scious purpose and unconscious variation produced developments
in his style which correspond very remarkably to the chief periods in his life, and which entitle us to say that he had an *early*
style, a *middle* style, and an admittedly *late* style. He examined
the problem of education and the state in two powerful books,
The Republic and *The Laws,* and his attitude to it in middle
life was widely different from the attitude of his old age. So we
must admit that not only the poet and his style, but the thinker
and his thought were transformed with the passing years. Every
attempt to find systematic unity in Plato's philosophy without
taking into consideration the historical facts of his development
falls into inevitable difficulties as soon as it tries to put all his
works on a level and treat them as equivalent authorities. Zeller
started by declaring that Plato did not write *The Laws,* because
it is so different from his principal works; in his history of
Greek philosophy he was forced to admit its authenticity, but he
had to discuss it in an appendix, because it was so unlike the
description of Plato's philosophy which he had built up from
the rest of Plato's major works.

But even if we admit these facts, we cannot accept all the conclusions which have been drawn from the idea that Plato underwent a constant development. In particular, this interpretation,
although so long accepted, breaks down when it comes to the
earliest dialogues. What we have said of their philosophical content makes it impossible to treat them as playful mimicry of real
Socratic conversations.[11] Nor can they be the reflex of a purely
Socratic period in Plato's thought.[12] As we have pointed out
again and again, it is a modern mistake to describe them as
ethical enquiries, and to believe Plato was exclusively interested
in 'ethics' at the outset of his career. That mistake becomes plain
as soon as we look at these enquiries against the broader background which Plato gives them in his later works. The virtues
discussed in these first dialogues are exactly the same as those on
which the Republic is founded. Courage, piety, self-control, and
justice are the old political virtues of the city-state and its citizens.[13] The first three are discussed in the early dialogues—each
in a separate work. Justice, which is the virtue most intimately
connected with the nature of the state, and indeed is its very
soul, is discussed in the first book of *The Republic.* It has often
been pointed out that this introductory book is half-independent

of the rest of *The Republic,* and that its form most closely resembles that of the early 'Socratic' dialogues. Some have even suggested that it was once an independent work which Plato incorporated in *The Republic,* in order to build the ideal state upon justice, with which it deals. Although many still believe this, it is really no more than a brilliant hypothesis. And yet, true or not, it does illustrate the close organic connexion between the early dialogues and the ideas underlying *The Republic,* in which the world of Plato's thought is revealed for the first time as a whole. Not only that first book, with its discussion of justice, but *Laches, Charmides,* and *Euthyphro* with their discussions of the nature of courage, self-control, and piety, even if they have no structural link with *The Republic,* still belong to the same realm of ideas. They are, as it were, the material of its foundations.

In the *Apology* Socrates' influence and the way he taught his fellow-citizens to approach true areté are related to 'the polis itself'. That stamps his mission as a political one.[14] If we look carefully, we shall see that Plato maintains that tone in all the smaller dialogues. We need only point to Socrates' conversation in prison with his old friend Crito, which deals with the citizen's duty to obey the law at all costs.[15] *Laches* emphasizes the political significance of its problem—the best way to educate the sons of two well-off citizens, in which the famous Athenian generals Nicias and Laches take part.[16] *Charmides* has several links to *The Republic* and its fundamental doctrines. It is the first dialogue to mention (as a 'riddle') the almost untranslatable idea τὰ ἑαυτοῦ πράττειν: 'to mind one's own business', 'to do one's own job and leave other things alone'.[17] The division of functions and social classes in *The Republic* is based on that idea.[18] And Plato several times points out the immediate importance to the lawgiver and to the government of the question around which *Charmides* is constructed: what is temperance, or self-control?[19] The science of politics appears in it (as in *Gorgias*) as a counterpart of the science of medicine.[20] And piety too, which is discussed in *Euthyphro,* is connected with politics: for the discussion arises from a problem of religious law. But in any case piety was for the classical Greeks a political idea, because it meant paying the proper honour to the gods of the state, who preserved the laws and institutions of the state.

After all this it is scarcely necessary to add that these separate lines of enquiry all meet in *Protagoras,* which shows the direction in which they have been moving by calling them all together 'the political art', πολιτικὴ τέχνη.[21] It is this political art or science whose elements Plato was investigating in his early dialogues, when he tried to define the nature of the fundamental political virtues. Later he was to build the true state upon these same virtues, and this is the beginning of that great work. Thus the central problem of *The Republic,* which is later revealed as the high point of Plato's educational activity—how men can acquire knowledge of the Idea of good—is foreshadowed in the very earliest of his books.

It is only when we see these youthful dialogues in this light that we understand the place Plato gave them in the whole scheme of his philosophy. Now we can realize that, from the very outset, the whole which he envisaged was the state. In his principal work on politics, he maintained that philosophers should rule the state because they possess knowledge of the good, and therefore they have that which is vital to society, understanding of the highest standards on which all human life must be based. Since his very earliest works, starting from different points, all lead with mathematical certainty to the same centre, it is evident that a fundamental feature of his thought is this architectonic awareness of the general plan, and that it marks an essential difference between the books of the poetical philosopher Plato and those of every non-philosophical poet.[22] He well knew the end towards which he was moving. When he wrote the first words of his first Socratic dialogue, he knew the whole of which it was to be a part. The entelechy of *The Republic* can be quite clearly traced in the early dialogues. But this way of writing is a new and unique thing. It is one of the greatest revelations of the Greek power of organic creation. Under the guidance of a powerful intelligence which seems in matters of detail to create with all the freedom of untrammelled play, and yet works steadily towards a supreme and ever-present end, Plato's philosophy appears to *grow* with the liberty and the certainty of a magnificent tree. It would be a serious mistake to believe that, when he wrote these little intellectual dramas, Plato's spiritual range was no broader than their foreground. Many scholars who have upheld the theory that his dialogues represent different stages of his development convict themselves of a failure both in aesthetic and in philosophic understanding, by assuming that in every one of his books Plato says everything he can possibly say.[23] That is what gives even the smallest of his dialogues its incomparable power—the fact that the neatly defined enquiry into one special subject, dry and limited as it may appear, always stretches out beyond its limits and vitalizes the vast philosophical background on which it is being conducted.

Socrates himself, in claiming that men should be educated to areté, thought of that as a political task, since it dealt with political virtue. There Plato had to make no change in Socrates' dialectic; he simply continued his master's work, from the first of his dialogues onwards, in maintaining that he who carried on that moral education was helping to build up the state. In the *Apology,* that is called service to Athens.[24] And in *Gorgias* the standard by which the work of Athenian statesmen is measured is Socrates' own greatness as a statesman and a teacher.[25] But even as early as that, Plato had reached the radical conclusion that Socrates' purposes could never be fully realized in any contemporary state. This we learn from Plato's own invaluable evidence, in his seventh Letter.[26] He and his brothers Glaucon and Adeimantus (whom he significantly makes into Socrates' pupils and interlocutors in *The Republic*) evidently belonged, like Critias and Alcibiades, to the rising generation of the old Athenian aristocracy. They felt that family tradition predestined them to lead the state, and they went to Socrates to learn political virtue from him. Having always heard from their elders the bitterest criticisms of the existing Athenian democracy, they gave ready ear to a teacher who said he wished to make the state morally better. For greedy, ambitious youths like Alcibiades and Critias, Socrates' teaching was oil on the flames. But after the overthrow of the democratic constitution, when Plato was invited by his uncle Critias to join the new authoritarian government, he immediately saw that it was totally incompatible with Socrates' teaching, and refused.[27] The conflict of Socrates himself with the Thirty Tyrants, and their command that he should stop teaching, were for Plato unmistakable proofs of the moral rottenness of the new state.[28] He got a second invitation to take an active part in political life after the fall of the Thirty and the restoration of democracy; but again he was repelled, this time by Socrates' conflict with the democratic state, and by its tragic outcome, so that he withdrew from all political activity whatever.[29] This repetition proved to him that it was neither the oligarchic nor the democratic constitution which had made the state the mortal enemy of its best citizen, but its utter moral degeneration in every one of its forms.

Now he thought it was plain that it could not be reformed by one man, however wise. To carry through his reforms, he would need friends and comrades of the same persuasion. In his seventh Letter, he says it was in that period that he acquired the profound hopelessness which remained thenceforth his fundamental attitude to the greatest problem of his life, the problem of the state. He became convinced that for him, inspired by Socrates' educational mission, it would be a senseless waste of time and energy to take an active part in Athenian political life: since he felt that the contemporary state, not only in Athens but everywhere, was lost, unless a miracle came from heaven to save it.[30] Socrates had been entirely taken up with his passion to teach. He had cared nothing for the power at which others were grabbing: since the State (αὐτὴ ἡ πόλις) for which he lived and worked was a purely moral order.[31] It could be brought into existence by itself alone. But Plato always had a genuine instinct for politics. The moral conversion which his thought and will underwent through contact with Socrates never went so far as to numb or destroy that instinct, produced by his birth and strengthened by his upbringing. Socrates had held back from taking an active part in political life because his power to help the state lay in another field.[32] Plato held back because he knew he did not possess the power needed to realize what he felt was good.[33] Nevertheless, his efforts were always directed towards bringing the best state into existence somehow, and uniting those qualities which are usually separate on earth, power and wisdom.[34] Thus, through Socrates' collision with the state, Plato very early reached the fundamental idea of his whole life: that state and society could never be improved until philosophers became kings or kings philosophers.

According to the seventh Letter, in which Plato at an advanced age described the development of his own political and philosophical views, he found himself drawn to hold these opinions and made them known to others even before his first journey to southern Italy and Sicily—i.e. before 389-8.[35] We need not take this to mean that he had actually worked out the whole thing. He mentions the voyage to Sicily as the particular date before which he had reached that conviction, because he is trying to explain why his arrival at the court of the tyrant of Syracuse (whose nephew Dion eagerly accepted his teaching) later seemed to him to be a dispensation of divine Providence. For it was his arrival which gave the first impulse to the later overthrow of the Sicilian tyranny. He is trying to show how Dion reached the idea which he retained throughout his life and always endeavoured to realize: that a tyrant should be trained to be a philosopher. He declares that he originated the theory that philosophers should be rulers, and converted Dion to it. Therefore he explains how and when he himself thought out the doctrine. According to this evidence, he reached it not so much because of his journey to Sicily as because of Socrates' death.[36] We should thus place it considerably earlier than 389-8. It really falls into the period when he was writing his first dialogues. This fact is of immense importance in reconstructing their philosophical background. It proves the conclusion we have already reached by analysing them: that their real purpose is to aid in building up a political science whose task is to construct the best state. This is the simple but convincing solution to the difficulties which have often been found in Plato's own description of his development immediately after Socrates' death, down to his first journey to Sicily.

The thesis that philosophers must become kings or kings philosophers if the state is to improve is familiar to us from *The Republic*. Plato lays it down just before describing the education of the future rulers of the state. It is an impressive paradox, which has made the whole passage so famous that, when he mentions it in his seventh Letter, he seems to be quoting himself. As long as the seventh Letter was thought to be spurious, this fact was taken as proof of its falsity. Scholars thought the forger had tried to give his work the stamp of authenticity by repeating one of Plato's best-known ideas. But they thought he had failed to notice that by doing so, he would make Plato imply that *The Republic* (placed by modern research somewhere in the 'seventies) was written between 400 and 390. Now that

we once more believe the Letter to be genuine, another difficulty
has appeared. It is genuine, and Plato is quoting himself in it;
he must have known *when* he wrote *The Republic*. Therefore
he wrote *The Republic* in the 'nineties! [37] Of course it is impossible to believe that this, his greatest book, along with all the
others which it presupposes and which we have learnt to look
upon as the work of thirty years of continuous thought and
writing, could have been written in the decade before his first
voyage to Sicily. Therefore other scholars reject the conclusion
above, but suggest that there was an earlier and shorter edition
of *The Republic*, from which Aristophanes got material for his
jokes about the empire of women in his *Women in Parliament*,
produced towards the end of the 'nineties. [38] But this suggestion
is no more probable than the other. In his seventh Letter Plato
does *not* say that he had written down the thesis. He says he
had 'spoken of it': and indeed it is extremely probable that, while
teaching and lecturing, he often expounded and discussed the
views expressed in his dialogues—before he wrote them down
to explain to the outer world the true essence of his philosophy
and his educational doctrine. [39] It took many years for him to
commit his essential ideas to writing. But in teaching by word
of mouth he could not wait for three decades before revealing
the aim of all his enquiries into the nature of areté. And (though
it is often overlooked) there is no need of elaborate arguments
to prove that he did not start teaching at the foundation of the
Academy (388), but that all the works he wrote in the 'nineties,
from the smallest dialogues down to *Protagoras* and *Gorgias*,
were meant to help him in carrying out an educational programme which he was developing in true Socratic fashion by his
own talks and conversations.

This gives us the background for the smaller Socratic works
of the 'nineties. It cannot be reconstructed unless we give them
their proper place in the realm of thought revealed by *The Republic* and by Plato's own account of his development during
that period, given in his seventh Letter. But what his contemporaries chiefly saw in them was the continuation of Socrates' dialectical enquiries, [40] which Plato must have undertaken on his
return from self-banishment after Socrates' death. The little
dialogues show how he carried on these discussions, and the
points on which his theoretical reasoning was mainly concen-

trated. Apparently he began by making perfectly clear the assumptions of the logical procedure employed in these dialectical enquiries, and the regular logical patterns which they followed. Our evidence is such that we shall probably never be able to determine how far Socrates himself had gone in that direction, and how much logic Plato had learnt from him.[41] Many scholars are inclined to underestimate Socrates' work in that field, and to ascribe all those first steps to Plato—Plato, from whose school the next two generations were to explore territory which it would take two thousand years to settle.[42] Socrates made an art of 'contradictory conversations' and gave them his whole life. Surely he must have found out a great deal about logic; he cannot have been merely a routine performer. And yet, when we read the writings of his other pupils, we find that they have very little, if any, interest in logical theory and its application. And Xenophon's brief remark that Socrates was tireless in defining concepts does not help us very much in understanding Socrates' ability as a logician.[43] Plato's description of his dialectic should certainly be the easiest to accept as true, provided we remember that the subject has been enriched and developed by a man with a genius for systematic abstract thought.

But when we weigh the evidence offered by these first dialogues about the state of Plato's dialectic at that time, we find ourselves faced by the same problem which hinders our efforts to estimate their ethical and political content. Those who believe that they represent an early stage of Plato's development, appreciably different from the later ones, think they prove he was already familiar with such fundamental elements of formal logic as definition, induction, and the concept. But, as we have said, they point out that there is no explicit evidence in them for the theory of Ideas, although it is characteristic of Plato's dialectic in his later works.[44] From this point of view it is difficult to think how, from such modest beginnings in abstract logic, Plato ever got so far as to teach that Ideas were independent entities. According to Aristotle, he held that the ethical concepts which Socrates had always studied belonged to a world of permanent reality different from the ever-changing sensible world; and anyone who understands Greek ways of thinking must agree that this account sounds the most natural one, although it is very

alien to modern thought with its nominalist presuppositions.[45]
The whole tradition of earlier Greek philosophy would make
Plato assume that, where there is knowledge, there must be an
object to know. Aristotle says Plato's first teacher Cratylus had
convinced him that we live in a world of constant flux, of perpetual coming-to-be and passing-away. Then, when he met Socrates, a new world opened to him. Socrates tried to discover the
nature of justice, piety, courage, et cetera, assuming that they
were permanent and unalterable things.[46] We should say that
Socrates' questions about the nature of the just, the pious, and
the brave were aimed at discovering the concepts or universals
underlying them. But, though that is now a common way of
thinking, it was not discovered in those days. In his later dialogues Plato struggles with it and gradually masters it; while
Aristotle fully understands the logical process of abstraction.
But when Socrates asked 'what is good?' or 'what is just?', that
certainly did not mean that he and his pupils had full theoretical
knowledge of the logical nature of universals. When Aristotle
says that Socrates, unlike Plato, did not hold the universals he
was studying to exist in a world apart from that perceived by
sense, he does not mean that Socrates possessed Aristotle's own
knowledge of the universals, that he fully understood they were
abstractions, and that Plato made the mistake of duplicating
them by affirming that an independent Idea of the just existed
to correspond to the concept of justice. It is true that Aristotle
thought the Ideas, in so far as Plato held them to be a world
of independent realities outside the sensible world, were a needless duplicate of this sensible world. He knew they were needless, because he had recognized the abstract character of universals. But this only makes it more certain that Plato had *not*
reached that point when he created the theory of Ideas or Forms
—far less Socrates. Plato was the first whose logical genius enquired into the nature of that Something which Socrates had
been trying to discover with his questions about the good, the
just, and so on. For him the dialectic way to the good, the just,
and the beautiful in themselves, on which Socrates had set out,
was the way of true knowledge. When Socrates had got far
enough on his way to pass beyond change to permanence, beyond
the manifold to unity, Plato believed that in that unity and
permanence he had grasped true reality.

If our interpretation is correct, Plato thought he was captur-
ing the essence of Socrates' dialectic in his theory of the Ideas,
and tried to formulate its theoretical assumptions. It implies a
new conception of knowledge as something different from sense-
perception, and a new conception of existence or reality, different
from that held by the old natural philosophers. Dialectic method
tries to discover the One underlying the Many. When Plato
calls that One a Form (in Greek an *eidos* or *idea*), he is using
words which were habitually used by contemporary physicians,
to whose method he so often alludes with approval.[47] The
doctor takes a number of different individual cases, which have
the same fundamental character, and reduces them to one form
of illness, one eidos. The dialectician does the same in investigating an ethical question—for instance in exploring the nature
of courage. He takes a number of different cases which we call
courage, and tries to reduce them to a unity. In Plato's early
dialogues we can see the dialectic process penetrating further and
further towards Virtue in itself, the unity in which Socrates
gathers together all the separate virtues. Again and again, the
enquiry into the nature of a special virtue, instead of distinguishing it clearly from the other virtues, as we should expect, ends
in pointing to the higher unity of everything which we call virtue,
to the good in itself, and to knowledge of it. In one of his later
books Plato says that the process of dialectic discovery is
synopsis—looking at all the manifold together and seeing it as
one Idea.[48] That is just what is done in the smaller dialogues.
The aim of the question proposed in *Laches*—what is courage?
—seems to be to define courage. But what is actually achieved
is not a definition of courage at all: instead of that, the dialogue
ends by pointing out that courage is like all the other virtues,
part of virtue in general. So the 'negative result' of the dialogue
is inextricably connected with the synoptic character of the dialectic enquiry. The question 'what is courage?' was asked not in
order to find out what courage is, but in order to define virtue
in itself, the Idea of the good. But the synoptic character of
dialectic, with its concentration on reducing many different things
to one Idea, appears not only within each individual work, but
even more clearly in Plato's skilful grouping of them all around
one centre. Starting with enquiries into the nature of all the
special virtues, he shows that any attempt to define one of them

inevitably ends in tracing it and all the others back to virtue in itself, from which alone it can be understood.

In view of this, it is really not very important whether Plato actually uses the technical words *idea* and *eidos* in these early dialogues.[49] He does not betray the fact, which is certainly a fact, that these enquiries into special virtues and the conception of knowledge of good in itself are intended to be the foundation for a reconstruction of the state. We cannot expect him to startle the reader by presenting him with a complete dogma such as the theory of Ideas before winning his interest and directing his attention to the problem as a whole. He never gives, in any of his books, a complete exposition of the theory of Ideas in this dogmatic way, even in the time when he believes it most firmly and mentions it most constantly. In the dialogues of his middle period, it is introduced only in isolated examples, and it is assumed that the speakers have long known it; or else a few main outlines are sketched in, enough for even the uninitiated reader to understand. It is seldom that he goes into it at any length. Aristotle gives a lot of details about the theory of Ideas in what is called its mathematical phase, when Plato was trying to interpret the Ideas as numbers; and it is astonishing for us to learn from him that Plato and his pupils in the Academy worked out a system whose existence could not even be guessed from the dialogues he was writing at that time. Only with Aristotle's help can we trace a few scattered signs of its existence in them.[50] The esoteric discussions of Plato's school were sharply separated from the side of his philosophy that he showed to the outer world. However, his reserve in dealing with the theory of Ideas in his first dialogues is not quite the same thing. It was the theory on which his ethical and political thought was founded, and he must have known that, although he was still treating it as an esoteric doctrine, he would one day reveal its outlines to the world. Anyhow, it is not quite accurate to say that there are *no* traces of it in the early dialogues. *Euthyphro,* which is generally thought to be one of them, several times calls the object of the dialectic enquiry an 'Idea', and there are other hints in dialogues of the same period.[51]

Now we have a picture of Plato's writing in the years just after Socrates' execution, which shows quite clearly the *organic unity* of all his books and all his philosophical thought. The little dialogues with which he began form an introduction to the central problem of his thought, from both sides, that of form and that of content. The central problem is: what is the best state? With it Plato connects Socrates' creed that virtue is knowledge. For if virtue is knowledge, then all our energies must be expended on reconstructing society upon that principle through education. Before Plato allows us to see the end he has in view, his early dialogues lead us to formulate the problem which must be understood before the end can be realized— the Socratic problem of the relation between virtue and knowledge. Of course, it is not until we read the next two dialogues, *Protagoras* and *Gorgias,* that we gain full understanding of its importance. There he surrounds it with all the vast implications which he knows it to contain. Therefore, if we stop with the little dialogues, we are still in comparative ignorance. Yet, we feel ourselves irresistibly urged forward, and we try to find the solution by taking a much wider view than before.

This description of Plato's method will be confirmed by his later works. As he wrote them, as he moved from the *Apology* to *Gorgias* and from *Gorgias* to *The Republic,* he must have had in mind the plan of taking his readers step by step upwards to the pinnacle from which they could look out to all the horizons of his thought. It would be too much to say that he planned the exact timing of every book, and knew before it was written how it would fit into the general scheme. But it is clear that the nineteenth-century development-theory criticized earlier in this chapter did not pay enough attention to the numerous connecting lines which Plato drew between his books, and which he meant to show us that they are all steps towards the revelation of a great and comprehensive system wherein every one, from the first step to the last, becomes fully intelligible.[52]

If we survey the course of Plato's work as a whole, and then turn back to its beginnings, we shall see that its ruling idea is to carry the reader along through Socratic conversations which gradually take him deeper and deeper into philosophy, and show him the connexion between its separate problems. In order to devise such a plan, Plato must have felt that philosophical knowledge was best approached as a sort of *education.* His dialogues are models of it, and propaganda for it. They are educational, not only because of their power to excite the reader's sympathy and anticipation and to release his own intellect from its trammels, but also because, by seeing the repeated failure of sincere efforts to reach the truth, he comes to realize the difficulty of true knowledge and to understand the hitherto unexamined presuppositions on which his life is built. He sees where the mistakes in his own thinking come from. He sees how unreliable common opinion can be. He learns that it is the highest rule of clear thinking to account to himself for his own judgments, and to expect others to account for theirs. He learns that this affects not only philosophical discussions, but the whole of human life and conduct. Inevitably, he wishes to arrange his life on that plan, and by doing so to give it an internal unity and a settled direction. Plato meant the educational power of Socrates, which he himself had experienced, to take shape through his dialogues, and to conquer the world by making it think more fully and clearly until it came to understand its own nature and purpose.

5

PROTAGORAS
SOPHISTIC OR SOCRATIC PAIDEIA?

IN *Protagoras* Plato for the first time lifts the veil that has hung over his earlier dialogues. It gives us a much freer survey of the problems he has already treated. The reader who has not observed their underlying unity is now made to see it, for they are all drawn together into one central problem. Ever since the *Apology* we have known Socrates' character as an educator. The problem on which he spent his life, the relation between virtue and knowledge, is worked out for separate virtues in the smaller dialogues.[1] Now, in a work of greater length and scope, we are introduced to the broad educational discussions which filled the age of Socrates and the sophists. In *Protagoras,* Plato's Socrates tries to pierce through that babble of words, to grapple with the fundamental claims made by the sophists for their paideia, and to oppose them with his own doctrine, his own educational programme.

Unlike the earlier dialogues,[2] *Protagoras* is played out on a broader stage, with more characters than surrounded the conversations of the historical Socrates. Plato makes his teacher fight in public with the greatest intellectual lions of his day, the sophists Protagoras, Prodicus, and Hippias. The scene is the house of the richest man in Athens, Callias, where these distinguished visitors are staying, and where every Athenian with social or intellectual interests has assembled to listen and admire. We need not ask whether or not this drama was really played at some time in Socrates' life. What Plato wants to show by choosing such famous actors is clear. He thinks of Socrates as something more than an Athenian eccentric. For all his close connexion with his city, and despite the ironic self-depreciation which kept people from realizing his true worth, the power and originality of his intellect far surpassed all the highly publicized thinkers of his day. *Protagoras* depicts his contest with the sophists' paideia as one of the decisive battles of his age, as the

struggle between two opposing worlds for the primacy in education. The conversation takes place before a large audience in a
wealthy house; the great sophists are impressive, even majestic
figures, followed by swarms of pupils and admirers; all these details enhance the importance of the occasion. And yet the entire
dialogue is lit with the brilliance of youthful gaiety, it sparkles
with humour and dances with whimsical wit, more than any
other of Plato's books. Others have richer language, others move
our emotions and stir our thoughts more deeply; but in clear and
penetrating character-drawing, and in taut and supple construction, none surpasses *Protagoras*.

Unfortunately, it is almost impossible here to say more of the
vivid life and subtle art of the dialogue. This means that we cannot show how, in every line, Plato appeals to our emotions by
expressing the character of the sophists' paideia and contrasting
it with that of Socrates. A historian cannot compete with an
artist, or try to recapture his effects. Even the wittiest and most
faithful paraphrase would fall far short of Plato's inimitable
originality. We must then be content to summarize *Protagoras*
in a few broad contrasts of light and dark.

A young pupil and friend of Socrates wakes him by banging
on his door one morning before dawn, and comes in to see him.
When he returned to Athens on the previous evening he had
learnt that Protagoras was in town, and he had been excited
by this great 'event'. He is determined to become Protagoras'
pupil, as many other well-born young Athenians had done, on
payment of high fees; and now he wants Socrates to introduce
him to the Master.[3]

Now comes a prelude to the main part of the dialogue. Dawn
has not broken, and the two stroll round the courtyard waiting
for daylight. There follows a conversation in the true Socratic
style. Socrates tests the firmness of young Hippocrates' resolution, and makes him clearly understand the enterprise on which
he is venturing.[4] He talks so unassumingly and puts himself so
simply on a level with Hippocrates that the young fellow has no
idea that the *real* master is walking beside him all the time.
(Besides, in this dialogue, Socrates is shown as a man in the
prime of life, in contrast to the venerable old age of Protagoras.) Hippocrates sees him only as an adviser and a friend who
can give him the entrée to the great stranger he admires so

whole-heartedly and uncritically. Yet, with a few well-aimed questions, Socrates makes him see that he neither knows Protagoras, nor understands what a sophist really is, nor realizes what kind of teaching he is going to get. This brings out a point which is to be very important later in the conversation between Socrates and Protagoras. If the young man was going to be trained as a doctor, he would study under the greatest doctor of his age, his namesake Hippocrates of Cos; and if he wanted to be a sculptor, he would study under Polyclitus or Phidias. Therefore, if he goes to study with Protagoras, it looks as if he meant to become a sophist. Hippocrates firmly rejects the idea.[5] Now appears one of the essential differences between sophistic education and technical education. Only some of the sophist's special pupils study his art in order to become sophists themselves;[6] the well-bred young Athenians who crowd round him listen to him 'for the sake of culture', as befits a free-born man who is not a specialist. But young Hippocrates does not know exactly what this 'culture' (paideia) is, and we feel that he is typical of all the other young men who are so keen about it.

Now that Hippocrates has been brought to make this confession of ignorance, his friend Socrates adds a warning admonition. Just as in Plato's *Apology,* where he insists that men must 'care for their souls',[7] he reminds Hippocrates of the danger into which he is putting his 'soul', by entrusting it to a stranger whose purposes he cannot explain to himself.[8] This throws the first sidelight on the character of sophistic education. Seen through Socrates' eyes, it looks very dubious. Protagoras comes from abroad to Athens, and offers (in return for a fee) to teach all kinds of knowledge;[9] the realistic Socrates feels that, as a social phenomenon, he is like the travelling merchants and pedlars who hawk their imported goods for money. But there is a difference, which is not in the sophist's favour. The merchant sells food and drink that can be taken home in one's own containers, and tested before eating or drinking them. But young Hippocrates 'must take into his very soul' the soul-food which Protagoras sells, and that without knowing whether it does him good or harm.[10] Even before the main conversation begins, we can now distinguish two types of teacher: the sophist, who crams people's minds indiscriminately with all sorts of knowledge (does he not typify Average Education throughout the ages, right down to this very day?) and Socrates, the physician of the soul, who holds that learning is 'the food of the soul' [11] and begins by asking whether it does good or harm. [12] Of course Socrates does not call himself a soul-doctor. But when he says that doubts about bodily food can be solved by the trainer or the doctor, one is forced to ask: who is the specialist who can solve doubts about the food of the soul? If this striking comparison were to be made, it would exactly describe the essence of the true teacher, as Socrates conceives him to be.

On the way to Callias' house, both Hippocrates and Socrates think over the problem of the true teacher. Daylight has come. It is not too early now to call on the sophists, who are beset with visitors from morning till night. [13] Callias' doorman is already exasperated—a sign that these two are not the first callers. At last they manage to get in, and find Protagoras walking up and down talking, followed by a chorus of admirers. On one side he has the host Callias with his stepbrother, Pericles' son Paralus, and Charmides son of Glaucon; on the other side is Pericles' other son Xanthippus, and Philippides, and Protagoras' most promising pupil, Antimoirus of Mende, himself a future sophist. Behind them walk some Athenians and more foreigners from all sorts of cities, following Protagoras as if he were Orpheus who had bewitched them with his voice. They are trying hard to catch everything said in the front row; and whenever the leaders turn, they all break left and right in military order, about-turn, form up again, and walk back the same way in reverse. [14] In the lobby opposite, Hippias of Elis is ensconced in an armchair, with other well-known Athenians and strangers sitting round him on benches, like students. He is expounding astronomical problems. [15] The third of the Graces, Prodicus of Ceos, is in an office which has been hastily cleared out and furnished as a guest-bedroom. He is still in bed, with lots and lots of blankets pulled round him. A number of distinguished visitors are sitting on sofas all around. From outside, it is difficult to hear what he is saying, because his deep bass voice echoes round the room and makes a vague booming noise. [16]

Socrates now introduces his young friend to Protagoras, explaining that he wants to become his pupil. He mentions that Hippocrates means to enter politics, and that he hopes to be helped in doing so by Protagoras' tuition. He adds the recommendation that he is the son of a rich and noble family, and is ambitious and capable. Protagoras accordingly explains the nature of his teaching.

This kind of *epangelma* or 'profession' was a regular device of the travelling sophist—a self-advertisement which was rather necessary in the absence of a regular professorial class with fixed income and standing.[17] We shall see that other wandering professions like that of the doctor had to advertise their skill in the same way,[18] and at that period it did not sound so odd as it does to us. It is difficult for us to get accustomed to the idea that, in the age of the sophists, before the foundation of settled schools like those of Plato and Isocrates, a teacher usually travelled to find pupils, and when he arrived in a strange city (ἐπιδημία, ἐπιδημεῖν) young men used to seek a chance to hear him. The epangelma, the teacher's 'profession', is one of the clearest proofs that a new social class had arisen, which was making a vocation out of educating young men. Until then, the only way a youth had been able to carry on his education was by private association (συνουσία) with older men of his acquaintance; and that in fact was the kind of relation Socrates had to his young 'companions'. Admittedly it was rather old-fashioned and unprofessional. So sophistic education had all the attraction of novelty, and Plato neatly embodies the enthusiasm it evoked in the figure of young Hippocrates. It might seem contradictory that Plato, who was himself the founder of a school, should attack the professionalism of the sophists with such violence. But his school was based on friendship (φιλία) and was meant to continue, on a higher level, the old form of higher education through personal association and conversation.

Protagoras does not recommend his art because it is new and up-to-date, but rather because it is old and long-established.[19] This is to counter the mistrust with which these sophists and their new-fangled education had been met in many countries, and which had induced many of them to avoid the name and to adopt some other designation—doctor, trainer, or musician.[20] They were accustomed to live on the educational prestige of the great poets, from Homer to Simonides, and to recoin the treasures of their wisdom into copy-book maxims of morality. Protagoras now alters the relationship. He describes those old heroes of the spirit as the ancestors of his own art, who chose to hide the fact that they were sophists one and all by calling themselves poets, and so avoiding the mistrust of their contemporaries.[21] In contrast to them, Protagoras, who does not fear the light of publicity, and thinks he would only excite greater mistrust of his culture by trying to disguise it, 'admits' he is a sophist, a professional teacher of higher culture, who 'educates men'.[22] He welcomes the opportunity to expatiate on the nature of this culture, before the assemblage in Callias' house. Socrates suspects that he is proud to have won a new adorer, and proposes to invite Prodicus and Hippias with their followers to hear him. Protagoras assents with pleasure.[23] After his eager admirers have hastily pushed chairs and benches together to make a lecture-room, and all are on the alert, the play begins. Protagoras formally professes that his teaching will make Hippocrates better and better every day.[24]

Socrates now asks in what way Protagoras' education makes his pupils better—thereby resuming the still unsolved problem of his preliminary conversation with Hippocrates about the nature and purpose of sophistic education.[25] He says that, if a young man were to become a pupil of Zeuxippus and Zeuxippus claimed to make him better, everyone would know he meant to make him better at painting; or if he went to be taught by Orthagoras of Thebes, everyone would know he would be made better at flute-playing.[26] But if he is taught by Protagoras, in what way will he become better? Socrates' question clearly means: what is the particular art (techné), the special knowledge of a particular subject, which the sophist claims for himself? Protagoras says he cannot answer for all those who call themselves sophists, for they themselves are not agreed on the point. Hippias, for instance, who is present and listening, is distinguished for his knowledge of the 'liberal arts', and in particular of what was later called the *quadrivium*—arithmetic, geometry, astronomy, and music. To mention these subjects would have answered Socrates' question well enough, in so far as they are all technical. But Protagoras says he prefers to teach the social sciences. He thinks that young men who have had the usual elementary schooling need a higher education to prepare them not for any particular profession, but for a political career. Therefore they do not wish to plunge into more technical studies;[27] they need something else, and he can give them what they need—the power to direct their own households well and to be most able in state affairs, both in word and in act.[28]

Although Protagoras does not call his ability a specialty or techné (unlike the mathematical subjects), he assents when Socrates asks him if he teaches 'the political art', and professes to make men good citizens.[29] Socrates says that that is a fine subject. But he adds that he does not believe it can be taught, and proves it by well-known facts. In the assembly of the people, and in public life generally, questions of architecture and shipbuilding and other special professions and arts are settled by the advice of the most distinguished specialist; if a layman tried to offer his opinion, he would be laughed off the platform or hustled off by the police.[30] But about political questions (in which there are no specialists because there is no special art concerning them), everyone, carpenter, blacksmith, or cobbler, merchant or sailor, rich man or poor man, noble or commoner, gets up and offers his advice, and no one shouts him down for talking about a subject he has not learnt from a teacher. People obviously think it cannot be taught.[31] The same applies to private life. The wisest and best men in Athens are unable to hand on to others the fine qualities which distinguish them. For example, Pericles, father of the two young men who are present, educated them very well in every subject for which teachers were available; but in his own wisdom he could neither educate them himself nor get others to train them. They have to 'graze about like mavericks' (νέμονται ὥσπερ ἄφετοι) in the hope of finding areté somewhere by sheer luck.[32] Socrates often comes back to the question why great men's sons do not resemble their fathers. Now he mentions other examples from the history of well-known families, especially of people actually present.[33] On these examples he bases his assertion that virtue cannot be taught.[34]

This is a philosophical restatement of one of the fundamental beliefs of the aristocracy which Pindar represented: it had been rather ignored than contradicted in the new rationalism of sophistic teaching.[35] The educational optimism of the sophists knew no bounds.[36] Their strongly intellectual conception of the purpose of education encouraged it, and indeed it seemed to fall in with the general trend of the age, with the democratic movement particularly.[37] But it was not only a class-prejudice that had made those old nobles doubt the universal efficacy of education.

They were proud of their virtues and traditions, which had
given birth to all the higher educational ideals of Greece; [38] and
they had learnt to distrust these novelties, after long and painful experience. Socrates' scepticism about sophistic education is a
restatement of Pindar's question about the educability of men.
He does not doubt the obvious successes of the sophists in intellectual culture,[39] but wonders if it is possible to communicate the
virtues of the citizen and statesman in the same way. That is
why neither Hippias of Elis, who specializes in mathematics, nor
Prodicus of Ceos, who specializes in grammar, but Protagoras
himself becomes the focus of the dialogue. For Protagoras was
the real leader of the school of thought which held the problem of ethical and political education to be the central one. He
thought that it could be solved by study of the 'social sciences'.
In this attempt to find a modern substitute, based on reason, for
the severe discipline of the old aristocracy, he showed a sensitive understanding of contemporary needs and changed conditions. And yet that very point shows the real weakness of the
sophists' paideia most clearly. In Socrates' words, 'I never
thought that human ingenuity could make men good', we hear
an exact echo of Pindar's belief that areté is a gift of the gods,[40]
and it is strange to see how that religious outlook mingles with
Socrates' sober realism, based on the experience of so many
futile efforts.

Socrates' objection is so fundamental that it compels Protagoras to keep the whole conversation on a far higher plane than
that of pedagogical technique. Not every sophist could have done
so, but Protagoras was just the man to meet such criticisms.
Plato felt he was a foeman worthy of Socrates' steel; and he
put great art into delineating him, through the long explanatory
speech he delivers in reply to Socrates. He would have been
a poor representative of the age of pedagogy if he had not had
his own reply ready for Socrates' fundamental question about
the limits of education. The question was based on a number
of isolated facts which could not be denied. Protagoras therefore approaches it from a different quarter, cleverly bringing in
his new sociological theories. He analyses the structure of society
with its institutions and its needs, so as to prove that, if we did
not assume that education was possible, they would all lose their

meaning and their justification. From this point of view education is an unassailable social and political postulate—particularly so in an up-to-date democracy, which sets such high value
on the individual citizen's common sense and his active co-operation in the work of the state. We have already examined these
theories of Protagoras about the sociological bases of education,
in our discussion of the sophists.[41] Plato gives him a long and
profound speech, and (remembering that he was a masterly
stylist) makes it a brilliant demonstration of all types of eloquence. Socrates admits he is beaten and overwhelmed; [42] but
what looks like uncritical admiration in him is rather his ironical
way of saying that he will not attempt to follow Protagoras
onto his own ground, where he holds undisputed supremacy.
Socrates' strength does not lie in his power to tell charming
mythical tales or make long didactic orations, but in the speed
and agility with which he sets a series of unanswerable dialectic
questions. And his dialectic art is triumphantly displayed in the
conversation which follows, as he endeavours to lure his opponent onto his own terrain. This makes the contrast between the
two sides complete: not only their basic views about the question
of education, but the methods they actually employ in teaching
are fundamentally opposed.

Socrates appears to join in the applause of the audience. He
asks for information on only one detail.[43] Protagoras had told
a myth to explain his conviction that men were educable. He
said that, after men got Prometheus' gift of technical civilization, but were in danger of being destroyed because of their
isolation, Zeus sent them a gift from heaven: the power to live
in society, political virtue, justice, self-control, piety, et cetera.
This gift kept earthly communities together. It was not given
to individuals specializing in it, but to all human beings equally,
and education in political virtue is simply and solely meant to
develop it.[44] Protagoras' reference to virtue in general and the
special virtues of justice, prudence, and piety gives Socrates a
chance to bring up his own particular problem—the nature of
these separate virtues and their relation to virtue as such.[45] He
proposes it to Protagoras in this form: is virtue a unity, and are
justice, prudence, and piety only parts of it, or are these different
names for one and the same thing? [46] The surroundings are
familiar. Suddenly we find ourselves back on the well-trodden

path along which Socrates' earlier conversations had moved: *Laches, Charmides, Euthyphro.* In his enthusiasm for this topic, Socrates appears to have entirely forgotten the question whether men could be educated and virtue taught; and Protagoras, with all the confidence of his recent success, boldly follows him onto the unfamiliar ground of these subtle logical distinctions, although (like the reader) he does not at first see their point.

In each of the little early dialogues, Plato had discussed one special virtue, and had always guided the discussion towards the problem of virtue in itself and its true nature. There too the idea that virtue might have 'parts' had been mooted. Now in *Protagoras* Socrates begins the enquiry in the same way, by asking about one special virtue. But here the problem of the relation between the separate virtues and 'virtue in itself' is not postponed to the climax or the conclusion of the dialogue, it is put forward right at the beginning as the real topic of discussion.[47] Socrates makes that perfectly clear at the outset. When Protagoras says that justice and prudence are 'parts' of virtue in itself, Socrates immediately tries to define 'part' more accurately. He asks if they are parts of virtue in the same way as the mouth and nose are parts of the face, or rather like the parts of a piece of gold:[48] i.e. are they qualitatively different from each other and from the whole, or just quantitatively? Protagoras, doubtless representing the common-sense point of view, takes the former alternative. When Socrates asks whether, possessing virtue, one must possess all its parts, Protagoras answers No: there are many brave men who are unjust, and just men who are not wise. The question appears to be complicated by the fact that wisdom (σοφία) is now treated as a part of virtue, an intellectual areté added to the moral ones.[49] But no doubt this is historically justified by the fact that Protagoras himself emphasized that side of virtue. He does not see that it will help his opponent, who thinks that virtue is knowledge! But we notice here that, however closely Protagoras and Socrates seem to agree in their high estimate of knowledge, the astronomical difference between them will come out in this same point—the difference between their views of the nature of knowledge. Protagoras does not know Socrates' thesis that virtue is knowledge, and he does not suspect that he is moving towards it. Throughout the conversation which follows, Socrates keeps him in the dark about his real aim, although we know it from the earlier dialogues. Just as a statesman with far-reaching plans must hide them from the ignorant mob when he takes his first steps, so at first Socrates appears to be asking a pedantic little question about the parts and the whole of virtue, with no ulterior end in view.

The difference between this dialogue and earlier ones on the same theme is that Socrates here does not show the relation of whole and part by discussing *one* virtue, but by comparing *all* the special virtues with one another in order to demonstrate their unity. Although he spends less time on details here, that is only because he has a longer argument to go through before reaching his conclusion, and must shorten the separate stages. Besides, greater use of detail would have brought in repetitions, almost inevitably. His discussions of special virtues in his earlier dialogues are quite clearly assumed to be known to the reader here, although Protagoras himself does not need to know them in order to follow the argument.[50] The question whether, if we possess virtue, we have all its parts is now divided by Socrates into several sections. First, he asks whether justice must be the same as piety; then he asks the same about prudence and wisdom; and finally about prudence and justice.[51] Starting with the virtues which have the greatest relative similarity, he tries to make his interlocutor admit that justice and piety are essentially the same, or at least very closely similar and related. Protagoras unwillingly admits this. Then Socrates does the same with the other pairs mentioned above, but leaves courage, which is psychologically most unlike the others, to the end. All this strikes Protagoras as very strange. Like most people who side with common sense, he is naturally inclined, when comparing different virtues with different names, to emphasize their differences rather than their resemblances. And he tries again and again to bring out that point of view.[52] But he cannot get through his opponent's guard. Socrates always manages to point out the kinship and the common basis of what seem to be different qualities; he does not even care about a few inaccuracies in his reasoning as he pushes onwards to his goal, the identification of the whole and the parts, the manifold and the unity. We know the 'synoptic' character of his dialectic from Plato's first dialogues,[53] and in this general view of all the special virtues its spiritual force is vividly manifested. Many modern scholars think it is wrong of Plato to skip so lightly over the differences between the qualities he is comparing: they have wholly misunderstood the point of his procedure.

Before reaching his goal, Socrates is compelled, by Protagoras' growing ill humour, to break off.[54] Much of the artistic tension of the whole dialogue comes from the relentless persistence with which Socrates keeps his end in view and refuses to leave the terrain of dialectic argument. However, he now gives Protagoras a breathing-space. Protagoras uses it to transfer the discussion of virtue and education to a new field, that of critical explanation of poetry, which was one of the fundamental types of sophistic paideia.[55] But again he meets his match in Socrates, who takes the lead in analysing Simonides' famous poem about true virtue, which Protagoras has chosen in order to display his skill.[56] By pretending to be perfectly serious, and skilfully distorting the meaning of the poem, he shows that by this method anyone can prove anything; and he reads into it his own thesis, that no one errs willingly.[57] It is an amusing episode, but it does not reflect much glory on Protagoras. After it, Socrates with some difficulty gets him to resume the unfinished discussion of virtue and its parts, by maintaining the daring theme that courage and wisdom are the same thing.[58] Protagoras refuses to admit this, and raises all sorts of logical and psychological objections to the way in which Socrates proves his point.[59] Socrates therefore sets out on a roundabout way to his goal. He begins by distinguishing the happy and the unhappy life; and defines the former as the agreeable and pleasant life, the latter as one full of grief and pain.[60] Doubtless the majority would agree with this definition, but not Protagoras: he thinks it is safer to distinguish good and bad pleasures.[61] Socrates next asks what he thinks about reason and knowledge.[62] He thinks they are 'the highest human powers'. Though Protagoras has not accepted the hedonism of the mass of men in ethical matters, Socrates says he is afraid that he might side with them in his estimate of reason. For most people do not really treat reason as a guiding force in their lives, but are ruled by the emotions. The ultimate question is this: can knowledge help men to act rightly, and if a man knows what is good, does that make him

proof against any influence moving him to do wrong?[63] Here
again Protagoras is ashamed to side with the majority—this
time from a sort of cultural snobbery. And actually, who should
assent to Socrates' high estimate of the power of knowledge in
life, if not a sophist, the most zealous upholder of culture?[64]

Socrates now quotes the objection which 'most men' would
make to Protagoras and him. Many people, they would say,
know 'what is best' but are unwilling to do it although they are
able to. If asked why, these people would answer that they 'gave
way to pleasure' (or 'to pain').[65] Anyone who is convinced that
knowledge of the good entails the power to do good must make
a satisfactory answer to this universal objection, and Socrates
and Protagoras must expect to be asked for an explanation of
what people call 'giving way to pleasure'.[66] Protagoras now
begins to guess that, having assented to Socrates' high estimate
of knowledge as a moral force, he may have to make some unexpected admissions. He feels that his opinion is ultimately the
same as that of 'most men', who think there is a long way between knowing good and doing it. But it is too late, he has
agreed with Socrates; and besides, he finds that the part he has
chosen harmonizes with his opinion of himself as an intellectual,
far above the profane mob. Still, he does not want to go any
further with the problem, and waves it loftily away. 'Why
should we enquire into the opinions of the mob,' he asks,[67] 'who
say anything that comes into their heads?' However, Socrates
insists that it is the duty of the champions of knowledge and its
value in conduct to put up an explanation that will satisfy the
man in the street: for he believes that the right answer to this
question is decisively important in defining the relation between
courage and the other parts of virtue. Protagoras is forced to
yield, and allows Socrates to represent him, as it were, in arguing
with 'most men' and their views. This means that Socrates puts
forward his own opinion and that of the majority in turn, and
carries the whole weight of the dialogue, while Protagoras has
an easier task, and merely listens.[68]

Socrates begins his dialogue with the multitude by pointing
out that when they say 'give way to pleasure' they mean the
psychical process of being drawn to fulfil a sensual desire, although knowing it is wrong. For example, one chooses momen-
tary pleasure instead of continence, although it is going to cause

trouble later. Socrates cross-examines them to find out *why* they
call this kind of pleasure ultimately harmful.[69] He compels them
to admit that they do so simply because it ends in greater pain.[70]
In other words, the aim or end (τέλος), with reference to which
they distinguish one pleasure from another, is simply pleasure.[71]
When they call bitter things good or sweet things bad, they mean
that the bitter things will end by giving pleasure, and the sweets
by giving pain. If so, then 'giving way to pleasure' really means
making an error of judgment, and choosing the smaller pleasure
instead of the larger, because the smaller one is closer at hand.[72]
Socrates exemplifies this by the image of a man who has to make
a decision, holding a pair of scales and weighing pleasure against
pleasure, pain against pain, and pleasure against pain.[73] He explains the meaning of the image by two other quantitative comparisons. If the safety of our life depended on choosing lengths
and avoiding shortnesses, the essential thing would be to discover an art of measurement to keep us from mistaking the short
length for the long one, and to banish the deceits of appearance
from our lives. Without such an art, our choice would waver
and wander, often misled by appearances, and we should often
repent of our choice. But the art of mensuration would abolish
the cause of mistakes and save our lives.[74] Again, if our welfare
depended on making the right choice between odd and even in
the mathematical sense, then arithmetic would be the art on
which human life should be based.[75] Since, therefore, most people
think the final standard of human life is to get a favourable
balance of pleasure, it is important to avoid the deceptions
caused by distance, which so often mislead us in making our
choice, by finding an art of measurement to help us to distinguish
appearance from reality.[76] What that art and knowledge is (says
Socrates) we shall enquire at some other time; but that it *is*
knowledge that gives the standard of our conduct has now been
sufficiently demonstrated, which proves the opinion upheld by
Protagoras and myself.[77] You asked us (he says to the multitude) what we thought was the nature of the psychical process
you call 'giving way to pleasure'. If we had immediately answered 'ignorance', you would have laughed at us. But now it is
perfectly clear that the nature of that process is nothing but
'the greatest ignorance'.[78]

Having answered the multitude in this way, Socrates now

turns, in Protagoras' name and his own, to the sophists who are present. They say they are fully convinced. Socrates gets them to admit, in so many words, that what is pleasant is good, and that that is the standard for human purpose and behaviour.[79] Protagoras too, reassured by this general agreement, assents, and makes no objection to the thesis, although he had begun by distrusting it.[80] So all the great educators gathered in Callias' house end by finding themselves reduced to the level of *hoi polloi*, with whose opinions Socrates had started. He has them all in the trap. The attentive reader has not failed to notice that he himself has never admitted the hedonist principle; he has only said it is the view of 'most people' and is the logical basis of *their* thought. But he leaves this point on one side, so as to character- ize, indirectly, the sophists as teachers. Without pause he goes on to use the admission which he has elicited from them. For if (as most people believe) pleasure is the standard of all that men will and do, it is clear that no one knowingly chooses that which is less good—i.e. less pleasant; and what is thought to be a moral weakness in the man who 'gives way to pleasure' is really a weakness of reasoning.[81] No one voluntarily aims at what he thinks to be evil.[82] Thus Socrates has brought the sophists to assent to his notorious paradox that no one errs willingly,[83] and he does not care at all whether they attach the same meaning to *err* as he does. For as soon as they admit that, it is easy for him to answer the question about the relation of courage and wisdom, which had been left open, and to add the last link to his chain of proof that virtue is one and indivisible. His thesis had been that courage and wisdom are identical. Pro- tagoras had admitted that all the other virtues were more or less closely akin to one another. The only exception he made was courage, and he said that punctured Socrates' whole argument:[84] for there were completely impious, unjust, incontinent, and un- learned men who were still extraordinarily brave. He had de- fined brave men as men who were bold in face of dangers that others feared.[85] If we define fear as expectation of evil,[86] Pro- tagoras (who has just said that courage is readiness to advance towards frightful things) contradicts the admission just made by everyone, that no one advances towards something which he knows to be evil.[87] According to this last admission, brave men must be the same as cowards, in so far as they do not willingly advance towards something they think is frightful.[88] The difference between them really is *what* they fear: the brave man is afraid of disgrace, the coward (because he is ignorant) fears death.[89] Here at last the deep meaning of Socrates' conception of knowledge emerges, now that we can see these contradictions face to face. It is knowledge of the true standard which inevitably dictates our choice and determines our will. And so courage is identical with wisdom. Courage is knowing what to fear and what not to fear.[90]

In Plato's smaller dialogues we saw the dialectic movement of Socrates' thought start forward again and again, but never reach its goal. Here for the first time we see it finish its course. The words in which he here formulates his result explain the purpose of the earlier dialogues. He says, 'The only reason I ask all these questions is to find out about virtue, and learn what it really is. If that could be discovered, I know it would clear up the question you and I have been talking about for so long, you asserting, and I denying, that virtue could be taught.' [91] Actually, the question about the nature of virtue must be settled before anyone can discuss whether or not it can be taught. But the result Socrates has reached—that virtue is knowledge, and that even courage fits into that definition—is not only the logical preliminary to any discussion of the subsequent question; it alone seems to make the teaching of virtue possible. Thus at the end of the dialogue the two speakers have changed places. Socrates, who thought virtue could not be taught, is now endeavouring to prove that virtue in all its forms is knowledge. And Protagoras, who explained that it *could* be taught, is striving to prove that it is certainly not knowledge—which, if true, would make it difficult to teach.[92] The drama ends with Socrates' astonishment at this remarkable contradiction; but for Plato this astonishment is clearly the origin of all true philosophy,[92a] and the reader closes the book with the realization that Socrates' creed, that virtue goes back to the knowledge of true values,[93] is to become the foundation-stone of all education.

In *Protagoras* Plato remains faithful to his Socratic principle of giving no dogmatic instruction. Instead, he enlists our sympathy for his problem, and makes it our own, by gradually building up knowledge in our minds under Socrates' guidance.

This dialogue itself might interest us deeply enough in the problem. But when, from the point reached at the conclusion, we look back over the enquiries into special virtues conducted in Plato's earlier dialogues, we can see that he assumes his readers will persevere with the same resolution and single-mindedness as he himself expends on dealing with the same problem in book after book, constantly opening up new perspectives into its depths. At the end of *Protagoras,* we are relieved by recognizing that, as we climb higher and higher, we have seen more and more of the structure and plan of the surrounding landscape. Reading the earlier dialogues on separate virtues, we had to guess, rather than know, that all these isolated enquiries were running towards the same central point of juncture, though all upon the same level. But at the end of *Protagoras* we are surprised to look down, and see that all those paths led to the summit on which we are standing—the recognition that all virtues are the same in nature, and that their nature is based on the knowledge of true values. All our earlier efforts to reach this conclusion take shape and meaning from the fact, now at last recognized, that they are all directed towards the problem of education.

Paideia first became an acknowledged problem in the age of the sophists. Under the stress of life and of intellectual development (which always affect each other) it moved to the centre of public interest. A 'higher culture' grew up, with its own representatives, the sophists, whose profession was 'to teach virtue'.[94] But now it is evident that, despite all their hard thinking about educational method and styles of teaching, and despite the bewildering multiplicity of subjects embraced in their higher culture, none of them really understood the assumptions on which his profession was based. Socrates did not claim to teach men, as Protagoras did—a point which our sources constantly emphasize.[95] But we are all convinced from the very outset (like all his pupils) that he is the true teacher needed by the men of his age: and the feeling is not created by some difference of method, or by the mysterious power of personality, but chiefly by the fact that, by referring the moral problem to the problem of knowledge, he has for the first time given teaching the fundamental assumption which the sophists failed to see. They had maintained that the culture of the mind was of supreme importance; but they could not justify that claim by mere worldly success. The men of that age were groping in darkness. What they needed was to recognize one supreme standard, which was binding on all alike because it expressed the innermost nature of man, and on which education could attack its highest task, the moulding of men to the pattern of true areté. All the skill and knowledge of the sophists could never lead to areté—the only thing that could was the deeper 'knowledge' about which Socrates so constantly enquired.

Just as the dialectic movement of the earlier dialogues comes to rest only in *Protagoras,* when Socrates' question about the nature of virtue is linked to the problem of education, so *Protagoras* itself leads on to new problems. It formulates them without answering them, and thus points onwards to later books. Socrates believes that virtue cannot be taught, and he does not profess to teach men. Yet Plato hints that this is merely an ironic screen for his deep awareness of the difficulties of that task. Really he is much closer to solving it than the sophists. All that is necessary is that the questions he sees should be thought out, and Plato suggests that that can be done. One of them, which urgently requires discussion, is whether virtue can be taught— for Socrates' proof that virtue is knowledge seems to have brought it near its solution.[96] But now it is necessary to investigate the true nature of what Socrates calls knowledge, for it is evidently not what the sophists and *hoi polloi* think it is.[97] This investigation we find in *Meno,* and to a certain extent in *Gorgias.* But *Protagoras* contains several other references to future discussions of the problems it raises. Such, in particular, is the question of the good life (εὖ ζῆν). Socrates mentions it in *Protagoras,* not for its own sake, but as a means to demonstrate the importance of knowledge for right conduct, by assuming the truth of the popular view that pleasure is the good. He makes it clear to the mob that, granting the correctness of that standard, they would need an art of measurement in order to make the correct choice and select the greater pleasure in preference to the less: so that even in that case knowledge is indispensable for the attainment of the good life. Thereby he reaches the end of his argument for the time being. Yet we cannot help asking whether this identification of the good with pleasure (which he makes the sophists, and some modern scholars, swallow without protest) is really his own view or not.[98] After the problem of the end of life (τέλος) has once been raised, it cannot fall back into oblivion again. We feel that in the careless ease with which he speaks in *Protagoras* he has been fooling the sophist, and perhaps us too; we want him to talk seriously to us on this serious question. That he does in *Gorgias,* which is the twin of *Protagoras,* and in its deep gravity forms the necessary complement to the other's nonchalant gaiety.

GORGIAS
THE EDUCATOR AS STATESMAN

THE first step towards understanding the relation between *Protagoras* and *Gorgias* is to escape from a very common error. Plato's dialogues are often called works of poetic imagination, and some have misinterpreted that description of them. They have been taken to be like Goethe's works—a series of confessions in which the author relieved the pressure of personal experience and private emotion upon his soul. Accordingly, since *Protagoras* is cheerful and *Gorgias* gloomy, scholars have decided that *Protagoras* is early and *Gorgias* later in Plato's life.[1] *Protagoras* has even been described as his first work, written before Socrates' death, and *Gorgias* has been explained by the embittering effect of that catastrophe on his mind. To do this is to misapprehend the thoroughly objective character of the Platonic dialogue. It cannot possibly be interpreted through the formula borrowed from modern lyric poetry, 'emotion recollected in tranquillity'.[2] True, the whole dialogue-form owes its inception to one mighty experience—the experience of Socrates' personality. But that explanation cannot be extended to separate works, so as to interpret each of them as the expression of a new situation in Plato's life and a new grouping of his emotions. That is debarred by the character of the experience on which the dialogue-form is based—its dependence on the personality of someone else makes it *objective,* not subjective. Of course Plato's own life and emotions do colour his dialogues to some extent, so as to influence the way in which he depicts Socrates. But if *Gorgias* is serious, it is not because it is the expression of a temporary state of gloom; and we need not assume that it was written near Socrates' death because of its splendid pathos, any more than we should use the same assumption to account for the funereal tones of *Phaedo,* which the same scholars place rather far away from Socrates' death and quite close to the cheerful *Symposium.* To put *Protagoras* at the very beginning of Plato's career is impossible for anyone who has followed our interpretation so far as to be convinced that it puts together and sums up on a higher plane the questions raised in the smaller Socratic dialogues, which belong to Plato's earliest period, and that, according to Plato's regular procedure, they are to be explained through illumination cast backwards from it. We shall later show that this mistakenly early dating of *Protagoras,* which tears it loose from its closest partner, *Gorgias,* has contributed to the misunderstanding of its philosophical meaning.

The parallelism between *Gorgias* and *Protagoras* is obvious. Gorgias of Leontini, who created rhetoric in the form which set the tone for the last thirty years of the fifth century,[3] is for Plato the embodiment of that art, as Protagoras is the embodiment of sophistry. Like *Protagoras, Gorgias* shows us the outward side of Socrates' teaching. The smaller dialogues showed his influence on his pupils and friends, but here we see him at grips with the intellectual giants of his day. The sophistic movement was a purely educational phenomenon, whereas rhetoric was the new culture as it affected the state in practice. In classical times, *rhetor* was still the correct name for the statesman— who, in a democracy, must be an orator first and foremost. Gorgias' aim was to train rhetors in that sense of the word. Socrates now challenges that intention, and develops his challenge into a discussion of the nature of rhetoric—as he does in *Protagoras* with education. But here the discussion takes a rather different trend. Gorgias does not make a long speech justifying his profession, like Protagoras, because there is not so much to say in its defence from a theoretical point of view. Obviously he cannot define his oratory except by its influence. The attempt to define it by its content, a method possible with other disciplines that use words as their medium, cannot succeed: because rhetoric is nothing but the art of words and language, aimed at persuading audiences through rhetorical form.

In *Protagoras* Socrates said he did not believe political virtue could be taught, because it was not a regular art with experts specializing in it.[4] But what he thinks is the chief fault both in the political education offered by the sophists and in rhetoric[5] seems to Gorgias to be its chief recommendation. He holds it is a proof of the greatness of his art, that it can make mere words determine great events in the most important sphere of life—

politics.[6] Thus Plato shows the true nature of rhetoric by letting us see that its practitioners are unable to define it objectively, and think its principal merit is to give power to the man who masters it.[7] Gorgias actually tells of cases where an orator's eloquence persuaded a sick man to take medicine or submit to an operation after the doctor (i.e. the specialist) had vainly recommended it.[8] And (he says) when there is a dispute in the assembly or any other meeting about choosing a specialist for some post, the specialist himself carries no weight, and it is the orator who counts.[9] It is his art which tells all the specialists and professional men the aim for which they must co-operate, and to which they must subordinate their knowledge. It was not the architects and shipbuilders whose skill Socrates praises that built Athens her fortifications and harbours. It was Themistocles and Pericles who persuaded the people to have all that done, and rhetoric gave them the power to do so.[10] These are the obvious facts to which Gorgias points when Socrates applies his severe standard of knowledge to rhetoric, and defines it as the ability, not to convince others of truth, but to suggest to them an appearance of truth and to lure the ignorant masses by the magic of this deceit.[11] But after Socrates makes this definition and stresses the danger that eloquence may be misused, Gorgias as a teacher of rhetoric counters with the declaration that the instrument need not be condemned because it is sometimes misused.[12] Every weapon can be misused. If a trained boxer were to beat his father and mother or attack his friends, that would be no reason for banishing his trainer. The trainer taught him the art so that he could use it rightly. The only person to be blamed and punished is he who misuses it.

This glosses over Socrates' difficulty, but does not solve it. When Gorgias says the teacher of rhetoric imparts his art to his pupils 'to employ justly',[13] he apparently assumes that he himself, as teacher of the art, knows what is good and just, and that his pupils also start by knowing it or else learn it from him.[14] He is depicted as an old gentleman who values bourgeois respectability just as much as Protagoras. Exactly as Protagoras at first had refused to assent when Socrates asked if good and pleasant were the same, so Gorgias thinks he can avoid the awkward question about the moral foundations of his profession by admitting that, if necessary, he could teach the knowledge of justice and injustice to someone who did not know it.[15] Of course this makes him contradict what he had said about the prevalent misuse of rhetoric.[16] But he is delivered from the dilemma by the interposition of his pupil Polus.

Polus represents the younger generation. He is not ashamed to admit what everyone knows, that rhetoric is absolutely indifferent to questions of morality. He tells Socrates, as forcibly as need be, that it is poor taste to embarrass a distinguished old master like this. According to this young realist, rhetoric tacitly assumes that what society calls its moral code is a convention and a sham. Of course people must pay lip-service to it, but in serious matters it need not keep anyone from making unscrupulous use of the power given by rhetoric.[17] This contrast between the half-ashamed love of power shown by the conventional older generation which had invented rhetoric, and the cynical amoralism of the younger, is a splendid example of Plato's art of displaying a spiritual type by developing all its characteristic forms, stage after stage. As the typical orator develops three main types in a dialectic of three stages, so the drama of *Gorgias* falls into three acts: as each new type enters, the intensity of the drama grows, and its significance deepens. First, Gorgias; then his pupil Polus; and then the third, the logically perfect type of the 'rhetorical man', the practical politician Callicles,[18] who frankly maintains that the highest moral law is the right of the stronger. The three types form a climax, in which the true nature of rhetoric displays itself more and more clearly at every stage. What differentiates them is their attitude to *power:* but although they differ, it is still power, tacitly or openly, admired in theory or sought in practice, which is the real 'object' of their art.

In the second part of *Gorgias,* Socrates' criticism attacks the claim of rhetoric to be a *techné.*[19] Our word *art* does not adequately reproduce the sense of the Greek word. Like *art, techné* emphasizes practical use. But *art* for us implies individual creation subject to no rule, whereas *techné* has the sense of well-established knowledge and ability, which we associate with *technique* or *profession.* The Greeks used *techné* far more widely than we use *art:* they used it for any profession based on special knowledge—not only painting and sculpture, architecture and music, but just as much, or even more, medicine, strategy, or helmsmanship. The word thus connotes the practice of a voca-tion or profession based not merely on routine experience but on general rules and fixed knowledge; and so it is not far from *theory*—the sense which it often has in Plato's and Aristotle's philosophical terminology, especially when contrasted with plain experience.[20] On the other hand, *techné* differs from *theoria* ('pure knowledge') by being always connected with practice.[21]

So, when Socrates asks Polus what rhetoric is, he is clearly asking whether it has the right to be called a techné. From *Protagoras* we know that this is the ideal of knowledge which Plato's Socrates has in mind as he searches for the norms of human conduct. For there he said that the good life could not be achieved without 'a techné of measurement', and, by putting that art in sharp contrast to Protagoras' political teaching, he implied that the latter had none of the rigorous character of a techné.[22] And there are others of Plato's Socratic dialogues which show that the techné was the ideal on which Socrates believed knowledge should be modelled. It is easy to see why, if we remember that the ultimate aim of all Plato's search for exact knowledge was a practical aim, namely, the science of the state.[23] According to the context, the word *techné* in Plato can be replaced by the word *epistémé,* to emphasize the fact that this political science is based on a complete theoretical understanding of reality. In this case Plato is postulating a new science of politics, and explains what it is by contrasting it with the political rhetoric of his day: the word *techné* was the obvious one to choose in order to stress the resemblances and differences be-tween the two.

Socrates declares that rhetoric is not a techné at all. He defines it as a knack acquired by experience—the knack of producing charm and giving pleasure. Therefore, it is very like cookery, which is also the knack of producing charm and giving pleas-ure.[24] Socrates explains to the astonished Polus and Gorgias that the two things are branches of the same business. Cookery too is not an art but a knack. The humour of all this reaches its height when Socrates lays down that the leading principle of these apparently so different activities is *flattery,* and goes on to divide that important genus into a system of four species. There are, he asserts, four species of flattery, each with a different object: cookery, rhetoric, make-up (or 'cosmetic'), and sophistry.[25] The mutual relations of these four types of flattery suddenly become clear at the moment when Socrates describes political rhetoric as a copy of a true art, which is part of the real art of the state.[26] It appears that the three other kinds of flattery are likewise copies of true and necessary arts. As the life of man is divisible into the life of the soul and that of the body, so each of them needs a special art to take care of it. The soul is to be cared for by politics. That surprising correlation throws a bright light on Plato's ultimate aim, the art of the state, and the entirely new meaning he attaches to it. The corresponding art of caring for the body has no name. Both arts—the care of the body and the care of the soul—are divided into two species: one is the care of the healthy soul and healthy body, the other the care of the sick soul and sick body. The branch of politics which cares for the healthy soul is legislation, while the sick soul is cared for by the practice of justice. Care of healthy bodies is gymnastic training, and care for sick bodies is medicine. All four of these arts serve the welfare and health of the body and the soul.[27] There are four copies corresponding to them. Legislation is copied by sophistry, justice by rhetoric, gymnastics by cosmetics, and medicine by cookery. These do not serve the best in man, but merely try to please him. So they work simply on experience, not as the real arts do, on established principles and with full knowledge of what is good for human nature.[28] The position of rhetoric is therefore fixed. It is for the human soul what cookery is for the body. This comparison of the copies and the true arts demonstrates that rhetoric is not a techné.[29] The essential characteristics of a techné are, first, that it is knowledge based on understanding of the real nature of its object; second, that it is therefore able to explain its procedure; and third, that it serves the good of its object.[30] None of these characteristics appears in political oratory.

After the paradox of Socrates' dialectic has revealed all its amusing side, it turns to show its serious aspect. It is not one of those intellectual fireworks that blaze up bravely and then go dismally out. Of course Socrates knows the stimulating psychological effect of making a statement which is unexpected and runs counter to ordinary experience: it excites one's interlocutor and leads to a spirited denial. But the true reason for his love of paradoxes lies deeper. They are meant to induce philosophical reflection.[31] To compare rhetoric with cookery—to dethrone the queen of contemporary politics and make her a contemptible scullion—does not change the facts of the case. But it gives a shock to his readers' estimate of the facts, a shock which extends until it affects all their ideas. His comparison is not made from the wish to injure. It is really and truly *seen* with all the visionary power of those eyes for which the ordering of things was far different from their appearance to the multitude's eye of sense. It is as if a chasm opened between appearance and reality: all human things have suddenly taken on a new value. Just as make-up relates to the healthy beauty of a body developed by gymnastic training, so the political culture taught by the sophists relates to the teaching of the true lawgiver. Just as the sauces and confectionery of a blue-ribbon chef stand to the health-giving rules and prescriptions of the doctor, so stands rhetoric, which tries to make wrong into right, to the activity of the true judge and statesman.[32] This makes the art of politics something poles apart from what the world calls politics. And so, even here in *Gorgias,* the kind of state-building and law-giving which Plato undertakes in his two greatest books is proclaimed as his conception of the great positive aspect of Socrates' work of 'caring for the soul'.[33] We cannot yet see the shattering results of this new idea, but it is evident that the signs by which we recognize it point to a complete transformation of the current philosophy of life. And indeed, in a passage later in *Gorgias,* Callicles describes Socrates' transvaluation of values as 'a revolution in our whole life' and condemns it.[34] The ideas which Socrates develops in his conversation with Polus provoke Callicles' passionate outbreak at the beginning of the third part of the book.

The strongest and most obvious objection made by Polus to Socrates' low estimate of rhetoric is that rhetoric actually does exercise a huge influence in politics.[35] The urge to obtain power is an impulse rooted too deeply in human nature to be disregarded. If power is a great thing, the faculty by which we obtain it is extremely important. So the problem whether rhetoric does or does not entail an exact knowledge of values, which seems to be a purely esoteric question of method, involves far wider decisions. It compels us to take up a definite attitude to the question of the nature and value of power. Polus' attitude to it is that of the man in the street. Just as in *Protagoras*, Plato is trying to show that sophists and rhetors have refined and elaborated the technical methods of educating and influencing people, but have terribly primitive ideas of the purpose to which they are to be put.[36] According to Plato, one's idea of this purpose depends on what one thinks of human nature. The greatest rhetoricians assume in practice that it is wholly sensual. Their highest hope is to be able to handle their fellow-men exactly as they wish. Although their political careers lie mostly in democracies, their ideal is to be like the despot who wields unlimited power over the property and lives of his subjects.[37] Even the lowest citizen has something of this power-lust in him, and is secretly full of admiration for the man who raises himself to the pinnacle of power.[38] Archilochus' philosophical carpenter, who says with his hand on his heart, 'I yearn not for the tyrant's power,' is obviously the great exception that proves the rule.[39] When Solon had completed his work as a legislator, he returned his absolute power to the hands of the people; and in his self-defence he says that not only his fellow-nobles, but even the people, sighing for freedom, thought he was stupid, and could not understand why he had not made himself a tyrant.[40] Polus is the same: he will not believe that Socrates does not envy the tyrant's power.[41] The last card he has to play is to ask whether Socrates does not think the King of Persia is happy. When Socrates answers 'I am not sure, for I do not know how much paideia and justice he has', Polus can only ask uncomprehendingly, 'Why, does all happiness depend on these things?'[42]

In this comparison between two diametrically opposite philosophies of life, the two concepts of *paideia* and *power* are sharply contrasted: and with good reason. Apparently they have little to do with each other. But (as the passage shows) Plato takes them to be opposing conceptions of human happiness— which means, of human nature. We have to choose between the philosophy of power and the philosophy of culture. This passage is particularly well suited to explain what Plato means by paideia. It is not merely a stage in a man's development, where he trains a certain number of his faculties;[43] its meaning is extended to connote the perfection of his character, in accordance with his nature. The philosophy of power is the doctrine of

force. It sees war and conquest everywhere in life, and believes
that that sanctions the use of force. It can have no meaning
except through the seizure of the greatest possible power.[44]
The philosophy of culture or education asserts that man has a
different aim: *kalokagathia*. Plato defines it as the opposite of
injustice and wickedness—it is therefore essentially a matter of
ethics.[45] But he does not hold that it goes against man's nature
to be trained to kalokagathia. Only it implies a different conception of human nature, which Socrates develops in detail. And
now the foundations of his criticism of rhetoric come to light.
As he conceives it, the real meaning of human nature is not
power, but culture: paideia.

If we were to describe the philosophy of power as 'naturalism'
(an obvious enough thing to do, from the Christian standpoint[46]), Plato would say we were doing it too much honour.
It was impossible for the Greek philosopher to think of opposing
nature, which was the highest norm and standard. But even if
we say that, according to the higher Greek conception of human
nature, the task of education was not to subdue nature but to
ennoble it, that interpretation does not cover Plato's meaning.
He did not think of nature (as the sophistic teachers did) as
raw material out of which education was to form a work of
art;[47] he thought it was the highest areté, which is only incom-
pletely manifested in individual man.[48] Again, his attitude to
power is not simply to condemn it as bad in itself. Here too his
dialectic takes the conception which is under scrutiny, and treats
it as a positive value, and transforms it. By 'power' Polus understands the ability of the orator or tyrant to do what he wants in
his state.[49] Socrates starts by granting that power must be a
real good if we are to pursue it; but he says that doing what
one wants, be one orator or tyrant, is not a good, because it is
without reason.[50] That is, he distinguishes true will from arbitrary desire. The man who does what he wants is running after
a sham good which he desires. But the only thing he can *will*
is a true good. For in desire he can always be deceived about the
value of the thing desired; but no one can knowingly will what is
bad and injurious. Socrates goes on to distinguish the end from
the means.[51] In acting, we do not will what we are doing, we
will the thing for whose sake we are acting. And that thing is
what is naturally good and healthy, not what is bad and injuri-

ous. The most drastic ways in which the tyrant shows his power
—execution, banishment, confiscation of property—cannot be his
end, only the means to it; and he cannot genuinely will them,
because they are not good but injurious. Therefore anyone who
executes, banishes, and confiscates as he likes, is not doing what
he wills, but only what seems desirable to him. Therefore, since
power is a good for the man who possesses it, the tyrant does
not possess any real power.[51a] No, he is really unhappy, for
perfect happiness consists in the perfection of human nature and
its proper value.

Still more unhappy is the unjust man if he is not punished
for his injustice.[52] For injustice is a sickness of the soul, as
justice is its health. Penal justice, which brings the evildoer to
account, bears the same relation to legislation as medical care
of a sick man does to the regimen of a healthy one—so runs
Plato's medical conception of ethics. Punishment is a cure, and
not (as the old Greek notion of legality had it) retribution.[53]
The only real evil is injustice. But it affects the soul only of the
man who does it, not of him who suffers it.[54] If the reason for
striving to get power is 'to protect oneself against injustice',
Socrates counters with the idea (quite unheard-of in Greece)
that it is less evil to be wronged than to do wrong.

The defeat of Polus represents the defeat of Gorgias. He
started up to defend Gorgias, and he put his case more out-
spokenly than Gorgias would have thought permissible. We have
no space here to go over all the stages of Plato's dialectic; we
can merely sketch the outlines of the argument which Socrates
puts forward with so much intellectual agility and moral fervour.
Even during his conversation with Polus, he makes the point
which Plato wants to impress on the reader as an essential
feature in the young man's character: he is well trained in
rhetoric, but quite ignorant of dialectic.[55] This makes Socrates'
art appear as the highest form of paideia. Although it could
conquer the listening multitude by numbing their minds, rhetoric
cannot face the concentrated attack of dialectic. Not only does
it lack logical precision and skilled, methodical tactics; its greatest defect is that there is no objective knowledge, no firm philosophy and view of life behind its words—it is inspired not by
an ethical code but simply by ambition, unscrupulousness, and the
lust for success.

However, it cannot be held to have suffered a final defeat till it has been defended by a stronger champion. A victory over him would really convince us of its annihilation. This champion now advances. He is Callicles, a fully trained orator, who has also some philosophical culture and practical experience of politics. His calibre as a personality is also more impressive than that of the two academic rhetoricians, the teacher and the pupil. He enters the dispute to beat down Socrates' niggling arguments. His predecessors had only defended their ground; he counter-attacks. He tries to elude or tear open the net of dialectical proofs thrown over him by Socrates, in case he is caught in it himself. He starts off at once with a long speech, in which he feels himself a master.[56] His quality is not intellectual subtlety so much as energy. After watching with horror the speed and skill with which Socrates thrusts one paralyzing paradox after another through his opponents' guard (paradoxes which Callicles himself thinks are merely eristic tricks), he abandons his role as a spectator and advances to crush Socrates with one fulminating stroke.

To the compelling spiritual conviction with which Socrates has morally crippled the defenders of rhetoric, Callicles does not oppose mere argumentation, as the school-rhetors Gorgias and Polus had done. He is a man of the world. He takes into consideration the whole of his opponent's personality. He sees what the others did not see, that Socrates' strength lies in the firm and incontrovertible spiritual attitude which he embodies. Socrates has spent his whole life in building the spiritual fortress from which he now makes his forays and his attacks in safety. But although that is a logical advantage, Callicles thinks it will really prove to be a disadvantage as soon as his apparently consistent thinking is brought up against experience and reality. Socrates has avoided reality all his life. His fortress is a brittle ivory tower, to which he has withdrawn in order to whisper to a few admiring youths,[57] and to work at the weaving of that network of dreams in which he tries to entrap the whole world. But it rips apart as soon as it is pulled into the light and gripped with a firm hand. Plato, in attacking the great power of rhetoric, well understands that he has not only to conquer the professors who teach it; he has to oppose the realism which was deep-rooted in the Athenian character, and which detested the exaggerations and extravagances of the new culture.[58] Rhetoric itself was part of that culture, but it had become acclimatized much more quickly than the theoretical elements represented by sophistic teaching and by Socrates himself, and was now a part of the routine of political life. The entrance of Callicles shows that rhetoric could now count on the support of all politicians and all citizens who held that Athens' real danger was the growing unreality of higher culture. Euripides had made the conflict between the man of action and the man of thought into a tragic problem in his *Antiope*. Callicles quotes a number of lines from the drama in his speech,[59] thereby acknowledging the tragic character of the conflict between him and Socrates. He takes the side of Euripides' Zethus, the man of deeds, who summons his brother Amphion, the Muses' friend, away from his laziness and his dreams to a life of energy and action.

Plato makes Callicles the flesh-and-blood embodiment of the widespread opposition to philosophy. Socrates hints that on some previous occasion he has heard him with some well-known Athenian politicians discussing how far the new philosophical culture should be carried.[60] The same problem appears in Pericles' funeral speech, where he praises Athens for its love of culture, but sets limits to that love, so as to satisfy the opposition, which held that Athens was politically endangered by her excessive intellectualism.[61] The problem had been raised by the appearance of the sophists. It was now brought up again, against Socrates, all the more urgently because it was growing clear that he affected the young men's attitude to politics far more directly than the sophists with all their political theories. In Plato's own lifetime this realistic reaction against the morality of Socratic philosophy was represented by Isocrates and his cultural ideal: it led *him* to found a school of his own.[62] But none of the opposition ever put their case so forcibly as Plato himself. He must have immersed himself deeply in their thought, to express it with such convincing vividness, such overwhelming force as he does through Callicles. He had obviously heard that kind of criticism from his early youth, on the lips of his closest relatives and friends. Many have suggested that Callicles is only a mask for some real historical personage in the Athenian aristocracy. It is quite possible; and psychologically it is even probable.[63] But it is enough to note that Plato had a sort of affection for the opponent whom he fought with such passionate energy, and worked hard to understand him completely before striking him down. Perhaps we have not given enough thought to the possibility that in his own character Plato had so much of that unruly will to power as to find, and fight, part of himself in Callicles. It does not appear elsewhere in his writings, because it lies buried deep beneath the foundations of the Republic. But if he had by nature been only a second Socrates, the real Socrates would hardly have had such an overwhelming effect on him as he had. His sympathetic portraits of the great sophists, orators, and adventurers show quite unmistakably that he possessed, in his own soul, all their powers, with their brilliant advantages and their terrible dangers; but they had been tamed by Socrates, and, like his poetic impulse, had bowed to and mingled with the Socratic spirit, to form a higher unity within his works.

Callicles is the first defender of rhetoric to counter Socrates' moral attack on it with the passion and energy of real life. Therefore he takes up once again the argument about rhetoric as an instrument of the will to power, which Socrates, by his dialectic re-interpretation of 'power', had changed into an ethical argument in his favour.[64] Callicles does not follow Polus in naïvely assuming that everyone naturally tries to gain power. He attempts to give the will to power a deeper foundation. He derives it from nature itself, which the Greeks always felt contained all standards of human conduct.[65] He starts with the well-known sophistic distinction between conventional or legal justice and natural justice.[66] He attacks Socrates for using both these concepts and interchanging them when necessary, so as to make his opponents contradict themselves. According to Callicles, everything which is a greater evil is naturally disgraceful: therefore to be wronged is *naturally* disgraceful, although it is *legally* disgraceful to do wrong. He says that it is unmanly and slavish to be wronged, for the slave cannot defend himself against wrong. Self-defence is for Callicles the criterion of a true man, and is a sort of ethical justification of the will to power, for it carries primitive conditions down to the present day.[67] But whereas the strong man naturally uses his strength to gain his will, law creates artificial conditions which hinder him in the free exercise of his powers. Laws have been made by the weak—that is, by the majority. They hand out praise and blame to suit themselves. By official laws and conventional morality they pursue a policy of systematic intimidation against the strong men who naturally want to have more than the weak; and they describe that will to power, pleonexia, as wrong and disgraceful. The ideal of equality is the ideal of the masses, who hate one man to have more than another.[68] By appealing to examples from nature and history, Callicles shows it is a natural law for the stronger to use his strength against the weaker.[69] The law of mankind puts the strong man in chains, by catching him young like a lion-cub, by bewitching and enchanting him with culture and education, by enslaving him to the ideals that have been devised for the advantage of the weak. But when a really strong man appears, he tramples down all the letters and fetters of the unnatural law, and suddenly the justice of Nature blazes forth. Callicles goes on to quote Pindar's words about *nomos,* king of all, mortal and immortal, who justifies violence with a high hand—like Heracles who stole the cattle of Geryon and proved that the property of the weak is naturally the prey of the strong. (Callicles takes Pindar's *nomos* to mean the same as his own 'law of Nature'.[70])

In this social theory based on the struggle for existence, education plays a minor role. Socrates had put up the philosophy of culture to oppose the philosophy of power. For him, paideia was the criterion of human happiness, which consisted in the kalokagathia of the just man.[71] But Callicles treats education only as a system for deceiving and hoodwinking stronger natures so as to maintain the rule of the weak. Moulding (πλάττειν) begins in earliest youth, as it does in taming wild animals. In so far as that moulding is moral, the strong man can only wish to cast it off when he awakes to realize how unnatural it is.[72] But that happens rarely, rarely. In spite of his hatred for law and education, these two allies in the service of the organized weaklings, Callicles is still quite tolerant, not to say generous, to philosophy. He thinks there is something attractive about it, if taken in moderation. But beyond that it spoils people.[73] He is evidently thinking of the sophistic education which he himself has had, and of the methodical training of the intellect which it offered; he does not regret the time he spent on it. But anyone who studies philosophy after a certain age, even if he is highly gifted, becomes soft and unmanly. He does not know

the laws of his own country. He does not know what to say
in private or public life. He does not know the pleasures and
desires which people have. In a word, he is inexperienced. Whenever he enters on any business, private or public, he looks ridiculous; and so he runs away and shuts himself up in his studies,
where he feels at home.[74] All this goes to show that it is good
for young men to spend some time on philosophy for the sake
of culture (paideia), but beyond that this 'liberal study' becomes
illiberal, enslaving and unnerving the whole character.[75] Now
Callicles has expressed the direct contrast to Plato's high conception of paideia as filling the whole of man's life, by saying
that it is merely a stage occupying a few years of one's education
in youth. But whenever paideia becomes philosophy, it is bound
to have the tendency of which he accuses philosophy—it claims
to dominate the whole life of man.[76]

Callicles ends his speech with a personal appeal to Socrates to
give up philosophy because immoderate study of it is spoiling
his great intellectual talents. With this appeal he mingles a
scarcely concealed threat of state sanctions against him. What
good would his philosophy of suffering wrong do him if someone
arrested him and took him to prison, accusing him of crimes he
had not committed? He could easily be saddled with a capital
charge, 'without being able to help himself'. He could be struck
in the face with impunity.[77] The allusion to Socrates' execution
long after this scene gives terrible force to these harshly realistic
words.

Socrates replies that he is glad to have found an opponent
who says what he thinks. If he manages to make Callicles contradict himself, no one will be able to object that (like Polus
and Gorgias) he did not dare to say what he thought. And he is
kindly disposed too, as his warning shows. And, thirdly, he is
well educated, 'as many Athenians would say'.[78] For these three
reasons his defence of rhetoric must be considered the complete
and final one. The bitter irony of this approval of Callicles' oration, within the dramatic structure of the whole dialogue, shows
that Plato intends, after his impending defeat, to make Socrates
appear as the image of true frankness, true kindness, and true
paideia.

Callicles' view of human nature, on which his doctrine of the
right of the stronger is based, depends upon identifying the good

with the pleasant. That is not particularly emphasized in his
own argument, but Socrates recognizes that it is its real primary
assumption, and proves this dialectically. But other upholders
of the same doctrine could be adduced to say the same thing, for
it was one of their regular arguments. In his *Truth* the sophist
Antiphon makes the same distinction between what is naturally
just and what is legally just; and he says the mark of natural
justice is that it is the same as what gives men pleasure.[79] The
same criterion appears in Thucydides, in the Melian dialogue,
where he makes the Athenians expound the doctrine that Might
is Right.[80] It is not clear at first what Callicles means by 'the
stronger', but Socrates induces him to define the phrase more
closely. He offers several definitions, and is forced to abandon
them one after another. At last he settles on one. 'The stronger'
means the man who is politically cleverer and bolder, whose soul
has not been softened: therefore mastery belongs to him.[81]
The question on which Socrates and Callicles at last take issue
is whether this born ruler must rule himself too.[82] It was part
of the Greek idea of the tyrant and despot that he could give
free rein to his maddest desires, without having to conceal them
in terror, like the slavish mob. His freedom is to be what man
'really is'. Socrates asserts that the true ruler must first learn
to rule himself; and Callicles, clearly in opposition to bourgeois
morality, declares that his ideal is to be free to do what he
wants. Socrates praises him ironically for this 'not ignoble freedom of speech'.[83]

By now the discussion has once more reached the point at
which we have found ourselves before: it was in *Protagoras,*
when Socrates, discussing the best life, asked the sophists
whether there could be any other criterion for it than pleasure.[84]
But the delicately humorous atmosphere of that conversation has
given place, in *Gorgias,* to the fate-laden gloom of tragedy. The
exaggerated vanity of the sophists was harmlessly comic, and
could be treated lightly; the brutally menacing tone of Callicles
shows the seriousness of the situation here, and the irreconcilable spiritual enmity between the protagonists of each side. In
Protagoras Socrates was teasing his opponents, with the sham
earnestness of a conjurer, deliberately concealing the distance
between his audience and himself. Here he reveals and points
to the universe-wide gulf that lies between him and hedonism.

He actually brings in religious imagery and symbols—the first hint that, behind the infinitely subtle dialectic distinctions in which his moral principles are concealed, there is a metaphysical transformation of the whole of life. 'Who knows,' he asks with Euripides, 'if life here be not really death, and death in turn be life?' [85] And he reminds his hearers of the Orphic imagery which called the unintelligent 'the uninitiate', which made a sieve the symbol of the soul of the insatiable lover of pleasure, and taught that in the next world he was punished by pouring water for ever into a leaky cask. Callicles despises a life without pleasure, calling it 'living like a stone'.[86] But neither here nor later in Plato's *Philebus* does Socrates uphold the ideal of a life devoid of all emotion. Just as he does there, he demands that pleasures should be divided into good and bad. By a close analysis of the pleasures and sufferings involved in thirst and its satisfaction, he makes Callicles admit that good is not the same as pleasure and bad not the same as pain, and that he himself makes moral distinctions between good and bad pleasures.[87] As a pendant to this he works out the idea that will depends on choice, and that what we always choose in willing is the good.[88]

Modern students of Plato have often pointed out that this definition of the telos is very different from the hedonistic definition of it in *Protagoras;* and have based their whole conception of Plato's development on this difference, assuming that he did not reach those lofty moral heights on which he stands in *Phaedo,* at any time before he wrote *Gorgias*.[89] Both in *Phaedo* and in *Gorgias* we find an inclination to asceticism and a tendency to think of death as a positive moral good.[90] The implication is that *Protagoras* is one of Plato's earliest works because it agrees with 'most people' in treating the good as identical with pleasure.[91] It is hard to imagine a more complete misunderstanding of the meaning of Plato's reasoning in *Protagoras*. Socrates is trying to prove to the sophists that, *even if* he assumes that the vulgar are correct in thinking that what is pleasant is always good, his thesis (so difficult for common sense to accept) that knowledge is essential for right conduct can be proved with perfect ease.[92] The only essential thing is always to choose the greater pleasure instead of the less, and not to make mistakes in calculation by thinking the nearer pleasure bigger than it is. To do this, one must have 'an art of measurement', although in *Protagoras* Socrates says he will not discuss it in any detail.[93] He has proved what he wanted; and besides that, while the sophists all agree, as if under a spell, to everything he says, he has exposed the full inadequacy of their moral beliefs. For it is surely obvious that in that scene Socrates tries to show the reader, not once but again and again, with suspicious pertinacity, that the identification of good with pleasure is *not* his own view but the view of the mob. He explains that, if they were asked, they could give no other motive for their conduct than pleasure and pain; and he cheerfully invites them to name any other telos they can think of. But, he adds in obvious triumph, they cannot think of any other.[94] The notion that when Plato in *Phaedo* [95] scornfully rejects this conception of human conduct, calling it a barter-business carried on with pleasures of various sizes, he is deriding himself, cannot be taken seriously. On the other hand, the 'art of measurement', which is the guise assumed in *Protagoras* by the desirable knowledge of true standards, is not merely a joke. We need only take good as the standard instead of pleasure—for Plato in *Philebus,* and Aristotle under Plato's influence in his youthful work *The Statesman,* describe good as the most exact of all standards. The measurement referred to is not quantitative but qualitative. And that is what distinguished Plato from the multitude with its lower scale of values. This telos is announced in *Gorgias,* and assumed in *Protagoras.* From the very earliest of Plato's works, the small Socratic dialogues, it lies behind his search for areté, in the form of the knowledge of good; and as *Gorgias* unmistakably teaches, the good is 'that through whose presence the good are good'; [96] that is, it is the Idea, the ultimate shape of every good thing.[97]

This conversation with Callicles has led to a result diametrically opposite to the point from which it started—the doctrine of the right of the stronger. If pleasure and pain are not the standard for our conduct, then rhetoric must relinquish the supremacy over the most important branches of life which the rhetoricians had said it enjoyed,[98] and along with it all other types of flattery, which have as their goal only the pleasure, not the good, of man.[99] The most important duty in life is evidently to determine which pleasures are good and which are bad—and that, as even Callicles laconically admits when Socrates asks him, is not 'in everybody's line'.[100] This is a succinct statement of a principle fundamental to Plato's ethical and educational doctrine. He does not advise men to trust their own moral sentiment as the supreme judge. He declares there must be a science, a techné, whose findings the individual must follow.[101] The conversation has turned back to its beginnings. Socrates' initial question whether rhetoric was a science or not now reveals its full meaning. There are two contrasting types of life, two *bioi*.[102] One of them is built upon the flattering quasi-arts—really not arts at all but copies of arts. We may call it, after one of its main species of flattery, the rhetorical ideal of life. Its purpose is to create pleasure and win approval. The other, its opponent, is the philosophical life. It is based on knowledge of human nature and of what is best for it: so it is a real techné, and it really cares for man, for the body as well as the soul.[103] Its therapy benefits not only the individual but the community too. Correspondingly, there is a flattery for the individual and another for the multitude. As examples of the latter, Plato mentions different types of poetry and music: flute-playing, choral and dithyrambic poetry, tragedy. All of these aim at pleasure alone; if rhythm, metre, and melody are subtracted from them, the remainder is nothing but *demegoria,* mob-oratory.[104] Later in Greek history this idea, that poetry was a part of eloquence, was universally accepted. This is its earliest appearance, but here it is meant disparagingly. Plato's radical criticism of poetry as an educational force, which is so essential to his philosophy, is announced here for the first time. It finds its real place in *The Republic* and *The Laws;* for it belongs to the general system of Plato's paideia, which is laid out in detail in those works. It is of the same type as his attack on sophistry and rhetoric in *Protagoras* and *Gorgias.* The public which the poet addresses oratorically is not the male citizen-body; it is a mixture of children, women, and men, slaves and free alike. But even the higher type of rhetoric, addressed to free men, is no better than the type we call poetry: for it too is aimed, not at good, but at pleasing the multitude, without asking whether it makes them better or worse.[105]

Callicles takes this opportunity, and makes his last attempt to defend the spiritual values of rhetoric. He admits that Socrates' destructive criticisms are true of contemporary political speakers, in order to elevate the oratory of great Athenian statesmen of the past into a model of truly educational art. (Thereby he tacitly accepts Socrates' standard for their valuation.) [106] Surely their very names—Themistocles, Cimon, Miltiades, Pericles—ought to silence all opposition. But Plato condemns them all without the flicker of an eyelash. If a statesman is great because he understands how to satisfy his own desires and those of the multitude, then they deserve the praise lavished on them by history. But if the statesman's real task is to give his work a definite form, an eidos, in the greatest possible perfection, to orient himself with reference to it—as the painter, the architect, and shipbuilder, and other craftsmen must do—and to reduce the parts composing the whole to an intelligible order so that every one fits every other, then those men were mere bunglers. As every work of art has its proper form and order, on whose realization its perfection depends, and as the human body has its own cosmos, called health, so there is a cosmos and an order in the soul too. We call it law. It depends on justice and self-control, and what we describe as virtues. The true statesman and orator will have his eyes on it when he is choosing his words and doing his actions and giving his gifts.[107] He will always be watching to see that justice comes into the souls of his fellow-citizens while injustice leaves them, that prudence and moderation grow in them while incontinence leaves them, and that every virtue grows in them while wickedness departs. The doctor does not glut a sick body with lots of sweet food and drink that do it no good; and the true statesman strongly disciplines the sick soul and does not indulge its fancies.

By this time Callicles is in an apathy. He scarcely seems to hear what Socrates says, although he is powerless to contradict him.[108] He cannot escape from Socrates' logical reasoning, but in his heart he is not convinced—indeed he says so later, and Plato adds 'as happens with most people'.[109] After silencing him, Socrates goes on with his reasoning, and follows it out to the very end by answering his own questions. In a short survey of the results already reached, he points out that all thinking about right conduct must be founded on the idea that the pleasant is not the same as the good and healthy. Therefore one should do what is pleasant only for the sake of the good, and not the other way about. A man, like anything else, is good because there

is an areté, an excellence or virtue, in him.[110] Areté or excellence
in a utensil, a body, a soul, or a living being, does not come
about by chance, but only by right order and deliberate art.
Everything becomes good when its own peculiar type of order,
its cosmos, becomes supreme and is realized in it.[111] Before Plato
the word *cosmos* had not been used to mean an orderly system
within the soul; but the kindred adjective *kosmios* had signified
modest, disciplined, orderly behaviour. Solon's law dealt with
eukosmia in the citizen's behaviour, especially in that of the
young. In harmony with all that, Plato now declares that the
self-controlled and disciplined soul is a 'good' soul.[112] (Remember that the Greek for 'good' [ἀγαθός] does not have merely the
narrow ethical sense we give it, but is the adjective corresponding to the noun areté, and so means 'excellent' in any way. From
that point of view ethics is only a special case of the effort made
by all things to achieve perfection.) Socrates shows that every
other type of virtue (piety, courage, and justice) naturally co-
exists with true sophrosyné.[113] In fact, he is bringing in here the
theme discussed in the little dialogues and *Protagoras*—the
unity of virtue.[114] What the Greeks called *eudaimonia,* perfect
happiness, depends (he says) on excellence in this way; and
when they called being happy 'doing well' (εὖ πράττειν) he declares they spoke more wisely than they knew, for *being happy*
depends entirely upon *doing well.*[115]

To reach this areté and escape its opposite must be the fixed
aim of our lives. All the energies of the individual and the state
should be devoted to reaching that aim, and not to the satisfaction of desires.[116] The latter can lead only to the life of a robber;
and the man who lives like that is hateful to men and gods,
because no community is possible on such a basis, and where
there is no community there can be no friendship. But wise men
tell us that heaven and earth and gods and men are held together
by community and friendship and orderliness and moderation
and justice, and that is why the universe is called the Order,
the Cosmos.[117] It is not *pleonexia,* the greed for more, that is
powerful among gods and men; it is geometric proportion. But
Callicles does not care about geometry![118] Thus, what seemed
to be a paradox, that it is less bad to be wronged than to do
wrong, is perfectly true. The real orator and statesman must be
just and possess knowledge of justice. The greatest disgrace is

not being unable to 'help oneself' against wrong and violence from outside, as Callicles asserts,[119] but being unable to help oneself against the severest possible injury, the injury one's soul suffers when injustice takes possession of it.[120] To escape suffering that injury, one needs not only good will, but ability and power (δύναμις). As the politician and orator strives to gain external power, to protect himself against *suffering* wrong, so Socrates says we must learn to protect ourselves against the danger of *doing* wrong. That protection can be given only by knowledge and the understanding of the good, 'the political techné': for since no one does wrong willingly, everything depends upon that techné.[121]

If it were only a matter of protection against suffering wrong, it would be enough to support the constitution which was in force at the time.[122] But when the country is ruled by a cruel tyrant with no paideia, he will be afraid of anyone who is a better man than he is.[123] So he can never become that man's friend; and he will despise anyone who is worse than himself. Thus the only friend left to him is the man whose character resembles his own, who praises and blames the same things, and who is ready to be ordered about by him. That man will become very powerful, and no one will wrong him with impunity.[124] Therefore ambitious young men in that country will conclude that the only way to get on is to copy the despot as closely as possible, and to admire and dislike the same things as he does.[125] But although this safeguards them against suffering wrong, it does not protect them against doing wrong. And so, by copying the tyrant, they will have the greatest evil in their souls, which will be corrupted and deformed by their imitation of him.[126] Of course there is the danger against which Callicles warned Socrates, that the tyrant will kill anyone who does not copy him. But Socrates does not fear that, because he has learnt that life is not the greatest possible good.[127] Still, he advises Callicles, who does not want to take *his* lonely path, to give up the code of Might which he flaunts to his friends, and copy the standards and the whims of his master, the Athenian demos—not only externally, but by growing as like him in his soul as he can manage: anything else is dangerous.[128] Suddenly Callicles, who had warned Socrates of the dangers of crossing those in power, is seen to be in the very same position himself. They are both faced with the same problem: how to behave to the 'tyrant' of their country who demands unconditional respect for his wishes—namely, the Athenian demos. Socrates has shown that he knows the consequences of his courage, and is ready to accept them for the sake of benefiting his fatherland. He, the representative of 'virtue', is the true hero. The other, Callicles, who upholds the mastery of the stronger, is really the coward, making himself a glib and supple imitation so as to become a ruler.

At this point Socrates very opportunely reminds his hearers of the fundamental distinction he made at the outset, between two methods of treating the body and soul: one directed to producing pleasure, the other to doing good; one flattering the lower side of man's nature, the other fighting against it.[129] Callicles and Socrates, it is now apparent, are the complete embodiments of those two methods. One is the flatterer, the other the fighter. We must choose. We cannot wish the state to have the deceitful sham arts, but rather the severe therapy of truth, that makes the citizens as good as possible. Neither the possession of riches nor the increase of power is worth anything to the man whose mind is not trained to real kalokagathia.[130] The philosophical educator who leads the state towards it is the state's only real benefactor, as Socrates observes, with a sideglance towards the statesmen whose services are publicly recognized in laudatory resolutions and immortalized in inscriptions.[130a] The attempt to raise the citizens to that stage must begin with the choice of political leaders. Since Socrates' political science is a techné, this choice is to be made by a regular examination.[131] If, he says, we were being examined for the post of state-architect, we should be tested to reveal whether we understood our profession, and who had been our teacher, and whether we had designed any buildings that would recommend us. It would be the same if we were candidates for a post as medical officer.[132] So, if politics is a true art, the future statesman must be tested to reveal what he has done in that department. Since it is the art of making men better, Socrates asks Callicles (as the only politician present) whom he has made better in private life, before he entered politics.[133] And then, after this half-joking question, he turns to examine the most famous statesmen of Athenian history, Pericles, Cimon, Miltiades, and Themistocles. Pericles, he says, made the Athenians lazy, cow-

ardly, talkative, and avaricious by introducing the dole-system.
When he took them over from his predecessors, they were relatively tame, but (as his own impeachment proved) he made
them savage. They sent Cimon and Themistocles into exile; they
voted to throw Miltiades into the *barathron*, the traitor's gulf.
All those men were like drivers who handle obedient teams so
badly that they are thrown out of the chariot.[134]

A statesman, in Socrates' sense of the word, has never yet
existed.[135] The famous Athenian statesmen were only servants,
not teachers, of their country.[136] They made themselves subservient to the weaknesses in human nature, and tried to use them,
instead of changing them by persuasion and compulsion. They
were not trainers and doctors, but confectioners, who filled the
body of the nation with fat and relaxed its once strong muscles.
Of course the consequences of that gluttony cannot be seen till
much later. Meanwhile we praise the men who served us the
sweet dishes, and say they made the state great, without seeing
that it is bloated and shaky because of what they did to it.[137]
For without self-control and justice, they filled it with harbours
and dockyards and fortifications and tributes and such rubbish.
But when the attack of the disease comes, people will not turn
upon the really guilty men, but on those who are ruling the country at the moment, although they are only accessories.[138] Still, it
will be useless to call the people ungrateful when it overthrows
and persecutes its leaders. The sophists foolishly do the same:
they profess to educate men in virtue and then complain because
their pupils wrong them by refusing to pay the fees.[139] There is
no real difference between the sophist and the orator; in fact,
the orator, who despises the sophist, is really as far beneath
him as the judge is beneath the lawgiver, and the doctor beneath
the trainer. A rhetor or a sophist who blames the people he has
'educated' is really accusing himself and his method of education.[140]

Therefore if Socrates is to choose between the two methods
of treating men—serving the Athenian people by flattery, or
fighting them to make them better—he can choose only the
second, and that although he knows the mortal danger he is
running.[141] Anyone who accuses him will be a bad man. And it
would not be strange if he were put to death. He expects that
that will be the result of his teaching, for, as he says, 'I believe

that I am one of the few Athenians, not to say the only one, to practise the true art of statesmanship, and the only living man engaged in politics.' If he is accused, he will be condemned like a doctor accused by a cook before a crowd of children. The cook would say, 'Children, this man has afflicted you with bitter medicines and hunger and thirst, while I have treated you with all sorts of delicious dainties!' The doctor would be shouted down when he answered, 'I did all that, children, for your health.' Likewise Socrates will be shouted down when he says, 'It is for justice that I say all this, and what I do I am doing for your sake alone.'[142] But he is not frightened by the prospect of this end. There is only one way for him 'to help himself'. That is to keep himself free from injustice; for the greatest evil, and the only one to be feared, is 'to reach the next world with a soul full of many injustices'.[143]

In *Gorgias,* Plato for the first time advances beyond the simple method of examination and enquiry which fills his earlier dialogues. Now he shows the philosopher at the point where this apparently purely intellectual enquiry (so important, in his view, for right conduct) reveals its vast scope and profundity, and where the game he has been playing with such inexplicable passion suddenly changes into a battle against the whole world, with life as the stake. To alter the metaphor, we might say that, after *Crito,* his first dialogues are bright and cheerful scherzi, charming to all lovers of the muses; but suddenly, in *Gorgias,* we are appalled by the grim deep-mouthed chords of the Socratic symphony, crashing through the gay music with heroic forebodings of death. *Gorgias* gives the first complete picture since the *Apology* of Socrates' teaching and *bios.* Out of what looks like the logical indecision of his conversations, there glows the relentless moral conviction of his life, sure of its ultimate aim, and therefore possessing that hotly sought knowledge which renders any faltering of will impossible. Seen from this point of view, his concentration on the Idea of Good takes on new meaning. The effort of the logos to reach its aim becomes the direct expression of the life that is entirely given up to that aim. What is for others nothing but words, which they hear without being convinced,[144] is the revelation of Socrates' true existence. Plato describes it to us in the firm conviction that in his master speech and reality were one and the same.[145] *Gorgias* shows us a new way of estimating life, which has its origin in Socrates' knowledge of the nature of the soul.

It is this metaphysical meaning of Socrates' fight against injustice that Plato displays to the spiritual vision of his readers, with all the vividness of true poetry, in the closing myth of *Gorgias*.[146] He tries every possible method of making our emotions too feel all that the logos has proved. His use of the myth does not imply that he is appealing to the irrational element in us as if it were a special or even a unique faculty of cognition. He shows us significant figures and actions which make a complete picture out of the lines drawn by logical analysis. So the function of the myth within the dialogue is to sum up and round off what has been said. Plato is using one of the devices of the sophistic lecture, but he has transformed it into an organic part of the Socratic dialogue. The essence of the Platonic myth lies in its co-operation with the logos to serve the same purpose. Long after the reader has forgotten the tortuous complications of Plato's logical arguments, he can remember the picture given by the myth, which becomes a symbol of the philosophical meaning of the whole work, and indeed of all Plato's doctrine and all his attitude to life.

The myth of *Gorgias* is based on religious conceptions of the life after death, remodelled with poetic freedom by Plato to suit his own purpose. The real Socrates can hardly have invented these boldly decorative variations on religious myths, even if he was sometimes interested in them. But the common belief that Plato, either on his travels or in some other way, fell under the influence of the Orphic mysteries or some similar cult, and mingled their beliefs with Socrates' moral teaching, is too coarse an interpretation of his intellectual and spiritual processes. His myths of the soul's destiny after death are not the dogmas of a mere religious syncretism.[147] So to interpret them is to underestimate Plato's power as a creator, although it is in them that it reaches its maximum intensity. Still, it is true that he used as material some eschatological conceptions of the kind usually called Orphic. They impressed him so deeply because he felt as an artist that a proper transcendental background was needed for the heroic loneliness of Socrates' fighting soul.

If a man who lived and thought like Socrates had not, as it

were, one foot in the unseen world, he would lose his equilibrium
—at least so it would seem to the dim eyes of sense. The truth
of his conception of life cannot be understood unless it is referred to such a Beyond as that imaged in the vividly realistic
language of Orphic eschatology: a place where the value or
worthlessness, the blessedness or damnation of man are finally
determined, where 'the soul itself' is judged by 'the soul itself'
without the defensive and deceptive clothing of beauty, rank,
wealth, and power.[148] This 'judgment', placed by religious imagination in the second life which begins after death, becomes a
higher truth for Plato when he thinks through all that is meant
by Socrates' idea of human personality as a purely inward value,
based in itself alone. If the soul's purity from injustice is its
health, and its infection with guilt is its deformity and sickness,
then the judgment in the next world is a sort of medical examination of the soul. Naked, it appears before the judge (himself
a naked soul); he examines every scar, every wound, every
blemish left in it by the sickness of its own injustice during life.[149]
Plato did not borrow *that* trait from Orphic myths; it is an
expression of Socrates' basic belief that the evil that men do
lives on in them and forms the nature of their souls. It means
a permanent weakening of the value of the personality. This is
the ground of the doctrine expressed in *Gorgias,* that happiness
is identical with moral perfection. The healthy souls, mostly
those which have striven for wisdom (φιλόσοφοι ψυχαί), are sent
to the Isles of the Blest. The souls which are found to be unhealthy, and are consequently despatched to Tartarus, are divided into curable and incurable: this leaves a way open for
the curable to recover after long suffering and painful treatment.[150] The incurables—mostly despots and tyrants, beyond the
power of any therapy—are used as eternal examples, *paradeigmata,* for the benefit of others.[151]

Gorgias closes with a warning against *apaideusia,*[152] ignorance
of 'the greatest goods in life'; and postpones practical concern
with politics to the time when we have freed ourselves of this
ignorance. Thus Plato reminds us once again of the educational
tendency of the whole dialogue, and of the whole Socratic philosophy; and thus he stamps his unique conception of the nature
of paideia deeply and indelibly in our memory. Paideia for Plato

is the soul's lifelong struggle to free itself from ignorance of the greatest goods, which bars its way to its true welfare.[153] These words point backwards, to the conclusion of *Protagoras,* where this same ignorance, 'false belief and error about things of the highest value', was described as the source of all evil.[154] There it was laid down that man is not capable of willingly choosing evil. The kind of knowledge referred to was not described in detail—its discussion was postponed to a later occasion.[155] *Gorgias* is the first revelation of the programme hinted at in those words, of Socrates' paideia, with its ethical doctrine and its transcendental implications. Therefore it is a decisively important stage in the great debate with Socrates which runs through Plato's dialogues, and which we have described as the process by which he became conscious of the philosophical presuppositions of Socrates' life and thought.[156] It is a many-sided process, concerning Socrates' method and logic quite as much as his ethics and his *bios. Gorgias* is the first work which brings out all those aspects of his character at once, although the real emphasis is on his morality. That is what defines its value as a document of Plato's paideia.

Plato's first dialogues presented the educational element in Socrates' conversations chiefly as a matter of method, even in their approach to their subject, the problem of virtue. Then *Protagoras* showed that Socrates' enquiries, all aimed at reaching knowledge of the highest values, were fundamental to the problem of education—although it did not show what form education on that basis ought to assume. All it revealed was the new evaluation of knowledge as the way to areté and the new demand for a techné of right conduct. If such a techné could exist, the education given by the sophists would be completely superseded or at least relegated to a secondary place. Now *Gorgias* attacks the problem anew, and works out the essential features and assumptions of the desired techné. It does this under the guise of a debate with rhetoric—which, as the end of the dialogue shows, is treated as essentially the same as sophistry. Still, Plato chose rhetoric for the target of his criticism, not just for a change, but because it is the force guiding the state, and therefore points to the connexion between education and the state. We have already fitted the early Platonic dialogues into this connexion (from internal grounds); *Protago-*

ras revealed it quite clearly; and now *Gorgias* expressly
acknowledges and defines it. As *Protagoras* shows, the sophists'
educational system too had attempted to prepare citizens for
life in the state. It had not only given instruction about the
state's workings, but attacked, as a theoretical problem, the
sociological influence of the state in education. But its aim had
been to train successful leaders for public life, who could learn
to fit into existing conditions and use them to their own advantage. So they had treated the relation between state and education as a very one-sided affair (from Socrates' point of view),
because they took the state holus-bolus as it was, and therefore
made an entirely degenerate form of political life the standard
of their education.

In opposition to that, *Gorgias* develops Plato's conclusive
view that the problem at the root of all education is to find, to
define, and to understand the standard by which it is to be
regulated. It presents Socrates as the only true teacher, because
he alone knows the telos. In the *Apology* and other early works,
down to and including *Protagoras,* Plato's Socrates (and here he
is the same as the real Socrates) ironically denies that he teaches
men—although Plato describes him as the only real teacher. But
in *Gorgias* he lays down that paideia in its ethical sense is the
highest good, the epitome of human happiness, and claims that
he himself possess it. Plato now ascribes to him his own passionate conviction that Socrates is the real teacher needed by the
state, and he makes him proudly declare (with an emotion which
is not Socratic but wholly Platonic) that he is the only statesman
of his age.[157] The statesman's true task is not to accommodate
himself to the mob, as the pseudo-paideia of orator and sophist
implies,[158] but to make men better. Still, *Gorgias* does not explain
what a state would look like if it exerted all its energies to reach
that aim. *The Republic* is the first book in which Plato shows us
that. *Gorgias* merely announces the aim—with a truly prophetic
zeal: it is to bring the state back to its educational task. In such
a state, and only in such a state, is it possible for an educational
ideal like that of Socrates, which takes human perfection as its
absolute standard, to be justified in its claim to be the basis of
all the art of statesmanship.

This is the first work in which Plato purposely expounds
Socratic paideia at some length as equivalent to the art of poli-

tics; and here he puts it in the most violent opposition to the
existing state. This opposition is quite different from that which
we hear of between the politicians and sophistic education. The
sophists, as a new phenomenon, excited the distrust of the conservatives. They were therefore on the defensive. Even when
they were helping the opposition by putting weapons into their
hands—for instance, with their doctrine that Might is Right,
or with their attacks on the democratic principle of equality—
they knew enough to pay lip-service to democracy (as Callicles
shows) and keep their advanced views for private discussion.
Of course Socrates himself had no such scruples; Plato makes
much of his frankness, and Callicles warns him of its consequences.[159] But *Gorgias* goes further. There, in a big, sensational
work, Plato eulogizes his frankness and turns the full glare of
publicity on the conflict between Socrates' educational ideals and
the realities of politics. Even the *Apology,* which showed Socrates in conflict with the powers that be, had put that problem
in the foreground; it did so without diminishing its harshness.
It showed that (as we have pointed out) Socrates' clash with
the state was not an accident, but an inevitable necessity.[160]
The early dialogues were chiefly concerned with re-creating the
form and content of Socrates' enquiries, and paid little attention
to the opposition between his political science and the state. But
Gorgias shows that this calm was only on the surface. It is the
first work in which Plato describes Socrates' paideia as a complete system; he conceives it as a foe of statesmanship as then
practised, and of the spirit dominating public life. In fact, he
reveals its true character through its opposition to and criticism of rhetoric, which, with all its glittering pomp and flattering
unction, he takes to be the true representative of contemporary
politics. He even points to the clouds gathering above it, from
which the storm is soon to burst.

But the novelty of *Gorgias* is that it is not Socrates but the
state that is on trial. Out of Socrates' injunction to his fellow-
citizens to care for their souls, Plato develops a philosophical
system of education; and he accepts the inheritance left him by
his master, the conflict with the state that had brought about
Socrates' death. In the *Apology* Socrates' death may seem to many
readers to have been a unique catastrophe, as it were the crash of a
meteor which struck and perished. In *Gorgias* it is the expression

of a permanent conflict, and one of the foci of Plato's thought. All through, his philosophy develops by working out the assumptions of Socrates' life and thought; and so in this vitally important point. Through his efforts to understand the implications and the inevitability of the conflict which had led to the death of 'the most righteous of all the citizens',[161] it had become the starting-point of all his philosophy of education. His seventh Letter explains this experience so vividly and illuminates its permanent philosophical significance for Plato so clearly that *Gorgias*, the work of art, and the Letter, an autobiographical sketch, serve as perfect complements to one another.[162] The Letter tells us that after Socrates' execution Plato felt it was impossible for him to come to terms with the contemporary state. This feeling is made objective in *Gorgias*. At the same time we see what concrete political significance Plato (more than any other of his pupils) read into his master's educational mission. Although he condemned the state which had despised and rejected Socrates, he did not therefore condemn the state as such. On the contrary, the failure of Socrates, 'the only true statesman of his age', is just what proves that the state must be brought into harmony with Socrates' teaching. It is not education that must be changed (as the men who accused and executed Socrates thought), but the state that must be radically revised. But what does that mean, for Plato? His criticisms in *Gorgias* are directed exclusively against Athenian politicians, past and present, so that it looks as if his passion for reform still aimed at a political revolution in his own city. Yet the seventh Letter shows us that, by that time, he had given up the idea.[163] How could the spirit of Socrates possibly penetrate and influence the wholly 'rhetorical' Athenian state? Behind the negation of *Gorgias*, there stands the affirmation, the philosophers' Republic. Overwhelming as its criticisms of the contemporary state are, *Gorgias* neither aims at armed revolution,[164] nor expresses the gloomy sense of fatalism and defeat which would have been understandable after the external and internal collapse of Athens at the end of the war. By rejecting the existing state in *Gorgias*, Plato clears the way to the 'best state' at which he is aiming, and which he wants to design, without discussing the possibility of realizing it now or later. He takes the first step by describing Socrates' paideia and its aim, in *Gorgias*. That marks the spiritual basis of his new political purpose, which is his one unshaken rock in a world-wide social collapse.

Plato's paradoxical declaration that the art of politics must be based on the sure and certain knowledge of the greatest goods in human life, and must be solely aimed at making the citizens of the state better, obviously arises from the synthesis of his own political ideals with his faith in Socrates' political mission. But this purely personal and psychological explanation is not enough to make us understand the political techné which involves both caring for the soul and building the state. We moderns are bound to feel that this is a mixture of two tasks which we usually keep far apart. For us, politics means policy, realistic policy; and ethics means individual morality. Although many modern states have taken over the education of children, it is difficult for us to accept without question the ancient Greek view (which is Plato's absolute ideal) that the law of the state is the source of all standards of human life, and that the virtue of the individual is the same as the virtue of the citizen. That harmony between state and individual had for the first time been seriously challenged in the age of Socrates. The ethics of the individual and the creed of the state began to drift further and further apart, as political life grew coarser and more realistic, and as individual morality grew more independent and refined. This breach of the original harmony between individual and civic virtue, which we have already described, is the assumption on which Plato's political philosophy is based. It was clear that the statesman's power of controlling the minds of the people, which had been accepted without question in the early city-state, had its dangerous aspect. In the existing conditions, it was bound to make the cultured and intelligent man either withdraw from politics into silence, or apply his own moral standards to the state, and thereby come into conflict, irreparable conflict, with it. On principle, Plato was against the individual's withdrawal from politics. He had grown up in the ancestral and social tradition that the best men available gave up their lives to the state. Socrates' harsh criticisms would hardly have impressed him so deeply as his books show they did, unless he had always, from his youth, shared the fine old belief that the polis was by nature the moral legislator for all its citizens. Even Socrates' clash with the Athenian democracy was not interpreted by Plato to mean that the time had come to render to the state that which is the state's, and to render to God that which is God's. He did not plan to keep man's best side away from the state's influence. He thought that individual and community belonged to each other; and that the state, and the state alone, could set a norm for that relationship. But the state's claim to dominate the whole soul of each of its citizens creates a problem of terrible difficulty, as soon as one man's soul decides that the universal standard of human worth and happiness lies within its own moral conscience. The state should not lag behind that moral development. Plato asserts that it has only one choice. Either it must become the teacher and the physician of souls; or, if it fails in that, it must be regarded as degenerate, unworthy of its authority. Plato's *Gorgias* implies the assertion that all the functions of the state must give way to its mission as a moral teacher. If one may say that the Greek polis was both State and Church, it was the latter aspect which vitally concerned Plato.

But, besides the traditional idealization of the state as dominating the individual life, there was another motive which led Plato to take his strange new attitude to politics. It was involved in Socrates' theory of virtue. Plato agreed with his master that right conduct was based on knowledge of the highest values; therefore these values could not be realized in human life by mere subjective opinion and emotion. To understand them was the work of the highest type of cognition possible for the human intellect. By his ironical confession of ignorance, Socrates himself had shown that the knowledge of the good was not possible for everyone. Therefore it is a mistake to interpret Socrates' characteristic disregard of tradition as something like the modern freedom of conscience. Plato always holds that the knowledge of good is the political techné; and thereby he brings out its essentially objective character. It is not something vague, something different from specialist knowledge; on the contrary, its ideal is like the specialist's. Therefore it is impossible for the common herd, and can be reached only by the loftiest philosophical cognition. Just at the point where we might expect to find the appearance of such modern ideals as personal conscience and free individual ethics, they are decisively rejected. Instead, we are referred to the authority of objective philosophical truth, which claims to rule the entire life of society, and therefore of the individual. If knowledge or science as conceived by Socrates is possible, it can, according to Plato, be fully effective only within the framework of a new spiritual society which he conceives, traditionally, to be a *civitas*.

MENO
THE NEW KNOWLEDGE

PLATO's first dialogues were attempts to reach the knowledge of areté by a number of different routes. They all led to the realization that the separate virtues—courage, prudence, piety, and justice—were simply parts of one whole virtue, and that the essence of virtue in itself was knowledge. In *Protagoras* and *Gorgias,* assuming the correctness of that result, Plato proceeded to show that it was the foundation of all education, and to sketch the outlines of the paideia which was to be based on it. In a long and profound dispute with the leading representatives of up-to-date education, he showed that the sophists, the only ones who ascribed great importance to knowledge, were not prepared to draw the inevitable conclusion that moral and political education ought to be founded on knowledge. Meanwhile the old-fashioned educators paid no attention to this idea whatever. In *Protagoras* Socrates tried to enlist the sophists on his side. But, as he strove to work out all the implications of his thesis that virtue must be knowledge, thereby going back on his original statement that it could not be taught, Protagoras on his part had been notably reluctant to recognize that he could not defend his claim to be a teacher of virtue unless he accepted Socrates' thesis that virtue was knowledge.

There it was made clear that this knowledge must be something different from knowledge in the usual sense of the word. But no attempt was made to say what kind of knowledge it was. *Protagoras* stopped with the proof that virtue must be teachable if Socrates were right in saying it was knowledge. There was just a hint that it was an art of measurement; but Socrates postponed the attempt to find out what kind of measuring art it was, and what sort of standards it used.[1] We need not assume that his remark was an allusion to any specific dialogue. Plato often treated the problem of knowledge—indeed, it is a problem which he never permanently solved. But at least that hint of his makes it clear that after the identity of virtue and knowledge has been proved, and the importance of that knowledge in education has been demonstrated, it is urgently necessary to make a special investigation to find out what kind of knowledge it is. The first dialogue to attack this problem is *Meno*. It is also the closest in date to the dialogues we have already discussed: therefore it is Plato's first answer to the problem posed in *Protagoras* —what kind of knowledge is it which Socrates considers the basis of areté?

Recognizing the importance of this problem in Plato's philosophy, scholars have called *Meno* 'the programme of the Academy'. This is an exaggeration which merely proves that they have misunderstood Plato by applying modern ideas to him. His school could never have accepted a programme which limited philosophy to the problem of knowledge—especially if we take 'knowledge' to mean those modern abstractions, logic and the theory of cognition. Even in *Meno,* the first comparatively independent treatment of the question, Plato takes care to point out that, for him, the problem of knowledge is organically connected with all his ethical enquiries, and derives its importance from them. Here as elsewhere he starts with the problem: How can we get possession of areté?[2] Of course he does not work it out in detail, and end by finding that it can be acquired only through knowledge. Instead, he deliberately centres the discussion on the origin of knowledge. But we must remember that, throughout, he means the knowledge of virtue and good—i.e. the new, Socratic knowledge. And that knowledge is inseparable from its object, and incomprehensible without it.

He begins by putting down, in a neat, methodical way, the usual answers to the question 'How do we acquire areté?' Can it be taught? Or is it got by practice? Or is it neither practice nor teaching, but nature that imparts it to us? Or is there some other answer? This was the traditional form of the problem, known to us from the elder poets—Hesiod, Theognis, Simonides, and Pindar—and taken over from them by their successors the sophists. What is new for Plato in this discussion of it is that Socrates begins by asking what areté is itself, before he tries to discover how it is acquired.[3]

The logical meaning of this problem, to which the discussions of separate virtues in the smaller dialogues always brought us, is explained with particular care and elaboration in *Meno*. More clearly than in any of them, Plato shows the reader exactly what are the implications of the question 'What is virtue in itself?' First of all, Socrates clarifies the distinction between virtue itself and the various forms which it takes. Meno has learnt from Gorgias his teacher to distinguish the virtues of a man and a woman, an adult and a child, a freeman and a slave.[4] Socrates, however, turns away from this 'swarm of virtues' which Meno brings in instead of the one virtue underlying them all.[5] For other purposes, he says, it might be useful to differentiate virtue by age, sex, and social position; but that cannot be done without first examining the one single Virtue in relation to the various people who have it and the various ways in which they employ it. That is its relative side, whereas we set out to investigate its absolute nature.[6] The 'something' through which all the separate virtues can be seen to be not manifold, but one and the same, Socrates calls the *eidos*.[7] It is 'that through which they are all the same', all virtues.[8] Plato gives it the name *eidos*, 'shape', because it is only through looking at it that one can explain to an enquirer what virtue really is.[9] The phrase 'looking at something', 'with one's eye fixed on something', (ἀποβλέπων εἴς τι), is common in Plato, and it vividly evokes what he means by *eidos* or *idea*. There is one single eidos of areté and one single eidos of other similar 'concepts'. (We should call them concepts, but Plato had not realized what that logical 'something' was, nor could he name it: so that we should do better to speak of 'entities'.) Such, then, are the eidé or Ideas of health, tallness, and strength.[10] In *Gorgias,* and often elsewhere, these virtues (aretai) of the body are mentioned as parallel to the virtues of the soul.[11] Therefore these examples are carefully selected, and once more prove that the Platonic eidos is always worked out in relation to the problem of virtue. If we want to know what health is, we shall not try to decide if it is different in a man, in a woman, and so forth: we shall try to discover the eidos of health, which is identical everywhere. So also with stature and strength, the two other virtues of the body. Therefore the same applies to the virtues of the soul: there is no difference whether justice, for example, or prudence, occurs in a man or in a woman. It is always the same.[12]

The discussion of this problem is deliberately kept within an elementary range, since its aim is only to explain the essential steps of Socrates' thought. Plato himself calls Socrates' conversation with Meno 'exercise (μελέτη) for answering the question about the nature of areté'.[13] Its nature is described first as the simple absolute, in contrast to the many different relations in which virtue can stand to various types of men, and secondly as different from what Plato calls the parts of virtue—justice, prudence, and so forth.[14] We have said that it makes no difference to the unity of virtue whether, for instance, it is the virtue of a man or a woman. But is not virtue, in so far as it is justice, different from virtue in so far as it is prudence? And is not the division of virtue into the different forms in which it appears apt to endanger the unity for which we are searching? In other words, is there not a genuine difference between justice, prudence, and courage? The smaller Socratic dialogues and *Protagoras* have shown us that the essential unity of all these parts of virtue is Socrates' fundamental problem.[15] There he said he was looking for 'all virtue' or 'universal virtue'. In *Meno* he identifies the essence of virtue with the sum of all that can be said, not about any part of virtue, but about virtue 'as a whole' (κατὰ ὅλου).[16] This is the first expression of a new logical idea—the universal (καθόλου)—and it makes its meaning incomparably clear. The eidos of good or of areté, of which Plato spoke, is quite simply this view of good 'as a whole'.[17] The singular thing here is that Plato also describes this good 'as a whole' as that which really and effectively exists; and that prevents us from identifying it with our logical 'concept', the 'universal'. Neither in the earlier dialogues nor here in *Meno* is a real definition of areté ever given; and it is clear that when he asks for the nature of areté he does not want a definition for an answer. Instead of that, the parts of virtue are once more discussed, and, as always, the discussion leads back to the problem of virtue in itself, i.e. to the Idea. The answer to 'What is virtue?' is not a definition, but an Idea. The Idea is the goal towards which Plato's thought, with its dialectic movement, always proceeds. That is clear enough from his very earliest dialogues, and *Meno* makes it clearer still.[18]

If we take at its face value this analysis of the logical procedure of Socrates' dialectic, as given by Plato, its most distinguished interpreter, step after careful step in *Meno,* we shall

find it almost impossible to fall into the mistake so often made
by philosophical students of it in classical and modern times. In a
way, Aristotle began it all with his notorious assertion that Socrates was the first who tried to define logical concepts, whereas
Plato hypostatized these universals as independent entities, and
thus made a superfluous double of the real world.[19] According
to this, Plato's Ideas presuppose that logical universals had
already been discovered. If so, they really were a bizarre dupli-
cation of the concepts existing in the human mind. Most modern
logicians have followed Aristotle in this reconstruction of the
mental process that led Plato to create the doctrine of Ideas.[20]
But there is this point. If what we call concepts were already
implied in Socrates' question 'What *is* X?' then Plato, in interpreting Socrates' question, went off in a quite different direction
from what seems natural to modern logicians. They find the
logical universal perfectly obvious and easy to understand; therefore they feel that what Plato's Ideas contain *over and above*
logical concepts is merely a disturbing and enigmatic addition—
for they assume that one must first grasp virtue-in-itself as a
logical concept before going further and crediting this concept
with existence in the ontological sense. However, *Meno* really
contains no hint of this double aspect of the word Idea. Although
we can clearly distinguish two aspects in Plato's Ideas, the logical
universal and the ontological entity, the two sides form an absolute unity for him. The question 'What is virtue?' points straight
to the οὐσία, to the essence and real being of virtue, and that is
just the Idea of virtue.[21] It is only in the later dialogues that the
relation of the Idea to the manifold appearances (which Plato
had theretofore rather vaguely called 'participation' of the individual in the universal) becomes a problem for him; and then
there appear logical difficulties of which he had not been aware
when he originally worked out the Ideas.

Thus, the misunderstandings of modern scholars have not
arisen from misinterpreting Plato's words—which would scarcely
be possible—so much as from ascribing to him later logical discoveries. Aristotle started with what seemed to him the obvious
fact of logical universals. He saw, quite correctly, that Plato's
Ideas contained logical universals. He inferred that Plato
thought those universals in his Ideas were the only true and
effective realities. This second step, Aristotle decided, must be

the reason for the mistakes made by Plato in defining the relation of the universal to the particulars. According to Aristotle,
he made universals into ontological realities, and ascribed to
them a separate existence apart from the things of sense. But
the truth is that Plato did *not* take the second step, and hyposta-
tize the universals: simply because he had not taken the first step
—he had not abstracted universal concepts as such. It would be
nearer the truth to say that, in his philosophy, the universal is
still concealed in the Idea. It is, as Plato describes it, the penetration of thought from the phenomena to the true nature of
areté, an act of intellectual vision, which sees the One in the
Many. In *The Republic,* he himself calls the dialectic thought-
process *synopsis*—seeing all the common characteristics in a
number of phenomena which fall under one and the same Idea.
That is the best word for the logical act described in *Meno*.[22]
On the other hand, dialectic method is here defined as 'giving
an explanation and taking it and testing it'.[23] That is an essential
point, because it keeps us from believing that when he talks of
the act of intellectual contemplation, he is thinking of something
entirely unchallengeable by other people. A dialectic answer, he
insists, must not only be true, but be supported by some admission which the speaker has obtained from his interlocutor. This
presupposes that, through questions and answers, people can
reach understanding of that which is seen by the act of intellectual contemplation. Later, in *The Republic* and the seventh
Letter, it becomes clear that patient and laborious pursuit of this
dialectic search for an agreement is the way to approach 'vision'
of the Ideas.[24]

It is difficult to say whether, beneath the analysis of the logical
content of Socrates' dialectic given in *Meno,* there is a system
of general logical rules; and, if so, how far it is a complete
system. It is indeed very probable that there is, even although
all the results reached in *Meno* are ultimately produced by study
of the one problem of virtue. Two significant facts should be
noticed: the highly conscious skill in logic which Plato shows
throughout the dialogue; and the large quantity of technical
expressions he uses to describe his separate methodical pro-
cedures. Before attempting an 'exercise' like this,[25] one must
know the rules that one wants to establish. Particularly notable

in this connexion is the skilful care Plato takes to explain logical processes by examples (*paradeigmata*) and to point out their function again and again. Thus the question 'What is virtue?' is explained by another sample question: 'What is a figure?' And the question whether justice is virtue or *a* virtue is explained by the parallel question 'Is a circle *the* figure or *a* figure?'[26] When Socrates says that other colours are quite as much colours as white is, and that a curve is a figure quite as much as a straight line is,[27] he is giving a logical explanation of what is meant by οὐσία (essence): for essence (as *Phaedo* also shows) does not admit the more or the less, and no figure is any more a figure than any other.[28] But in qualities or relations there can be a more and a less. Later, these same facts are laid down in Aristotle's doctrine of categories; but Plato knew them too, and, as *Meno* shows, he knew them from his youth.[29] (A logical analysis of his earlier dialogues from this point of view would be profoundly interesting.) It is then quite obvious that *Meno* does not contain his first fumbling attempts to understand the logical character of Socrates' dialectic, but that it is based on a full knowledge of logic. Socrates makes his enquiry with the help of a pupil who is a good average representative of the students at the Academy.[30] In this way Plato makes his readers conscious of the elementary logical problems without understanding which they cannot comprehend his dialogues. He knows perfectly well the limits imposed on his explanation of these technical matters by literary form; and still he manages to give even laymen an idea of the difficulty and the charm of this new range of problems.

Mathematics plays a special part in *Meno*. It is certain that Plato was always deeply interested in it, for even his early dialogues show his exact knowledge of mathematical problems. When he sketched the outlines of the new ethical and political techné in *Gorgias*, he modelled it on medicine. Now, in *Meno*, the model is mathematics. That is obviously true of his method. At Meno's very first attempt to define the nature of areté, Socrates suggests that as a model he should try to define what a figure is.[31] In the second part of the dialogue, when Socrates and Meno make a fresh start to define areté, mathematics is brought in once more. They still have not discovered what areté is; but since, for educational reasons, they are particularly interested to know if it can be taught, Socrates now poses the problem by asking what sort of thing areté must be to be teachable. For this method of 'hypothesis' he appeals to the geometrician.[32] (We can dispense with an analysis of the example he uses—inscribing a triangle within a circle.)

But mathematics is used not only to exemplify right method in details, but as a general illustration of the type of knowledge at which Socrates is aiming. The resemblance between the two is that both start from phenomena perceived by sense, which represent the thing which is really being studied; but that thing itself does not belong to the world of sense. It can be cognized only in the soul, and the organ of cognition is the logos. Socrates makes this clear to Meno by taking his slave, a young man with some talent but no education, and questioning him in front of his master, in such a way that the slave himself, using a rough diagram, discovers the theorem of the square on the hypotenuse.[33] The execution of this educational experiment is the high point of the dialogue. Plato is giving us a glimpse of the meditations which led him to decide that the source of scientific certainty was purely intellectual and apart from sensible phenomena. Of course, without the help of Socrates, the slave would not be capable of making all the steps which led him to understand that complicated mathematical system of facts; and he makes all the mistakes which a naïve person who starts all his thinking with sense-perception must inevitably make, before he grasps the real reason for things. But at last he realizes that things *must* be in this way and no other; and the realization comes solely from his own inner vision. As soon as he has clearly grasped the nature of the fundamental mathematical relations involved, that vision works with absolute and ineluctable conviction. And it is not the instruction he has received which produces his conviction, but his own reason and his insight into the necessity of things.[34]

In order to adumbrate the nature of this intellectual vision, Plato introduces ideas from the world of religious myth. Since the Greeks could not imagine knowledge without an object known, and since, on the other hand, the human mind in its present state (exemplified by the mind of the slave doing the geometrical proof) has never seen or known anything like the truth seen by the intellect, Plato interprets the potential existence of mathematical knowledge in the soul as a sight seen by it in a previous life.[35] The myth of the immortality of the soul and its migration through various bodies gives that supposition the form and colour needed by our mortal and finite imagination.[36] In *Meno* Plato cares less about assuming immortality as the necessary foundation for his concept of the moral personality [37] than about providing a background for his new theory that we are all born with knowledge in our souls. Without such a background, the innate knowledge would have to remain a vague and colourless supposition. Combined with the doctrine of pre-existence and transmigration, it opens up a number of unexpected avenues for thought and fancy; and the knowledge of good in itself, for which we must always strive, is shown to be perfectly independent of all external experience, and to have an almost religious value. It is mathematically clear; and yet it impinges on our human life like a ray from a higher universe. All through Plato's work mathematics takes this position: it is ancillary to the theory of Ideas. It is always the bridge which we must cross to understand them; [37a] and it must have been so, even for Plato himself, when he set out to find a logical definition of the knowledge sought by Socrates and of its object.

With this, Plato felt he had fulfilled the purpose of Socrates' life; and at the same time he had taken a long step beyond him. Socrates had always finished by confessing his ignorance. Plato pushed impetuously on towards knowledge. And yet he took Socrates' ignorance to be a sign of his true greatness, for he thought it was the birth-pangs of a new kind of knowledge struggling to be born of Socrates' travailing mind. That knowledge was the vision within the soul, which *Meno* is the first attempt to define and describe, the vision of the Ideas. So it is not mere chance that in *Meno* Plato casts a new, positive light on his master's 'ignorance'. It was not that Plato himself had suddenly seen it in that light for the first time. But it had been impossible for him to show it to others thus until he could expound to them the strange character of that knowledge which drew all its certainty from within. When young Meno, at Socrates' invitation, attempts to define virtue, and ends with a false definition which (as Socrates explains to him) offends against a basic rule of dialectic, he says in his disappointment that others have told him Socrates possesses the dangerous art of leading people into an impasse, from which they can go neither forward nor back.[38] He compares him with the electric eel, which numbs the hand that touches it. But Socrates turns the edge of the metaphor by saying that the eel must electrify itself too, for he himself is the victim of his *aporia,* his helplessness.[39] But Plato then uses his mathematical example, in the episode with the slave, to show that that helplessness becomes the true source of learning and understanding.[39a] Obviously he sought, and found, in mathematics a perfect parallel for Socrates' aporia; and the example encouraged him by showing that there can be an aporia which is the most important precondition for the real solving of a difficulty.

The mathematical episode in *Meno* serves to show that *aporein,* 'to be helpless', is fertile ground for educational seed. It is the first stage on the way towards the positive knowledge of truth. In this gradual progress of the intellect towards complete self-awareness, the role of sensory experience is to awaken the soul to 'recollection' of the essence of things seen by it from eternity.[39b] The explanation of that role is that Plato (as he maintains in other passages) thought sensory things were copies of the Ideas. In *Meno* the theory that knowledge in the Socratic sense is recollection is only outlined; so too is the doctrine of immortality and pre-existence, which is worked out in detail in *Phaedo, The Republic, Phaedrus,* and *The Laws.* The essential thing for Plato is the realization that 'truth about being exists in our soul'.[40] This realization sets in motion the process of searching and methodical advance to self-awareness. The search for truth is nothing but the opening-up of the soul, with the contents that naturally lie within it.[41] This answers a yearning harboured deep within it, as Socrates hints.[42] In *The Symposium* and elsewhere Plato elaborated this into his doctrine that Eros is the origin of all spiritual effort. Several times Socrates rejects the word 'teach' (διδάσκειν), saying that it does not describe the process correctly, since it seems to imply filling the soul with knowledge poured in from outside.[43] The slave recognized the mathematical theorem to be true, not because he was taught it, but because 'he himself produced the knowledge out of himself'.[44] As Plato in *Protagoras* and *Gorgias* explains the ethical outlines of his new paideia by putting it in contrast to the sophists' ideal of education, so here in *Meno* he unfolds the profound conception of knowledge latent in Socrates' thought by contrasting it with the sophists' mechanical conception of the learning process. True learning is not passive reception, but a laborious search, which is possible only if the learner spontaneously takes part in it. Plato's whole description makes it clear that scientific or philosophical enquiry has a moral effect, and steels the character.[45] The Greek mind was active and energetic; and it looked within itself for the grounds defining its thought and action. These two qualities are perfectly expressed in Plato's *Meno*.

The Platonic conception of knowledge, after being elucidated in the mathematical episode, illuminates the conclusion of the dialogue, where the old problem, 'What is areté?' is once more attacked.[46] We have already said that for Plato the problem of the nature of knowledge is nothing but an offshoot of the problem of areté. Therefore it was to be expected that, after the discussion of knowledge was ended, the attempt would be made to learn something from it about the main question.[47] In the first section, before the discussion of knowledge, areté was defined with deliberate naïveté as the ability to acquire all kinds of good things.[48] That definition is still on the level of old-fashioned popular morality—and indeed Plato never breaks wholly away from tradition. This provisional definition was then brought closer to the rigorous ethics of philosophy by the addition of 'justly'.[49] But that does not define the relation of justice to the whole of virtue; it has not made the nature of virtue any clearer, because of the logical error of defining virtue by a part of itself (justice). Thus, it assumes that the object of enquiry is already known.[50]

Socrates' definition that virtue is knowledge is not mentioned at this stage of the investigation; but it has always been obvious that the purpose of the discussion of knowledge in the middle of *Meno* helps to introduce Socrates' conception of knowledge in order to define areté. This definition now follows, in the form of the hypothetical definition mentioned above (p. 167): if virtue is teachable, it must be knowledge.[51] Obviously none of the things so keenly desired by the world—health, beauty, wealth, power—really is good for men, if it is not accompanied by knowledge and reason.[52] So this reason—phronésis, that tells

us which are true and which are false goods, and which of them
we ought to choose—must be the knowledge we are looking
for.[53] In *The Republic* Plato calls it the science of right choice
and declares that the most important thing in life is to get this
kind of knowledge.[54] It is built upon the unshakable foundation
of the Ideas, the patterns of the highest values, which the soul
finds within itself when it reflects upon the nature of the good,
the just, etc.; and it has the power to determine and guide the
will. This at least is the direction in which we must look for the
answer to Socrates' question 'What is virtue?'

But Plato prefers to end the conversation with a truly Socratic
aporia. We recognize in it the old dilemma which was the culmination of *Protagoras:* if virtue is teachable, it must be knowledge; and if so, Socrates alone can reveal the true meaning of
education.[55] But experience seems to show that there are no
teachers of virtue, for hitherto even the greatest Athenians, past
and present, have been unable to transmit their own ability and
character to their sons.[56] Socrates is perfectly willing to admit
that they possess areté. But if it were knowledge, it should have
been effective as an educational force. Since it is not, it must
be based on 'right opinion',[57] which comes to men only by 'divine
dispensation', θεία μοῖρα,[58] but which does not enable them to give
account of their actions, because they do not possess 'understanding of the cause'.[59]

So, at the end of *Meno,* we seem to be no further forward
than we were in *Protagoras*. But it only seems so. Really we
have come to see more and more of the new conception of knowledge at which we arrived, with the help of mathematical examples, in the central part of *Meno*. It is a new type of cognition,
which cannot be learned from anyone else, but, if the thought
in the soul of the enquirer is led on in the right way, arises of
itself. The charming thing about the skill with which Plato
arranges these Socratic dialogues is that, even here, when we
have come near enough to grasp the result, he does not hand it
to us, but makes us find it ourselves. But if the dilemma he proposed in *Protagoras* [60] were to find a solution, it would justify
the educational claim made by Socrates there and in *Gorgias*.
It is true that the new paideia is not teachable as the sophists
understood teaching: so Socrates was right to say that he did
not teach men—not by giving them information. But by asserting

that virtue must be knowledge and making his way towards that
knowledge, he took the place of those false prophets of wisdom,
as the only real educator. In the concluding section of *Meno* he
is deliberately put in contrast with this background of sophistic
paideia, because a new figure, Anytus, enters the conversation,
and the talk turns to the right method of education. The problem with which the dialogue begins, and through which it develops Socrates' conception of knowledge, is, 'How does man
acquire areté?' From the very beginning the discussion of it has
been moving towards education. Like *Protagoras, Meno* ends
with a dilemma. Since the sophists' teaching cannot make men
virtuous, and since the areté of the statesmen who possess virtue
naturally (φύσει) is incapable of being transmitted to others,
areté seems to exist only by divine dispensation—unless a statesman (πολιτικός) can be found who can make someone else a
statesman too. But that 'unless', so easily overlooked, really
holds the solution of the dilemma: for we know from *Gorgias*
that Plato paradoxically thought Socrates was the only true
statesman, the statesman who made his fellow-citizens better.
Meno has shown how his type of knowledge is evoked in the
human soul. And so, at the end, it is evident that Socrates
believes areté is *both* natural *and* teachable. But if these words
are taken in the usual pedagogical sense, then it is *neither* teachable *nor* naturally implanted—unless it is innate like a talent or
a disposition which cannot account for itself.

But Socrates' educational mission does not depend only on the
methodical character of knowledge as he conceives it and as
Plato explains it in *Meno,* with the assistance of dialectics and
mathematics. The philosophical knowledge of the Ideas, born
from the mind's reflection on its own inner cosmos, is shown in
Plato's dialogues to be always the same thing in different lights:
it is the true fulfilment of man's natural disposition. In *Euthydemus* Socrates' phronésis is described as the way to perfect happiness and to true success.[61] There his gospel has an almost universal import, and it is certainly unthinkable without his consciousness that he is giving men a firm foothold in life by knowledge of the highest goods. In *Phaedo* its strength, rising above
and looking beyond the world, appears in the serene, mystical,
last hours of the master. There it is shown to be the philosopher's daily and nightly preparation for death.[62] But this con-

stant intellectual arming of himself for dissolution leads to his highest triumph: his death is a sort of apotheosis, and he leaves his pupils with calm cheerfulness, like a truly free man. There knowledge is described as the soul's collecting itself [63]—one of the immortal psychological images invented by Plato: it 'concentrates' itself from among the dispersed senses, all pressing outwards to the sensory world, and bends to its own proper inward activity. *Phaedo* is the clearest expression of the contrast between man's spirit and his senses.

But the philosopher's 'practice' (his *askésis*), his surrender of his whole life to knowledge and to permanent concentration, was not meant by Plato as a symbol of a devoted but one-sided life. Because of the hugely preponderant importance which it gives to man's spiritual side over his corporeal, it is the most natural kind of life. The man who has accustomed his soul to leave his body in this life, and has thereby become sure of the eternity which he carries in his spirit, has lost all fear of death. In *Phaedo,* the soul of Socrates, like the swan of Apollo, soars up to the fields of pure Being before it leaves his body.[64] In *The Symposium* Plato shows him as the highest type of Dionysiac man. The knowledge of eternal beauty to whose vision he rises is the highest fulfilment of Eros, the basic impulse of human life, the great daemon which holds the cosmos together internally and externally. And finally, in *The Republic,* the philosopher's knowledge is revealed to be the source of all the legislative and social powers of the soul. So Socrates' philosophy is not only a new theory of cognition, but the most perfect vision, θεωρία, of the cosmos of human and daemonic powers. Knowledge is central in that picture, because knowledge of its meaning is the creative force which leads and orders everything. For Plato, knowledge is the guide to the realm of the divine.

THE SYMPOSIUM
EROS

In *Lysis,* one of the most charming of his smaller dialogues, Plato enquired what was the nature of friendship. This was his first handling of a theme fundamental to his whole philosophy, which was fully and absorbingly discussed in the great books on Eros written in his maturity, *The Symposium* and *Phaedrus.* No less than the examination of the special virtues in his early dialogues, this discussion forms part of the great structure of Plato's political philosophy. His teaching about friendship is the nucleus of a theory of politics which treats the state primarily as an educational force. In *The Republic* and his seventh Letter, he explains that he gave up all political activity because he had no trustworthy friends and comrades to help him in rebuilding the polis.[1] When society is suffering from a great organic disorder or disease, its recovery can be initiated only by a small but basically healthy association of people who share the same ideas, and who can form the heart of a new organism. That is exactly what Plato means by friendship (φιλία). It is the fundamental form of all society, in so far as society is not only a natural but a moral and spiritual association of human beings.

Therefore the problem covers a far wider field than any conception of friendship existing in our own highly individualized society. We can understand the meaning of the Greek *philia* more clearly if we trace the working-out of the concept as far as the subtle distinctions and systematizations which Aristotle introduces into his theory of friendship in the *Nicomachean Ethics*: for his teaching on the subject is directly derived from Plato's. He elaborates a complete scheme of all possible types of human association (φιλία), from the simplest basic forms of family life to the various types of states and constitutions. The root from which this social philosophy sprang was the theorizing of Socrates and his pupils, especially Plato, about the nature of friendship, and the unique importance it had in Socrates' life and teaching.[2] Like the whole ethical movement which stemmed from it, the profounder conception of friendship which it produced was immediately felt and declared to be a contribution to solving the problem of the state.

The superficial psychology of Plato's time taught, very inadequately, that friendship was based either on similarity of character or on the attraction of opposites.[3] That comparison, or matching, of souls does not go very deep; and in *Lysis,* his first bold attempt to strike deeper, Plato coined the new concept of 'the first beloved' (πρῶτον φίλον), and maintained it was to be assumed as the source and origin of all friendship between human beings.[4] It is because of our general love for this ultimate object of desire that we love any individual thing.[5] That is what we are trying to attain or realize in every kind of association with other men, whatever its character may be. In other words, Plato is endeavouring to discover the principle that gives meaning and purpose to human society. *Lysis* hints at the nature of this principle when it sets up the concept of 'the first beloved' as a guide. And there is another such hint in *Gorgias,* where Plato says that a true society of men who live the life of bandits is impossible; society can exist only among good men.[5a] The other Socratic dialogues presuppose the Idea of Good as a fixed point of reference; and so too, in the discussion of the nature of friendship, it is assumed to be the absolute and final standard. For, although Plato does not say so expressly, the understanding reader will realize that 'the first beloved', for whose sake we love all other things, implies the highest value, Good in itself.[5b] Thus, as early as *Lysis,* we catch a glimpse of the view which is to be fully revealed in the two great books on Eros: every kind of society must be based on the idea that human beings are bound together by an inner standard established in their souls and by the law of a supreme Good which binds together both the world of men and the whole universe. Even in *Lysis,* the first principle beloved by all was shown to transcend this world of ours: for it is not the Good *we* love, but the Good desired and striven for by all things. Similarly, *Gorgias,* rejecting the doctrine of the right of the stronger, teaches that human society is part of the supreme symmetry of the universe—namely, the agreement of all things with one ultimate standard, which is meanwhile defined no further.[5c]

Plato's art reaches its height in *The Symposium*; and no words could possibly do it full justice either by analyzing the content of that great dialogue or by paraphrasing its language. All that we can do here is to mark its main themes, from the point of view of paideia. Plato showed by its title that it did not centre on one principal character, like most of his dialogues. It is not a dialectic drama like *Protagoras* and *Gorgias*. And it is very far from such purely scientific works as *Theaetetus* and *Parmenides,* which are dry methodical investigations of one definite problem. It is really not a dialogue at all in the usual sense, but an oratorical contest between a number of distinguished public characters. Men representing every type of Greek culture are gathered at the table of the tragedian Agathon. He has just won a brilliant victory in the dramatic competition, and is, so to speak, not only the host but the guest of honour. But in that small circle, Socrates wins the prize in the oratorical competition—a victory that is more important than the applause of that audience, more than thirty thousand strong, which had hailed Agathon's success in the theatre.[6] The scene is symbolic. Not only the tragic poet Agathon, but Aristophanes, the greatest comic poet of the age, takes part in it; and since their speeches are incontestably the finest of all those delivered until Socrates, last of all, takes up the theme, *The Symposium* is the palpable embodiment of that superiority of philosophy over poetry maintained by Plato in *The Republic*. But philosophy could attain such heights only by becoming poetry—or by creating poetic works of the noblest kind, to transcend any small dissensions of opinion and to bring its true essence before men's eyes, with all its imperishable power.

Plato gave the discussion of Eros a highly appropriate setting by his choice of scene. From earliest times, the symposium had meant to the Greeks the milieu where manly areté was celebrated in poetry and song. We find this to be true even in Homer.[7] And Xenophanes, who posed as a reformer of the vanishing past, addressed his criticisms of Homeric theology to the ready ears of intelligent men at symposia,[8] while the aristocratic educational maxims of Theognis were sung at banquets. In fact, Theognis believed that his poetry would survive because it would still be sung at feasts after his death; and his hopes were not in vain.[9] His educational teachings were closely connected with his love for the young nobleman Cyrnus, to whom his maxims are addressed; and it is that connexion between the symposium and educational Eros that is the basis of Plato's dialogue. But education in the philosophical schools was particularly closely linked to the tradition and usages of symposia; for the symposium became one of the regular meeting-places for teacher and pupil, and thereby took on an entirely new character. The numerous philosophical and scholarly works of post-Platonic Greek literature which have the word *symposium* in their titles [10] bear witness to the transforming influence exercised on that type of association by the entrance of the philosophical spirit, bringing with it deeper problems and richer ideas.

Plato was the founder of the new philosophical form of the symposium. His literary presentation and philosophical re-interpretation of the old-established custom went along with his organization of the intellectual life of his school. In his later years, that new significance of the symposium becomes plainly evident. Among the titles of the lost works of Aristotle and others of Plato's pupils, there are mentioned elaborate rulebooks for behaviour at the symposium—the kind of thing desiderated by Plato himself in *The Laws*.[11] At the beginning of that work, he devoted two whole books to the educational value of drinking and of wine-parties, which he defended against the attacks of some critic. This new code of behaviour at drinking-parties (it will be discussed in more detail later) grew out of the now established habit of holding symposia as a regular function in the Academy.[12] In *The Republic* Plato supports the Spartan custom by which all the men dined together at *syssitia*,[13] but in *The Laws* he says that one of the most notable failures in Spartan education was the absence of drinking-parties—its aim being to inculcate only courage, not self-control.[14] There was a gap which he did not intend to leave unfilled in the education given by the Academy. Isocrates' school took up the opposite attitude—thus reflecting the sobriety of its leader, who held that the young men of Athens were ruined by excessive drinking.[15] He must have felt the same about Eros. But Plato pressed both these mighty forces, Dionysus and Eros, into the service of his ideal. He was inspired by his faith that philosophy could impart a new meaning to all living things, and change into positive values even those which border on the danger-zone. He was sure

that he could infuse that spirit into all the contemporary world;
he felt that all those natural instinctive energies which his
paideia would vainly strive to combat ought instead to contribute to it. His teaching about Eros was a bold attempt to
bridge the chasm between Apollo and Dionysus. It was, he held,
impossible, to neglect the inexhaustibly renewed energy and
enthusiasm of man's irrational powers, if one hoped to reach the
height of illumination which was possible for the spirit looking
upon the Idea of Good. The thought on which *The Symposium*
is based is the union of Eros and paideia. As we have shown,
this was not a new thought. It was traditional, and the advance
made by Plato lies in this: at a time of sober moral enlightenment and rationalism, when it seemed certain that the male Eros
of old Greece, with all its undoubted evils and with all its lofty
ideals, would be relegated to oblivion, he revived it, and purified it, and ennobled it. He gave it immortality in this last form,
as the highest spiritual flight of two closely united souls towards
the realm of eternal beauty. We know nothing of the personal
experiences which may have been responsible for that refining
process. But they inspired one of the greatest works of poetic
imagination in the literature of the world. Its beauty lies not only
in the perfection of its form, but in its blending of genuine
passion with the winged flight of pure thought, and with the
power of moral self-emancipation which is expressed with triumphant courage in the final scene.

We have seen that Plato's method of thinking and writing is
always the same: it is a combination of two elements, an effort
to attain ideals of universal validity, and a lively awareness of
all the concrete facts of the life in which he is living. This is
shown by the form of his dialogues, which always centre upon
definite situations and real men, and ultimately upon one spiritual
situation which is viewed as a whole. Within that immediate
frame, Socrates tries, with the assistance of his dialectic, to reach
some understanding with his fellow-men about all sorts of goods
common to them all. This leads to a discussion of the speakers'
common problems, and they work together towards a common
solution which will embrace all the divergent points of view.
More than any other dialogue, *The Symposium* is the product
of just such a definite intellectual and moral situation. It must

be taken as a chorus of the real voices of that age, above which at the end we hear the voice of Socrates rising victoriously to lead all the rest. Its attraction as a drama lies in the masterly way in which the characters are differentiated; Plato has individualized the various conceptions of Eros and drawn them together into a rich but unified symphony of contrasts. It is impossible here to reproduce the full variety of all these aspects of the subject; but really they are all indispensable for the understanding of Socrates' Diotima speech. That speech is the pinnacle of the whole structure, and the others have not inaptly been compared with terraces leading up to it. We need only try to imagine the discussion of Eros in the usual form of a Socratic dialogue, with its continuous series of attempted definitions, to realize why Plato chose to make *The Symposium* a collection of independent speeches, and thereby abandoned his usual strictly dialectic procedure. Socrates is not, as in most dialogues, the leader of the whole company, but only one of many speakers—the last of them all, in fact, which is a role suited to his characteristic irony. For this reason, dialectic does not appear until the very end of the book, where it forms a complete contrast to the highly coloured rhetoric and poetry which have preceded it. Praise of Eros is the theme chosen for the competition. This subject provides a perfect motive for the peculiar structure of the work, which in its turn is accounted for by the place where the speeches are delivered, and the motive for their delivery; a series of improvised orations by different speakers would not allow the subject to be treated in a connected and factual way. An encomium is a work of rhetoric: and that is true, most of all, of the encomium on a mythical theme, which was a favourite show-piece for rhetoricians of the time. During the period in which he wrote *The Symposium,* Plato composed another work of the same kind, *Menexenus.* Therewith, for a time, he entered into open competition with his rivals, the Athenian schools of rhetoric—for the funeral eulogy of *Menexenus* was also a favourite field for rhetorical display.

Phaedrus (the first speaker in *The Symposium,* who is the real 'father' [16] of the idea of praising Eros) puts his suggestion purely as a challenge to perform a rhetorical exercise, which he expects to carry out with the help of the oratorical tricks he has

learnt from the sophists. He has often reproached the poets because they, whose function is to praise the gods in hymns, have
never glorified Eros; [17] and now he undertakes to fill that gap by
giving an encomium of Eros in prose. To set out deliberately to
rival poetry like this is characteristic of the rhetoric practised
by the sophists. Here and in the subsequent speeches, Plato's art
displays all its mastery. All the intellectual types at the feast,
each with its own appropriate style, are reproduced and paro-
died. Like a true pupil of the sophists, Phaedrus is very lavish
in quoting the maxims of the classical poets, and rivals Hesiod
and other authorities in celestial genealogy by giving the family
tree of Eros, 'oldest of all the gods'.[18] The main theme of his
speech is the social aspect of Eros: it is Eros who excites ambition and instils areté, without which no friendship, no community,
no state, can exist.[19] Thus, at the outset, the discussion aims at
finding a high moral justification for Eros, rather than defining
his nature more accurately or distinguishing his various aspects.

However, the second speaker, Pausanias, tries to fill this gap.
Declaring that the subject is too vague, he undertakes to define
it as closely as is necessary. Thereby he follows the first speaker
in postulating an ideal ground for erotic relationships, and makes
the ideal clearer. Still in the mythologizing tone set by Phaedrus,
he points out that since Aphrodite is twofold, her assistant Eros
must also be two: there is an Eros Pandemus and an Eros
Uranius.[20] It will be remembered that, in the same way, Hesiod
had distinguished two contrasting Erides, spirits of strife, in
Works and Days; he substituted them for the single Eris of
tradition.[21] Plato here seems to be following his example.
Pausanias goes on to say that the common Eros, general indiscriminate lust, is contemptible and cheap, aiming simply at the
gratification of sensual desire; while the other, divine in origin,
is eager to serve the true welfare of the beloved, helping him
in attaining perfection.[22] This second Eros he claims to be an
educational force, not only in the negative sense ascribed to it
in Phaedrus' speech, by deterring the lover from evil conduct,[23]
but in its full active nature, by serving the beloved so that he
can develop his personality.[24] According to this conception, it
must be assumed that sensual attraction 'coincides' with ideal
aspiration, in order to justify the physical side of Eros; [25] but

Pausanias, who is defending this species of love, obviously finds it difficult to make its two aspects match, and it is quite clearly nothing more than a compromise. Probably this type had many followers at the time, so many as to induce Plato to describe it fully here. When we compare Pausanias' speech with Diotima's, we notice that Pausanias bases his distinction between the worthy and the unworthy Eros on grounds which lie outside Eros, and not originally within his nature.

He makes a particularly illuminating attempt to use the uncertainty of prevailing moral judgments on the matter to support his theory. He does so by citing and comparing the different views held about male Eros in various countries.[26] In Elis and Boeotia—that is, in the most primitive, least intellectually developed regions of Greece—homosexual love is perfectly respectable. On the other hand, in Ionia (upon the Persian frontier of Greece), it is severely condemned. Pausanias declares this is due to the influence of the barbarians with their own political attitudes. Every despotism is based on mistrust, and in such a regime warm friendships are always suspected of leading to conspiracies. One actual case was, according to half-legendary tradition, the foundation of the Athenian democracy by Harmodius and Aristogeiton, two lovers sworn to live and die together. Was the Athenian cult which had honoured them ever afterwards not a sanction of their love? Pausanias takes pains to prove that it is the ideal spirit dominating such friendships which, in the eyes of Athenians and Spartans, distinguishes them from the satisfaction of purely sensual lusts, and makes them acceptable to public opinion. The attitude of Athens and Sparta was neither whole-heartedly in favour of them nor against them, as other states were. It was complicated and equivocal. It was halfway between the extremes. Therefore, Pausanias believes that he can make cultured Athenians more sympathetic to his own idealized and educational type of Eros by explaining the political and ethical imponderables on which it is based.

It is worth noticing that Pausanias does not speak of Athens alone—he brings in Sparta too. Sparta would seem to be a particularly important authority in ethical questions; but actually it is a poor witness in his favour. The view maintained by Pausanias is essentially of Spartan origin, as is the tradition of homosexual love itself. It began in a period which was much

less remote from the contemporary Dorians than from other
Greeks—in the age of the migrations, when the warrior tribes
lived in a perpetual standing camp, as indeed the fighting
Spartans still did. It had spread through other regions of
Greece, but it was still strongest in Sparta. And when Sparta
was overthrown and lost its social prestige, which happened not
long after *The Symposium* was written, pederasty quickly died
out, at least as an ethical ideal—to survive only as the despicable
vice of the *cinaedi*. Even in Aristotle's ethical and political systems it plays no part, and when Plato was an old man writing
The Laws he condemned it out of hand as unnatural.[27] Thus,
even Pausanias' method of approaching the subject through
historical comparisons shows that *The Symposium* marks the
frontier between early and late Greek feeling. Eros holds the
same position in Plato's thought as the polis and the old Greek
traditions it represents: that is, they are still fully real and alive,
more so for Plato than for almost any other Greek of that
transitional age, but it is only their ideal self which, transfigured,
is carried over to the new era, and linked with its metaphysical
centre. The attempt to compromise by uniting old and new was
evidently too weak. Plato could not be content with Pausanias'
conception of Eros.

Next speaks Eryximachus. He represents a third type of
spiritual tradition. Being a doctor, he starts from the observation of nature,[28] and does not, like his predecessors, confine himself to the facts of *human* life. Still, he does not depart from
their rhetorical formulation of the subject: in spite of his broad
general interpretation of the nature of Eros, or even because
of it, he can still praise him as a great deity. This cosmic interpretation of Eros had begun as early as Hesiod, who placed
him at the beginning of the world in his *Theogony,* hypostatizing
him as the basic creative force which manifested itself in all the
creations of later dynasties of gods.[29] The early Greek philosophers like Empedocles and Parmenides took over from Hesiod
this conception of a cosmological Eros, and tried to use it to
explain details of natural science. They said that Eros caused the
elements to combine into various physical forms. The first
speaker, Phaedrus, had made a learned allusion to these old
philosophers, when he used them to support the half-humorous

genealogy he constructed for Eros.[30] But now Eryximachus
argues systematically that the creative force of Eros is the principle accounting for the coming-to-be and passing-away of the
entire physical world, since it is the basic love, the creative force
whose regular rhythm of filling and emptying pulses through
and vivifies all things.[31] At first glance, it does not seem possible to start from this physical hypothesis and maintain any moral
distinction between the various manifestations of Eros, as
Pausanias had done, starting from the current *nomos,* from
social convention. But Eryximachus too, as a physician, expressly
lays down that there is a distinction between a good and a bad
Eros.[32] He holds that the difference between health and sickness,
which runs through all nature, is a sort of general denominator
on which the above moral distinction must be based. Health is
the proper blending of opposites in nature. Sickness is a dangerous disturbance of their concord and harmony; and he holds that
that harmony is the essence of Eros.[33]

Now we begin to understand why Plato chose a medical man
to represent the naturalistic attitude.[34] It was in order to bring
out that distinction, the point of which is that Eros can be subjected to a scale of values. As *Gorgias* shows, Plato always conceived his moral teaching and his paideia as a counterpart to
the medical doctrine of the sound and unsound nature and its
proper care (θεραπεία). The medical conception of the bodily
physis resembles Plato's conception of the spiritual and ethical
physis in this—it implies a standard, a norm to which the *physis*
ought to conform. Eryximachus holds that the rule of the
healthy Eros over all realms of the cosmos and all human arts
is the principle of well-being and of all true harmony. His doctrine of harmonious concord is based on Heraclitus' theory of
opposites [35]—which had greatly interested other medical thinkers
of the period, as we can see particularly from the pseudo-Hip-
pocratic treatise *On diet.*[36] The function of medicine is to bring
about harmony between opposing physical forces; and that of
music is to produce the correct blend and commixture, the symphony between high and low tones. Of course it is not hard to
see that in the basic relationships of rhythms and sounds, the
simple elements of which they are composed are really akin, and
complement one another: at that stage it is impossible to speak
of a 'twofold' Eros. But when we come to real musical composi-

tion, or to apply rhythm and harmony to men—'which is called paideia'—then we need great art and skill.[37] We ought to be kind to decent men (κόσμιοι), and to preserve their Eros; and we should use it as a means to instil decency into those who are not yet decent and well-behaved. That Eros is the heavenly one, Eros Uranius, love for the Muse Urania. But Eros Pandemus, love for the Muse Polyhymnia, must be applied with caution: its enjoyment is permissible, but care should be taken that it does not bring about incontinence—just as the doctor must know how to use and control the arts of cookery.[38]

In this speech Eros becomes such a comprehensive allegorical force that it almost loses its definite character. But next comes the comedian Aristophanes, with a tirade full of brilliant wit. He goes back to the concrete facts of love, and tries to interpret them in a bold poetic vision. He is thinking principally of the mysterious power of Eros over mankind, which is really impossible to compare to anything else.[39] This all-powerful yearning within us can be explained only by the peculiar nature of the human species. He goes on to tell a grotesque myth. Mankind were once, he says, spherical in shape. They had four arms and four legs, and moved rapidly about by revolving wheelwise. But the gods, in fear of their strength and their threats to heaven, bisected them. This amusing but profoundly meaningful fantasy expresses the truth which we sought for in vain in the three earlier speeches. Eros is born from man's metaphysical yearning after the wholeness which is for ever impossible to the individual nature. That yearning shows man to be merely a fragment, always striving to be reunited with its appropriate other half, as long as he exists in helpless separation.[40] Aristophanes is considering love as part of the process by which the self attains perfection. It can do so only through its relation to another, to a beloved, who will complement the powers in it which need completion, help them to take their place in the original whole, and thereby at last enable them to become properly effective. This symbolism draws Eros right into the process of educating and building up the personality. Aristophanes is looking at Eros not merely as love between two persons of the same sex, but much more universally, in every form in which it appears.[41] The passion which lovers feel for each other makes them unwilling to separate even for a moment. But those who spend their lives together like this cannot explain what they really want from each other. Obviously it is not sexual union alone that makes each of them enjoy being with the other so much, and be so anxious for it. The soul of each of them wants something else which it cannot name, but can only guess at with dim forebodings.[42] Aristophanes suggests that they might be restored to a physical unity by having the appropriate halves joined together —but that is only a fantastic image of the inexpressible spiritual harmony and wholeness which he says is the true aim of Eros. In *Meno,* knowledge is interpreted to be the recollection of pure being seen in a previous life. So here, Eros is explained as man's yearning to return to the whole nature which he had originally had in an earlier age of the world, and thereby as an exciting aspiration towards an eternal Unattained. This unattainable thing, in Aristophanes' myth, is described only as that which we have lost, and which we seek to recover once more. But if we look at it through the speech of Diotima, it is obviously a first vague allusion to the standard of ideal good in which all true human friendship and love are fulfilled.

The last speech before Socrates takes up the theme is made by the young host, Agathon. A finely wrought and delicately coloured eulogy of Eros, it is a calculated contrast to the roaring extravaganza of Aristophanes. The comedian's speech had broadened the theme of Eros from homosexual love between men to the nature of love in general; and now the popular tragedian (often laughed at by contemporary comic poets for being a ladies' man) pushes male Eros into the background and speaks of love in its most universal form. He says he will not follow the other speakers in praising the benefits conferred by Eros on men, but will start by describing the god's nature, and then go on to his gifts.[43] His description of Eros is hardly psychological at all—it is impossible to avoid noticing that when we compare it with Aristophanes' speech, which centred upon the effect of Eros on the human soul. However, it is full of noble idealization. Agathon treats the perfection of Eros very seriously, inferring that he must be perfect, since he is divine. But since every encomium of Eros personifying him as a divine force must necessarily derive his qualities from man, to whom he manifests his power, it is always significant for the psychology of the eulogist to note whether he praises him as a reflection of the beloved, or of the lover. Agathon does the former. He is naturally amorous himself, and he gives Eros characteristics which suit an adorable being rather than a passionate lover.[43a] With Narcissus-like devotion, he makes his portrait of Eros a mirror-image of himself. From that point of view the purpose and significance of his speech, at that precise place in the general scheme of *The Symposium,* will become plain from later developments.

He says that Eros is the noblest, fairest, best of all the gods.[44] He is young, elegant, and tender, living only in flowery and perfumed places. Force never touches him: his rule is one of free will. He possesses all virtues—justice, self-control, courage, and wisdom. He is such a great poet that he can teach others to write poetry. Ever since he has inhabited heaven, the regime has changed from one of cruelty to one of beauty. It is Eros who taught most of the immortals their arts and skills. So says Agathon, and he ends his encomium with a prose-hymn to Eros, so exquisitely balanced in structure and so euphonious in harmony that it is equal to any poetry ever written.[45]

Plato chose to make that speech the immediate background for the speech of Socrates. He took Agathon, the exquisite sensualist, the subtle aesthete, as the proper foil for the philosophical ascetic who was so infinitely superior to him both in the strength of his passions and in the depth of his knowledge of love. Socrates now does what the others did before him. He sets out to counter the disadvantage he suffers from following so many brilliant speakers, by handling the subject in a different way. He says he approves of Agathon's procedure in defining Eros first, before describing his actions; [46] but he himself treats the theme in a radically different way from his predecessors. He does not undertake to exaggerate the importance and beauty of Eros through rhetoric, but (as always) tries to find out the truth about it. And so, even in his first tentative steps, in his brief preliminary conversation with Agathon, when the methods of dialectic are (for the first time in *The Symposium*) half-seriously and half-jestingly brought into play, we are recalled from the airy poetic superlatives of Agathon's speech to the solid earth of psychological truth. Every Eros, says Socrates, is a desire for some-

thing—a desire for something which one lacks.[47] Therefore, if
Eros strives to attain the beautiful, he cannot himself be beautiful (as Agathon maintained) but must be lacking in beauty.
From this negative dialectic thesis, as from a root, Plato makes
Socrates' and Diotima's doctrine of Eros grow and unfold. But
it unfolds not in dialectic form, but in the form of a myth opposed to Agathon's, and explaining how Eros had his birth from
Poros (Plenty) and Penia (Poverty).[48] Yet, with astonishing
sureness of touch, Plato deliberately refrains from allowing Socrates' controversial genius to triumph and silence all others—for
this is an occasion for unrestrained cheerfulness and bold imaginative flights. As soon as the first questions have been asked,
Agathon rather charmingly capitulates, and acknowledges that
he feels as if he didn't know what he had been talking about; [49]
Socrates leaves him in peace. This takes the edge off the pedantic
cross-examination by accurate logical processes, which would be
out of place in good society. But Plato manages to complete the
dialectic conversation by putting it far into the past, where the
exhausting and terrifying questioner Socrates himself becomes
the naïve examinee. He repeats to the guests a conversation on
Eros which he had had long ago with the Mantinean prophetess
Diotima.[50] This makes all he has to say appear to be not his
own superior wisdom, but the sage's revelation. Plato deliberately chose and developed this image of initiation into the mysteries. The godlike Diotima introduces her adept to the knowledge of Eros, by instructing him step by step—a process in which
the reader is meant to distinguish between the lower and the
higher degrees in the rites leading to the last revelation. In
Greek religion the mystery-cults were the most personal form
of religion, and it is as a personal revelation of his own that
Socrates describes the philosopher's ascent to the summit on
which the yearning for eternal beauty inherent in all Eros is
finally satisfied.

Eros is not beautiful; but of course he is not ugly. This established, it follows that he is somewhere between beauty and ugliness. Similarly, he is between wisdom and ignorance. He has
nothing of either, but stands midway between them.[51] This proof
that he comes somewhere between perfection and imperfection
also demonstrates that he cannot be a god. He possesses neither
good nor beauty, nor yet happiness—all essential qualities of

godhead.[52] Still, he is not a mortal. He is something between
mortal and immortal. He is a great spirit: a daemon acting as
intermediary between gods and men.[53] This gives him a vitally
important place in Platonic theology. He closes the gap between
the earthly and celestial realms; he is the bond, the *syndesmos*
that binds the whole universe together.[54] His nature is twofold,
a heritage from his dissimilar parents, Plenty and Poverty.[55]
Forever partnered with want, he is nevertheless overflowing
with riches and full of inexhaustible energy, a great huntsman,
a daredevil, a plotter, a never-failing spring of spiritual energy,
constantly seeking wisdom, a terrific magician and wizard.
In one day he can live and flourish, die, and revive again;
and whatever he gains always flows away from him again; so
that he is never either rich or poor.[56] Thus the allegorical
genealogy of Eros which Socrates substitutes for Hesiod's
version is corroborated by the description of his nature. By
assigning Eros a place midway between beauty and ugliness, wisdom and ignorance, divinity and humanity, wealth and poverty,
Socrates contrives to connect him with philosophy. The gods do
not philosophize, or educate themselves—for they possess all
wisdom. Fools and ignoramuses, on the other hand, do not aspire
to knowledge—for the real evil of their ignorance is that, without knowing anything, they yet believe they know. Only the philosopher strives to achieve knowledge—for he knows that he
does not possess it, and he feels his lack of it. He stands midway
between wisdom and ignorance. Therefore he alone is both
capable of culture and honestly and seriously concerned to obtain
it. Eros too, from his whole character, belongs to the same category. He is a true philosopher, standing midway between wisdom and folly, and absorbed in constant striving and yearning.[57]
Agathon had depicted him as all that is lovely and beloved; now
Socrates paints a rival picture, with lines drawn not from the
beloved but from the lover.[58] He contrasts that which is never
motionless but always aspiring, for ever striving to perfect itself
and win eternal happiness, with that which rests motionless
within itself, happy and perfect.

Diotima now turns from her enquiry into the nature of Eros,
to discuss his value for mankind.[59] But it is already clear
that his value will not lie in any social effects he brings about,
as other speakers have suggested—in his power to inspire ambi-

tion and honourable shame (so Phaedrus), or in the lover's
readiness to assist in the education of the beloved (so Pausanias). These suggestions are of course not false; but it is soon
made plain that they are not the whole truth. Diotima gives a
genuinely Socratic interpretation of the desire for the beautiful
(it being agreed that Eros is such a desire) : she says it is man's
yearning for perfect happiness, eudaimonia.[60] Every strong and
deep urgency of our nature must ultimately be connected
with happiness, and must be deliberately guided and controlled
with reference to it. For it implies a claim and an aspiration to
one ultimate supreme possession, a perfect good—and indeed
Socrates holds that every act of will necessarily wills the good.
Thereby Eros, instead of being only a special case of the act of
willing, becomes the most clearly visible and convincing expression of the fundamental fact of all Platonic ethics—that man
can never desire what he does not think to be good for him.
Despite that, the name *Eros* and the verb *eran* are not used for
every kind of willing, but kept for a definite type of desire.
Plato points out that this fact can be paralleled in other words
like *poiésis,* 'poetry', which simply means 'making', but is kept
for only one particular kind of making. In reality, this new
awareness of the arbitrariness with which the true meaning of
words like *eros* and *poetry* is 'curtailed' in everyday speech is
part of Plato's work in extending these concepts and filling them
with a universal content.[61]

Thus the concept of Eros becomes an epitome of all human
striving to attain the good. Once again a remark made by an
earlier speaker, correct in itself and indeed profound, has been
reinterpreted from the new and higher standpoint of Socrates'
present speech, and relegated to its appropriate place. It was
Aristophanes who said that Eros was a yearning for the other
half of our selves—that is, for wholeness. But it is truer to say
that by wholeness we must understand perfection and goodness.[62]
We must take the completed whole to mean not a chance individual but the true self. We must understand that the good is
that which is natural and essential to our nature, and that that
which is foreign to our nature is the bad. Only if we do that can
the essence of all Eros be taken (as Aristophanes took it) to be
love for that which was 'once' part and parcel of our 'old nature'.
Then it is the desire 'to possess the good for ever'.[63] That is very

close to Aristotle's definition in the *Nicomachean Ethics* of the higher self-love (φιλαυτία) which is the final stage of moral perfection.[64] He took over this principle from Plato, and the source from which he took it was *The Symposium*. Diotima's words are the shortest and best commentary on Aristotle's conception of self-love. Eros interpreted as love for the good is at the same time the urge of human nature towards real self-fulfilment and self-completion, and is therefore the impulse towards education and culture in the truest sense.

Aristotle follows Plato in another point too. He derives all other types of love and friendship from this ideal love of self.[65] Now we may recall what we said above on the Narcissus-like love of self evidenced in Agathon's speech.[66] Agathon's ornate little oration is, in this respect as in others, the complete opposite to Socrates' speech. For the philosophical self-love which Socrates reveals as the ultimate basis of all Eros, the yearning to attain one's 'true nature', is poles apart from self-satisfaction and self-admiration. Nothing is so remote from true Socratic *philautia* as the narcissistic selfishness which, if it were psychologically misinterpreted, might be identified with it. Eros for Socrates means the aspiration of the man who knows he is still imperfect, to mould his own spirit and his own reason, with his gaze steadily fixed on the Idea. It is in fact what Plato means by 'philosophy': the yearning of the true self within us to take shape.[67]

When Plato lays down that the object of Eros is the perfection of the final good for which he yearns, he has converted a seemingly irrational impulse into something highly intelligible and meaningful. On the other hand, the most real and obvious meaning of Eros—yearning for one beautiful thing or person— seems to be entirely lost in this new interpretation. Plato knows this, and does it full justice in the second part of Diotima's speech. The next question to arise is this: from Plato's lofty standpoint, what kind of activity or desire really deserves the name of Eros? We are surprised to get an answer which sounds neither exaggeratedly metaphysical nor morally improving, but is solidly based on the natural process of physical love. Eros is the desire to have offspring by a beautiful person.[68] The only mistake in the usual definition of it is that it confines this desire to the body, whereas it has a perfect analogy in the life of the soul too.[69] Still, it is a good idea to begin by thinking of the physical act of begetting, because it makes it easier to explain the nature of the corresponding spiritual process. The physical wish to beget is a phenomenon existing far outside the sphere of human relations.[70] If we are certain that all Eros is the desire to help one's own true self to be realized,[71] then the impulse in animals and in men to beget offspring and reproduce themselves is an expression of the desire to leave someone like oneself behind.[72] The laws of mortal existence make it impossible for us to be immortal. Not even the human ego, which believes that it retains its identity throughout all the changing phases of life, is self-identical in the true sense. It is constantly renewed, both soul and body.[73] Only the divine is for ever absolutely the same. And thus the only way in which mortal and finite beings can infinitely prolong themselves is to beget offspring like them in species although individually distinct. That is the meaning of Eros, which, as a physical impulse, is simply the impulse of our bodies to be immortal.[74]

But Plato affirms that the same is true of man's spiritual nature.[75] The spiritual self is areté, which flows outward into the life of the community, as fame. Homer knew that well. And Plato was wise enough to adapt the old Homeric conception of areté, so truly and ancestrally Greek.[76] Therefore Phaedrus was entirely right in saying that ambition (φιλοτιμία) was one of the effects of Eros,[77] but the meaning of his remark was deeper than he knew. All spiritual Eros is begetting: it is the impulse to perpetuate oneself in a love-act or creative work, such that it will live on in the memory of men and have an enduring and living effect. All great poets and artists are begetters and creators of that type; and most of all those who found and organize states and communities.[78] He whose soul is full of the wish to beget looks for something beautiful by which to beget. If he finds a soul which is beautiful, noble, and talented, he greets the whole man, and makes many speeches to him about areté, and the character and pursuits which a good man should have, and he sets about educating him (ἐπιχειρεῖ παιδεύειν). So in contact and association with him, he begets the offspring he had had within himself for so long. Both present and absent, he remembers his partner and shares with him in bringing to perfection that which he begot, so that their parentage is a far stronger link than any share in children begotten of the body, and their love is more lasting than that of marriage, because they share in more beautiful and more immortal children. Homer and Hesiod, Lycurgus and Solon are for Plato the highest Greek representatives of this Eros—for through their works they have begotten all kinds of areté. Poets and legislators are alike in the educational force of their work. Plato regards the spiritual history of Greece from Homer and Lycurgus down to himself as a single unity. Poetry and philosophy, although he believes their conceptions of reality are widely and deeply separated, are united by the ideal of paideia, which springs from Eros, the love for areté.[79]

Up to this point, Diotima's speech moves on the loftiest heights of Greek tradition by interpreting all the creative work of the spirit as a manifestation of Eros. Eros, as the educational force which holds together that whole spiritual cosmos, seems to be the right avatar for Socrates, the latest embodiment of that force. But Diotima says she is not sure whether he is capable of understanding the higher mysteries and ascending to the summit for the final vision.[80] Since the object of this vision is the supreme Idea, Plato evidently wants to point out how far the discussion has been Socratic, and how far it goes beyond Socrates himself. The argument so far has contained an obvious progress from the physical to the spiritual. In the last part of the speech this progress becomes the basic structural principle. Plato carries on the image of the mysteries, and sketches an elaborate scheme of advancing stages (ἐπαναβαθμοί) to be climbed by the man captured by true Eros,[81] either from his own impulse or from the stimulus of others; and he finally calls this spiritual ascent *pedagogy*.[82] We must not think he meant the educational influence of the lover on the beloved—which was previously mentioned, and to which he alludes even here.[83] Eros is now the force which educates the lover himself, by carrying him from lower to higher stages. This ascent begins in early youth, with admiration of the physical beauty of one person, which inspires the lover to 'beautiful speeches'.[84] But then the true pupil of Eros realizes that the beauty of one body is practically the same as that of another. So he loves beauty in all bodies, and recognizes that they are one and the same; his dependence on that one person dwindles and vanishes away. Of course this does not mean that he has a number of indiscriminate affairs with separate individuals, but that he comes to appreciate beauty in itself. Next he notices spiritual beauty, and prizes it more highly than physical beauty: he prefers the charm of a soul even when it is in a rather unattractive body.[85] That is the stage at which his Eros becomes able to educate others, and brings forth speeches designed to make young men better.[86] Now he becomes able to detect the kindred beauty of all customs and laws—a plain allusion to the synoptic function of dialectic, as described elsewhere by Plato. The dialectic process, which looks at the numerous visible beauties and sees in them one invisible 'beauty in itself', is symbolized in Socrates' entire description of the stages in the mystery of Eros. It ends with his recognition of the beauty of all science and knowledge. And therewith, the lover is free from the slavery which has bound him with the chains of passion to one man or to one admired custom.[87] Now he turns to the 'wide sea of beauty', and, after studying all kinds of knowledge and science, he sees the divine beauty in its own purity, free from all individual phenomena and relationships.[88]

Plato contrasts the many 'beautiful sciences' with the one science (μάθημα) which has as its object Beauty itself.[89] The sciences are not beautiful in the sense in which we speak of 'fine' arts or 'belles' lettres. Plato thinks that every type of knowledge has its own peculiar beauty, its own special value and meaning. But all scientific enquiry into special subjects must end in knowledge of the essence of beauty.[90] Even that sounds rather strange to our ears: we usually think of beauty first of all in the realm of aesthetics. But Plato gives a number of clear indications that this is not what he means. He says that only the life spent in perpetual contemplation of this eternal beauty is worth living.[91] This evidently does not mean one single lofty moment of vision, one absorbed instant of ecstasy. Only an entire life spent in concentration upon this end (τέλος) is enough to satisfy Plato's demand.[92] Of course this does not mean a lifelong trance, a dream of beauty unbroken by the irruption of life. We must recall that Diotima has already defined Eros as the desire to make the good one's own 'for ever'.[93] That also means permanent possession, a state lasting throughout life. 'Beauty itself', or, as Plato also calls it here, 'divine beauty itself',[94] is not essentially distinct from the Good of which he wrote in the earlier passage. Here he says that the ultimate aim of all wandering through the separate sciences (μαθήματα) is the science (μάθημα) of beauty.[95] That corresponds to the dominant position given to the Idea of Good in the system of paideia he works out in *The Republic.* There Plato calls it 'the greatest subject of study' (μέγιστον μάθημα).[96] Beauty and good are only two closely allied aspects of one and the same reality—two aspects which were fused into one by general Greek idiom, since the highest human areté was called 'beauty-and-goodness', καλοκἀγαθία. This 'beauty' or 'good', this *kalokagathia* in its pure state is, we understand, the highest principle of all human will and action, the ultimate motive which works with its own inward necessity, and at the same time the ground for all that happens in nature. For Plato holds that between the moral and the physical cosmos there is perfect harmony.

Even in the first speeches about Eros, Plato brought out the fact that Eros implies a yearning towards moral beauty: the speakers mentioned the lover's ambition and his anxiety that the beloved should be perfect and attain excellence. That gave Eros his place in the moral structure of society. Similarly, in Diotima's description of the various stages in love's mysteries, she mentioned that even the lowest of them all, love for physical beauty, evoked 'beautiful speeches'. That means speeches characterized by a feeling for higher things, for noble ideals and honourable aspirations. The beautiful activities and sciences which appear at higher stages are, in their turn, not merely aesthetic functions, but embody goodness and perfection, that which gives real meaning and direction to any kind of act or knowledge. Thus the progress through love's various degrees reveals, with growing clarity, that beauty is not one single beam of light falling on one point of the visible world to illumine it alone, but the striving of everything and everyone towards goodness and perfection. As we climb higher, as we behold more and more plainly the depth and universality of this power, our desire grows stronger and stronger to see it in its purity and to know it as the moving force of all life. And yet, when Plato says that the general Idea

of beauty will at last be seen separately from its individual manifestations, he does not mean in practice that those who see it must
quit this world. It is only that it will teach them to apprehend
the supreme power of the principle of good and beauty throughout all reality, and to make it fully significant in their own lives.
For then they will understand that the principle which in the
external world they discovered to be the ground of all existence
can be rediscovered in the spirit's utmost self-concentration, and
will prove to be the soul's own essential nature. If our interpretation of Eros is correct—if the yearning to make Good one's
own for ever is the same as self-love in its loftiest sense—then its
object, eternal goodness and beauty, must be the very heart of
the Self. The 'pedagogy' of Eros, as Plato calls it, with its various stages, really means the process by which man's true nature
is formed out of the raw material of individuality, the construction of his personality upon the basis of the eternal within him.
The radiance which Plato's description of 'the beautiful' throws
upon this invisible ideal flows from the inner light of the spirit,
which finds in it its focus and the ground of its existence.

The humanistic significance of the doctrine put forward in *The
Symposium,* that Eros is man's instinctive urge to develop his
own higher self, needs no exegesis here. The thought recurs in
The Republic, in another form: Socrates says the purpose of all
paideia is to help the inner man to rule over man.[97] Humanism
is based on this distinction between man the individual as given
by nature, and man the higher self. It was Plato who made it
possible for humanism to have this philosophical foundation,
and it was *The Symposium* in which it was first laid down. But
in Plato humanism is not merely an abstract theory. Like everything else in his philosophy, it grows out of his knowledge of the
unique character of Socrates. That is why any account of *The
Symposium* which confines itself to searching for the central
dialectic core of doctrine, by dissecting the speeches of the guests
and in particular the philosophical revelation given by Diotima
to Socrates, must needs be too narrow. No doubt there is a
doctrine at the centre of the whole dialogue, and Plato takes
no trouble to conceal it. But it would be wrong to think that
his real purpose was to amuse those of his readers who were

experienced in dialectic, by allowing them to extract the logical quintessence from a number of different sensuous disguises.

He does not end *The Symposium* with the revelation of the Idea of beauty and the philosophical interpretation of Eros. It culminates with the scene in which Alcibiades bursts into the house at the head of a band of drunken friends, and makes a daring speech extolling Socrates as the master of Eros in the highest sense, the sense revealed by Diotima. Thus, the long succession of encomia on Eros ends with an encomium on Socrates. He is the embodiment of Eros: and Eros is philosophy.[98] His educational passion [99] attracts him to all handsome and talented youths. But in the case of Alcibiades the profound spiritual attraction which emanated from Socrates reverses the usual relationship of lover and beloved—so that ultimately it is the much-beloved Alcibiades who is vainly yearning for the love of Socrates. For the Greeks, it was the very height of paradox that such a beautiful and adorable youth should be in love with the grotesquely ugly Socrates. And yet the new feeling for *inner* beauty which is announced by *The Symposium* makes itself powerfully felt in Alcibiades' speech, when he compares Socrates to the statuettes of Silenus sold in art-shops, which open to reveal images of gods inside them.[100] At the end of *Phaedrus*, Plato makes Socrates pray for inward beauty, since there is nothing else to pray for: and that is the only prayer in the whole of Plato, a pattern and an example of the philosopher's prayer.[101] There is something tragic about Alcibiades' love for Socrates, whom he follows and yet flies, because Socrates is his own conscience, accusing him to himself.[102] The tragedy is that a great nature, eminently fitted for philosophy, should through ambition degenerate to a selfish power-hunter—just as Plato shows in *The Republic*.[103] His complicated psychology—admiration and adoration for Socrates, mixed with fear and hatred of him—is fully exposed in the magnificent confession at the end of *The Symposium*. It is the tribute involuntarily paid by a strong man to Socrates' unmistakable strength, and the shrinking of the weak, ambitious, and selfish man from the moral greatness of true independence, which he feels for ever unattainable. Here Plato answers not only those who condemned Socrates for having had Alcibiades as a pupil (such as the sophist Polycrates, author of a pamphlet against the master), but Isocrates, who thought it was ridiculous to say that Socrates had been the teacher of such a distinguished man as Alcibiades.[104] Alcibiades wished to be his pupil, Plato says, but his nature was not capable of self-mastery.[105] The Socratic Eros blazed up in his soul for a moment, but it did not kindle into an enduring flame.

THE REPUBLIC

PART I

INTRODUCTION

FROM the very start, Plato's thinking is aimed at solving the problem of the state. At first invisible, that theme emerges more and more clearly, until it is unmistakably the aim of all the dialectic enquiries of his earlier books. As we have seen, Socrates' discussions of the several virtues, even in the earlier dialogues, were directed towards discovering political virtue;[1] while in *Protagoras* and *Gorgias* he viewed the knowledge of good in itself as the political art which would solve all difficulties.[2] If we keep these facts in mind, we shall scarcely need the witness of Plato's seventh Letter [3] to understand that *The Republic* is his central work, in which all the lines drawn by his earlier writings now converge.

Plato's modern readers, judging him by modern patterns of thought, used to spend much energy searching for his 'system'. But at last they became content to realize that—whether for artistic or for critical motives—he refrained from constructing a fixed body of doctrine like other philosophers. He wanted to show knowledge in process of becoming. But subtler-minded scholars observed that there were large differences between the constructive contents of his various dialogues. The most constructive of all is called *The Republic,* or *The State.*[3a] It follows from this that he chose to give unity to all his thinking on social and ethical problems, not within an abstract logical system, but within the vivid and tangible form of the state. Similarly in *Timaeus* his ideas on physics are expounded, not as a logical system of natural principles, but as a clear and palpable picture of the origin of the universe.[4]

But what does the state mean to Plato? His *Republic* is not concerned with constitutional law, nor with the art of government, nor with legislation; in fact, it has nothing to do with politics in the modern sense of the word. He does not start with an actual historical nation like Athens or the Spartans. Although he deliberately confines himself to Greece, he is not bound to any particular region or city within it. The physical conditions of his city are never mentioned. They concern him neither geologically nor anthropologically. The training described in *The Republic* has nothing to do with the *race* which lives in the city —the entire population. The vast majority of the people, with its business life, its customs, and its ways of living, is not mentioned, or else remains wholly on the periphery of the discussion. It can perhaps be found in the 'third class' of the citizens, but that class is only a passive object of government,[5] and even as such is not described in any details.

In *The Republic* Plato neither describes these aspects of political life nor offers any standard applicable to them. They are left out as unimportant. But book after book of the whole work is given up to an impassioned discussion of poetry and music (2-3), and of the value of abstract science (5-7). In book 10 poetry is discussed once more, from a new point of view. Books 8 and 9, with their examination of the various forms of state, look like an exception to this rule. But there too a closer inspection shows that Plato is thinking of these political patterns only as expressions of different spiritual attitudes and types of soul. The same is true of the problem of justice, which opens the discussion and leads to all that follows. It would surely make a vast theme for jurists, not only in our own day, but in Plato's also— for his contemporaries were the first to interest themselves in problems of comparative political science. But even here he pays no attention to practical law. The question 'What is justice?' leads to the theory of 'the parts of the soul'.[6] The ultimate interest of Plato's *Republic* is the human soul. Everything else he says about the state and its structure (the organic conception of the state, as it is called, which many believe to be the real core of *The Republic*) is introduced merely to give an 'enlarged image' of the soul and its structure. But even in the problem of the soul, Plato's interest is not theoretical but practical. He is a *builder of souls*. He makes Socrates move the whole state with one lever, the education which forms the soul.[7] The meaning of the state, as revealed in Plato's greatest work, is no different from that which the preceding dialogues, *Protagoras* and *Gorgias*, led us to expect. Its highest virtue is education. After all that has been said in previous chapters, this way of describing it cannot appear strange. In his account of the state and society, he has philosophically set forth one of the permanent and essential presuppositions of Greek paideia.[8] But simultaneously he brings out in the form of paideia that particular aspect of the state whose weakening he thinks responsible for the progressive degeneration and debasement of contemporary politics. Thus *politeia* and *paideia*, which for so many men even at that time were only vaguely related, became the two foci of Plato's work.

When we regard the book from this point of view, we cannot but stand astonished at the attitude of a distinguished modern historian of philosophy trained in the positivist school: he holds that *The Republic* contains many fascinating thoughts, but objects to its preoccupation with education.[9] He might just as well say that the Bible was a very clever book, though it talked too much about God. But we need not laugh at him: he is not an isolated case. In fact, he is typical of the nineteenth-century misunderstanding of *The Republic*. Philosophy and scholarship had soared too high above the scholasticism of the humanists, and had come to despise all 'pedagogy' so arrogantly that they forgot their own origins.[10] The problem of education had been of supreme interest even in the age of Lessing and Goethe; but philosophers were now incapable of realizing the scope it had had in Plato's day and in the classical period generally—when it was the centre of all spiritual life and the source of all the deepest significance of human existence. A century earlier, Rousseau had come far closer to understanding *The Republic* when he said that it was not a political system, as might be thought from its title, but the finest treatise on education ever written.

THE PROBLEM OF JUSTICE LEADS TO THE IDEAL STATE

Gorgias closed with the paradox that Socrates was the greatest statesman of his age. Ever since then we have been waiting for Plato to fulfil the promise he made there.[11] Of course it is clear enough, even in *Gorgias*, what the Platonic Socrates means by so describing himself. But this transference of 'politics' from

the sphere of selfish lust for power to that of Socratic education and soul-shaping—what would its results be when put into
practice in a real state? How would it change the nature of that
state? Plato was a poet, with the desire to make every truth
a visible image; and he was a statesman, with a passion for
reformation. The two sides of his character were combined in
his desire to create 'the best state', in spirit at least, upon this
foundation, and to set it up as a paradeigma before the eyes of
mankind.

The idea of a 'best state' was not new in itself. The Greeks
had an innate impulse to aim at perfection in every branch of
art and knowledge. It was active in political life too, where it
acted as a goad, to make them discontented with the inadequacy
of existing conditions: even the rigorous laws that threatened
with death any revolt against the country's constitution could
not prevent men from imagining some better political life than
that which they lived.[12] Social conditions in particular had for
many years been the object of keen speculation. Long ago, in
ages of chaos, the old poets had evoked pictures of *eunomia,* an
ideal state of law and order. The Spartan Tyrtaeus, as a conservative, had proclaimed that that perfect order was identical
with Spartan tradition.[13] Solon went further, and derived the
perfectly just state from the eternal ideals of moral reason.[14] In
the era of the sophists, thinkers went further yet: they set out
now to give concrete proposals for bettering social evils in the
state, and Hippodamus and Phaleas (whose Utopias we know
in outline from Aristotle's report)[15] drew up plans for a just
and permanent social order constructed in the spirit of contemporary rationalism—its schematic form, indeed, is reminiscent
of Hippodamus' highly geometrical schemes of town-planning.
Among other prescriptions, Phaleas' ideal state involved equal
education for all citizens, as a bond to hold society together
from within.[16] Towards the end of the Peloponnesian war, an
unknown sophist writing on the reconstruction of the state centred his discussion on the problem of getting the citizens to be
virtuous and obedient to the state's laws.[17] His point of view was
far different, however, from that of *The Republic:* he thought
that every problem—even the authority of morals and society—
had an economic solution. He held that economic factors were
the basis of confidence, of credit both within the state and in

intercourse with nationals of other states, and that the state's inability to establish this kind of authority by its own legal powers must lead to tyranny. His chief concern, therefore, was in reaching practical solutions of the value of which he was already convinced, and which must essentially have corresponded to the views current in the Greek democracies after the conclusion of the ruinous war. But still, his book is highly significant: it shows the kind of atmosphere in which Plato's theory of the ideal state was constructed.

Plato is not content with assuming one type of constitution and giving advice for its betterment, or with discussing the relative value of different kinds of constitution, like the sophists.[18] He is more radical in his approach. He starts with the general problem of justice. The symphony of *The Republic* opens with the familiar Socratic theme of areté, in the same key as Plato's earlier dialogues. At first (as in the early dialogues) the state is not mentioned at all. Socrates seems to begin by discussing one single virtue. But the discussion has an important historical background, which, though invisible, is present to the eye of the historian. In order to understand the opening of the book, we must think back to the disputes about the ideal of justice which had taken place in the century before Plato. Justice was political virtue in the highest sense. As the old poet said, it contained all other virtues in itself.[19] Long before, when the constitutional state was coming into being, that line had pregnantly expressed the new significance of the concept of virtue; and now it was once more actual and up to date for Plato. But now its sense had changed and become deeper. For the pupil of Socrates, it could not signify mere adherence to the laws, that legality which had once been the rampart of the constitutional state against a world of autocratic feudal or revolutionary forces.[20] Plato's conception of justice transcended all human institutions: it went back to the origin of justice within the soul. What the philosopher calls justice must be based on the most inward nature of the human spirit.

Two hundred years earlier, the solution to centuries of party struggle had seemed to be that all citizens should be bound to obey the rule of universal law.[21] But subsequent developments had shown that this solution involved serious difficulties. Laws had been meant to last for a long time—perhaps for ever. But they came to need improvement or extension. And yet experience showed that everything depended on the particular element in the nation which undertook to extend and improve them. Whether it was a small governing class, a majority of the citizenry, or a single ruler, it appeared inevitable that while it ruled it would alter the laws to its own taste—and that meant to its own interests. Justice meant so many different things in different states that it looked like a purely relative conception.[22] Yet if one tried to pass beyond these variations to find some ultimate unity, it could—or so it seemed—be found only in the unsatisfactory definition that justice in any one place meant the expression of the will and of the interests of the party which happened to be stronger. Accordingly it became simply a function of power, which has no moral principle in itself. The doctrine that the interests of one are subordinate to those of all was recognized by all governments at all times, but interpreted by every ruling class in its own way. But if justice is equivalent to the advantage of the stronger, then all our struggles to attain a higher ideal of righteousness are mere self-deception, and the political order which is aimed at realizing that ideal is nothing but a painted screen for the relentless battle of selfish interests. Many sophists and many statesmen of the age of the sophists had actually drawn that conclusion and thrown off all moral restraint—although the average decent citizen did not realize it. Plato was bound to begin any far-reaching investigation of the problem of the state by examining the claims of this naturalistic doctrine: for if it were correct, then all philosophizing was useless, or worse.

In *Gorgias* he had personified the deliberately unscrupulous power-politician in the figure of Callicles, and singled him out as the real opponent of Socrates.[23] There he had described the battle between power and education for the human soul as the central spiritual problem of his age.[24] And now in *The Republic*, when Socrates sets out to explain his own political art, we naturally expect him to go back to the same problem. In the first book of *The Republic*, the quarrelsome sophist Thrasymachus is chosen to represent Callicles' philosophy of power for its own sake; and, despite Plato's deliberate and artistic variations, there are many other repetitions of the thoughts and emotions of

Gorgias. Plato obviously considers that the doctrine of the right of the stronger is the perfect foil to set off his own attitude to the state.[25] But in *The Republic* he does not simply lay out his own thesis of education as a systematic contrast to the thesis of the will to power, as he had done in *Gorgias;* he reaches it by a long circuitous route. His preliminary discussion of the Machiavellian conception of state and justice as governed wholly by power is merely an introduction, and the positive exposition of the Platonic system of education is the real theme of the work.

In the first book, Socrates controverts the doctrine that justice is only the expression of the will of whatever party happens to be stronger, in his usual way—by setting up the true nature of justice in place of the positive law of one time or place. With this, the discussion seems to be finished.[26] But Plato's brothers, Glaucon and Adeimantus—two splendid representatives of the élite of Athenian youth, with all its unwavering endurance, keen intellectual powers, and noble aspirations—challenge Socrates at this point. They ask him for something far greater than he has given them. They treat all that he has said as only a prologue, and they say they are still not fully convinced that justice *in itself alone,* without reference to its social advantages and without reference to bourgeois conventions, is a supreme good. Glaucon and Adeimantus make two speeches, one following immediately upon the other, to develop this problem in that rigorous form which is the only one that can convince the young men of their generation: is justice a good thing which we want for its own sake? or is it simply a means to getting some particular advantage? or is it one of those things which we love both for their own sake and for their advantageous results?[27] For the moment, Glaucon represents those who hold that doing injustice is good in itself and suffering it is evil, but who lack the power to live according to this strong man's morality—so that they welcome the protection of law as a compromise, a middle way between the highest good (which is doing wrong with impunity) and the highest evil (which is suffering wrong).[28] He illustrates the idea that justice is forced upon us, by bringing in the story of Gyges' magic ring, which gave its wearer the power of becoming invisible whenever he turned the seal inwards.[29] Suppose any one of us owned that ring: would he have such adamantine spiritual strength as to resist temptation? Who would not set out to gratify all kinds of secret wishes which are condemned as wicked by the moral order of our own society? Thus Glaucon grasps the difficulty at its root. We have already observed the importance, in sophistic discussions of the objective validity of moral and civic laws, of the question why men so often behave differently before witnesses and alone. Some of the sophists attributed men's public conduct to the artificial compulsion of law, and held that their private conduct showed the true standard of nature—which was nothing but the urge to obtain what was pleasant and avoid what was unpleasant.[30] In the story of Gyges' ring, Plato found a brilliant symbol for this naturalistic conception of human effort and power. We can appreciate the true value of justice in man's life only if we compare the life of a thoroughly unjust man whose true character remains hidden, with that of a man who is thoroughly just, but either does not know or does not care how to maintain the external appearance of virtue, which is so much more important. Would that comparison not turn out greatly to the advantage of the life led by the wicked man? And would the just man not be persecuted, tormented, and miserable?

Yet Plato is not content even with that moving image of the problem of the purely inward value of justice. He puts another speech in the mouth of Glaucon's brother Adeimantus, to make Glaucon's view still clearer.[31] First Glaucon had spoken for the modern eulogists of injustice. Now we are to hear their opponents, those who praise virtue, the great poets from Homer and Hesiod to Musaeus and Pindar. Do they not praise the ideal of justice simply because of the rewards which the gods give the just man?[32] Do they not elsewhere say that justice is a fine noble thing but difficult and painful, while they often make out injustice as profitable and even claim that the gods can be corrupted?[33] If the authorities for the highest virtue, poets and educators of the nation, believe this, what kind of life is a young man to elect when he must make the choice in practice? Adeimantus is evidently speaking in deep spiritual perplexity: his words (especially towards the end of his speech) are utterances of his own personal experience.[34] Plato makes him the representative of the younger generation to which he himself belonged. That is why he chose his brothers to be interlocutors in the dialogue, to push the discussion forward and to formulate the problem which Socrates is to attack. They are two splendid supporters for the monument which Plato is raising to Socrates in this, his greatest work. The ground on which it is built is the painful doubt of these young representatives of the genuine old Attic kalokagathia, who come to Socrates as the only man who can find a solution for the troubles of their conscience.

Adeimantus describes the spiritual difficulties of himself and his contemporaries with ruthless vigour: every word he speaks is a criticism of the traditional methods of education by the old classical poets and the renowned moral authorities who have left the sting of moral doubt to fester in the soul of those young men who are thinking out these problems uncompromisingly to the end. Plato and his brothers were the products of that old-fashioned education; but they felt they were also its victims. Did any of these teachers really believe in the essential value of justice, the value which young men claimed the ideal must have if it were to be worth believing in?[35] What they saw and heard around them in public and private life was just crafty unscrupulousness, veiled by compulsion in lofty phrases; and they were sorely tempted to give in and make their pact with that world. As Adeimantus describes it, the still small voice of conscience would soon be silenced by the experience that injustice quite often goes undetected; and the religious fear that God sees and knows all could be quieted by a little dose of atheism, or by ritual obedience to some mystery-cult promising purification and absolution for all sins.[36] And so he agrees with his brother Glaucon in asking Socrates to convince them—not that justice is socially profitable, but that it is good in itself for the soul of the man who possesses it, just like seeing and hearing and clear thinking; and that injustice is unhappiness. And he wants to hear what are the effects of justice and injustice (whether they are detected or not) upon the essential core of human character. With this formulation of the problem of justice, the discussion has reached a climax, from which all the meaning of life—both moral worth and happiness—has been transferred exclusively to the inner life of man. How that can be, the young questioners of Socrates cannot say, without his help; yet they see quite clearly that that is the only way to escape from the out-and-out relativism which is involved in the theory that justice is what the stronger party wants. Justice must be something in the soul, a sort of spiritual health, whose existence it is impossible to doubt—unless, like the written laws of the state, it is simply a reflex of the changing influences of power and party.[37] It is beautiful to see that Socrates does not announce this dogma pontifically to an incredulous audience, as in *Gorgias*,[38] but instead, two young men, struggling to find some moral certainty for themselves, draw that conclusion from their own spiritual doubt, and only turn to Socrates so that his superior intellect can solve their enigma. This casts a distant light on Plato's definition of the state, which is destined to grow out of *this* ideal of justice: it is rooted in the inner depths of the personality. The soul of man is the prototype of Plato's state.

The close relation of the state and the soul is hinted at in the remarkable way in which Plato comes to discuss the state. The title of the book makes us think that now at last the state will be announced as the true ultimate aim of the long discussion of justice. And yet Plato treats the state simply as a means to explain the aim, nature, and function of justice in the soul. Since there is justice both in the soul and in the state as a whole, we must be able to spell out its character in the state, that larger although more distant picture, in bigger and clearer letters than in the individual soul.[39] At first glance this looks as if the state were the prototype of the soul. But for Plato they are exactly similar: their structure either in health or in degeneration is the same. Actually the description he gives of justice and its function in the ideal state is not derived from the realities of political life but is a reflection of his theory of the parts of the soul, projected in larger proportions onto his picture of the state and its classes. He makes the state grow up before our eyes out of its simplest elements, in order to discover the point at which justice becomes necessary in it.[40] That does not come to light for some time; but the principle underlying it is invisibly active in the first beginnings of the state, in the division between various trades and vocations that is necessary as soon as some craftsmen and farmers join to form even the simplest community.[41] This principle—that everyone should do his own job (τὰ ἑαυτοῦ πράττειν)—is for Plato connected with the nature of areté, which is the perfect functioning of everything and of every one of its parts.[42] It is easy to understand this of men working together in society, and less easy of the co-operation of 'the parts of the soul.' The essential nature of justice becomes plain later, when Plato draws the conclusion prepared for by his comparison of state and soul.

REFORM OF THE OLD PAIDEIA

We have gone too far ahead of the argument, and must return to Plato's description of the origin of the state. He distinguishes two phases in its growth. The first, which is a simple society composed of the most essential trades and professions, he calls 'the healthy state'; the second, where luxury and ease have increased along with the apparatus of civilization, he calls 'the swollen and sickly state'.[43] The latter contains not only farmers, builders, bakers, tailors, and cobblers, but a host of people concerned with the superfluous things of life. The state, however, is healthiest when it is stripped and economical. The inevitable result of filling it with sickening excess is greed for more land: it cuts off a piece of its neighbours' territory and appropriates it. We have now discovered the origin of war, which always starts from economic causes.[44] (Here Plato accepts war as a given fact of nature, and carefully postpones discussing whether war is good or bad, until another occasion.[45]) The next step, naturally, is the appearance of soldiers. In contradistinction to the democratic principle of Greek city-states that all citizens are obliged to bear arms, and in harmony with his own thesis that everyone should do his own job, Plato sets up a class of professional soldiers, 'the guards'.[46] This was an anticipation of the professional army of Hellenistic days. Contemporary strategists had already moved far in that direction by instituting the much criticized mercenary armies.[47] Plato prefers to create an entirely distinct military caste inside the citizen body. But by calling them 'guards' he restricts their function to defence. The idea he is working out is a rather remarkable mixture: it is partly a description of an actual and inevitable process, with an implied moral condemnation (war being taken as a sign that the original order of society has been disturbed), and partly an idealized fiction, an attempt to make the best of the now indispensable class of soldiers. The second of these two themes soon predominates over the other, so that we suddenly find ourselves playing the part of creative artists, whose task is to choose the fittest natures and educate them correctly so as to mould, with skill and imagination, the pattern of the brave and intelligent guard.[48]

Here and elsewhere, Plato places the strongest emphasis on the importance of choosing the prospective guards carefully if their education is to succeed.[49] The method of selection is not complicated. It depends rather on the teacher's flair—of which Plato gives a brilliant example in defining the right nature for a guard to have. Physically, the future guards should be keen to perceive, agile to catch what they have sighted, and strong to fight once they have caught their prey. And for fighting they need courage. The natural foundation of courage is the same emotional element which is peculiar to well-bred horses and dogs. Plato uses the same kind of comparison in describing the spiritual standards for choosing guards and for educating women.[50] This shows the true aristocrat that he was, with his admiration for good breeding, and his liking for horses and dogs, the faithful companions of the gentleman's leisure hours of hunting and sport. If the soldier is to be a true guard, he must, like a good dog, combine two apparently contradictory qualities—mildness to his friends and pugnacity towards his enemies. Plato humorously calls this a philosophical quality, because dogs and guards alike love what they know and hate the unknown.[51]

After explaining the selection of the guards, Plato proceeds to describe their education—their paideia.[52] He expands his description into a long treatise, which in its turn leads to still longer excursuses on the education of women and the education of the ruler in the ideal state. He justifies his detailed account of the guards' education by pointing out that it will help to illustrate the main theme, the enquiry into the position of justice and injustice in the state; and his young interlocutor expressly agrees to the remark. But even if we believe that, we are bound to feel that, as we go deeper and deeper into the details of the guards' education, we are completely losing sight of what is ostensibly the main theme, the enquiry into justice. Of course in a work like *The Republic*, which has the form of a long, involved conversation, we must inevitably assume that many passages which offend our sense of system and order are determined by the style of the book. Still, the three treatises (on the education of the guards, the education of women, and the education of the ruler) do have such an independent air, and the big question about the nature of justice and the happiness of the just man is so hurriedly answered when we come to it, that we must assume that Plato deliberately chose to reverse the proportion between the two connected enquiries. The discussion of justice is the main theme, since the whole book grows out of it and since it leads to the decisive problem of finding a norm. But the length and philosophical intensity of Plato's discussion of the question of paideia proves that it is really the principal theme: it is indissolubly connected with the method of gaining knowledge of standards, and therefore, in a state which strives to realize the highest standard, naturally becomes the chief concern.

Plato's proposal to educate the guards on a system legally ordained by the state was a revolutionary reform of unimaginable historical consequences. Modern states of every kind have claimed it as their right to dictate the education of all their citizens (particularly since the age of enlightenment and absolutism), and that claim goes back to Plato's *Republic*. In Greece too, of course, especially in democratic Athens, education was largely conditioned by the spirit of the state's constitution; but according to Aristotle there was no education by the state and its officials, anywhere except in Sparta.[53] Aristotle's allusion to this example makes it certain that both he and Plato, in calling for state-supervised education, were thinking of Sparta. In *The Republic* Plato does not discuss how the state educational system is to be organized. He explains that problem later, in *The Laws*.[54] Here he is exclusively concerned with the content of education; in trying to work out the fundamental lines along which it is to run, he is finally led to discuss how we can see and recognize the highest standard. The natural way to educate both body and soul, he decides, is the traditional Greek system of paideia, divided into gymnastics and 'music'; and so he takes that as his basis.[55] In criticizing this, we must recollect his remark elsewhere that every educational reform is harmful to the state. Despite his radical criticism of certain aspects of traditional education, he has a conservative's wish to cling to things that have proved their worth. Of course people usually emphasize his negative criticism, which, without doubt, admirably reveals his new philosophical principle. But much of his charm, and much of his powerful influence on the development of culture, are due to the lively tension between his radical ideas and his conservative respect for a tradition controlled by reason. Therefore, before we listen to his criticisms, we must understand quite definitely that he constructed his new philosophical system of education on the foundations (revised, no doubt, and transformed, but unshaken) of traditional Greek paideia. His decision to do so became the pattern followed by later philosophers, and had wide historical importance. In the first place, it assured the continuity and organic unity of the development of Greek culture, both formally and substantially. It avoided a break with tradition at the moment of tradition's grave danger, when the rationalistic spirit of philosophy turned from the contemplation of nature to reconstructing culture by the light of cold reason. In the second place, Plato's active admiration of old Greek paideia and for the living heritage of the Greek people gave his own philosophy its historic character: for it reappeared and was completed in his constant criticisms of poetry and music, the powers which had hitherto held the mastery over the Greek soul. Therefore his criticisms are not (as some modern scholars think) mere digressions in his philosophy; they are essential parts of it, and their importance is primary.

CRITICISM OF 'MUSICAL' EDUCATION

Plato declares that we must begin with the education of the soul—namely, with 'music'.[56] *Music,* in the comprehensive Greek sense of μουσική, is not simply a matter of sound and rhythm, but also (and, according to the emphasis Plato gives it, principally) of the spoken word, the *logos.* In describing the education of the guards, Plato does not so far reveal his philosophical principle, but with his first sentence he points out the direction in which it lies. All the philosopher's interest in speech lies in discovering whether a given sentence is true or false. Not only the informative value of a word, but its educational value, depends on its truth. This makes it even more of a paradox when Plato insists that education begins, not with the truth, but with 'a lie'.[57] What he means is the myths, the legends told to children; and even he can think of no other way to begin teaching. But here as elsewhere in *The Republic,* when he deliberately allows the use of deceit, he still makes an essential restriction

on its employment—a restriction which is clearly a serious attack
on traditional methods. The stories we are to tell children are
in general not taken to be true; and yet they contain a modicum
of truth. Now, in education as in everything else, the beginning
is extremely important, because it occurs at the easiest and most
sensitive stage of man's development. That is the age when he
is most easily shaped, when he takes on any stamp (*typos*) that
is imposed on him. Nothing therefore could be more inappropriate than the carelessness we show in telling children stories
of all sorts of men. The ideas they get into their heads from
these stories are often absolutely opposite to the convictions they
are required to hold when they grow up. Therefore Plato declares that the tellers of tales and legends should be carefully
controlled, because a child's soul is more permanently shaped [58]
by them than his body by the hands of the trainer.

Plato goes so far as to say that the same *typos* or mould
should be marked on all stories, large and small.[59] The founder
of a state cannot of course write poetry himself, but he must
clearly understand the general moulds in which the poets are to
cast their stories. Plato sometimes speaks of a type, and sometimes, in the plural, of types. He does not mean that poets are
to be confined to a fixed number of prescribed patterns, in a
rigid typology, but that all notions involving moral value which
the poet's work implants in the child's mind must (especially if
they concern God and the nature of human areté) conform to
a general shape and outline. If we read Homer and Hesiod
to-day, we are confronted with many scenes which we should
criticize in the same way if we used our moral judgment. But
usually we think of them simply as meant for our amusement;
and that is how most of his contemporaries thought of them. In
strict fact, no one would say they were ideal for children. Nor
should we print in a book for children the story about Kronos
eating his sons and daughters. At that time, there were no children's books. When quite young, children were given wine to
drink, and real poetry to nourish their souls. But when Plato
starts with the stories told to children, his criticism of poetry is
not narrowly pedagogical: he does not simply want a collection
of bowdlerised legends *ad usum Delphini*. Behind what he says
lies the profound difference of principle between philosophy and

poetry, which dominates his argument about education, and becomes acute at this point.

He was not the first Greek philosopher to attack poetry. There was a long tradition of criticism behind him; and although it is naturally impossible to be precise about his predecessors in this particular critical attitude, it would be a historical error to underestimate the strength of the tradition and its influence on him. He begins by attacking Homer and Hesiod for portraying the gods as too like human beings. That was the first point made by Xenophanes in his satiric attack on epic poetry.[60] Heraclitus had repeated the attack, and up-to-date poetry (personified in Euripides) had sided with the philosophical critics.[61] But did not Aeschylus and Pindar thoroughly sympathize with this criticism of the Homeric Olympus? did they not—although abstaining from negative criticism—put the whole weight of their moral earnestness, the whole energy of their personal conviction, into substituting their own purer conception of godhead for the old bad one? There is one unbroken line of thought from those early critics of Homer's heaven to the Christian fathers, who took their moral and religious arguments against the anthropomorphic Greek gods directly, and often word for word, from the pagan philosophers. The first such critic is really the poet who wrote the *Odyssey*—for he is obviously taking pains to make his gods (particularly Zeus) behave more nobly than they do in the *Iliad*.[62] Plato took over certain detailed arguments directly from Xenophanes, such as the criticism of the battle between the gods and the giants, and of the feuds of one immortal against another.[63] The ultimate source of his complaint is the same as that of his predecessors. Like them, he tests the stories which the old poets tell by the standard of his own morality, he finds them unworthy of what he believes divinity ought to mean, and he judges them false. Xenophanes had already attacked Homer 'because he was always the teacher of all men',[64] and because he knew that he himself possessed a higher truth.

Plato's attack moves along the same lines, but it goes far further. He is not casually criticizing the bad influence of poetry on popular thought; in *The Republic* he is revising the entire system of Greek paideia. Poetry and music had always been the foundations of the education of the mind, and had involved religious and moral education too. Plato thinks this idea of the power of poetry so natural that he never tries to find exact reasons for it. But whenever he speaks of the nature of poetry, he either assumes that quality, or expressly uses it in his definition. It is particularly difficult for us to understand it to-day, not long after modern 'art' has painfully and victoriously torn itself away from the 'moralizing' tendency of the eighteenth and early nineteenth centuries. We feel absolutely certain that the enjoyment of a work of 'art' has nothing to do with morality. Whether that is true or not does not concern us here. The point is that the Greeks did not think it was. Of course we must not think they all shared Plato's views of the poet's educational mission and its lofty implications; but these views were certainly not peculiar to Plato. They were held not only by the representatives of early Greek tradition, but by most of his contemporaries. The Attic orators often cite the laws of the state to establish the exact letter of the ordinance to which they are appealing. And in the same perfectly natural way they often quote the utterances of the poets, when they have no written law to cite and must appeal to the unwritten law.[65] It is to the power of this unwritten law that Pericles proudly refers in his eulogy of Athenian democracy. Although we call it unwritten, it is itself codified in poetry. If rational grounds for an argument are lacking, a line of Homer is always the best substitute, and even philosophers are not ashamed to quote him.[66] The authority of poetry, taken in this way, can only be compared with that of the Bible and the church fathers in a simply religious Christian century.

We cannot understand Plato's criticisms of poetry unless we remember that the Greeks thought it was the epitome of all knowledge and culture, and that the poet's utterance was a standard for all men to admire. Plato now sets out to measure that standard against the higher standard which he knows he possesses through his philosophical knowledge. The idea of superior standards is at the bottom of what Xenophanes had already said: he complained that Homer's and Hesiod's description of the gods was 'unfitting'.[67] But Plato's entire thought from beginning to end was expressly aimed at finding the highest moral standards of conduct. Judged by such a criterion, the old poets' ideals were partly noble, partly contemptible. Looked at from a still higher point of view, Plato's criticism of poetry is bound to take on an even more radical form. If we judge it by the knowledge of true being which philosophy opens up to us, the world which poets describe as though it were real must inevitably melt into a world of appearances alone. Plato, of course, takes different views of poetry, now treating it as a standard for regulating conduct, and now as a means of reaching the knowledge of absolute truth. He does the latter in the tenth book of *The Republic,* during his final discussion of poetry—which he there calls the copy of a copy. But there he is looking at it from the loftiest pinnacle of pure knowledge. Here, in describing the education of the guards, he is on a lower stage—that of mere opinion, *doxa,* on which all 'musical' education moves. Therefore he takes a more tolerant attitude. Here he preserves poetry, as the best method of education, and as an expression of higher truth,[68] but therefore he must relentlessly change or suppress anything in it which is incompatible with the standards of philosophy.

Modern readers have not always understood how Plato's criticism is connected with the peculiar relation between the poet and the people in Greece. Even the 'historical approach' of the nineteenth century was not entirely capable of freeing them from the philosophical and moral preconceptions of their own day, in judging the past. Scholars tried to apologize for Plato, or to prove that his statements were really more harmless than they seemed. They explained them psychologically, as the rebellion of his reason against his poetic imagination, or historically, as due to the increasing degeneration of poetry in his own time. But these explanations, though not entirely devoid of truth, misconceived the fundamental principles of Plato's attitude. They were too bound up with the political view that 'art is free.' The Greeks had often been cited by those who were struggling to liberate art from the guardianship of church and state; and Plato would not fit into that picture very well. So they tried to retouch it, in order to keep him from looking like the Lord Chancellors, the Comstocks, and other bureaucratic censors of art. But he was not trying to explain how a censor's office could be organized with the greatest practical success; and if the tyrant Dionysius had been willing to realize Plato's Republic he would have balked at this point—or else he would have had to obey Plato's stern verdict and burn his own plays first. The real meaning of the reform of poetry by philosophy in *The Republic* is spiritual; and it is political only in so far as a state-building force is contained in the expression of every spiritual ideal. That is what gave Plato the right to lay down that, in his newly constructed society, poetry ought to be written in conformity with the Ideas, or else be weighed and found wanting. He did *not* want to burn all the poetry that did not correspond with his standard; he did not question its aesthetic merits. But it was unfitting for the lean energetic state he was constructing, and suitable only for the rich overfed state.

And so poetry was doomed by the unique value with which the Greeks had invested it. In the same way the state was impugned by its own claim to moral authority, when Plato measured it by Socrates' moral standard—a standard which its mundane character for ever prevented it from attaining. Of course neither poetry nor the state could be abolished as factors in education, but in Plato's Republic they had to surrender their former leadership to philosophy, the knowledge of truth: because philosophy was able to tell them how they must change in order to justify their educational claims. In reality, they refused to change: so that the only visible effect of Plato's criticism was the unbridgeable gulf which thenceforward was to divide the Greek soul. But there was one positive result of Plato's apparently vain yearning to reconcile the aspiration of art towards beauty with its high educational mission. That was the philosophical poetry of his own dialogues. By the criteria set up in *The Republic,* his writing was entirely up to date, and quite supplanted the older type of poetry—even if, in spite of all attempts at imitating it, it remained unique. But why did he not say right out that his own books were the real poetry that should be given to teachers and pupils? Simply because he was pretending to record not his own thoughts, but a dialogue between others. In his old age he abandoned the pretence, and told the degenerate world that his own *Laws* was the type of poetry it needed.[69] Thus, dying poetry once more manifested its supremacy in the work of its greatest accuser.

Most of what Plato says about the education of the guards is concerned with the 'types' of poetry which are to be excluded from it. He has two reasons for doing this. By declaring that all ideas which are morally and religiously unworthy should be eradicated from 'musical' education, he makes us aware of his conviction that all education ought to be governed by a very lofty standard. All his criticism and selection of myths according to their moral and religious value presupposes an inexpugnable principle. It first appears here indirectly, in practical employment; and when Socrates gets his hearers to agree that it should be valid, their agreement is only an emotional one, not intellectual. But even there we feel that the principle needs a deeper philosophical justification. This stage points on to a higher stage of insight, to be reached later, when Plato will reveal the true significance of the norm that he here takes as a dogmatic assumption. His first point is the 'types of theology'— patterns for everything said about the nature and conduct of gods and heroes.[70] The accounts of them previously given by poets are compared to a bad portrait [71] : the poets really mean to tell something like the truth about them but they are simply not able to do it. They speak of feuds and violence between the gods. But Plato is unalterably certain that God is completely good and free from faults. Malevolence and maleficence and all the demoniac qualities which legends attribute to God are really false to his nature. Therefore he cannot be the cause of all the evil in the world. Therefore he is only in a limited way responsible for what happens to man: it is not he, as the poets claim, who puts all the trouble in our lives.[72] The old Greek belief that the gods entrap an erring mortal in guilt so as to destroy him and his house is ungodly and blasphemous. But, if so, then the whole world of Greek tragedy collapses. The sufferings of the innocent are never caused by God; and when a guilty man suffers it is not a disaster but a blessing. Plato illustrates all these arguments by copious examples and quotations from the poets. Therefore he proscribes all legends which show the perfect, unchangeable, and eternal Divinity changing its shape and putting on all sorts of mortal appearances, or which make God responsible for deceit and error. Poetry of that kind is not only to be excluded from education, but to be expelled from the Republic altogether.[73]

For good and sufficient reasons, Plato's sharpest attack on poetry is made at this point. It concerns the poet's conception of God and of divine government. It is one of the most essen-

tial characteristics of early Greek poetry, from Homer to Attic
tragedy, to treat the destiny of man as dependent on the power
of the gods. Our lives cannot be explained by themselves alone,
on purely psychological grounds. They are joined by invisible
threads to the power which controls the universe. Our effort to
achieve our ideal culminates in heroic areté; but above us stands
divine moira, inflexible and inevitable, to which all the will and
the success of mortals are ultimately subjected. The spirit of
Greek poetry is *tragic* because it sees in our mortal destiny the
indissoluble link between every event, even the noblest of human
endeavours, and the rule of heaven. Life became more and more
rationalized in the sixth century, and the Greeks began to feel
that men were responsible for their own actions and sufferings.
But even that change of feeling did not invade the moral sentiment of thinkers like Solon or Theognis, Simonides or Aeschylus,
so far as to destroy the last strong core of belief in moira—the
belief which is still active in fifth-century tragedy, the belief that
'whom the gods wish to destroy, they first make mad'. Misery
deserved and misery undeserved, each is 'moira of the gods':
for God is the cause of everything that happens, be it good or
bad.

The conflict between this religious conception and the ethical
idea that man is fully responsible for the results of his actions
runs through all Greek poetry, although sometimes beneath the
surface. It was bound to come to a head when Socrates preached
his radical doctrine that all human life should be judged by
ethical standards. The world of areté in which Plato constructed
his new order is based on the assumption that each individual
shapes his own moral course through life towards what he has
seen of the Good. This absolutely excludes the rule of moira.
What is called moira by those who think like the old poets is
not the will of heaven. If God were capable of leading men into
evil, despite their efforts to avoid it, we should be living in a
world in which paideia had lost all its meaning. And so, through
Socrates' belief that men 'naturally' will the good and are capable of apprehending it, Plato is led to make a great transformation in the pre-Socratic conception of the world. In early
days, the Greeks thought of God chiefly as the power which is
the cause of everything: their poets and their philosophers were
in harmony on that point. Plato does not shrink from the con-

sequences of abandoning this belief. He admits that the realm of good and of freedom is counterbalanced by the realm of necessity (ananké) which his predecessors had described as 'Nature'. But (as *Timaeus* shows) he holds that the world of nature is merely *matter,* in which the *form,* which is the divine Idea of Good, realizes itself as the higher Nature. Everything which does not harmonize with the Good is an exception, an imperfect manifestation of pure being, and therefore an abnormality. Plato's paideia could not exist in the world as Democritus conceived it. Democritus' world was the world of the old poets, dominated by moira; but it was that world pushed to the scientific extreme. Plato held that the great enterprise of educating men was impossible unless teachers and pupils had a new conception of the universe, as a true cosmos, a world-order in the Platonic sense—unless they were both guided by a single good principle—and unless the whole work of education was in harmony with the law of the universe. In a universe of that kind paideia is truly the work of God, as Socrates calls it in the *Apology,* where he proudly acknowledges he is devoted to it as 'the service of God' and dedicates his life to it.

After laying down the rules for describing the gods, Plato proceeds to an argument, also supported by copious quotations, that poetry tends to prevent courage and self-control from developing. All his criticism of traditional paideia is based on the doctrine that there are four main virtues—piety, courage, self-control, and justice. He does not include justice here, but at the end he explains carefully that we do not yet know what justice really is, and what importance it has for our life and happiness.[74] In this section, too, he treats the old poets rather harshly. By his grisly descriptions of the underworld (he says) Homer would teach the guards to fear death. Of course he does not suggest banning Homer entirely, but he does make excisions in him (ἐξαλείφειν, διαγράφειν), he cuts out entire passages of the epic, and he does not shrink from rewriting the poets on the plan he demonstrates later in *The Laws.*[75] A scholar devoted to the true tradition must think this is the most violent depravation of despotism and arbitrary will: for of course he holds the poet's written words to be inviolable. But that view, although we all hold it almost instinctively, is the product of a culture which has

reached its close, which holds the works of the ancients to be
treasures preserved by fortunate chance, and which can think of
only one reason for altering them—the discovery, from a purer
textual tradition, of what the poet originally wrote. But let us
remember that even when poetry was still alive, there had been
a number of remarkable approaches to Plato's plan of rewriting
the poets, which greatly mitigate the violence of his proposal.
For instance, Solon had already invited his contemporary, the
poet Mimnermus, to rewrite a line he had published. The tender
pessimist had written that after the sixtieth year man should
die. Solon asked him to rewrite it, and say 'after the eightieth
year'.[76] There are many cases in the history of Greek poetry
where a poet, wishing to combat or correct the views of a predecessor about the highest human areté, actually takes over his
predecessor's poem and pours his own new wine into the old
bottles.[77] That is nothing but rewriting one's predecessors. And
the rhapsodes who transmitted Homer's and Hesiod's poetry by
word of mouth must, oftener than we can now prove, have
altered them so as to remake them closer to their hearts' desire.

Of course, this peculiar phenomenon cannot be understood unless we remember that poetry had an authoritative educational
meaning and prestige, which was just as natural to the Greek mind
as it is strange to ours. If a poem had become classical, to alter it
to correspond with a changed set of standards was natural enough,
though rather naïve, and at the same time it was somehow a
sign of honour. All the philosophers borrowed this idea of
epanorthosis and used it in interpreting the poets; and from
them it was taken over by the Christian fathers. 'Give the coin
a new stamp' was the slogan of a tradition which was not yet
dead, but which continued to be active as long as its representatives were aware of their share in it as inheritors and active
transmitters.[78] So those who charge Plato with a rationalist's
lack of understanding for the poets are themselves guilty of
some historical misunderstanding of what poetic tradition really
meant to him and his generation. For example, when he says in
The Laws that the old Spartan poet Tyrtaeus, who praised
courage as the crown of manly virtue and whose works had remained the Bible of Sparta right down to Plato's own day,
should be rewritten with 'justice' substituted for 'courage',[79] it
is easy to see what a grip the poetry of Tyrtaeus must have had

on the soul of a man who felt it was only through rewriting him that he could fulfil his twofold debt to the poet and to the truth.

But Plato does not attack the thing so naïvely as the older thinkers had done when they refashioned some old coin of wisdom. His stern censor's frown is lightened by a gentle irony. He has no quarrel with those who try to keep a place for aesthetic pleasure, and say that Homer's descriptions of Hades make the epic more poetic and more enjoyable for us. Only the more poetic these descriptions are, the less suitable they must be for the ears of boys and men who are to be free: for *they* ought to fear slavery more than death.[80] So also he relentlessly cuts out of Homer all dirges for famous men, and also the inextinguishable laughter of the Olympian gods, which will make readers too free in giving way to their own laughter. Insubordination, voluptuousness, avarice, and bribery also are excised, as tending to corrupt the soul. The same kind of criticism is exercised upon the epic characters.[81] Achilles, who takes ransom for Hector's corpse from Priam and expiatory money from Agamemnon, offends the moral feeling of a later century just as much as his tutor Phoenix, who advises him to take a gift and be reconciled with Agamemnon. Achilles' defiance of the river-god Spercheius, his abuse of Apollo, his insults to the corpse of the noble Hector, and his murder of the prisoners at the pyre of Patroclus deserve no credence. The morality of the Homeric heroes makes it impossible for them to be divine—or else they are wrongly described.[82] From all these points Plato does not conclude that the Homeric epics are rather old-fashioned and crude because they reflect the thought of a primitive age. He sticks to his thesis that poets ought to give examples of the highest areté, whereas Homer's men are often far from exemplary. To explain that fact away by historical arguments would miss the whole point of the thesis, because it would be to deprive poetry of the normative force on which its claim to guide mankind must rest. Poetry should be measured only by an absolute standard. Therefore it must either be expelled or be subjected to the rule of truth, which Plato holds up to it.[83] That 'truth' is the extreme opposite of what we understand by artistic realism, although such realism had indeed existed in the generation before Plato. He thought that to describe the ugliness and weakness of men or apparent faults in God's government of the world was to put down only the appearance of things, not the truth. And yet he never suggests for a moment that poetry ought to be abolished altogether as an educational force and replaced by the abstract knowledge which is philosophy. On the contrary, the bitter energy behind his criticisms arises ultimately from his knowledge that nothing can replace the formative power of the master-pieces of music and poetry which have been admired for hundreds of years. Even although philosophy may be able to find the redeeming knowledge of a supreme standard for all life, Plato would still feel that half its educational task remained unfulfilled until the new truth put on the vesture of a new poetry, like a soul which gives form to a body.

The effect of musical works depends not only on their content, but very largely on their form. Accordingly, Plato's criticism of the accepted musical education is divided into two parts. The first, which we have examined, deals with the myths; the second, with language and style.[84] His discussion of poetic style (λέξις) is particularly interesting because it is the first passage in Greek literature to set out and to treat as established certain fundamental poetic conceptions which we first meet in a larger systematic context in Aristotle's *Poetics*. However, Plato does not give his theory of poetry for the sake of theorising. His theory is a criticism of poetry as *paideia*. Earlier, he had derived all arts from the same root—the pleasure we take in imitation;[85] but when he describes the various types of poetic speech we see that he is using 'imitation' in the limited sense of dramatic or mimic imitation. The types of poetic representation are:

1. pure narrative, like the dithyramb
2. representation through dramatic imitation
3. representation by a mixture of narration and imitation, where the narrator's personality is concealed: as in epic, where narrative and direct speech (a dramatic device) succeed one another.[86]

Naturally, Plato could not assume that his readers would understand this without some introduction. It was a new approach to the question, and he illustrates it in detail with examples from the *Iliad*.

Here again he has to decide which of the foregoing types of

poetry will be permitted to exist in the perfect state. To answer this question, only one datum is needed: which of them is required in the education of the guards? Still driving home the principle that everyone should thoroughly understand his own job and do nothing else, he explains that the qualities of a good guard will not admit the wish and the ability to imitate many other things. Usually even a tragic actor cannot act a comedy properly, and a reciter of poetry is seldom fit to take a part in drama.[87] The guards are to be a professional class, understanding only one kind of work: the defence of the state.[88] The old paideia tried to educate not specialists, but universally capable citizens. Plato does indeed claim its ideal of kalokagathia for his own guards too,[89] but by his unfavourable comparison of the amateur's efforts to act in drama with the highly specialized professional acting of his own day, he transfers the question of allowing dramatic poetry in the guards' education into a test-case between two rival abilities, which it would be wise not to bring into conflict. It is a strange but comprehensible thing that Plato, himself a universal genius, should be so emphatically in favour of such businesslike specialization. It is obviously a sign of the internal conflict which, here as in many other points, forced him to take a rather unnatural solution. From the fact that human nature 'is split up into minute subdivisions' he draws the conclusion that it is better for a soldier to be deliberately one-sided.[90]

Well: that is a harsh and exaggerated way of arguing. And yet, beneath it lies Plato's profound understanding of the truth that imitation (especially continuous imitation) influences the character of the imitator. All imitation means changing one's soul—that is, abandoning its own form for the moment, and assimilating it to the character of the model, whether the model be good or bad.[91] Therefore, Plato lays down that the guards shall have nothing to do with acting, except in representing figures possessed of true areté. He entirely forbids imitating women, slaves, men of low character or conduct, and *banausic* persons (those who have no share in kalokagathia). And a well-behaved young man will not (except in fun) imitate the voices of animals, the rush of rivers, the roar of the sea, the crash of thunder, the howl of the wind, the creaking of wheels.[92] There is one way of talking for gentlemen and another for their opposites. If a candidate for the guards imitates anyone, he should choose to imitate noble characters.[93] He should have only one style—as is proper for a gentleman—and not have a mixed style full of harmonies and rhythms, with constant variations in them.[94] A versatile virtuoso who understands all these variations is to be honoured and welcomed in the Republic, and sprayed with perfume, and crowned with a woollen crown, and then escorted to another city, because there is no place for him in the pure educational state. The Republic admits only a poet who is more severe and less a purveyor of pleasure.[95] Plato goes so far as to depreciate dramatic poetry in favour of narrative, and thinks that even in epic the dramatic element constituted by direct speeches should be limited as far as possible.[96] Of course, his treatment of this point starts from the ardent devotion of young men of his class to dramatic poetry and the theatre. Plato, who was himself a passionate lover of tragedy before he met Socrates, must have seen the injurious effects of this passion in himself and in others. He is clearly speaking with the energy of personal experience.

In Greek culture, poetry and music, 'blest pair of sirens', were inseparable sisters. The same Greek word, *music,* designates them both. So after he has laid down rules for the content and form of poetry, Plato proceeds to what we should call music proper.[97] Lyric poetry is a borderline case, in which music blends with the art of language into a higher unity. But after he has explained his rulings on the content and language of poetry, by illustration drawn chiefly from poetry which is spoken—epic and drama—he has no need to give special treatment to lyric poetry, which is sung. The rules established for the other two types hold good for it.[98] But the various musical modes or 'harmonies' must be discussed without reference to language. There is another non-linguistic element which enters into both the poetry of song and the music of the dance: namely, rhythm. Plato lays down as the supreme law for the combination of the three—*logos, harmonia,* and *rhythmos*—that sound and rhythm must be subordinate to language.[99] Thereby he demonstrates that the rules he had laid down for poetry are valid for music also, and proves that it is possible to treat language, harmony, and rhythm from one single point of view. Language is the direct expression of reason, and reason must be supreme. That, however, was very emphatically not the state of music in Plato's day. On the stage, acting had conquered poetry, and created what Plato calls *theatrocracy* [100]; and so in concerts, poetry was subordinate to music. Such descriptions as we have of musical life in that period agree in censuring music for its gushing emotion and exaggerated thrills.[101] Music was emancipated, and had become a demagogue.

The best justification for Plato's criticism is that it convinced all the musical theorists of antiquity that he was right. But he was not trying to restrain our degenerate world: after all, its nature is to be unrestrained, and he lets it go its own way. It will be cured by its own excesses. When the time comes, there will be a natural swing back to the opposite pole. And we must not forget that Plato was thinking of the healthy, lean, muscular state, which existed 'first', not the fat podgy one which came 'afterwards' and had to have cooks and doctors. He simplifies it by radical methods. Instead of taking a finished process and forcing it backwards, he stops it before it can start. His rules about music show, even more clearly than his restriction of poetry to certain 'patterns', that he is not trying to set out a full-scale theory of art. Instead of overloading his discussion with technical detail, he works like a true legislator, and strikes out a few bold firm lines to fix the limits beyond which men must not go. Therein he shows himself a skilful artist—although, as historians, we may deplore his reticence, since the scant facts we learn from him are the basis of our knowledge of the harmonies of Greek music. It is impossible for us to give a detailed description of Greek 'gymnastic' and 'music', although they were the foundations of paideia in the archaic and classical periods. There is not sufficient evidence. That is why there is no separate treatment of them in this book. Instead, they are discussed wherever they are mentioned in poetry and philosophical thought; and we may console ourselves by reflecting that neither Plato nor we are primarily concerned with technicalities. Plato himself often says that professionals will have to decide technical points of harmony; and thereby hints that Socrates was acquainted with the musical theories of Damon, the great innovator of that era.[102] And so all we learn is that the mixed Lydian and hyper-Lydian 'harmonies' were to be banned, because they were appropriate for dirges and lamentations, which had already

been forbidden in the discussion of poetry. Likewise the soft
Lydian and Ionian modes, suitable for drinking-parties, were to
be censored, because drunkenness and voluptuousness were improper for the guards.[103] Socrates' interlocutor, Plato's young
brother Glaucon (who personifies the interests of the educated
young men of his time), proudly shows off his expert knowledge
of musical theory by observing that this would leave only the
Dorian and Phrygian modes; but Socrates will not attend to
these details. Plato is calling our attention to the fact that Socrates is a really cultured man, who has a flair for the essentials,
but does not care to compete with specialists. A professional
must make a point of exactitude, but for an ordinary man of
culture it would look pedantic and unworthy of a free-born
citizen.[104] Therefore Socrates says broadly that he merely wants
to preserve the kind of music whose tones and accents imitate
those of a brave man facing danger, wounds, and death, or of
a man of sober character and decent behaviour in peace-time.[105]
He condemns both variety in musical modes and multiplicity in
musical instruments. Instruments, he says, are not to be valued
by the number of the modes they produce or the range of their
strings. Flutes, harps, and cymbals are absolutely banned. Only
the lyre and the cithara are kept—because they are suitable for
nothing but simple music; and in the country only the shepherd's
pipe is to be heard.[106] This reminds us of the story that the
Spartan officials prohibited the brilliant Timotheus, the greatest
innovator in modern music, from appearing in Sparta, because
he had abandoned the seven-stringed cithara of Terpander, hal-
lowed by tradition, and played an instrument of more strings
and richer harmonies. The tale need not be true, but it shows
very clearly how the Greeks felt a fundamental alteration in the
structure of music to be a political revolution, because it changed
the spirit of education, on which the state depended.[107] That
feeling was not peculiar to conservative Sparta. It was just as
strong, or stronger, though differently expressed, in democratic
Athens—as we can see from the violent attacks on modern music
throughout contemporary Athenian comedies.

Rhythm, the orderly pattern of movement, is inseparable
from harmony.[108] We have explained elsewhere that the Greek
word originally did not imply movement, but in many passages
meant a fixed position or relation between a number of things.[109]

The Greeks could see a pattern in repose as well as in movement, in the time of dance, song, or speech, particularly in verse. According to the ratio between the long and short units in a rhythm and their connexion with one another, various kinds of order or pattern appear in the movements of the feet or of the voice. Here too, Socrates prefers not to go into technical problems, which are for specialists; but he catches up something from them that excites his educator's imagination: the theory that harmony and rhythm can have an *ethos,* a moral character. It is the basis of his choice of harmonies. Only those modes are allowed which express the ethos of a brave or temperate man.[110] Likewise, from the many possible rhythms, he chooses only those which imitate the same two moral attitudes. And thus the doctrine of ethos becomes the basis of both musical and rhythmic paideia. Plato assumes it, rather than proves it. The fact that he takes it over from Damon, the leading musical theorist of Socrates' time, shows that he is not expounding something specifically Platonic, but describing a musical attitude peculiar to the Greeks, one which from the very earliest times, consciously or unconsciously, had determined the predominant position of music and rhythm in Greek education and culture.

Giving an outline of education in the eighth book of his *Politics,* Aristotle develops the theory of musical ethos still further. He is following in Plato's footsteps. But, as often, he interprets even more clearly than Plato the feelings of the average Greek. He agrees that music and rhythm have an ethical content, to which he attributes their educational value.[111] He holds that the ethos of various modes and tones expresses spiritual feelings of various kinds. Then, after asking whether the qualities which we apprehend by hearing and call *ethos* are found in the realms of other senses—taste, touch, or smell—he concludes that they are not [112]; and who will gainsay him? But he asserts that there is no ethos even in impressions received by sight, for instance, those communicated by the fine arts: with a few exceptions in sculpture and painting, and even then to a very limited extent.[113] According to Aristotle, such paintings and statues are not really expressions of an ethos, but only signs of one, manifested through colours and shapes. For instance, ethos cannot be found in the work of the painter Pauson, but it does appear in that of Polygnotus and certain sculptors.[114] On the other hand, musical works are direct imitations of an ethos. An admirer of Greek sculpture may retort that Aristotle was so unfair in assigning much ethos to music and little to visual art because he had no eye for sculpture and painting; and he may support this by pointing out that he declared the ear to be the spiritual sense-organ, whereas Plato said the eye had the closest kinship with the spirit.[115] But the fact remains that no Greek ever thought of giving painting and sculpture and the enjoyment of visual art a place in paideia, whereas the educational ideals of Greece were always dominated by poetry, music, and rhythm. (What Aristotle says about the value of drawing has nothing to do with the appreciation of fine art, and cannot be taken to contradict this point.[116])

Plato too mentions painting only cursorily. He gives it a word after discussing musical education, and lines it up with weaving, interior decoration, and architecture. Sculpture he ignores.[117] It is not entirely clear how far he ascribes these arts an ethos like music and poetry[118]; but evidently they are brought in more for the sake of completeness—as expressions of a general spirit of propriety and severity or of tasteless extravagance, and as factors contributing to the creation of a certain good or bad social atmosphere.[119] They are not, however, the real pillars of paideia.[120] To realize the educational influence of such an atmosphere was a peculiarly Greek ability, but even in Greece it was only Plato who felt it with such intensity and subtlety. We shall come across it again when we discuss the education of the philosophical ruler.[121] Even when education became more and more intellectualized, the Greeks never forgot that it was a process of growth. The words for *education* and *child-rearing,* which originally were almost identical in meaning, always remained closely akin.[122] The main difference is that *paideia* came more and more to connote intellectual education, and *child-rearing* the pre-rational stage of a child's development. But Plato brought the two ideas together on a higher plane: he did not think of the problems of intellectual education in isolation, as the sophists did, but was the first to recognize that for intellectual education too there are certain preconditions relating to climate and to growth.[123] Despite its lofty intellectualism, Plato's idea of education was that it was like a slow vegetable growth—a notion which was almost wholly absent from the individualistic methods of the sophists. And that takes us to one of the foundations of his political and social policy: the knowledge that man does not live in isolation, but thrives only in an environment which is appropriate to his nature and disposition. There must be a state, a polis, if there is to be any education. The state is necessary, not only as a legislative authority, but as the social atmosphere surrounding the individual. It is not enough for 'musical' culture, the nourishment of the soul, to be pure. The products of every art and craft, everything that has form, must likewise reflect the spirit of nobility and join in the effort to produce decent behaviour and perfection of soul. From his earliest infancy, every citizen must, as it were, drink in healthy air from these surroundings.[124]

But even though arts and crafts help to define the spiritual atmosphere, music remains 'the most important nourishment'.[125] Here as elsewhere, Plato is not by any means fettered by tradition. He sets out to consider whether music is justified in holding the traditional supremacy among the arts which is assigned to it by Greek paideia. He concludes that it is fully justified, because rhythm and harmony 'sink furthest into the depths of the soul and take hold of it most firmly by bringing it nobility and grace'. But it is not only because of the psychological power of music that Plato considers it vital: music trains us, more precisely than any other subject, in recognizing what is right or wrong in a beautiful work and its performance.[126] Anyone who is properly educated in music takes it into his soul while he is still young and his spiritual growth is unconscious; and he develops an unerring accuracy in enjoying what is beautiful and hating what is ugly, so that when conscious reason comes later, he can welcome her like a friend.[127] In his system of education for the guards, Plato intends that after the work of the Muses has moulded them unawares into a certain intellectual pattern, philosophical teaching will later reveal to them in full consciousness the highest knowledge; and so philosophical knowledge presupposes musical education. While he thus foreshadows the existence of a second, higher type of culture, he reveals more clearly the limits of musical education, which had been the only type of superior intellectual training available in earlier Greece. At the same time, he gives it a new importance by showing that it is the indispensable preparation for pure philosophical knowledge, which, without the foundation of musical knowledge, would be left hanging in the air.

Those who know Plato will observe that this is not simply a subtle but more or less irrelevant philosophical epigram. It is a basic educational truth, deduced from Plato's theory of knowledge. According to Plato, even the keenest intellect cannot enter directly into the realm of knowledge of values, which is the climax of all Plato's philosophy. His seventh Letter says that the process of knowledge is the gradual and lifelong assimilation of the soul to the nature of those values which it endeavours to understand. Good cannot be understood, as a formal, logical, external notion, until we have managed to share something of its inward nature. Knowledge of good *grows* within us as Good itself becomes a reality taking shape in our souls.[128] Therefore Plato holds that the best way to sharpen the eye of the mind is to train the character—a process in which the pupil unconsciously has his nature so changed by the highest spiritual forces, poetry, harmony, and rhythm, that he can finally grasp the nature of the supreme principle by being educated into it. In his homely way, Socrates compares the slow process of shaping a man's ethos with elementary lessons in reading and writing.[129] It is only after we have learnt to recognize in all words and combinations the *A*'s, *B*'s, and *C*'s which are the simplest elements of everything written that we can really be said to know how to read. And so we are not 'musically' educated until we have learnt to trace and to cherish as far as possible, wherever we find them imprinted, the 'forms' of self-control and temperance, courage, generosity, nobility, and all qualities akin to them.[130]

CRITICISM OF ATHLETICS AND MEDICINE

Plato has now set up one half of his paideia, 'music', and turns to the other, 'gymnastic' or athletics.[131] He himself is actually more interested in musical education, but physical training is also vitally important for the education of the guards, so that they must practise athletics from their earliest childhood. Now we can see why Plato discussed musical education first. It was not merely (as he originally said) because it must start first.[132] It comes before gymnastics in principle also: an efficient body cannot make the soul good simply because it is fit itself, but conversely a fine soul can help the body to become perfect.[133] On this fact Plato bases the plan of his educational system. He means to give the young a full intellectual and spiritual education, and then leave them to look after the details of physical training themselves. Here, as in 'musical' education, he is content to give a few fundamental outlines,[134] enough to be precise without being long-winded. For centuries the Greeks had held the athlete to be the highest type of physical strength; and since soldiers have to be 'athletes in the greatest contest', it would seem logical that the guards' training should be modelled on the highly developed training of the athlete.[135] Like athletes, for instance, they must not eat and drink to excess. On the other hand, many of the dietetic rules followed by boxers in training are too exaggerated for Plato. He thinks they make the athlete far too sensitive and too dependent on his diet, and certainly the athlete's long hours of sleep are unsuitable for guards who are to be vigilance personified. They ought to be able to stand any change in food, drink, or weather, and their health ought not to be a thing of 'razor-edge delicacy'.[136] So Plato wants a different type of gymnastics, a simplified one (ἁπλῆ γυμναστική) similar to the 'musical' system he had prescribed in education.[137] Just as instrumentation and harmony had been cut down to simplicity,[138] so physical training ought to be freed of extravagance and revert to the strict minimum.[139] He thinks there are two symptoms of *bad* paideia: lawcourts and hospitals. We should certainly not believe it the height of civilization to develop them elaborately, and the educator must aim at making them superfluous in his state.[140]

The parallel between the doctor and the judge is familiar to us from *Gorgias*. Plato's reference to it shows that it is an essential part of his educational theory.[141] It is complemented by the parallel between the legislator and the gymnastic trainer—they deal with the healthy soul and the healthy body, whereas the judge and doctor treat the sick soul and sick body.[142] In *The Republic* the general plan is the same, except that here the parallel to gymnastics is not legislation, as in *Gorgias,* but 'musical' education: for it contains all higher standards of human conduct, and anyone who has mastered it does not need legislation in the juristic sense.[143] The part played by legal justice in society corresponds to that played in matters of physical health by medicine—which Plato calls 'pedagogy attendant upon illness'.[144] But the moment when a man falls ill is too late for a real educational influence to intervene. The development of medicine in Plato's time, and the ever stronger emphasis on diet, which was then beginning to dominate several medical systems, prove that philosophy, with its claim that healthy men deserved care as much as invalids, represented the most advanced views on the question, and indeed had largely helped to advance them.[145] The education of the guards gives Plato an opportunity to devote much attention to the preservation of health: since gymnastics, which are necessary for that purpose, take up a good deal of time in the life of such professional soldiers. Theirs is, in fact, the ideal case. Everyone who has read the medical writing of the Greeks knows how medicine varied according to the social rank of the patient and the type of work which he did. Quite often the directions physicians give are only meant for the rich man, who has time and money enough to live only for his health, or, it may be, his illness.[146] That kind of life will not fit into Plato's world, where everyone has his own work to do. How could a sick carpenter spend weeks on a cure that kept him from practising his trade? He has only one choice: work or die.[147] But even a well-to-do man, if he is ill, cannot follow the occupation recommended in Phocylides' realistic maxim: 'Get a livelihood, and then practise virtue'.[148] What virtue could he practise at home or in public life, if he were always looking after his health to an immoderate degree, with a hypochondriac care far above the ordinary limits of gymnastics? And above all he would be unable to practise the culture of the spirit, learning and meditating—if he did, he would surely blame philosophy for his headaches and dizziness.[149] Actually, there is a natural affinity between Platonic philosophy and a body which has been made thoroughly healthy by strict training. Nothing could be more alien to it than the morbid streak many readers have found in it. In *Phaedo*, Plato preaches the soul's separation from the world of the senses, so that it can collect itself to contemplate pure abstract truth; but the spirit of gymnastic paideia described in *The Republic* is the necessary complement to that preaching. We cannot see the real Plato unless we look at both these pictures together.

Plato has no intention of depreciating the doctor's art, or discarding it altogether. But of course he looks at the doctor in a different way when speaking of his position in the contemporary world and of the part he is to play in the ideal state. In the primitive but healthy Republic created by his magical imagination, he models the function of medicine not on the sophisticated medical science of the fourth century, but on the healers of the old heroic age described in Homer. The real statesman of health, he thinks, is the god Asclepius himself.[150] It was he who found out how to treat healthy men who had suffered some local and temporary injury, so as to relieve it. But the Homeric poems do not show him and his sons treating thoroughly corrupt and infected bodies. When Eurypylus is seriously wounded, the servant-girl looking after him brews him a mixed drink which would kill even a healthy man nowadays. Menelaus' wound from the poisoned arrow shot by Pandarus is sucked clean by Machaon, son of Asclepius, and then poulticed. This shows that in the heroic age doctors knew the truth represented by Hippocratic medicine: a healthy nature recovers by itself, if it is assisted by the right remedies. But bodies which are ill through and through should be allowed to die, just as the judge executes men whose souls are hopelessly infected by vice and crime.[151] It is thoroughly perverse to make gymnastics into a remedy for chronic illness, instead of handing over the education of healthy men more and more to medicine. Herodicus is the chief culprit mentioned in this connexion—he had made a great reputation by mixing gymnastics and medicine in what Plato held to be the wrong way. All he did was to torture himself and others to death. By carefully and deliberately putting obstacles in death's way, he was an unconscionable time a-dying, and finished by attaining a great age.[152] In the ideal state the guards will have no need for jurymen and law-courts, thanks to their 'musical' education; and similarly their gymnastic training will make it unnecessary for them to consult doctors.

Why do the guards have to do all the exercises and undergo all the exertions prescribed by gymnastics? Not to gain physical strength, but to develop courage.[153] So it is wrong to believe (as Plato himself seemed to assume at first) that gymnastics is to train only the body and 'music' the soul.[154] Both are meant first and foremost to mould the soul. But they do it in different ways, and the effect would be lopsided if one were put before the other. A purely gymnastic training would make a man too hard and violent, and too much music would make him soft and tame.[155] If he were to let his soul be constantly lapped in soft Lydian airs, he would first of all be tempered, as steel is tempered and made usable. And then he would dissolve away altogether till his soul had no sinews left.[156] On the other hand, if he spent all his time training hard and eating heavily without cultivating any musical and intellectual interests, he would first of all be filled with pride and energy, thanks to his physical strength, and grow more and more courageous. But even if he were naturally apt for learning, his mind would become deaf and blind if it were never fed on learning and study. He would become a misologist—a brain-distruster, hating the Muses. He would not be able to persuade by argument, but settle everything by force and brutality, like a beast.[157] That is why God gave us gymnastics and music together, the inseparable unity of paideia. They are not separable as physical training and intellectual education. They are forces which mould the spirited and the rational sides of human nature. Anyone who can blend them in the proper harmony will be a greater darling of the Muses than the legendary hero who first put together all the strings of the lyre.[158] Plato could not have put the essence of his doctrine better than in that simile, with which he closes his description of the guards' education.[159] It is indeed a highly refined instrument, with numerous strings: dumb for those who cannot play it, and intolerably monotonous for those who play only one string. But to sound several strings at once, and produce not shrieking dissonance but a sweet concord, is the difficult art of true paideia.

THE POSITION OF EDUCATION IN THE PERFECTLY JUST STATE

If the Republic is to be preserved, there must always be someone in it who has the art of guiding it by maintaining this balanced paideia [160]—or, as Plato says when he takes up this thought later and elaborates it, there must always be an element in the state in which the founder's spirit lives actively on.[161] This requirement involves a new and greater problem: the education of the educator. It is solved by the development of the philosophical ruler. Plato did not begin this subject immediately after discussing the guards' education, as he might have done in a systematic treatise. He felt it was better to separate the two internally connected forms of paideia by a long interlude which both excites our interest and increases the importance of the subject. But he never for a moment deceives the reader about the direction in which his argument is moving: for he immediately asks which of the guards is to rule the state.[162] He does not need to prove that the ruler can only belong to the guards, since they represent the highest military and peaceful virtues in the state. He holds that no one should exercise the highest power without possessing the best education. But education does not finish as soon as a young man is trained to be a guard. Those who are to become rulers are specially selected —on a principle of which at first we hear only that it is applied while they are undergoing the guards' training.[163] The young aspirants are constantly watched and tested to see which of them possess the essential qualities of leadership—practical wisdom, talent, and care for the common weal. By temptation of all kinds, their incorruptibility and self-control are put to the proof, and only those who succeed in passing through tests lasting not years but decades are accepted as guards in the true sense. The others, by comparison, are called helpers or auxiliaries.[164]

This system of character-testing implies that, for all Plato's lofty view of the influence of education, he does not believe that it will produce mathematically equal results. He takes into account the variations in individual nature. From a political point of view, also, the principle of rigorous and deliberate selection is highly important for the structure of his Republic, since the preservation of the class-system depends upon it. The class-system assumes a certain regular recurrence of inherited qualities—those which are desirable for the maintenance of each of the three classes. But Plato believes it is always possible for members of the upper classes to degenerate and for members of the third class to produce highly talented children. By insisting on careful selection and elimination, he makes it easy for these elements to rise or fall to their proper place.[165] A ruler needs a particularly strong character. Doubtless this is true of any state, but it is truest in Plato's 'best state'. There are absolutely no constitutional guarantees against the misuse of that

unparalleled, almost unlimited power which he puts in the hands
of its rulers. The only real guarantee to ensure that they will
be the guardians, not the masters, of the Republic—that they
will not degenerate from watchdogs into wolves tearing their
own sheep—is their good education.[166] It is clear, from the interpretation we have given, that it would be wrong to criticize
the 'lack of guarantees' in the Republic exclusively from the
standpoint of constitutional law and political experience, and to
blame Plato for naïvely imagining that a state could be ruled
without the complicated apparatus of a modern constitution. It
seems perfectly clear that Plato had no intention of treating
the problem seriously—because he was not interested in the
state as a technical or psychological problem, but was regarding it merely as a frame and a background for education. We
may reproach him for this, accusing him of deifying education;
but the fact remains that his real problem was paideia. Paideia
was for him the solution of all insoluble questions. It is not for
any political reason that he crowds the greatest possible power
into the hands of those who dislike it most. His rulers are the
noblest products of education, and their duty is to be the noblest
educators.

Plato leaves it an open question whether the education of
the guards, which is primarily aimed at creating as fine an
average type as possible, is sufficient to achieve that aim.[167] But
even if this leaves the specific content of the ruler's education
indefinite, he goes on to describe the ruler's life in such a way
as to show that the new state is dominated by the educational
ideal. Meanwhile, political problems are dismissed with notable
curtness. The external life of the ruler is to be one of the
greatest frugality, poverty, and severity. He has no private
existence at all—not even a home of his own or meals at home.
He is an entirely public man. His bare necessities in food and
clothing are supplied by the community, but he can have no
money and no private property.[168] It is not the duty of a real
state to make its ruling class as happy as possible, although it
may be happiest in its divine independence of earthly goods.
The ruling class is meant to serve the happiness of the whole
community, and the happiness of the community can be ensured
only if everyone does his own work and nothing else. For, according to Plato, the life of every individual takes its meaning,

its justification, and its limitations from the function he performs as a member of the social whole, which closely resembles
a living organism. The supreme good which it must realize is
the unity of the whole.[169] But note this: although the rights of
the individual are curtailed, they are not supplanted by those
of the state. The state is not expected to become as rich and
powerful as possible. The things to which it aspires are not
power and economic prosperity and the limitless accumulation
of wealth. Its endeavours to acquire power and riches are limited. These are external goods, and the state wants to obtain
no more of them than will help to maintain the desired social
unity.[170]

Plato does not think this is an impossible ideal. He believes
it would be simple to carry his plan through, if the citizens
would only maintain one thing: that one thing being good education, on which the state depends.[171] If it is faithfully maintained, it will stimulate superior characters in the community,
and they will eagerly grasp at it, and so excel their predecessors.[172] Plato's conception of the social organism does not depend, according to his ideal, on individual preference or arbitrary will. He thinks it is the absolute norm, derived from
human nature, from the nature of man as a social and moral
being. Therefore the system must be *static.* There is no progress in it, no development. Any departure from its standards is
degeneration and decay. The essence of an ideal state is that
anything different from it is bound to be worse. If anything is
perfect, we cannot wish to improve it—only to preserve it. But
it can only be preserved by the methods through which it was
created. Therefore the one essential thing is that education
should not be changed.[173] A state like this can suffer nothing
much from external changes, but a change in the spirit of its
'music' would alter the character of its laws.[174] Therefore the
guards are to build the citadel of the state on the highest spot—
that is, on 'musical' education.[175] If it degenerates, it will auto-
matically and almost negligently spread unlawful customs and
conduct throughout society. On the other hand, it is through it
that right customs can be set up again—respect for age, piety
towards parents, proper hairdressing, clothing, footwear, and
posture.[176] Plato makes fun of elaborately detailed legal codes.
He thinks they are a simple-minded exaggeration of the power

of language, written or spoken. The only way to reach the legislator's ideal is by education; and if education is really effective, laws are not needed. Of course, Plato often describes the
rules he gives for setting up his Republic as 'laws', but all his
laws are concerned solely with the establishment of education.
It is education which is to do away with the state of constant
law-making and law-changing (as was the rule in Athens in
Plato's day) and render superfluous all special ordinances concerning the police, markets, harbours, insult and injury, as well
as civil lawsuits and the constitution of juries.[177] Politicians carry
on a hopeless battle with the hydra. They keep trying to cure
symptoms, instead of striking at the root of the trouble with
the natural cure, which is right education.

Greek and Roman admirers of the Spartan *eunomia* describe
it too as a state educational system which made specialized legislation unnecessary, because of the citizens' rigid observance
of the unwritten law dominating their whole lives. We have
pointed out elsewhere that this conception of Sparta was really
created in the fourth century under the influence of revolutionary political ideas like Plato's paideia [178]; but that does not
necessarily mean that Plato himself, in planning his educational
state, borrowed nothing from Sparta's example. Contempt for
the mechanism of modern administration and legislation, abolition of incessant lawmaking in favour of the power of morality
and an official educational system to dominate the whole of life,
introduction of a public mess-table instead of private meals for
all the guards, state supervision of music, and the respect for
music as the citadel of the state—all these are Spartan traits.
But it was only a philosopher who had grown up in opposition
during the decay of Athenian democracy, who could describe
Sparta as a political system in which extreme individualism was
happily avoided. The pride of Athens was its constitutional
state, with its respect for the written law and its principle of
legal regulation of every detail, its maintenance of equal rights
for every citizen, high or low, and its intricate administrative
machinery. Of course Plato's depreciation of these principles is
an exaggeration which can be understood only if we recall the
spiritual danger of Athens in his day. He had come to the tragic
conclusion that laws and constitutions are mere forms, which
have no value unless there is a strong moral core in the nation

so that they can be protected and respected. Conservatives even believed that what actually held democracy together was something entirely different from what democratic ideology praised as its support. They said it was not really the citizens' new-won and jealously guarded freedom of criticism, but the suprapersonal power of custom and tradition—which is often exceptionally strong in a democracy, which even the citizens themselves do not realize, and which the nationals of different types of states seldom appreciate. The continuous life of this unwritten law had been the strength of Athenian democracy in its heroic age; its collapse transformed liberty into lawlessness, despite all the laws which could be written. Plato believed that a severe education on the pattern set by Lycurgus was the only way to restore—not what so many of his fellow-nobles yearned for, the old aristocracy of birth, but the old code of custom which should bind the state together once more. We should be misunderstanding the background of emotion and of contemporary politics which lies behind Plato's educational proposals, if we expected him to create an evenly balanced blend of all the elements in the life of the state. It is with passionate moral conviction that he puts, in the centre and focus of his discussion of the state, the one great truth which he had learnt through the agonies of his time and the sufferings of its greatest man. The outward aspect of Plato's education may be very un-Athenian, but the deliberate 'Spartan ethic' which animates it was impossible anywhere else than in Athens. Its inmost spiritual essence is absolutely un-Spartan. It is the last effort of the Athenian democracy's educational will, which now, in the last stage of its development, turns to make head against its own collapse.

Now, finally, let us ask what the education of the guards has to do with justice. After all, we did set out to discover what justice is. Plato has already stated that a thorough investigation of the problem of education would be useful in discovering the nature of justice.[179] This promise is fulfilled. To begin with, we were doubtful whether the long enquiry into the education of the guards was really a way of discovering justice, or perhaps Plato thought it worth making for its own sake [180]; and now we have found that the whole structure of the state is based on right education—or, more precisely, is identical with right education.[181] Now, if this is correct, we have not only found the aim of true education, but have realized true justice: all we have left to do is to understand more fully what justice means.

For this purpose, Plato goes back to the earlier motive he gave for constructing the state: he said he described it in order that, when it was finished, we could recognize justice in it.[182] There was never any real doubt that he conceived justice as a quality dwelling within the human soul; but still he thought it was easier to use the analogy of the state to make its nature and effects in the soul quite clear. And now we see that it was his *organic conception* of the state which induced him to make that comparison. He believes that justice in the state is the principle by which every member in the social body fulfils its proper function as perfectly as possible.[183] The rulers, the guards, and the working class—all have their fixed and definite duties, and if every one of the three classes does its job as well as it can, the state which is made by the collaboration of the three will be the best conceivable state. Each of them is characterized by a special virtue: the ruler is to be wise,[184] the soldier brave.[185] The third virtue, prudent self-control, is not a virtue in the same sense—it is not a quality peculiar to the third class, but it is specially important for it to have. It is concord between the three classes, based on the voluntary subordination of that which is by nature worse to that which is by nature or training better. It is to penetrate all three classes, but its principal demands are made on the class which is expected to be loyally obedient.[186] Thus each of the four cardinal virtues of the old city-state code has found its right place in the state, and its appropriate social class—all except justice, which has no special position, no class left to attach itself to. And so the intuitive solution of the problem lies before our eyes. Justice is the completeness with which every class in the state expresses its peculiar virtue in it and fulfils its specific function.[187]

But we must recall that this does not really interpret justice in the exact sense. It is only its enlarged image, projected on the social structure: so we must look for its nature and origin in the soul of man.[188] There are the same parts in the soul as in the state. The wisdom of the rulers corresponds to reason in the soul, the bravery of the guards to the spirited element in the soul, and the self-control of the third class (which always seeks out profit and pleasure) corresponds to the libidinous part of the soul when it subordinates itself to the highest insight of reason.[189] Plato does hint that this way of proving the theory of the parts of the soul is rather sketchy, but he says he does not want to use too subtle a method to solve the problem, one which would lead too far away from the main theme.[190] How could the psychological distinctions between the various classes in the state have arisen, if they had not already existed as distinct or distinguishable elements in the soul?[191] Just as one part of the body can move while another remains still, so in our souls the lustful element desires, the rational element sets limits to the desire, and the spirited element beats down the desire and allies itself to reason.[192] The soul contains forces which restrain as well as forces which urge and strive: it is their interplay that creates the harmonious completeness of the personality. It is impossible, however, to create this unity, unless each part of the soul 'does its work'. Reason should rule, and the spirited element should obey and support it.[193] Their concord is the product of the right mixture of 'music' and gymnastics.[194] This kind of culture braces the intellect and feeds it with noble thoughts and knowledge, while it leaves the spirit free, under constant control, and tames it by harmony and rhythm. If they are both educated in this way, if each learns its part correctly, they should both together control the desires. Desires form the greater part of the soul, and they are naturally insatiable. They can never be induced to do their work by being satisfied. If satisfied, they will become big and strong, take over power, and upset their owner's entire life.[195]

So justice is not the organic political system which ordains that the cobbler shall make shoes and the tailor sew clothes.[196] It is the quality of the soul through which every one of its parts does its work, and through which the individual is able to control himself and unite the conflicting forces which make up his soul.[197] We might use the analogy of the organic state, and speak of the organic cosmos of the soul. If we do, we have reached the very centre of Plato's thinking about state and education. The parallel between doctor and statesman which was so strongly emphasized in *Gorgias* now recurs, at this decisive point.[198] Justice is the health of the soul, if we take health to mean moral perfection.[199] It does not lie in separate actions, but in the ἕξις, the permanent state of having a *good will*.[200] Just as health is the greatest physical good, justice is the greatest good of the soul. So the question whether it is healthy and advantageous for the soul is exposed in its full absurdity [201]: for justice is the health of the soul, and departure from its standard is illness and degeneration.[202] Life without it is not worth living— for even a life without physical health is intolerable.[203] The comparison between the medical and the political problem shows that justice is an inner quality, independent of all changes in external power. It is a realm of true freedom. But this does not exhaust its significance. Plato goes on to the further conclusion that there is only one form of justice, but many forms of its degeneration; and so once more he reminds us of medicine. There is one 'natural' state based on justice, and one just soul corresponding to it; but there is a multitude of degenerate forms of state and soul.[204] Thus immediately the task of education is widened, to take in a huge new territory. Until now it seemed to be confined to moulding the normal and 'natural' type of state and soul. Now we see that it must include the unnatural types of state and the degenerate forms of individual culture corresponding to them.[205] These two parts are the physiology and pathology of virtue. One essential purpose of Plato's *Republic* is to connect them, and his method can be fully understood and justified only by bringing in medical science. But for the time being Socrates does not go further into this fascinating pathological eidology.[206] He turns to the question of the education of women and their position in his state. And so begins a new act in the great philosophical drama of paideia.

THE EDUCATION OF WOMEN AND CHILDREN

This excursus on the community of wives and children has excited more sensational interest, both in Plato's own day and afterwards, than any other episode in *The Republic*. Socrates himself is reluctant to expound his paradoxical proposals, for he is afraid of the storm of anger it will call forth.[207] But he believes it is the logical sequel of what he has said about the guards' paideia.[208] After being brought up in utter devotion to the service of the community, with no home, no property, and no private life, how could a guard be the head of a family of his own? If every accumulation of private wealth is to be condemned because it fosters economic selfishness in individual families, and thereby prevents the realization of complete unity among the citizens, Plato can scarcely avoid condemning the family too as a legal and ethical institution. So he abolishes it.

This extreme logical deduction shows more clearly than anything else how utopian *The Republic* is. But Plato's political idealism, with an almost mystical adoration for social unity, rejects every compromise. Of course he is still bound to explain, as he promised, how this moral and social revolution can be possible.[209] The only proof that it is desirable is that it is necessary, in order to establish the absolute unity of the social group by restricting the individual's rights. Actually the endeavour to make the individual wholly and permanently a servant of the state [210] is bound to produce conflicts with the life of the family. In Sparta, where men of the ruling class spent almost their whole lives in fulfilling their military and civic duties, the family played a very subordinate role, and the morals of the women (in what was otherwise a very puritanical state) were ill reputed throughout Greece. It is mainly through Aristotle that we know about these criticisms of Spartan wives.[211] But they go back beyond his day: for all Greece had been shocked by the panic of the heroic women of Sparta during the Theban invasion, after the disaster of Leuctra.[212] The resemblance of Plato's Republic to Sparta, because of the absence of family life in the ruling class, is even more pointed by Plato's borrowing of the Spartan custom of communal meals for the men.[213] Probably that was why he felt he ought to find a nonSpartan solution for the problem of the position of women and their relation to husbands and children. He very significantly restricts the community of women and children to the guards, who are immediately in the service of the state, and does not extend it to the mass of the working population. The Church later solved this same problem by directing priests, its own ruling class, to remain unmarried and childless throughout their lives. Plato, who was not married himself, did not adopt that solution—both because he did not, like the Church, believe that marriage was morally worse than celibacy, and because the ruling minority in his state was physically and spiritually the cream of the crop, so that its offspring were necessary to produce a new élite. The prohibition of private property (including the possession of a wife), blended with the principle of racial selection, leads to the doctrine that the guards must have wives and children in common.

Plato is first concerned with the *education* of the women who are to be the wives of the guards. Actually, they are to be not only wives, but guards themselves.[214] He holds that the women of the guards are capable of making a creative contribution to building up the community, but he does not expect, as we should do, that they will make their contribution through family life. He is opposed to the prevailing view that they are meant by nature only to bear children, bring them up, and look after the household. He admits that they are generally less strong than men, but thinks that does not keep them from taking their share in the guards' duties.[215] Now, if they are to do the same work as men, they should have the same upbringing (τροφή) and education (παιδεία). Therefore the women of the ruling class must be schooled in 'music' and gymnastics just like the men, and also trained for war.[216]

Plato is quite clear about the effects of this law. It is a revolutionary innovation, which will provoke hearty laughter. Women will do exercises naked in the palaestra along with men —and not only young women, but old wrinkled ones, just as elderly men often take regular exercise in the gymnasium. But Plato does not think morality will be endangered by his regulations. And whatever we may think of the proposal, the very fact that it could be made shows what a revolutionary change had taken place in the relation of the sexes since the Periclean age, when Herodotus, telling the tale of Gyges and Candaules, wrote that a woman stripped off her modesty together with her clothes.[217] Plato observes that the barbarians thought nakedness was disgraceful even for men; and the moral feeling of the Greeks of Asia Minor, who were influenced by them, was not far different.[218] Greek art seldom depicted women naked in the archaic period, nor even in the fifth century. But under the influence of athletic training and its ideal of physical areté, which radically changed the long-established feeling for moral decency and seemliness, sculpture had for many years depicted the naked bodies of male athletes.[219] This then marks the profoundest dif-

ference between Greek and oriental art. The ideal of paideia
gave direction and ethos to Greek art by making it admire athletics. So now Plato's new rule that women shall strip for gymnastics is symbolic of the changing views of the fourth century,
when artists turned to portraying women in the nude.[220] That
must have been generally felt as a revolutionary innovation in
art—not less revolutionary than Plato's recommendation of
athletics for women. He knew quite well that it would arouse
opposition; but in reply he asked how long it was since men
had begun to exercise naked, and had stirred up thereby the
same tempest of scorn and anger. According to the tradition he
is following, it started in Crete, was imported from there to
Sparta, and finally spread to all Greek cities.[221] As we read in
Thucydides (in his archaeological excursus) the last relic of opposition to complete nakedness at the Olympic games, namely,
the loincloth, had been given up not long before his time, and
was worn only by the Asiatic nations.[222] But in proposing naked
exercise for women, Plato was perhaps thinking of Sparta, for
there are several traditions of Spartan girls stripping for
exercise.

But by admitting women to men's vocation, is Plato not contradicting his own principle that justice in an organic state
means that everyone performs his own natural function? The
point of it is that those who are differently equipped by nature
should do different jobs.[223] Plato, however, believes that this
application of his principle is a dialectical error. It takes the
concept of *different equipment* in the absolute sense, instead of
concentrating on the particular kind of activity in relation to
which we are similarly or differently equipped. A man who is
not equipped to be a cobbler is not to do the same work as a
man who is. But if one man is bald and another has a fine head
of hair, they might both (despite that particular difference in
their equipment) be qualified to become cobblers. No doubt the
natural difference between men and women influences their lives
more profoundly than that, but still they may both be equally
well equipped for the same vocation.[224] Man's superiority means
that he is better than woman in every sphere, even in those
which are declared to be woman's province by those who maintain she is a domestic creature—cookery, baking, and weaving;
but there is no one work which man or woman alone can do

and which is impossible for the other sex.[225] Women are very
successful in medicine and music: why not in athletics too, or in
the handling of weapons?[226] Therefore training of women in
'music' and gymnastics is not contrary to nature. The existing
situation is against nature, for it makes it impossible for woman
to develop her natural gifts.[227] This is the logical result of a
process which began in the age of Pericles and Euripides. Of
course in early Athens women were neither physically nor mentally trained. They were confined to the house. Since then, they
had evidently been taking more and more part in the intellectual life of the day, and particularly in its educational interests. The increasing number of great female characters in
tragedy shows that woman had been discovered to be a human
being; and her right to education was publicly discussed.[228] Plato
adds some Spartan touches to his plan for women's education.
But if we subtract from it the regulations which are aimed at
building them into Amazons, what remains is essentially the
modern programme for the education of women. Plato makes
the point that it is not only possible but highly desirable to
realize the programme: it strengthens the unity of the state by
making the education of men and women entirely homogeneous,
and gives those who are to be rulers that superiority over the
governed which is demanded by their position.

BREEDING AND EDUCATION OF THE ÉLITE

Plato defines the best state as the rule of the best. This, he
thinks, is a principle which is in harmony with nature and is
therefore absolutely inevitable in the state of divine perfection.
The rule of the best men and women is literally 'aristocracy'[228a];
but the relation of this type of aristocracy to constitutions which
actually exist is not investigated, meanwhile. What he means by
'the best' he does not fully define until he has expounded in detail the principle of selection—namely, the education given to
the inner circle of guards who are destined to rule the Republic.
But the description of woman's education has taken us to the
point where, after finishing their musical and athletic training,
they are ready to fulfil their function as mothers of the next
generation. So Plato now introduces his regulations for the relation between men and women and for the bringing up of chil-

dren. This is their proper place in logical sequence; but also, it
is the most natural thing to make the discussion of women's
education lead up to the one indispensable prerequisite for the
guards' education. This prerequisite is the racial selection of
the class that is destined to rule the state.[229] Plato's 'aristocracy'
is not a nobility of birth, if that implies that anyone born into
it has a right to an important position in the governing caste.
Incapable or unworthy men and women are to be degraded (see
p. 235), while capable and worthy ones are to be promoted,
from time to time, into the ruling class. Still, Plato holds that
birth does play an important part in forming the élite of his
Republic. He is convinced that in general the children of the
rulers will be as distinguished as their parents—that is, if the
parents are carefully chosen and mated. If the rule of the best
men and women is to be founded on the best education, the best
education in its turn demands the best natural abilities. The age
of Plato was familiar with that principle, chiefly from the educational theories of the sophists.[230] But the sophists simply took
physis as they found it, without thinking of producing it by deliberate policy. Breeding for quality was really a relic of the
aristocratic code of early Greece. Any nobleman who was thoroughly convinced that φυά, hereditary type, was the root of all
true virtue, was bound to be anxious to preserve the precious
inheritance of blood. Theognis had addressed protreptic poems
to the impoverished nobles of his city who were endeavouring
to retrieve their shattered fortunes by marrying the daughters
of rich commoners; he had prophesied that the mixture of
breeds would be fatal to the preservation of the old nobility of
blood. He is the first who is known to have laid down that selective marriage (as in animal breeding) is necessary to maintain
the noblest human families.[231] Plato takes over this principle in
the intellectualized form that the best children can be produced
only by the best parents [232]; and he declares it necessary to preserve the élite, once established, by a special system of breeding
officially controlled. Old Theognis certainly never dreamed that
the thing could be carried so far as that. The intermediate
stage between his aristocratic theory and Plato's is the Spartan
paideia, which paid particular attention to producing healthy
children in the ruling caste of Spartiates. At the time Plato was
growing up, the Athenian aristocracy had been very interested

in the theory behind Spartan education. Xenophon says it was
specifically a Spartan rule to begin the severe Spartan discipline
with the conception and birth of the baby.[233] Critias' prose essay
eulogizing Sparta as a model state started off with the same
principle. It maintained that both parents should do gymnastic
exercises and take strengthening food before conception and
pregnancy began.[234] That essay leads us straight to Plato.
Critias was his uncle; he must have heard these ideas discussed
and read the book itself when he was quite young. There are
two or three other points in *The Republic* which look as though
they came from it. The principle (revived in the Renaissance by
aristocratic humanists like Ulrich von Hutten) that aristocracy
of birth must vindicate its privileges by true *virtus* was probably
held by the aristocratic opposition party in democratic Athens:
for how else could they have justified their existence? Plato himself thought that no one could claim a leading position in the
state unless he had ability far above the average of mankind.
But he did not expect to take an aristocracy of blood and train
it for virtue; he wanted to choose those who represented the
highest areté, and with them to create a new élite.

This view led Plato, who had already prohibited the guards
to have a private life and property of their own, to conclude
that they ought to have no marriage either—in the sense of a
permanent union between man and wife. He replaced it with
temporary connexions, as an impersonal method of breeding the
best children. None of his regulations shows more bluntly, and
for us more shockingly, how he demanded that his ruling class
should surrender all personal interests to those of the state.
This destroys the last relic of individuality, the right which no
other state had ever ventured to challenge, the individual's
right to his own body. For when Plato in another context describes the propertyless state of the guards by saying they literally own nothing but their bodies, he is really exaggerating,
considering his own views on the relation of husband and wife.
He can only have meant that they 'possessed' their bodies, not
that they could use them freely. Of course he does say that
young men and girls will fall in love through proximity,[235] which
means that they can have some personal emotions. But still they
are forbidden to yield to such feelings, and to enter any union
that is not sanctioned by the government.[236] Plato is deliberately

vague about the matter, but it is perfectly clear that this does not mean simply obtaining formal permission from the officials. It means that the officials will have personal knowledge of those who apply to get married, and then make the choice they believe to be 'most useful'. That is Plato's definition of what he calls 'holy marriage'.[237] He is evidently trying to use religious sanctity to cast a halo around the temporary sexual unions which he substitutes for permanent marriage and life together. For the same reason he suggests the institution of special festivals at which the couples will be united with the singing of hymns and the offering of sacrifices.[238] But no personal affection or independent will is allowed to influence the selection of the partners. He even permits his officials to use tricks to make sure that the best men marry the best girls and the worst the worst, for the benefit of the community.[239] The number of unions to be consummated depends on the number of citizens the state needs.[240] Since (according to Plato) the perfect state is small and easily supervised rather than a large confused mass, and since the size of the population must therefore be restricted, that rule will tend not to increase but to diminish the number of births taking place in it. Plato's policy of breeding is meant not to increase the quantity of the citizens but to improve their quality.

For the same reason, he ordains definite ages for parenthood. Women are to bear children, for the state, only between the ages of 20 and 40, and men to beget children only from 30 to 55.[241] These are the years of the prime of life (ἀκμή). Young folk and the old are to have no right to produce children.[241a] These eugenic principles are borrowed from Greek medical theory: for Greek physicians had made special studies of the right ages for parenthood. In the Republic, the government will make it easy for the best men and women to marry, hard for the inferior ones.[242] Mothers are entirely relieved of the care of babies. Nurseries are to be set up in a special quarter of the city, where the healthy babies can be brought up. Mothers are admitted in order to suckle them, but none of them knows her own baby: the love that each of them feels for her own child ought to be shared with them all.[243] The Greeks, as Plato well knew, had very strong instincts of family affection. It was a powerful support for the structure of society, and Plato desired to use it. He simply wanted to keep it from being exclusive, to extend the feeling of solidarity which it fosters among the members of one family to the whole citizen body, to knit the whole state into a single family, in which all the grown-up men and women could feel themselves to be the parents and teachers of all the children, and the children would treat them all with the respect due to parents.[244] Plato's supreme aim is to make the joys and sorrows of every citizen the joys and sorrows of all.[245] His axiom is that the best state is the state where most citizens think 'mine' means not something individual and separate, but something common to all—because such a state is the most unified.[246] He illustrates it clearly by comparing it to a body, all of which feels the pain when one finger is hurt. The comparison also illuminates the connexion between his radical attitude to the individual and the family and his organic conception of the state.[247] The life and conduct of every individual derive their whole meaning from the whole. Community (κοινωνία) joins; privacy (ἰδίωσις) separates.[248] He does not attempt to extend the radical deductions about marriage which he makes from this principle as far as the working-class which supports the Republic. His principles are restricted to the class that governs and defends the state. Therefore it is chiefly through them that the state is a unity; and, after that, through the voluntary subordination of the lower class, which Plato hopes will be induced by the selflessness of the rulers. That is, the rulers of the state will be not masters, but helpers, and they will treat the common people not as servants, but as breadwinners and providers.[249]

But where does the state itself, the Whole, derive its supreme value and its claims to loyalty? Surely the idea of wholeness and community can be interpreted in very different senses and taken to cover very different spheres? Nowadays we are most apt to believe that 'the nation' means the men and women whom nature and history have made representatives of that particular whole; and that 'the state' is the form in which the nation politically exists and acts. In that case, the purpose of breeding future rulers would be to create an élite of virtue within the racial stock that makes up a particular nation. But that is not what Plato wants. His perfect state is a city-state. In that he is in harmony with the general realities of political life and the trend of Greek history. He does call his Republic a Greek city now and then,[250] but it does not represent the whole Greek nation—for there are other Greek states with which it can be at peace or war.[251] Therefore its existence as a state is, essentially, not even based on the fact that its citizens are Greeks. It might just as well be brought into existence among barbarians—perhaps it did exist among them, once upon a time, entirely without our knowledge! [252] The thing that justifies the Republic in Plato's eyes is not the ethnic character of its population but the fact that it is a perfect whole, with *all* its parts forming a unity.[253] That is how we are to understand its character as a polis, or city-state. Plato's ideal state was neither a big nation-state nor a world empire, but a city-state. Looking at it from what is sometimes called the historical point of view, we might think that that was simply because he clung to the facts which history happened to put before his political experience. It was not. The city-state was part of his absolute ideal. He felt that a small but tightly closed state would be a more perfect unity than any state with a larger territory or denser population.[254] The Greek conception of political life could develop in its full matchless intensity only in the city-state, and actually died with its death. Plato felt that his state was more genuinely and fully a state than any other. He was convinced that the people in it would realize the highest form of human virtue and human happiness.[255] And both the racial selection which he recommended, and the education for which it was to prepare, were devoted to the service of that ideal.

MILITARY TRAINING AND MILITARY LAW

The fact that they are all Greeks, members of a single nation, is not the decisive factor in the lives of the citizens of Plato's Republic. Still, the growth of Greek national feeling in the fourth century has left clear traces in *The Republic*.[256] Plato used it to establish a new ethical code for war. He begins by laying down certain fundamental principles—what we are nowadays inclined to call principles of international law, because modern wars are usually between different nations, so that rules for their conduct depend not on the internal law of individual countries but on agreement between nations. But as long as the Greeks retained their political freedom, most wars were between

Greek states; and although non-Hellenic peoples were often involved, a war waged exclusively against foreigners was a rare
thing in Greece. So Plato's rules for the conduct of war are
chiefly aimed at regulating war between Greek armies.[257] But
not even in that limited area do they depend on international
agreements. Plato simply prescribes them for his own perfect
state, without assuming that they will be adopted by other countries. His rules for the conduct of war between Greeks are
really only an epitome of a code containing the full rules of
military law, as learnt by his soldier-guards.[258]

Plato does not give them much space among the regulations
for 'musical' and athletic training. He merely cuts out of Homer
the passages likely to make soldiers afraid of death, and he
specifically points out that physical exercise is meant as preparation for war, in order to keep it from degeneration into specialized athletic training.[259] But he does not explain how to give
his soldiers fighting morale. Long after finishing the account of
musical and gymnastic education, after the digression on the
education of women and the community of wives, he inserts a
passage on military training. This comes after his account of
the rearing of children (τροφή), who, he says, are to be accustomed to warlike sights and sounds at an early age.[260] But his
allusion to accustoming children to war is only a device which
he uses to bring in his regulations for the conduct of war, which
really have little to do with childhood.[261] They are a sort of appendix, which is significantly separated from the main description of the education of the guards.[262] The separation involves
a problem which is not only one of structure. Why did Plato
shrink from arranging the book so that the 'musical' and gymnastic paideia of the guards and their military training came
close together? Not simply because military training is to start
before the real paideia; but because he thought of musical and
athletic education as an organic unity, fixed by historical tradition and justifiable on rational grounds. He did not wish to
insert anything into it that was not closely connected with it.
The fighting qualities of the guards, however, came from a different tradition altogether. In describing the paideia of 'music'
and gymnastics, Plato had been careful to establish a higher
spiritual harmony between the two naturally disparate forms of
Greek culture, physical and spiritual.[263] On a higher level, he

does the same thing for the guards' military training and their musical-gymnastic education. These two types of education had never yet been fully unified anywhere in Greece. In Sparta military training was more important than anything else, while in Athens the two years of cadet-training given to all citizens were far less essential than gymnastics and music. Plato is trying to bring both these currents of educational tradition together into a single stream.

Modern professional soldiers are likely to be disappointed when they read his plan for military training—just as teachers of music are, when they read his plan for music-lessons, or sports coaches when they read his system of gymnastics. At that time, the art of war—strategy, tactics, and technique—was very highly developed, and mechanized warfare was becoming more important every year. Here as elsewhere, Aristotle is more up to date than Plato, and emphasizes his neglect of that point.[264] But just as he did in 'music' and athletics, Plato excludes all purely technical matters from military training, and reduces it to what is genuinely paideia.[265] His intention is that the guards, both male and female, shall become true soldiers. Primarily that does not mean that they are to be expert in the use of weapons, but that they are to take on a certain definite spiritual mould. The decisive point about Plato's musical paideia was, as we have seen, that it shaped the character: that was why it had to start early when the soul was pliable, and mould it unawares into a shape which it would later know and strive consciously to maintain.[266] Plato proceeds in the same way to educate his small but élite soldiery. They are to learn war from childhood. Potters' children learn pottery by standing by and watching or helping their fathers at work; and the guards' children must be taught just as well as that.[267] But when they are taken into battle they are to be kept out of danger. Therefore special precautions must be taken for their safety. They are put in charge of the most capable and experienced of the elder guards, who are to be their guides and guardians, and help them to get out of the battle-zone at once if anything happens to endanger them.[268] We might think that they would not learn so much about war by simply watching battles as by regular practice in war-games.[269] But here again Plato is not trying to produce technical expertness. He is trying to shape their character.

Therefore he hardens them by making them accustomed to the terrifying sights and sounds of real war. He is, it seems, thinking of Tyrtaeus' eulogy of old Spartan courage, where the poet compares it with all other personal and social distinctions, and concludes that none of them can be seriously compared with patriotic self-sacrifice—since no other makes a man able 'to see bloody slaughter' and to hold his ground unafraid, 'biting his lips with his teeth'. Tyrtaeus thinks the ability to stand and watch a battle is the highest proof of courage and valiant steadfastness.[270] That ability, and not a collection of military devices, is the 'experience' of war that Plato means.

That is the sum and substance of the military education given to the guards' children. Plato simply assumes that they will learn the use of weapons and other soldierly skills. If we are right in suggesting that the rule of watching battles (θεωρεῖν) has an ethical significance, then we can easily understand why Plato adds a complete code of military ethics, with regulations for the conduct of fighting men towards one another and towards the enemy. The worst disgrace of all is to leave one's post in battle, or throw away one's weapons, or commit other such misdemeanours from cowardice. Plato degrades any soldier guilty of this, and puts him in the working class as an artisan or a farmer. The customary penalty in Greece was *atimia,* loss of civil rights; and Plato's substitute for it shows what a privileged position the guards in the perfect state possess.[271] Members of the working class—aye, in the catalogue they go for citizens, but this kind of penalty shows that they are at best only second-class citizens.[272] Any soldier who is taken prisoner by the enemy is not ransomed, but is left to the enemy as booty.[273] (According to ancient rules of war, that meant that he became a slave, or was killed out of hand.) Anyone who distinguishes himself in the field is crowned with garlands and congratulated; he even gets special sexual privileges as long as he is serving in that particular campaign. Plato is not thinking of 'war weddings'. The sexual connexions of his guards both in peace and in war follow his rule for breeding the best children. That is exactly why brave men are specially favoured, and concessions unknown elsewhere in *The Republic* are made to their personal inclinations.[274] Plato humorously refers to Homer for authority in this exceptional case, and recalls how Ajax after winning glory in battle was distinguished by honourable and nourishing gifts of 'whole chines of beef'.[275] At sacrifices and festivals, the hero is rewarded by being addressed in hymns, and having a seat of honour, and getting specially chosen food and drink. Those who die gloriously in battle are counted as belonging to the golden breed—that is, they become heroes and get a shrine which can be approached only with religious respect.[276] Those who survive, and die of old age after a life full of service to the nation, are given the same honour.[277] Both the form and the content of this military code remind us of Tyrtaeus' poem eulogizing the soldier's courage in face of the enemy as the highest virtue, and describing the entire system of honour to dead and living heroes on which the Spartan state was based. We have already discussed it, as a monument to the Spartan educational system.[278] It was not one point only (that about watching the battle) that Plato took from him; he took the whole soldierly code, and built it into his state. Whether he also took from Tyrtaeus the exaltation of courage as the supreme virtue is another question. The Republic is built upon justice, which excludes the possibility that courage is meant to dominate it. Courage was the basis of the Spartan code, and we shall see in *The Laws* how Plato takes issue with it and criticizes it severely.[279]

Plato's code is quite old-fashioned in its rules for the behaviour of soldiers to one another, their honour, dishonour, et cetera. But it is very modern in prescribing for their relations to the enemy.[280] He derives these principles from one source alone—the general feelings of equity held by cultured Greeks in his own day. According to Plato, that is where national sentiment ought to become active, not to construct a Hellenic state, but to act as a moral brake on the internecine conflicts of the Greek states among themselves. It was that ruthless policy of state to state, during the Peloponnesian war and in the years of collapse after it, that made all the best of the Greeks yearn for peace and concord. Although their yearning was unlikely to be fulfilled in practice in a world whose highest law was the entire independence of separate city-states, it did make the public conscience more sensitive about the murderous brutality with which the Greeks had hitherto waged their wars. Both the aim—annihilation of the enemy—and the methods—savage cruelty and enslavement—of this kind of war came to seem unnatural among people who were conscious of a community of language, customs, and descent. It was senseless suicide for the Greeks to destroy one another, with their country and their civilization exposed on all sides to the growing pressure of hostile nations. And the danger grew with the weakness of the Greeks. The years when Plato was writing his Panhellenic code of rules for war saw the resurgence of Athenian power, and the creation of the second naval confederacy, which was to maintain itself only by exhausting wars against Sparta and her allies. So Plato's suggestions are a highly contemporary appeal to the warring blocs of states composing the Greek people.

Plato's rules are meant to cover war both against Greeks and against barbarians. But they are not based on any ideal of universal humanity and kindness: for they make a difference of principle between the treatment of Greeks and the treatment of non-Greeks. The humane treatment they enjoin is meant wholly or chiefly for Greeks. By nature, Greeks are kinsmen and friends: barbarians are strangers and enemies.[281] This is just the principle which underlies Isocrates' Panhellenic teaching, and which induced Aristotle to advise Alexander to rule the Greeks like a leader and the barbarians like a despot.[282] Plato does not start out with the general principle, but with one specific statement which cannot fail to convince. It is wrong, he says, for Greeks to enslave a Greek city.[283] But that same recommendation, that Greeks should spare other Greeks, is backed up by a reference to the danger they run from the barbarians. Therefore he forbids his Republic to have Greek slaves, and instructs it to use its influence on other states to induce them also to refrain.[284] He hopes the result of this will be to make the Greeks turn against the barbarians rather than their own fellow-countrymen.[285] In this his thought is parallel to that of Isocrates;[286] he does not, however, expect that war against the barbarians will unite the Greeks, but merely lays down this thesis in general terms. Yet later, in his Letters, he applied the same policy to the war between the Sicilian Greeks and the barbarians, and gave the Carthaginian danger as the reason why they ought to unite.[287] That is, he has one unvarying view of the relation between Greeks and barbarians. He expects them

to be at war. But he would prefer not to call a fight between
Greeks 'war', since war is possible only between strangers, not
between kinsfolk. He distinguishes war (πόλεμος) from civil
strife (στάσις)—it was a favourite topic of contemporary orators—and says that only the latter should be used to describe
hostilities between Greeks.[288] Thereby, he takes it as equivalent
to war within one single state, and applies the same legal standards to judging it. Thus he forbids devastation of fields and
burning of houses—since, he says, they are not usual in civil
wars in any civilized state in the fourth century, but bring down
the anger of the gods on the perpetrators and stamp them as
'unpatriotic'.[289] Similarly in a war between Greek states, the
opponents should not regard each other entirely as 'enemies'.
The victor should be content with calling the guilty ones to account.[290] The worst injury he would allow one enemy to inflict
on another is the destruction of his year's crops.[291] He adds that
no matter what acts of hostility one state may execute against
another of the same nation, the two should always remember
that their natural purpose is not to destroy their opponent, but
to be reconciled with him.[292]

Besides these rules for war between Greeks, Plato also gives
general regulations for all wars without distinction. It is (he
tells us) unworthy of a free man to strip a corpse on the battlefield for the sake of greed. The same applies to a refusal to
allow the enemy to collect his dead. The only thing a soldier can
rightly take from a dead foeman is his weapons.[293] But the Republic is forbidden to hang up captured arms as offerings in the
temples of the gods, which might profane them instead of deco-
rating them.[294] These regulations arise partly from moral self-
respect, partly from a purified religious faith. They complement
his rules for treating enemies who happen to be Greeks, in so
far as both sets of precepts aim at humanizing warfare. Plato
himself admits that the Greeks do not fight as he wishes them
to. Therefore his rules are not merely a summary of the current conventions of war, but a bold attack on existing conditions. He finds them barbarous—and he says so indirectly, by
maintaining that contemporary rules of warfare ought to be
kept for wars between Greeks and barbarians.[295] In his day it
was customary to enslave prisoners of war. We must remember
that, if we are to understand what a huge advance in morality

had been made, an advance that is reflected in his rules for the
conduct of war. Even in the seventeenth century Hugo Grotius
(the great humanist who was the father of modern international
law) said in his *De iure belli ac pacis* that it was not unnatural
to enslave prisoners. At the end of his chapter called 'De iure
in captivos' he quotes the Byzantine historian Gregoras to prove
that the Rhomaei and Thessalians, Illyrians, Triballians, and
Bulgarians, because they were all Christians, kept the rule of
taking plunder but not enslaving the enemy, and killing no one
except in battle. It was only after the age of Grotius that Christianity attained what the Platonic Socrates had vainly endeavoured to urge on the Greeks as necessary for national self-
preservation.[296] But Grotius himself remarks that the Moham-
medans followed the same rule in fighting their co-religionists.
So we must broaden his statement. Neither the ancient city-state
nor the national ideal of the fourth century, but the universal
religious fellowship of Christendom laid the foundations for
the fulfilment of Plato's hope. That religious foundation was
something far broader than the Greek nation which Plato had
addressed. But it was similar to the Platonic scheme in this: it
was not an abstract universal brotherhood of man; instead, it
was identical with the concrete Christian or Mohammedan
brotherhood, whose component nations continued to belong to
it even in time of war.

THE REPUBLIC: TRUE HOME OF THE PHILOSOPHER

Now the perfect state has been completely planned. Plato
drops the subject before the book is half-finished, before it has
reached its central climax. The question now confronting us is
this: can the perfect state be realized, and if so how? [297] Plato
tries to survey his own work with a certain detachment, and his
attitude to it is highly significant. 'Socrates' compares himself
to a painter who has just finished a wonderful picture: it is the
ideal portrayal of the perfectly just man, showing his nature
and his happiness.[298] The significance of the portrait is enhanced
by the contrasting figure—that of the supremely unjust man in
his misery. Plato calls his work a paradeigma—it is both a picture and a pattern.[299] This comparison between Socrates' Utopian ideal and a picture of a handsome man shows what Plato

thought was the true subject of *The Republic*. It was not first
and foremost the state itself, but man with his power to make
the state. Though he also speaks of a paradeigma of the state,
we cannot compare the state with the picture of the ideally
handsome man.[300] The picture really corresponds to the character of the truly just man, the man whom Plato himself describes as the subject of his painting.[301] The perfect state is only
the proper space which he needs as a frame and background
for his portrait. Plato's description of his own work thus agrees
with the results of our analysis. *The Republic* is primarily a
book about the making of human character. It is not a political
work in the usual sense of *politics*—only in the Socratic sense.[302]
But the great educational truth vividly expounded in *The Republic* is the close correlation of character and environment, the
portrait and the background. This is not merely an artistic principle: it is also a law of the moral world. The perfect man can
be shaped only within the perfect state; and vice versa, to construct such a state, we must discover how to make such men.
That is the ground for the universal correspondence between
the inner structure of man and state, for the resemblance between both patterns. And from this point of view new light is
cast on Plato's constant assertions that the social atmosphere is
vitally important in forming the citizens of his state.

But he also tells us how we should look at Socrates' philosophical 'picture'. Every paradeigma is absolutely perfect, and
we admire it whether it can become real or not.[303] The very
nature of it is that it cannot be realized, and at most can be
approximated.[304] By recognizing that, we are not complaining
that the ideal itself is imperfect. It is a philosophical work of
art, and therefore, like the picture of the perfectly handsome
man, it is always valuable for its beauty, which is independent
of practical considerations. But when Plato describes the picture drawn by Socrates as a model, he is thinking of the un-
quenchable human instinct for imitation. The whole of Greek
paideia is founded on two very old Greek ideas—paradeigma
and mimesis, the model and its imitation. Plato meant *The
Republic* to be a new stage in the development of paideia.
Rhetoricians in his day often spoke of mythical and historical
paradeigmata, and used them as patterns and models for conduct in exhortatory speeches. We have already shown that this

idea goes back to the earliest Greek poetry, which, in relating legends and describing mythical characters, gave them that significance.[305] It was in that interpretation of myth that the educational value of poetry was thought to lie. Therefore, when Plato calls his ideal state and his ideal man a myth too,[306] he means not only that they are unreal, but also that they are models for the real to imitate. There is a similar conception in plastic art: the word *canon* means a human figure which is aesthetically perfect in all its forms and proportions.[307] But Plato's paradeigma is also intended to be an ethical model. Therein his work continues the tradition of early Greek poetry, and enters into competition with it. He fully understands the charm possessed by the ideal figures of poetry, and their power to influence us to imitate them. And he feels that this power is absent from philosophical thought, which is directed towards abstractions and universal ideas. So, before his poetic eye, the universal concept of a virtue changes into the type of character that embodies it. Justice is incarnated in the perfectly just man.[308] This is not an isolated case. He needs new paradeigmata, and so he creates ideal human figures to correspond to all moral attitudes and modes of life; and this mode of personifying a quality in a type-personality became a regular part of his thought. It is against this background that we must understand 'the perfect state' and 'the truly just man' in *The Republic*. They are to be inspiring models, and Plato means them to become tangible realities through our imitation of them.

But how are we to set about realizing them? If the ideally just man can come to life only in a perfect state, the kind of education which is to create his type must ultimately be a question of *power*. Of course, contemporary states treat the struggle for power as a self-evident aim (as *Gorgias* showed),[309] and therefore do not feel called to the educational duty which Plato considers the essence of the state. He believes it impossible to find a constructive solution to the problem of moulding human character in the Socratic manner, and thereby healing the social ills of the age—*unless political power and political wisdom coincide*. Hence comes his famous axiom: the political troubles of the world will never end until philosophers become kings, or rulers take to philosophy.[310] This axiom he places in the very centre of *The Republic*. It is not a brief and brilliant epigram.

It is the ideal solution to that tragic conflict between philosophical education and the state which we have shown to exist
in Plato's earlier works.[311] The conflict had been symbolized in
the death of the just man on whom Plato's thought was focused
throughout his early life. At that time it seemed to mean a
complete severance between reason and the state.[312] But in *The
Republic* there arises, behind the strife and suffering of that
gigantomachy, the vision of a new cosmos which shall absorb
the positive values of the old order and take over its forms.
Plato calls for the rule of the philosopher because of his conviction that the constructive force in the new world that is being
born will be philosophy—i.e. reason, the spirit which the state
tried to destroy in the person of Socrates. Only reason, which
had created the perfect state in idea, could translate it (if it
had the power) into reality.

Now, for the first time in *The Republic*, philosophy comes
into the foreground. Until now it had been concealed behind its
work, its newly created ideal state; but now it boldly advances
its claim to supremacy. This claim does not spring from the
usual will to power, and its apparent contradiction of Plato's
earlier criticisms of the state and its power is only nominal.[313]
Behind the condemnations of *pleonexia*, greedy aggrandize-
ment, in the 'power-state' which were expressed in *Gorgias*, lay
the claim of philosophy itself to rule. Plato did not condemn
power as bad in itself; he merely subjected the concept of power
to a thorough dialectic clarification which purged away the
stains of selfishness from it.[314] He freed it from arbitrary whim,
and turned it back to pure will, since the unalterable aim of the
will is, by nature, the good. No human being wants to be mistaken about what he considers good and beneficial. Real power
can consist only of the ability to fulfil the natural aspiration to
attain this end. Therefore true power assumes genuine knowledge of the good. And so, paradoxically, philosophy becomes
the way to true power. In *The Republic* also, Plato proves
that the claim of philosophy to supremacy is directly justified
by its nature. Of course it must be defined more accurately—
especially since it is introduced here without any previous discussion. Plato first of all takes us aback by his provocative thesis
that the philosopher ought to rule, and then justifies it by explaining the nature of the philosopher, showing just why he is

meant by nature to rule.[315] As soon as he lays down this principle, we recall the painfully elaborate discussions in his earlier
books about the problem of right conduct, of true virtue, and
of real knowledge; and suddenly we understand that they were
all making towards one goal, which is now revealed. Plato cannot possibly have meant, in this brief passage of *The Republic,*
to give a description of the philosopher's character which would
be as vivid and impressive as that given in his earlier dialogues.
Here, as elsewhere, he assumes that his earlier books are known
to the reader. Still, the artistic structure of *The Republic* en-
courages us to imagine that this is the first time we have been
made to think seriously about philosophy. And in a way that is
true. The claim of philosophy to rule the state casts a surprising new light upon it, and even its most orthodox worshipper
is bound to feel that this makes him revise his whole conception
of it.

It is very moving indeed to watch how Plato, with complete
and utter trust in the power of philosophy, enthrones her at the
centre of life and sets her the most strenuous of practical tasks.
Nowadays she is lonely and deserted. She can hardly understand
that it was only through her struggles with these mighty tasks
that she put on the power and majesty of her early creative
period. Yet there is truth in Hegel's melancholy epigram that
Minerva's owl does not begin her flight until the dusk has fallen;
and it is that tragic realization that casts its shadow over Plato
in those final heroic efforts of the human mind to rescue the
state from its destruction. But even an aging civilization has its
youth; and Plato's philosophy is the youthful energy of its
epoch. Therefore it enlists the enthusiastic young men whom
Plato likes to picture crowding around Socrates, in a crusade
to preach a new birth to the aging and sceptical and hyper-
civilized state of the fourth century. That was what philosophy
felt to be her duty: not so much because she was herself a
power invested with a great historical tradition, glorified by
many honourable titles and functions—discoverer of nature,
solver of the riddle of the universe, explorer of the cosmos—
but because she felt herself inspired by Socrates with a new
strength, the power to impart to mankind the reviving knowledge of the true standards of human life.

It is under this aspect that Plato explains the nature of philosophy in *The Republic*. He outlines a brief catechism defining its nature by the object of its knowledge. The philosopher is a man who is unwilling to surrender to the manifold impressions of his senses, and to be driven around all his life on the uncertain sea of opinion. His mind is bent on the unity of existence.[316] He alone possesses true knowledge and wisdom. Below the manifold individual phenomena, he can detect the permanent and universal foundation of things, the 'idea'. Only he can define what is just and what is beautiful in itself. The opinions of the masses about these and all other problems veer about in the twilight between reality and unreality.[317] Statesmen are no different from the masses. They look for guidance to all sorts of constitutions and laws—but, as Plato says in *The Statesman*, these are only imitations of truth.[318] Therefore if a man knows no better than to copy them, he is only an imitator of imitations. The philosopher is the man who has a clear paradeigma, a pattern to imitate, within his own soul.[319] When everything else rocks around him, he holds his gaze fixed upon that standard. The ability to apprehend it is the power of vision which the true guard needs more than anything else. If a philosopher can combine that with experience and other good qualities necessary for the practical government of the state, he is far superior to the general run of statesmen.[320]

This description of the philosopher illuminates the intellectual attitude and the point of departure of Plato's theory of the state itself. He holds that the greatest weakness of the political and moral world is its lack of a supreme authority to fix aims to be attained and rules for attaining them. It was in the effort to create such a power that democracy had been born. It had solved the problem of creating it by accepting the will of the majority as the supreme legislative authority. This system depended on a lofty estimate of the reasoning powers of the individual, and it was for long considered to be the most advanced of all types of constitution. Yet, just like the others, it suffered from human imperfection. As it developed in the great Greek cities, it came more and more to be a tool in the hands of unscrupulous agitators, trained by the particular type of educator known as a sophist. Plato describes them as being like animal trainers, who spend their lives trying to learn the whims of 'the big beast'—the mob—and who are intimately acquainted with the noises it makes to signify pleasure or anger. Their art consists of handling it correctly, and managing it just as they wish through flattering it and carefully suiting themselves to its varying moods.[321] This makes the approval of the mob into the highest standard of political action—and that spirit of conformity gradually invades the whole of life. If people have to conform to the prevailing methods of winning the mob's approval, true education, oriented towards the lodestar of permanent standards, will become impossible.[322] From his very earliest writings, Plato makes great play with Socrates' criticism of political orators for not knowing the facts about their subject. In *Gorgias* he compares this kind of rhetorician's politics with the attitude of the philosopher, who subordinates every action to the knowledge of his highest aim, the good.[323] He backs this up in *The Republic* by laying down that knowledge of the highest norm, which the philosopher carries in his soul as a permanent model, is the touchstone of the true ruler.[324]

With this in view, we can understand the entire structure of *The Republic*. Plato holds that philosophy is a saviour in time of need, because she possesses the solution to the most urgent of all social problems. If we assume that knowledge of the highest standard, in Plato's sense, is possible,[325] it is inevitable that we should start from that point to reconstruct the collapsing state. Its real monarch, the fountain of all authority and power, must be the knowledge of the Truth. And that is naturally not possible for the masses—only for a few. Plato does not start psychologically, from the problem of handling the masses. He starts from the claims which the highest moral and intellectual type of man must make on the state in order to devote himself wholeheartedly to his duty.[326] In the name of the higher element that exists in man, he declares that the philosopher must rule. And the most obvious peculiarities of his Republic—the organic interconnection of the three classes, and its authoritarian government—arise simply and solely from the one basic principle that the state must be ruled by the knowledge of absolute truth. It is a simple construction, logically perfect. Not one stone can be taken away from it; not one can be replaced by another. Suppose we deprive the ruler of his character as a philosopher possessing absolute knowledge. According to Plato, we thereby destroy the foundations of his authority:

for it does not depend on any mystic personal leadership, but on
the power of truth to convince. And in the Republic everyone
will voluntarily submit to the rule of truth, because everyone has
been brought up in its spirit. The knowledge of the highest
standard carried in the soul of the philosopher is the keystone
of Plato's educational Republic.

Knowledge of the ultimate standard is the foundation of the
Republic. And yet, when Plato infers that only the philosopher,
who possesses that knowledge, is fit to rule, he is confronted by
the facts of experience. Philosophers are usually rather vague
and helpless in practical life.[327] This section of *The Republic* is
mainly concerned with answering the objection raised by Callicles in *Gorgias,* that philosophy was good enough 'for paideia'
if it were practised for a few years in youth, but as a permanent occupation it debilitated men and made them unfit to cope
with life.[328] Both in *Gorgias* and in *The Republic* Plato rejects
this narrow conception of paideia as something that ought to be
studied for a limited time and then dropped. In reply, he offers
a metaphor—a vivid picture that could easily be converted into
a cartoon for the front page of a satiric political magazine.[329]
Imagine, he says, a ship's captain who is very big and strong,
but rather deaf and short-sighted, and rather ignorant of navigation too. He is the public. He is surrounded by sailors arguing about the course to steer, and each claiming he ought to be
the steersman. They are the allegorical embodiment of the politicians who are each trying to grab the supreme power in the
state. They do not believe steering is an art, nor that it can be
taught; they all think they can steer perfectly well by themselves. If anyone opposes them and keeps them from steering,
they use force and toss him overboard. And they drug the true
steersman, the only man who could guide the ship securely, and
keep him from practising his art; and they sail on drinking and
feasting. Whenever anyone helps them in terrorizing the captain and grasping power for themselves, they call him an able
navigator. The only true navigator, who has learnt his art properly, they call a useless star-gazing fool.

Plato is very anxious to distinguish the education of his philosopher (concealed under the mask of the true navigator)
from the 'paideia' referred to by Callicles, which might occupy

the sons of noblemen like himself for a few years, before they started 'life in earnest'. Compared with that paideia, the science which the 'navigator' has acquired seems to be very dry, and anti-humanist, and set on producing results. It is admittedly vocational training; it is employed and fulfilled in the practice of the profession it teaches. So Plato seems not to agree with the attacks levelled by sophists and humanists against professionalism in education. At first that seems rather paradoxical in a man who values knowledge for its own sake.[330] But it is clearly a way of defending Plato's paideia against the charge of complete and deliberate uselessness, which was levelled against it by contemporary educational authorities, particularly Isocrates.[331] It has a purpose. It serves a vocation. The vocation is the noblest possible for any man, that of saving the lives of those who are in the same ship. Plato chose the image of the ship's steersman to bring out two points. The first is that the navigator's knowledge is indispensable for the safety of his fellow-men, and the second is that other men cannot realize what it really means. The crew thinks he is only an eccentric fellow gaping at the stars, and talking nonsense and wasting his time,[332] because his work involves far more theory and method than they could possibly understand. Another interesting point in this passage is that Plato several times points out that the helmsman's methods can and must be *learnt,* although the silly sailors think it is all a matter of practice.[333] This is a reference to Plato's discussion of the political techné in *Gorgias,*[334] and at the same time it reminds us of the beginning of *Protagoras,* where Socrates was doubtful whether political virtue could possibly be taught.[335] At the end of *Protagoras,* of course, his doubts were removed when he saw that virtue meant knowledge of the Good.[336] In *The Republic* Plato does not permit Socrates to have any doubts. By using the simile of the true art of navigation (which can be learnt) he prepares for the subsequent explanation of his own art of political navigation, the ruler's philosophical education.[336a]

But the image is not a sufficient refutation of the charge that philosophers are useless. It is only the first step into a profound analysis of the philosopher's position in the political community.[337] The widespread scepticism about the philosopher's political ability is based principally on psychological grounds.

Therefore the answer to it must go deeply into the psychology of the philosopher. But Plato does not treat him as an isolated figure. His analysis is a masterly description of a type. It not only describes the characteristics of a particular class in the abstract, but explains its interactions with its social milieu. He takes the opportunity to reject many of the qualities usually attached to the name of philosophy. But in his resolute defence of true philosophy, every concession to its critics changes into an accusation against the world. His description of the philosopher's fate becomes piercingly tragic. More than any others in his work, these pages are written with his heart's blood. Now he is thinking not only of the doom of Socrates, which had become symbolic, but of his own high intentions, and of the 'failure' of his powers before the task he had once thought of as his own.

Strictly speaking, his defence of the philosopher begins before he says anything of the criticisms against him. Hitherto he has defined the philosopher only by the object of his knowledge [338]; but now he gives a description of the philosophical character [339] which is indispensable for the understanding of his theory that the philosopher must rule—especially for modern readers, who are too apt to think that the Greek word *philosopher* means *scholar*. His *philosophos* is not a professor of philosophy, nor indeed any member of the philosophical 'faculty', arrogating that title to himself because of his special branch of knowledge (τεχνύδριον).[340] Still less is he an 'original thinker'—how *could* there be so many original thinkers in existence at one time as Plato needs for the administration of his Republic? Although, as we shall shortly see, he uses the word to imply a great deal of specialized dialectical training, its root meaning is 'lover of culture', a description of the most highly educated or cultured type of personality. Plato sees the philosopher as a man of great intellectual power, quick apprehension, and real eagerness to learn. He is averse to all petty details; he is always anxious to see things as a whole; he looks down on time and existence from a great height. He does not prize his life, and cares little for external goods. Display is foreign to his character. He is magnanimous in everything, and has considerable charm too. He is 'a friend and kinsman' of truth, justice, courage, and self-control. Such a type, according to Plato, could be produced in reality. It would be the product of early and constant selection,

perfect education, and the maturity brought by years.[341] His
character of the philosopher does not at all resemble the typical
pupil of the sophists. The 'intellectual' who is known for constant criticism of others is greatly disliked by Plato, and is
driven out of his temple.[342] His principal emphasis is on harmony between mind and character. Therefore he sums up his
philosopher quite simply by calling him *kaloskagathos*, 'a gentleman'.[343]

The real onus of the charge that the philosopher is useless
falls on those who cannot use him. Natures like his are few and
far between. Besides that, he is exposed to very serious danger
from the mass of the public, and constantly threatened with corruption.[344] The danger is partly rooted within himself. Each of
the good qualities he possesses—courage, self-control, et cetera
—can become a hindrance to true philosophical culture, if it is
isolated from the others and developed disproportionately.[345]
Then again, he can be impeded by good looks, money, strength,
influential relatives, and other such 'advantages'.[346] Healthy
development depends on the proper nourishment, season, and
environment: these general requirements for every well-bred
plant and animal are specially important for the strongest and
finest natures.[347] The most gifted character is apt to become
worse than the average man, if he is spoilt by bad 'pedagogy',
bad upbringing.[348] The philosophical nature grows wonderfully
on good ground, but produces the opposite of all its noble qualities, if it is sown and nourished in the soil of bad education—
unless it is helped by 'divine chance'.[349]

Students of Plato meet this idea, in this connexion, more than
once. It is that prodigies, inexplicable by ordinary human reason,
may occur, and that they are not brought about by pure accident, but by the miraculous power of a protecting deity.[350] It is
the expression of a religious interpretation of certain events
which are both paradoxical and deeply significant. We find this
same 'divine chance' in Plato's letters. For example, he thinks
it was a divine chance that, during his first stay in Sicily, he converted Dion, the nephew of the tyrant, to enthusiastic support
of his doctrine of the educational function of the state, and that
Dion later headed the revolution which overthrew the despotism
of Dionysius. This means that Plato unintentionally became the
primary cause of this important historical event, through his

teaching. We naturally ask whether the whole thing was chance, or he was a tool in the hands of a higher power.[351] In later years, after what seemed to be the collapse of all his direct efforts to realize his hopes, this concatenation of events acquired the importance of a religious problem. And there is something of this quality of personal experience in *The Republic,* when he describes the miraculous preservation of the man meant by nature to be a philosopher from all the dangers which threaten him during his education in a dangerously corrupt environment. That is what makes his description of the life of the philosopher in this world seem so tragic: it seems that only a miracle, a divine chance, can permit a philosopher to grow up in it; and most such natures go bad before they are ever fully grown.

When Plato says the chief danger to the young philosopher is unsuitable education,[352] he seems to be agreeing with the general complaint about the corrupting influence of the sophists— the complaint to which Socrates himself had fallen victim. But in fact it is quite contrary to his conception of education to ascribe a decisive influence to any particular individuals. He holds that all education is spiritually a function of the community, whether it is 'free' or officially directed by the state. Believing that right education can exist only in the perfect state, he constructs an ideal state to be the frame for this perfect education. Therefore he does not think the teachers are responsible for the faults of the existing educational system. It is the community that is responsible. The men who blame the sophists for the degeneration of young men are themselves the greatest sophists.[353] It is actually the influence of the state and society that educates men and makes them into whatever society wants. Public meetings, law-courts, the theatres, the army, and all other assemblies where an excited crowd applauds or boos the speeches of an orator—these are the places where men of every age are moulded. No young man, no private or individual education (ἰδιωτικὴ παιδεία) can withstand that power.[354] In such a position the individual is bound to follow the crowd's approval or disapproval, and to take its judgments as his standard of conduct, if he wants to remain alive. No one can mould character and personality otherwise than in conformity with this 'paideia' conducted by the crowd—unless perhaps he is saved by special divine interposition.[355] The salaried individuals (μισθαρνοῦντες ἰδιῶται) whom we call teachers and educators cannot help teaching us what the mob tells them to, since the mob directs public opinion. Their terminology of things honorable and shameful is, if closely examined, the same as the crowd's.[356] The real weakness of the sophists' teaching, which professes to give men higher culture, is that all their judgments of value are derived from that source. In the present world the most successful teachers are the men who are most expert in the sounds and words that 'the big beast' loves.[357] They have made a career out of adapting themselves. Thus contemporary education and pedagogy is for Plato a caricature of real paideia.[358] When he asserts that it is impossible for true paideia to exist in this world, or for a young man with a philosopher's character to be saved (which can be achieved only through the right paideia) unless by a special miracle from heaven,[359] this is a general but unmistakable reference to the fact that Plato himself was originally preserved by finding Socrates, the true teacher. That was the exceptional case, where one single personality imparted to his pupils good of eternal value. But for his independence of the crowd's ideas, that teacher of all teachers was not paid; he had to pay with his own life.

Quite clearly, the Athenian democracy of his own day is the historical background of Plato's picture; but his description of 'the crowd' is general. It is not the Athenian mob, but any mob. This is plain from his definition—the mob does not know what is good and right *in itself*.[360] To know what is good in itself is the mark of the philosopher, and Plato thinks it is self-contradictory to speak of a philosophical crowd (φιλόσοφον πλῆθος).[361] The crowd's natural attitude to philosophy is hostility. The same is true of the man who makes a career of flattering the crowd: he is equally hostile to philosophy. How is the philosophical nature to assert itself against that enmity, and to do full justice to the inward urge it feels? Surely it will simply be used as a tool by men who foresee the great future in store for it, and play up to its baser instincts? They tell the young man he will rule over Greeks and barbarians, and inflate his mind with foolish and futile conceit.[362] Here Plato is obviously thinking of characters like Alcibiades and Critias, whose faults had been laid at the door of their teacher Socrates.[363] He does not, like Xenophon, attempt to disown them.[364] He accepts them as former students of philosophy, and uses them as examples of the philosophical character which has the highest gifts, but is spoilt by its environment. There is, he admits, something 'philosophical' in these political adventurers. They have a dash and brilliance that raises them high above the average—for a paltry nature can do nothing big, either good or bad. Only the philosophical nature is capable of mighty things. Only such a man has the choice of becoming one of the greatest benefactors of mankind or one of the dazzling scoundrels who bring the most dreadful harm upon their people.[365]

We can most profoundly understand Plato's dream of the philosopher-king if we compare this Alcibiades-like character with the description of the mature philosopher—a description which takes on new colour and new life from the contrast. The comparison is the work of a man who had been intimate with men like Alcibiades and Critias, who felt that he was of the same intellectual caliber as they, but who knew where their paths separated. At the same time, he saw their difficulty sympathetically, from the inside, for he was describing the tragedy of a member of his own family. The corruption of young men like that robbed philosophy of those who were meant by nature not to be the devilish opponents of truth, but rather to stand like archangels around its throne. And now their empty places were invaded by upstarts who were unworthy and incapable of such lofty paideusis, and were scarcely fitted to strengthen public confidence in the philosopher's vocation to be a ruler of men.[366] Plato felt himself surrounded by these miserable imitations. Few, very few were those who escaped the general corruption. Perhaps a cultured man of noble character, compelled to live as a foreigner in exile, and involuntarily isolated from these injurious influences, or else some great soul, born in a small town and despising it, will turn towards the life of the spirit; perhaps such a man may be kept out of politics by illness, or he may be a specialist in some work which he rightly scorns, and so find the way to philosophy.[367] They are strange companions, those who survive the dangers surrounding them—and they are very plainly reminiscent of real members of Plato's circle.[368] It is strange too to read such ironic self-depreciation, just after the serious and lofty announcement of philosophy's claim to the throne of the world. That is the transition to a passage of profound resignation, with which Plato concludes his defence of philosophy.[369]

'Those who join this little group, taste the blissful sweetness of this treasure, and really see how crazy the crowd is, so that absolutely no one does anything sane and sound in politics, and they have no ally with whom they could fight for justice and survive, but are like a man fallen into a den of wild beasts, unwilling to join in their crimes, unable to resist all these savage creatures by himself, and doomed to die too soon before he can help his country or his friends, useless to himself and to others, —after they understand all this, staying quiet and doing their own work, as though standing behind a wall in a storm of wind-driven dust and sleet, when they see others infected by lawlessness, they are content if they can live out their life here pure of injustice and unholy acts, and say good-bye to it cheerfully and pleasantly, full of good hope.'

The philosopher has descended from his lofty claim to rule the true state. Quietly he retires to a corner out of sight,[370] where the real world will not come near him. We know now the aspect of the state which he would build if he had the power. But after that soaring flight of the spirit, he is still in the same situation as in *Gorgias,* savagely criticized and cruelly threatened by rhetors and politicians. Without the belief that he can transform the real state of his own day, without the intention of entering the struggles of the political arena, he is, just as in *Gorgias,* the true man misunderstood by the world. The focus of his life is beyond the sphere of success, publicity, and power, inhabited by those of his contemporaries who are counted great. His true strength is his withdrawal from effective public life. In the *Apology* Plato had depicted Socrates as realizing at the end of his life why his *daimonion* had always warned him not to take part in politics. He tells the jury frankly that no one can expect to make head against the mob for long if he openly opposes their crimes. Anyone who really wants to fight for justice must do so in private life, not as a politician.[371] This shows it is a mistake to think, as many scholars do, that Plato's resigned admission in *The Republic* is his first surrender of his original hope of influencing the contemporary state. The seventh Letter says as clearly as possible that Socrates' death was the great crisis in Plato's political aspirations,[372] and that is confirmed by the *Apology*. The tragic confession of *The Republic* is the same in substance, although it has far higher poetic intensity—the result of Plato's long and agonized brooding over his destiny. Socrates' simple avoidance of politics on principle, which he acknowledges in the *Apology,* has here changed into a sort of religious renunciation, in which Plato seems to collect his strength in silence for a final trial. That is the attitude we see in the eschatological myths of *Gorgias* and other dialogues.

It is because the world misunderstands him that the philosophical man described by Plato is different from all the earlier ideals of personality drawn by Greek poets. They had all been expressions of a virtue that was rooted in the real city-state. The citizen community saw them as the glorious poetic incarnation of its own highest aspirations, its own understanding of the world. But Plato's idealized description of philosophical virtue and the philosophical man stands in direct contrast to civic virtue as practised by the community—and thereby the community ceases to be a community. His involuntary separation from it is caused by his feeling that he possesses a more profound knowledge of the truly valuable things in life than others—even if the others are in the vast majority. The philosopher makes a virtue of his own defect, which is that of being in the minority. What others think of, in terms of practical politics, as society, looks to him like a mere mob. Opposite it there are a few survivors, saved from all threats and dangers and kept pure by their philosophical nature; and they begin to look like a new society, the community of the school or the sect.

The appearance of such schools is a historical fact of immense importance, which even to-day essentially affects and conditions the relation between individual and society. Behind the school or the little community there always stands an intellectual personality, who is the active force, who speaks with the authority of his own deep knowledge and who gathers around him associates with the same attitude to life. When Plato works out a plan for an authoritarian state, we must not forget that his great principle of making philosophical truth the highest standard (a principle impossible of execution in practical politics) really originated from a huge enlargement of the individual's claims to true freedom, and not from a denial or misunderstanding of their value. This assertion of intellectual independence had one direct practical effect on the structure of Greek society: the creation of communities like schools or colleges. Such was the Academy founded in Athens by Plato himself. Of course there have always been teachers and pupils. But it would be a historical anachronism to imagine that there was anything like a Platonic school among the pre-Socratic philosophers. Its only prototype was the Pythagorean order in southern Italy. Since Plato founded the Academy immediately after returning from his first tour among the western Greeks, during which he had been closely associated with the Pythagoreans, it would seem that the two institutions were connected. The Pythagoreans were a society maintaining a fixed rule of life. Similarly Plato's philosophical βίος seems to presuppose knowledge of that rule— although it is pure legend that deliberate cultivation of the philosopher's life, and the word *philosophy* itself, are derived from Pythagoras.[373] Despite all Plato's political theorizing, his school was not active in Athens as a political group, as the Pythagoreans had been until the annihilation of their order. In the seventh Letter, when discussing the political enterprises of his favourite pupil Dion of Syracuse, he gives explicit reasons for his decision to refrain from revolutionary activity in Athens. He felt towards his native city as a son who is grown up and independent feels towards parents whose conduct and principles he cannot approve. When necessary he expresses his disapproval, but it does not release him from the duty of piety, and does not justify him in using force.[374]

As a matter of fact, the existence of the Academy would have been possible nowhere else than in democratic Athens, which allowed Plato to speak even when he criticized his own state. The Athenians had long thought it was a grave crime to condemn Socrates, and they considered his heirs as increasing the glory of the city—which, although its political power was waning, was more and more coming to be the intellectual focus of Hellenic society. Cloistered and remote from the world, sheltered physically too from the noisy bustle of the city, on the peaceful green hill of Colonus, the Academy produced a special type of men. Plato describes them with affectionate irony in a digression in *Theaetetus*.[375] They do not know where the marketplace is, nor the law-courts and the public assembly; they are as ignorant of the pedigrees of noble families as of the details

of city gossip. They are so deeply immersed in mathematical
and astronomical problems and their gaze is so unwaveringly
directed on regions above, that they are not at home here in
this world, and stumble even over things that cause no trouble
to men with open eyes and sound brains. Yet Plato is quite convinced of their value, of the divine spark in their minds. Therefore the fact that they are inevitably misunderstood by their
fellow-men simply makes him exaggerate his description of them
into a caricature—so as to infuriate the Philistines and thereby
bring amusement and satisfaction to the understanding lover of
that strange philosophical character. The philosophical man
looks on life with a true artist's freedom, although without any
conceited attempts at originality and deliberate Bohemianism.
This portrait is probably more like the true philosopher than
the ideal blend of physical and mental culture set up by Plato
for his guards to attain. But his account of the studies of the
philosopher in *Theaetetus* closely resembles the higher education of the philosophical ruler in *The Republic*. That education illustrates his remark in *Theaetetus* that the philosopher's
knowledge is not so easy as sense-perception, which we all have
from birth: it 'grows up in him' only after much trouble and
long education (paideia).[376] *The Republic* shows us something
of the structure of this paideia in Plato's Academy; and in this
particular part, Plato is giving not only an ideal, but a slice of
reality.

After he has described how the philosopher resigns himself
to being misunderstood and remaining far from the world, it is
difficult for his readers to recur to the idea that the philosopher
is the ruler of the state of the future. The real philosopher, as
described to us in the preceding pages, looks a little silly when
measured against that lofty ideal. Yet Plato feels that is simply
another proof of his theory (in which he draws a parallel between the growth of plants and the growth of the human soul)
that education can be ruined by the wrong environment. The
philosopher is indeed a miraculous birth; but if he is trans-
planted to unsuitable soil, such as the states which now exist,
he is bound to be crippled in his growth, or else to grow like
them.[377] On the other hand, if he is moved to the favourable
surroundings of the ideal state, he will reveal his divine origin.[378]

This is the clearest indication of the fact that Plato's ideal state is simply the ideal society which is necessary for the full development of the qualities of the philosophical nature. Conversely, by making his philosopher the ruler of the state, Plato puts a spirit in it which is fit to maintain his educational system and establish a tradition. He, and he alone, fulfils the prescription in which the construction of the ideal Republic culminated—that there should be a supreme authority presiding over education.[379] Philosophical education as it had existed up to Plato's time could not possibly attain its highest aim, which was to be 'political' education: because it was always placed in the wrong period of life. It had always been only 'a paideia and philosophy for young men'.[380] This is another challenge to the sophists' characteristic ideal of studying philosophy 'merely for the sake of culture'.[381] Plato now produces his own programme, which gives a far more comprehensive meaning to culture by making it a process demanding all one's energy and all one's life. People would alter their ideas of the educational power of knowledge, if they could once get to know what real knowledge was, and test it. The idea of knowledge which is unattached, and sought for its own sake alone, is still strange to them.[382] They know of it only in the form of brilliantly clever, elaborately cunning types of oratory, which have no purpose or importance in themselves and serve simply to satisfy the passion for argument and the desire to show off.[383] Men must first realize that those whom they believe to be philosophers are not true philosophers. They will not despise the philosophers for being unworldly when they understand this: it is impossible for anyone who has dedicated his life to the observation of high and divine laws to take part in that all too human envy and spite, in the strife and backbiting of those whom the world falsely believes to be scholars and intellectuals, though they are really no more than bold intruders into the house of philosophy.[384] A man must be filled with divine calm and orderliness, if he attempts to understand the divine world of pure being which is ordained for all eternity.[385]

Just as in *Theaetetus,* the typical philosopher in *The Republic* has a notably close resemblance to a mathematician and astronomer, in comparison with the Socrates of Plato's earlier books. *The Republic* and *Theaetetus* were written during the same period of Plato's life, and the same theme in this connexion appears in both—that the nature of the philosopher comes to resemble the object of his study, the divine.[386] But in *The Republic*, although the philosopher is compelled in his present surroundings to lead a predominantly contemplative life, that is not the end of his whole existence. In the ideal state, he will move out of the sphere of pure contemplation into that of action. He will become a 'demiurge'. He will exchange the only creative work he is permitted in this present world, that of moulding himself (ἑαυτὸν πλάττειν) for the work of moulding other men's characters (ἤθη), either in private life or in public service.[387] Thus he will become the great painter who gazes within himself and works out the picture of the perfect polis.[388] We remember how Socrates, when he finished sketching his ideal Republic, compared himself to a painter who had done a picture of a perfectly handsome man.[389] The difference is that Socrates was constructing a model for reality to copy; while here the philosopher's 'picture'—the ideal state—is itself the new reality modelled upon the divine paradeigma in his soul. The painter is the statesman; the state itself is the *pinax,* the canvas, on which, after it has been thoroughly cleansed, the portrait of the new type of man takes form and colour. In him are blended the characteristics of eternal justice, beauty, self-control, and all other virtues, as well as traits which we observe in real men. He is indeed a blend of ideal and fact; and thus, under the hand of the philosophical artist, there grows up, not the 'godlike being' (θεοείκελον) that Homer depicted in the personages of his epic, but something corresponding to him, a 'manlike being' (ἀνδρείκελον).[390]

Here once again Plato emphasizes the parallel between poetry and philosophy, which guides all his thinking and all his character-drawing. The philosopher is able to compete successfully with the paideia of the poet, because he has a new ideal of humanity. In this passage Plato completes his transposition of the heroic ideal of character into the philosophical ideal, and orients his greatest work towards the polestar of humanism that guides the Greek spirit throughout its journey. For humanism means education which is deliberately modelled on a certain ideal conception of human nature. Plato offers his own philosophical humanism as a direct challenge to the sophis-

tical type, which was not governed by any such ideal as his, and
which he had described as assimilating itself to whatever kind
of state happened to exist at the moment. His humanism does
not shun politics on principle; still, its political attitude is dictated, not by the realities of experience, but by the ideals which
it holds to be the true reality. It is constantly ready to serve
the state, although not in this world but in the divinely perfect
world of the future. It feels bound to retain its right to criticize every kind of real state, because it looks not towards any
temporal model, but towards eternity.[391] Plato places the ideal
portrait of the 'human' or the 'manlike being', as a symbol of
the real meaning and content of the true state, at the opening of his discussion of the ruler's paideia. It is impossible to
mould men without an ideal of humanity. The process of 'self-
moulding' to which philosophical paideia is confined in the real
world of to-day, acquires a higher social significance because it
is preparing the way for the ideal state. Plato does not believe
that this relationship is a mere fiction, an As If. Here as
elsewhere he says the ideal state is possible, though it is difficult to realize.[392] Thereby he supports the idea of the 'future'
for which the philosopher is moulding himself, and keeps it
from melting into pure imagination; the possibility that the philosopher's 'theoretical life' may at any moment change into the
practical gives it a wonderful tension and excitement entirely
absent from 'pure' science. It is because of its intermediary position, between pure research devoid of any purpose in the realm
of practical conduct, and the wholly practical, political, and
success-loving culture of the sophists, that Plato's humanism
stands above them both.

THE REPUBLIC

PART II

THE PAIDEIA OF THE RULERS: THE DIVINE MODEL

IMMEDIATELY after Plato finished his description of the guards'
education, he pointed out that the rulers, who were to preserve
the spirit of true education in the ideal state, ought to have special training themselves.[1] But the subject was postponed, while
he discussed the education of women and children and the community of wives.[2] Still the doctrine that the philosopher must
have supreme power, which as it seemed was introduced only
as a precondition for the realization of Plato's other theories,
naturally leads back to the education of the ruling class,[3] after
the problem of 'saving the philosophical character' proves to be
the same as the problem of giving the philosophical nature the
right education.

The athletic and 'musical' training of the guards is at bottom
the traditional Greek paideia, which as far as intellectual things
went was ruled by custom and tradition [4]; but it has been revised
from a philosophical point of view. Plato bases it on ideas of
that which is good and just; but he does not prove these ideas
to be accurate, he merely assumes their validity. Its purpose is
to create right harmony and right rhythm in the soul—not to
understand the reasons why that particular type of harmony
and rhythm is good. At this stage of education it is impossible
for the learner to understand the reasons. But the man who
constructs and supervises the whole scheme of education—
namely, the ruler—must understand the reasons before his work
begins. His special education is intended to make him understand them: therefore it must be philosophical. Although it
comes at a later stage in time than the training in music and
gymnastics, it is really earlier by nature and definition. The
whole plan of education must begin with it. Plato connects it
with the first stage, by bringing in the paradeigma, placed mid-

way between them both, as the special possession which destines the philosopher to be a ruler and an educator in the highest sense of the word.[5] The supreme standard, the 'pattern' with reference to which he outlined the guards' paideia, he calls the greatest subject of study (μέγιστον μάθημα), because it is the hardest to understand and at the same time the most important knowledge that the ruler of the Republic must possess.[6] The word *mathéma* contains the one decisively new factor in philosophical education compared with all earlier stages of paideia: the fact that, instead of teaching through paradeigmata in the form of poetic personages or separate moral injunctions, its educational paradeigma is one universal knowledge, in fact, the knowledge of one single object. The inflexible and incorruptible character which Plato expects his rulers to have must be coupled with the highest intellectual ability and trained by the most accurate educational system (ἀκριβεστάτη παιδεία).[7] He must be no more afraid of the difficulty of learning than he was of other things, when, after the exertions of physical training, he begins 'the gymnastics of the mind'.[8]

Hegel said, in a famous epigram, that 'the way of the mind is roundabout'. The natural route seems to be the one which leads straight to its goal. But it is often broken by a deep invisible chasm; or blocked by other obstacles to direct access. To overcome these difficulties by taking a circuitous route to the goal, however arduous it may be, is the nature of all systematic research, and particularly of philosophical thought. Indeed, it looks rather as if Hegel's epigram had been inspired by a hint in Plato, which he had expanded into a more general formula. In laying down the necessity for the rulers to have special training, Plato reminds us [9] how he had previously described his treatment of the problem of the four virtues, in which the guards' education culminates, as brief and sketchy, and how he had pointed out that 'a long detour' would be necessary for a full understanding of the subject. He said then that it was not needed in the lower stage of the guards' education. But at the start of the true philosophical education he reverts to it, declaring that those who are to be rulers of the Republic must now take this detour, or else they will never get to know 'the greatest subject'. There have been disputes about what he meant by the detour; but, although his language in the passage where it is first mentioned is rather ambiguous,[10] the way in which he picks up the metaphor of the detour, at the beginning of the philosopher's education, makes it impossible to doubt that he means the path of philosophical education which the rulers must traverse. If we take it to mean a system of education for future statesmen, 'political culture', it is very appropriate that Plato's system of mathematical and dialectical training should be called a 'detour'.[11] The name shows the novelty of the programme—namely, Plato's demand that men who are to engage in active practical life should prepare for it by long years of purely intellectual training. Plato formulates the principle which makes him think the detour necessary, in the following way: 'We must observe the greatest accuracy about the greatest truths'.[12] That is Socrates' old demand that the politician should have exact and specialized knowledge of the highest aim of all human conduct. To satisfy it, Plato puts forward the science of dialectic, developed by him from Socrates' art of conversational debate.

But before giving any details of the stages of the 'detour', he diverts our eyes, and points to the end of the journey, the steep pinnacle we have to climb. Heretofore it has simply been called 'the greatest subject'. It is nothing more or less than the Idea of Good—that *because of which* all justice, beauty, et cetera, is profitable and beneficial.[13] Unless we know it, all our knowledge is useless. What would be the good of possessing something that was good for nothing? By describing 'the good' (as he usually calls it) as 'the Idea of Good', he means, first of all, universal goodness (as the word Idea signifies), the unity of all goodness in contrast to the various objects which we call 'good', because, as Plato puts it, they have some 'share' in the Idea of Good. This way of looking at it is strange to the ordinary man; and yet even he recognizes a sort of *summum bonum* by reducing everything he thinks valuable to the pleasure that he derives from it.[14] But ever since *Gorgias* (and indirectly ever since *Protagoras*) we have realized that this vulgar assumption that pleasure is the highest good does not fit in with the distinction between good and bad pleasures, although most people take it for granted too.[15] Cultivated men are inclined to take wisdom and reason to be the highest good. But when asked what kind of knowledge they have in view, they answer 'knowledge of the good'.[16] Other dialogues prove that Plato has no intention of condemning the two opposing views out of hand. They are both aiming at the real 'human good', which, according to *Philebus*, is composed of both pleasure and intelligence in the right blend.[17] But neither pleasure nor reason is in itself the highest good.[18] Those who support one or the other of them agree (as Plato shows in *The Republic*) in assigning a higher value to Good itself than to the thing they believe supreme—as we said, they put *good* pleasures above *bad* ones, or judge knowledge of the *good* superior to all other kinds of knowledge.[19] However, we do not need the preliminary definition of the Idea of Good in order to appreciate its importance in the education of the ruling class. We need only take into account the most universal mark of good, the one which everyone knows—namely, that good is the thing about which no one is voluntarily mistaken.[20] If we do that, we can realize how wrong it would be to hand over the government of the state to a ruler who was in the dark about this, the most vital of all problems.[21]

Plato does not try, even in the succeeding sections of the book, to define accurately the nature of Good itself. In fact, he never gives a definition of it anywhere in any of his books, although the discussion often leads towards that point. Among his later works, *Philebus* is the one which contains a systematic examination of the question raised here, whether pleasure or reason is the highest good. But even there, Plato does not attempt to close by giving an exhaustive definition of the Good. Instead, he deduces three of its characteristics—beauty, symmetry, and truth [22]—and uses these criteria to determine whether pleasure or reason is nearer to good. In *The Republic* he makes Socrates first of all take refuge in the 'ignorance' affected by the real historical Socrates, when his interlocutor Glaucon asks him not merely to give the opinions of others but to state his own belief about Good.[23] But elsewhere in the book he is not such a sceptic, but declares that the art of political navigation can really be taught [24]; and so Plato does not allow him to maintain his pretence of ignorance. But he makes Glaucon suggest that his hearers would be very glad if he would give his views about the Good even in the same summary way in which he had discussed civic virtue before.[25] As we recollect, he had not given a final definition of the four virtues. Instead, he had outlined

their position and function in the soul, by paralleling them with
the various social classes and their functions in the state.[26] He
does the same now with the problem of the Good—he avoids
any technical philosophizing, and instead he illustrates the position and influence of the Good in the world by means of a
visual analogy. It is an image (*eikon*) that combines poetic
force and vivid logical clarity; and it all at once reveals that
which, throughout his earlier works, had been deliberately
shrouded in mystery or vaguely indicated in the distance—the
position and meaning of the Idea of Good, the supreme principle of Plato's philosophy.

During the course of the discussion, it has become doubtful
whether it is possible to apprehend the Good through any intellectual definition. The image that Plato substitutes for such
a definition shows that we must approach the problem in another
way. In his dialectic, 'to see' had come to describe the act of
the mind in putting many particulars together to realize the
single idea behind them. He himself sometimes calls this act
synopsis.[27] But since the last stage of the dialectic way towards
'seeing' the Idea of Good cannot possibly be described in writing, he explains it by quoting its 'analogon' in the visible world,
the world of sight. Eternal good displays its nature, he tells
us,[28] in its son Helios, the Sun, the highest visible god in heaven.
He does not say that the Sun's parent is a god—that would be
assuming what we are trying to discover. Therefore the visible
symbolism of his theology first of all includes only the son.
When Glaucon hints that he would like some time to hear the
same kind of 'story' about the parent, Socrates puts him off by
saying he wishes that he could tell one, and that his hearers
could understand it. He alludes briefly to his remarks earlier in
the dialogue, about the theory of Ideas, and to his more detailed exposition of it elsewhere in his dialogues.[29] Then, in conformity with the distinction between idea and appearance, he
distinguishes two worlds, the intelligible world, known through
thought, and the visible world, known through sight. We call
the world known to sense-perception the visible world, because
sight is the noblest of our senses.[30] The reason Plato gives for
thinking sight the noblest of the senses is that the eye needs
light as a medium to see by, and light is a peculiarly noble thing.

The fundamental reason why the eye sees and the outer world is visible is the god who sends down light, Helios. (Now we remember the doctrine which was mentioned and discarded earlier in the dialogue, that knowledge itself is the Good,[31] and we begin to see the significance of the comparison. What he means to point out is that good is real, objectively real, independently of our consciousness.) What is the relation, he asks, of our power of sight to the heavenly god of light? Neither our sight nor our eyes *are* Helios himself.[32] We might perhaps say that the eye is the most sunlike of our sense-organs; but it becomes capable of seeing only through the light which it takes in as it flows towards it from the sun. It is through that light that the eye is able to see the sun itself; but the sun is not sight. It is the source of light, and therefore it is the cause of all sight.

Now we have got very close to understanding the process of knowledge, and the part played in it by the Idea of Good. The soul is like the eye.[33] If we do not turn it towards that region from which daylight streams forth in brilliant rays, but towards the world of night, dimly lit by the stars, the eye will see poorly and blindly as though it did not possess the pure power of sight. So with the soul. If it turns its gaze to that world which is brightly lit by the rays of truth and reality, then it understands, and thinks, and reasons. But if it looks towards the darkly confused region where things are always coming into being and passing away, it produces nothing but opinion, it is weak-sighted, it vacillates, like something devoid of reason.[34] What gives truth to the things the soul apprehends, and what gives it understanding to know them, is the Idea of Good. It is the primary cause of knowledge and truth. We can know it too, just as we can see the sun, by which we see other things. But it is far nobler than either knowledge or truth, just as the sun is nobler than our sense of sight.[35] As the sun is the source of light, making the visible world visible, so the Idea of Good is the source of truth and meaning, and makes the thinkable world thinkable. Therefore our knowledge is not the Good, any more than our sense of sight is the sun.[36] Yet, just as the eye is the most sunlike (*helioid*) of all our organs, knowledge and truth are the most goodlike (*agathoid*), the closest to the basic form of good. But the parallel casts its light still further. The sun gives the visible world not only its visibility, but its powers of growth and nutrition, although it is not itself the process of becoming. Similarly, the intelligible world derives not only its intelligibility from the Good, but its reality too—although the Good itself is not reality, but is even superior to reality in nobleness and power.[37] This dual significance of Good as the cause of all knowledge and all being allows us to call it the monarch of the invisible, intelligible world, as Helios is the king of the visible world.[38]

Greek philosophers before Plato had usually described the highest principle in the universe—whether it was the material substratum which bestows life, or the spirit which controls everything—simply as God, or 'the divine'.[39] From the very first, Greek philosophy had been concerned with nature, the nature (*physis*) of reality or 'being'. That is the origin of what we call science. However, there has been a tendency ever since the nineteenth century to allow the scientific aspect of Greek philosophy to obscure its religious aspect, or even to discard the religious aspect as mere window-dressing. This makes it practically impossible to understand Plato, who is far more religious than any of his predecessors. We cannot appraise his central doctrine of the Idea of Good except against a religious background. Plato is the greatest of all classical theologians.[39a] Without him, neither the name nor the subject of theology would exist. His remarks about the nature of God are distributed all through his works, and their importance is various. It is impossible here to discuss the vexed question of his theological beliefs. We must be content to discuss it where it comes within the purview of his paideia in *The Republic;* and we may limit ourselves to pointing out its place in the whole system of Plato's paideia, and stressing the theological function of the supreme principle towards which he leads his readers.[39b]

According to Greek ideas, Plato, by making the Idea of Good monarch of the intelligible world, like the sun in the world of sight, gives it the same divinity as the God of other thinkers, even though he does not actually call it God.[40] It looks as if he had purposely avoided doing that, because it was so obvious that the reader could fill it in without help, and also because it was important to distinguish his supreme being from the gods of everyday religion.[41] But if we recall his description of the 'outlines of theology' affecting the poetry to be read in the

guards' school, we shall see that nothing deserves the name of
God better than the Idea of Good: it is fully covered by his
definition of the divinity, as that which never does evil and
always does good.[42] That is the dogma underlying his criticism
of epic and tragedy for misrepresenting the gods. As we have
seen, it is based on the belief that the supreme principle is the
Idea of Good. Perhaps that is another reason why he does not
call it God—because he would not add anything essential to
it by doing so. On the other hand, the statement that God can
do nothing but good makes the nature and activity of God himself answerable to that standard which is the Idea of Good.[43]
Actually, the leading proof of the 'divine' character of the
Good is that it has made Plato's God into a 'measure' like
itself. For, as Plato says in *The Laws,* God is the measure of
all things;[44] and he is the measure of all things because he is
the Good. The Idea of Good here is the supreme standard
which is the basis for a conception that appears early and survives late in the development of Plato's thought: the conception
that philosophy is the supreme 'art of measurement'. Such an
art could not, as the sophists and the mass of ordinary men believed in *Protagoras,* use the subjective scale of pleasure and
pain. It must employ an entirely objective standard.[45] But here
we can adduce another piece of evidence. Aristotle, in one of
his early dialogues, *The Statesman,* where he is evidently still
thinking along Platonic lines, calls the Good 'the most exact
measure'.[46] There are two points of interest about that remark:
it shows the close connexion between the Good and the exact
political art of measurement desiderated by Plato, and it provides a welcome link between the Idea of Good in *The Republic*
and the God defined in *The Laws* as 'the measure of all things'.

For Plato's ontological realism, the Idea of Good is not an
idea in our sense of the word, but is itself good. In fact, it is the
Good in its most perfect form, just as the Idea of beauty is
itself beautiful, and indeed the most beautiful being that there
is. Moreover, to be good means, for Plato, to be happy.[46a] The
Greeks held that one of the most essential aspects of God's
nature was happiness. The Homeric gods are simply called 'the
blessed'. If we are right in explaining that Plato held the Idea
of Good, as the pattern of everything in the world that deserves

the name good, to be 'God', then it ought also to be called happy; and this would be supported by Plato's thesis that areté (= being good) is the same as happiness. Absolute Good is the reason for the existence of every kind of areté in the world: therefore it must share in happiness, *eudaimonia,* or rather it must be the ultimate source of happiness. In a later passage of *The Republic* which has not always had the attention it deserves, Plato actually says that the Idea of Good is the happiest thing in the universe.[47] We now see that the Good is the supreme paradeigma of which the philosopher carries knowledge in his heart.[48] To replace the gods and heroes of legend, who were the models of areté in human form set up by the paideia of earlier Greece in the works of the great poets, Plato's new philosophical paideia in *The Republic* sets up divine Good as the perfect paradeigma. And thus the great saying in *Theaetetus,* that the philosopher's life according to areté is 'assimilation to God', becomes the noblest expression of Plato's paideia;[49] and the connexion between the Idea of Good and the education of the philosopher in which it is to be 'the greatest subject' is made perfectly plain. If God is by nature good, if in fact he is Good itself, then the highest areté attainable by man is a process of coming to resemble God. For, as the smaller dialogues have already shown, the basis underlying all the separate virtues (aretai) is Good-in-itself, absolute, perfect goodness. These books were all investigations of the nature of different virtues, but they all served the same purpose: instead of defining the virtues, they led back to the principle of Good in itself, which is revealed in *The Republic* to be the divine principle (ἀρχή) of all being and all thought.[49a] Yet this does not seem to harmonize with Plato's assertion that *humanity,* 'that which is like mankind', is the aim of the philosophical painter. (The assertion was made at the beginning of his description of the higher paideia.)[50] But there he said that the 'humanity' drawn by the painter was parallel to the 'godlike' being described by the epic poet, and stated that the new pattern of mankind was to be so mixed of ideal and real elements that it should be as 'God-beloved' as possible.[51] So even there the ultimate standard is not man, in his individual contingent nature, as it was in the paideia of the sophists who made man the measure of all things. Complete humanity is possible only through endeavour to approximate to the divine, that is, the eternal measure and standard.[52]

But we have got ahead of Plato's argument. At first, he seems to be interested only in the metaphysical aspect of the Idea of Good. It is as if he had entirely forgotten its relation to the function of educating men and women. This has very often misled commentators into taking the sun-metaphor out of its context, and interpreting it as an independent symbol of Plato's metaphysics or of Plato's theory of knowledge—particularly because it comes at the close of the sixth book, and so looks like a high point of the discussion, which is not what Plato meant. The metaphor illustrates how the soul acquires knowledge—but that knowledge is knowledge of the Good: therefore it is inextricably connected with the problem of acquiring virtue. Even when Plato is making the most remote and difficult metaphysical deductions from Socratic principles, the structure of his thought still bears signs of the educational basis on which it is founded. The metaphysics of paideia is an ontology culminating in the Idea of Good. Reality, or Being, in Plato's thought, is not unconnected with man and his will. The Idea of Good which gives meaning and value to Plato's whole world of ideas is the natural aim of all endeavour. To know it, we must make our character and conduct resemble it. But it cannot be known within this immediately obvious world of sense, it is hidden from our eyes by several barriers. The first step towards flooding the eye of the soul with its light, and thereby making the world of truth visible to it, is to cast off those obstructive veils.

Therefore Plato joins the sun-metaphor closely on to a metaphor describing the stages by which knowledge moves from the emptiest sham of appearance to the vision of the supreme reality. It is a mathematical image. The progress of knowledge, he says, is like a line divided into two unequal parts.

$$\underline{\quad\quad A \quad\quad /\!/ \quad\quad B \quad\quad\quad}$$

Each of its parts is divided in the same ratio as the entire line.[53]

$$\underline{\quad A^1 \;/\; A^2 \;/\!/\; B^1 \;/\; \quad B^2 \quad}$$

The two main sections, A and B, represent the visible and the intelligible world, or else (in terms of the theory of ideas) the world of *opinion* and the world of *reality* and *knowledge*. In section A, symbolizing the visible world, there are two subsections, A¹ and A². Of these, A¹ covers everything that is only a copy, such as shadows, reflections in water, and images in bright smooth surfaces. The other subsection, A², represents the world of plants and animals in which we live, and all sorts of artificial objects. The shadows and reflections which occupy the first class are the copies of the things in the second: the same objects appear in both subsections, in different degrees of truth and reality. Then the same relation must exist between the objects which occupy the third subsection, and those which occupy the fourth: for the division of the entire line and the subdivision of its two sections in the same ratio shows that Plato is thinking of a regular proportion. Of course his real meaning is not adequately expressed by the various geometrical sections, for he is not concerned with the quantitative relationship between the various sets of objects, but with the relative degrees of their reality and of the exactitude of our knowledge of them. It is only the second section of the line that takes us out of the realm of opinion into that of scientific enquiry and knowledge and truth —that is, the region within which the education of the philosophical ruler is to take place. Here for the first time Plato reveals the idea underlying his method of teaching. It is a gradual progress, by which the pupil is lifted above the world of sense and finally climbs the heights of philosophical truth.

The first subdivision of section B contains the special arts and skills dealing with objects (the τέχναι),[54] like mathematics, which begin with hypotheses and reach new knowledge by following out their logical consequences.[55] They use visible figures as images. Yet they do not really prove their truths to be valid for the visible figures; they prove them about the Triangle in itself and the Circle in itself which are the true objects of their thought.[56] Because they abstract the truth from sensible objects and try to see the essence of the mathematical objects (circles, triangles, angles, et cetera) with the eyes of the mind, they are very close to the highest philosophical methods of reaching knowledge. But on the other hand they are tied to the world of sense and the stage of knowledge which is appropriate to it (i.e. opinion) in two ways:

(1) they start with hypotheses built around sensible figures, although their theorems do not really concern the visual images at all;

(2) they do not attempt, in principle, to rise above these hypotheses which are taken as true ('adopted'), and because they follow them out logically right to the last possible deduction, they are forced to treat them as principles (ἀρχαί) at the same time.[57]

It is only in the last subsection of the line, B², the second part of the intelligible world, that we come to a kind of knowledge that starts from hypotheses, not in the same way as mathematics, but in the manner signified by the word *hypothesis:* that is, as bases on which to stand, and from which to move upwards to the absolute, the principle of the universe.[58] This kind of knowledge is the real or pure logos. It rises to grasp the highest principle; from there, by holding onto what is just next to it and within its reach, it descends again to the end without the help of any sense-perception; and thus, moving from Ideas to Ideas, it finally rests at Ideas.[59]

Several times Plato points out how difficult it is to make the various stages of this progression easily understandable in a brief compass. He does so by making Socrates' interlocutors, who are quite well trained in philosophy, fail completely at first to understand what he means, and end by grasping only the outline of his argument.[60] But Plato is evidently not concerned about putting down on one page the last secrets of his logic and methodology—although most of the commentators, who revel in this passage, think he is. He is merely trying to give a bold diagram of the various stages of knowledge, right up to the pure dialectic dissociated from any sensible image whatever, the type of knowledge which leads up to the universal principle, the absolute, and therefore can go down again, and show how everything else is derived from that principle. It is only that form of thought which deserves the name of intellect (*nous*). Compared with it, mathematical thought is only understanding (*dianoia*), while sense-perception of the material world is only opinion (*pistis*). The fourth and lowest stage is pure guesswork or conjecture (*eikasia*):[61] its objects, as seen from the stage above it, the stage of sense-perception, are mere copies.[62] Similarly any sensible reality (e.g. a wooden sphere) is itself only a 'copy' of the kind of reality with which the mathematician deals (the sphere in itself).[63] Plato does not say that the type of reality dealt with by mathematical knowledge is merely a copy of that which is apprehended by dialectic. But he must have something like that in view when he says that the universal propositions taken as principles by the mathematician are merely hypotheses for the philosopher, from which he rises to the true principle.[64]

The mathematical ratio which illustrates these four stages leads from the sun-metaphor, which forms the climax at the end of the sixth book, to the image of the cave at the beginning of the seventh. Until now the process by which the philosopher's knowledge rises to grasp the Idea of Good has only been described in abstract terms. But the image of the cave symbolizes it with supreme poetic force and vividness.

THE CAVE—AN IMAGE OF PAIDEIA

'And now', Socrates begins the famous parable,[65] 'compare our nature, from the point of view of paideia and lack of paideia, to an experience like this'. He imagines men in an underground cave, which has a broad entrance open to the light. They have been chained down there since childhood, by their legs and neck, so that they cannot move, and cannot turn round and look behind. They have their backs to the entrance. Above and behind them, some distance off, a fire is burning: its rays fall above the heads of the prisoners on the back wall of the cave, towards which they are looking. Between them and the fire there is a road, along which runs a low wall, like the stage of a marionette-theatre, upon which conjurors show their puppets. Behind the wall there are people carrying along all sorts of objects and figures made of wood and stone, some talking and others silent. The objects show above the wall, and the fire throws their shadows onto the back wall. The prisoners cannot turn round, so that they have never seen anything all their lives except the shadows. They naturally take the shadows for reality, and the echoes of the voices for the speech of the shadow-figures.

Now, if one of them were released from his chains, and compelled to climb up and look towards the light, he would not be able, because of the dazzling brightness, to see the things whose shadows he used to look at; and he would not believe it if anyone told him everything he had seen hitherto was all nonsense, while he was now looking at a world of higher reality.[66] Instead, he would be quite convinced that the shadow-pictures he used to see were the true reality, and he would turn away with smarting eyes into the cave once more. He would need long practice before he would see the upper world. At first he would be able to see only shadows, and then the reflections of men and things in water; then, much later, the men and things themselves. Thereafter he would look at the sky and the stars at night; and finally he would be able to gaze at the sun—not its reflection in water or elsewhere, but itself in its purity and in its right place. Then he would recognize that it is the sun which produces the changing seasons and the years, and controls everything in the visible world, and is somehow the cause even of the things which he and his fellow-prisoners used to see.

When he remembered his first home, and the wisdom he had there, and his companions in prison, he would be delighted with the change, and pity them. Now, supposing there were honours and distinctions for the prisoner who was best at recognizing the shadows as they glided past, and at remembering which of them came first and which last and which came together, so that he could best foretell which were coming (Plato is thinking of the politician who works purely by experience), the freed prisoner would scarcely yearn to return, and envy his comrades their honours. Instead, like Homer's Achilles, he would prefer to 'work as a lowly serf' in the upper world of reason rather than be king in the world of shadows.[67] But if he went down again into the cave, and tried to compete with the others at identifying the shadows as before, he would be ridiculous, because he would be unable to see in the dark: his fellows would say he had spoilt his eyes while up above. And if he tried to set them free and take them up, they would kill him if they could get hold of him.

Plato himself gives the interpretation of this parable. It is quite clear as soon as we connect it with the two preceding metaphors, the comparison of the Idea of Good to the sun, and the mathematical ratio between the different degrees of knowledge and reality.[68] The cave corresponds to the visible world. The fire which illuminates it corresponds to our sun. The ascent to the world above it represents the soul's ascent to the intelligible world. Socrates gives all this as his personal 'hope': God knows if it is true, but it is how it seems to him.[69] The concept of hope in this sense is specially used of the expectations which initiates in the mystery-religions have about the next world: here it is transferred to describe the soul's expectations of passing from the visible to the invisible world.[69a] And besides, the apprehension of true being *is* a passage from time into eternity. In the region of pure knowledge the last thing which the soul 'with difficulty' learns to see is the Idea of Good. But when one has seen it, one must conclude that it is the cause of everything right and beautiful, and that anyone who wants to act sensibly in private or public life must have seen it.[70] The true philosopher's unwillingness to take part in the affairs of men, and his longing to stay in the upper world, are easy to understand in view of this simile; and we can understand why he looks ridiculous coming down from these divine visions to the bad world of men, when his eyes are still blinded with the light above, and are not yet used to the darkness. But the confusion felt by the eye of the soul when it comes from light into darkness is different from the confusion it suffers when going from the darkness of ignorance into the light; and anyone who thoroughly understands the situation will not laugh, but congratulate the soul on its passage from dark to light, and commiserate it on the opposite.[71]

We have given this whole section pretty much in Plato's own words, not simply because it is the finest piece of poetic imagination in the book, but also, and chiefly, because it is vitally important to our enquiry here. The parable is a profound one; since classical antiquity it has been interpreted innumerable times, and widely different meanings have been drawn from it. But we are uniquely fortunate in one thing: Plato has added his own explanation, which is clear, brief, and complete. It directs our attention to the exact point which he wishes to make. Thereby it keeps us from wandering off into problems which are extremely important but need not be investigated any more closely in this connexion. Such, for instance, is the problem of philosophical method, in which modern thinkers are particularly

interested. What he says about it in this passage is to be explained by his other dialogues: it cannot contribute much to
explaining them. Therefore we shall confine ourselves to summarizing what Plato himself says about the significance of the
two images for his main theme.

The image of the sun and the image of the cave (which, as
we have pointed out, are linked into a unity by the simile of the
divided line) are one single metaphorical expression of the nature of paideia. Every book on Greek philosophy discusses these
images, saying that they are impressive symbols of Plato's
vision of the universe. But very few pay any attention to the first
sentence of the seventh book, which leads into the image of the
cave. There Plato actually states that it is an image of paideia:
or, more exactly, that it represents the nature of man, and its
relation to culture and 'unculture', paideia and apaideusia. Any
reader who can understand more than one sentence at once in
a logical connexion must see that this remark points in two
directions, forwards and backwards. Paideia has of course been
referred to before—it is imaged in the sun-simile and in that of
the divided line, which describes the four grades of reality.
There the highest aim of paideia was defined—it is the knowledge of Good, the supreme measure, the measure of all measures. Plato pointed out previously that this image is the first
step towards describing the philosopher-ruler's education: he
said that the Idea of Good is 'the greatest subject of study'.[72]
Now the image of the cave shows the relation between *our
nature* and this goal.[73] It treats paideia not in the absolute
sense, as in the image of the sun, but from the point of view
of humanity as the transformation and enlightenment of the
soul till it reaches the point when it can see the vision of the
supreme reality. By directing our attention away from the ultimate aim to the emotional experience of this inward process
of education, he makes us more capable of understanding its
methodical progress in mathematical and dialectical teaching.
Before taking us into the dryly rational discussion of the cultural value of such studies, he shows us the nature and the significance of the entire spiritual process by describing the vision
of the ascent of the soul towards light and true reality. He
makes us feel the whole impact of the emotion accompanying

this process; and by describing the metamorphosis of the soul he explains the *liberating* work of knowledge, which he calls paideia in the very highest sense.

PAIDEIA AS CONVERSION

After reading his earlier dialogues, we are bound to expect that, somewhere in *The Republic,* he will draw the necessary deductions from the revolution in the conception of knowledge that is first foreshadowed in *Meno*.[74] Even in his earliest books he had taken care to show that Socrates' 'ignorance' was the *aporia* or doubt of a man who was endeavouring to conquer and to make more profound the existing concept of knowledge. What *The Republic* says about this subject is bound to be far less precise than the dialogues which are written as special studies of the problem of knowledge. In it he is merely setting in order the results they reached. His own interpretation of the images of the sun and the cave absolutely excludes the usual conception of paideia—that knowledge is poured into an ignorant soul as if the power of sight were given to blind eyes.[75] True education means the awakening of abilities asleep in the soul. It starts the functioning of the organ by which we learn and understand; or, to continue the visual metaphor, it turns the soul round to the source from which light (= knowledge) flows. As if the only way our eye could face towards the light were by turning the whole body round, so we must turn 'with our whole soul' away from the realm of becoming, until it can bear to look at the brightest pinnacle of reality.[76]

Therefore the essence of philosophical education is 'conversion', which literally means 'turning round'. 'Conversion' is a specific term of Platonic paideia, and indeed an epoch-making one. It means more specifically the wheeling round of the 'whole soul' towards the light of the Idea of Good, the divine origin of the universe.[77] There is an important difference between this experience and conversion to the Christian faith, which was later named after the philosophical concept, conversion. That is the fact that the philosopher's knowledge is rooted in objective reality. On the other hand, as conceived by Plato, it is absolutely free from the intellectualism of which it is often wrongly accused. The seventh Letter shows that the spirit of this knowledge can kindle only in a soul which through long years of endeavour has reached the closest possible kinship with the object—i.e. Good itself.[78] The living manifestation and activity of this phronésis is a virtue, which Plato distinguishes from the ordinary virtues by calling it the philosophical virtue— because it is grounded on conscious knowledge of the eternal principle of all good.[78a] By comparison, the 'so-called virtues' (temperance, courage, et cetera) which were the aim of the guards' education, seem more closely connected with physical virtues such as strength and health. They were not pre-existent in the soul, but were created in it by custom and practice.[79] The philosophical virtue, phronésis, is the one comprehensive virtue which Socrates sought for throughout his life. It belongs to 'a more divine part of us', a part which is always present, but which cannot be opened up unless the soul is made to face in the proper direction and turn round to the Good.[80] Philosophical culture and the philosophical virtue corresponding to it are higher degrees of ordinary culture and ordinary virtue, because they are a higher degree of reality. If, as the soul strives to mould itself by striving towards wisdom, there is any progress towards a higher level of being and therewith to higher perfection, then that progress is, as Plato says in *Theaetetus,* 'becoming like God'.[81]

The incessant secret excitement that marks the efforts of Socrates and his friends in Plato's dialogues, as they endeavour to acquire knowledge of virtue in itself and of good in itself, here at last comes to rest. This is the end it has been striving to reach—even although it can never really enter a state of permanent possession and unmoved satisfaction. From the individual's point of view, the inmost nature of philosophy is constant struggle to imitate the paradeigma, 'the pattern that stands in the realm of Being'.[82] But in an idealized state that is considered to be entirely grounded on this philosophy (or phronésis) which appears throughout it as its architectural principle, philosophy must necessarily seem final, complete, and irresistible. Knowledge of the 'starting-point of everything',[83] the cause of all good, is the principle of government in that state. Apart from the variation in phrasing, there is no difference between this principle and the fundamental statement in *The Laws* that 'God is the measure of all things'.[84] The state described in *The Laws* is 'theonomic', ruled by God, but it is not the opposite of the Republic—it is modelled on it. Although it gives philosophical knowledge only as much scope as befits the lower plane of ontological reality on which it is built, it maintains that supreme principle. Plato says in *Phaedo* that the discovery of the good and of the final cause is the historical turning-point in the philosophy of nature, where the pre-Socratic and post-Socratic worlds divide.[85] Aristotle constructed his history of philosophy in the first book of the *Metaphysics* around this notion.[86] The statement is no less true of political philosophy than of natural philosophy. In natural philosophy Socrates' discovery led Plato to distinguish between physics and the highest philosophy which is the theory of Ideas, and is ultimately theology. In politics Plato's conviction that the Idea of Good is the end of all action leads to the rule of the philosopher-king (who represents the new religion of the spirit) over the Republic inspired by the pure Idea.

Plato's pupils believed that when he proclaimed the Good to be the ultimate cause of everything in the universe, he was founding a new religion. This is made quite certain by Aristotle's laudatory poem on the altar of Philia. They thought also that Plato's belief that being good was the same as being happy was made manifestly true at least once in this world, in the person of their master.[87] Following the tradition of the Academy and the orientation given to philosophy by Plato, Aristotle called his 'first philosophy' *theology*.[88] Another of Plato's pupils, Philip of Opus, edited *The Laws,* adding an appendix of Plato's wisest thoughts, which he conceived as *theology* too.[89] He cannot have compiled it and published it along with *The Laws* without the consent of the Academy.[90] Now, he takes as the basic principle of the state described in *The Laws,* not the doctrine of the Idea of Good (although he is obviously thinking of it as a model), but the astronomical theology of the 'visible gods' mentioned in *Timaeus*.[91] That corresponds to the distinction between the empirical reality described in *The Laws* and the reality apprehended by pure phronésis described in *The Republic*. As a matter of fact, it was Plato who founded theology. That revolutionary concept never appears in history before Plato's *Republic,* where 'outlines of theology' are sketched out to help in employing the

knowledge of God (= the Good) in education.[92] Theology—
study of the highest problems in the universe by means of
philosophical reason—is a specifically Greek creation. It is the
loftiest and most daring venture of the intellect; and Plato's
pupils had to combat the widespread Greek feeling (really a
vulgar prejudice) that the jealousy of the gods forbade men to
understand such high matters. They could not appeal to the
authority of a divine revelation which they possessed, but to the
knowledge of good which Plato had taught them, good whose
nature cannot admit jealousy.[93]

This makes theology a higher and purer work of the intellect than any mere religion—any worship which is based on
mythical ideas accepted through faith. At an earlier stage of
culture, the state had founded its system of discipline upon religion. Although piety had been undermined by the spirit of
rational doubt, Plato's contemporaries still held it to be one of
the four cardinal virtues of the citizen of the polis. Along with
the other three, Plato takes it over from that religious and
political tradition. It interests him from the beginning of his
career as a philosopher. He gives it a dialogue to itself, soon
after Socrates' death—the *Euthyphro*. Even there the traditional conception of piety is critically compared with the new
Socratic concept, which measures all things not only on earth
but in heaven against one standard, the Good.[94] It is not merely
coincidence that makes *Euthyphro* the first Platonic dialogue in
which the Ideas are mentioned.[95] Then in *The Republic* piety,
eusebeia, is included as one of the 'so-called virtues' in the first
stage of paideia, the education of the guards.[96] On the higher
plane of reality represented by the philosophical culture of the
rulers, it has disappeared. Together with the other three civic
virtues of the average man, it has merged into the higher unity
of 'wisdom'—which is itself a divine part of the soul and can
know the divine in its purest aspect, as the Idea of Good.[97]
Piety in the ordinary sense has been replaced by the philosophical form of it created by the Greeks, theology, which now
becomes the basic principle of the state. We might well adapt
Spinoza's title, and call *The Republic,* Plato's chief work, in
which he lays this ideal foundation of paideia, a *Tractatus
Theologico-politicus.* Despite the close connexion between religion and the state, the Greeks never had a priesthood sup-

ported by dogma. But in Plato's *Republic* Hellas produced a bold ideal worthy to be matched with the priestly theocracy of the Orient: a ruling class of trained philosophers, their claim to rule founded on the ability of the human mind to seek out and find the good which is God. We have pointed out above that, although Plato thought of his state as a Greek polis, its Greekness was only the material of which it was built.[98] The divine Idea of Good expresses itself as the formative principle in that material; and thereby the rational element which has been active in Greek political life ever since the ideal of the constitutional state was born, the element that strives to create universally valid laws and standards, now rises to the highest possible universality. Its visible symbol is the comparison of the good with the sun, which lights up the whole world.

But before we study the actual process of acquiring philosophical knowledge which corresponds to that conception of education, a new doubt arises—about the possibility of the philosopher's rule. Earlier we had discussed whether he was *capable* of ruling. Now we must ask whether he will be *willing* to rule, which means descending from the heights which he has so laboriously climbed to see true reality and being.[99] As far as his qualifications go, the image of the cave shows that what we call practical statesmen have a very poor insight into truth. Some of the folk chained in the cave acquired a certain dubious distinction among their fellow-prisoners because they managed to learn the commonest sequences of shadows recurring in the endless procession against the back wall of their cave. These (says Plato) are the men who handle power by experience alone without principle; and it is in their hands that government now lies.[100] According to the cave-parable, the uneducated man (ἀπαίδευτος) is one who has no fixed aim in his life;[101] and modern statesmen are the most notable embodiment of the type, for their subjective 'aim', suggested to them by ambition or power-hunger, does not deserve the name of 'end' in Plato's sense. If we follow him in saying that the supreme criterion for judging one's vocation to be a ruler is the possession of an absolute aim, then the philosopher, because of his paideia, is the only man who is truly entitled to rule. But how can he be induced to leave his 'isles of the blest' and take on a burden which

will pretty certainly keep him from continuing his studies? [102]
The 'isles of the blest', as an image for the paradisal *vita con-templativa,* are such an apt invention that they have been used
by many authors since, to describe what we might call 'the ivory
tower'. They appear again in the work of Aristotle's youth,
Protrepticus, where, as Plato's pupil, he expounds his own ideal
of philosophical life; and through him they spread to the literature of later antiquity and beyond.[102a] Despite the attraction
which Plato and Aristotle give to the life of pure contemplation, it was always meant ideally to culminate in action; and
action is what justifies it. The original political meaning of all
Greek paideia now emerges triumphant at the moment of its
greatest conflict and danger, through the intellectual and ethical
significance which Plato once more imparts to it. How and when
the philosopher is to do his duty must be defined more closely
later, but Plato lays down the principle to begin with: the philosopher *must* go back down into the cave.[103] He must be persuaded and compelled to help those who were his fellow-
prisoners. This strong sense of social duty distinguishes Plato's
ideal of spiritual culture from the philosophy of the pre-
Socratics. It is one of the paradoxes of history that those
thinkers who were interested in the study of nature more than
man should have played a far more active part in practical
politics than Plato, whose whole thought was centred on the
problem of practice.[104] He believed it was only in the ideal Republic that a philosopher could get the right education and become a practical statesman, and it was only in the ideal Republic
that he would be fully responsible to the community. Plato felt
no active gratitude to the degenerate state of his own day: for
if a philosopher could grow to maturity in any such state, it
was very sure that the public and the state's institutions had
done nothing whatever to help him.[105] That would all be different in the Republic. There the philosopher would have
society to thank for his paideia, and therefore for his whole
intellectual existence: so he would be ready to 'pay the cost of
his upbringing'. Despite his reluctance, he would be impelled by
his feeling of gratitude to take the office assigned to him, and
fulfil it to the best of his ability. Therefore the best state will
be that which is governed not by those who love power, but by
those who positively dislike it.[106]

MATHEMATICS AS PROPAIDEIA

What kind of knowledge can effect the 'conversion of the soul'? Obviously Plato does not believe that it can be done through a single experience, a sudden movement of the soul, an instantaneous flash of light which bursts upon a man without any trouble on his part. Nor can it be achieved by the ordinary education of the guards—that is, by the traditional methods of Greek paideia: for athletics deal with the world of coming-to-be and passing-away, with growth and diminution, while 'music' only creates rhythm and harmony in the soul, without giving knowledge.[107] Professional skills (τέχναι) are all vulgar artisan work, and cannot be considered in a discussion of education.[108] But beyond those things there is still one type of knowledge which is used by more or less everyone, and which is extraordinarily well suited to convert the soul from the visible world to the world of thought. This is the science of numbers, arithmetic.[109] Legend says it was founded by the hero Palamedes, who fought in the Trojan war, and showed the generalissimo Agamemnon how to use the new art for strategic and tactical purposes. Plato makes fun of this story, which implies that Agamemnon had not been able to count his own feet, far less his army and navy. Seriously, however, the science is indispensable for the education of the ruler, because of its military value.[110] This practical argument should not be taken as ironical. Plato later extends it from arithmetic to the other mathematical sciences, and, as we know, the development of the art of war in the fourth century demanded an increasingly large knowledge of mathematics.[111] But arithmetic as Plato means it to be studied is more than an ancillary subject for generals. It is one of the humanities, for without it a man is not a man.[112] Primarily, this refers only to a rather primitive stage of arithmetical learning—the numeration and distinction of concrete quantities. But Plato looks beyond that to a type of science which is especially fitted to carry our thought into the region which we are trying to attain—into the realm of Being.[113]

This is the entirely new point of view from which Plato looks at the cultural value of arithmetic and of all mathematics. We need not expect him to discuss the content of mathematical

problems, or even to detail the course of study to be pursued. Just
as he did with gymnastics and 'music', he gives only the boldest
outlines to define the spirit in which the subject is to be treated.
He mentions the various mathematical disciplines in order.
Therefore there are some repetitions in his brief survey, since
in dealing with each one he drives home his point once more:
that mathematics is meant to stimulate *thinking*. He admits that
so far it has never been used for that purpose. (We may recall
what we said of the sophists' introduction of mathematics as
an educational discipline, and the realistic reasons they gave for
it.[114]) Plato takes over the sophists' high valuation of mathematics, but he does not follow them in placing its value in its
practical usefulness. When he says it is valuable for strategy,
he is simply making a concession to the rulers' education which
he has planned. The future statesmen's journey up to philosophy
is so difficult that it assumes they will have a great deal of pure
love for culture—so much so that when Plato mentions the
practical importance of these studies, he can scarcely think of it
as detracting from the real reasons he gives for studying mathematics.[114a] He makes particular fun of mathematicians who discuss geometry: he says they behave 'ridiculously' in arranging
their proofs as if geometrical operations were concerned with
action (*praxis*) and not knowledge (*gnosis*).[115] Again and
again, with an impressive wealth of metaphors, all pointing in
the same direction, he describes mathematical knowledge as
leading or drawing towards thought, purifying and kindling
the soul, calling out or awakening the reason.[116] The young men
and women who are to rule the Republic are to have not only
a layman's but a specialist's knowledge of arithmetic.[117] They
must learn to appreciate the beauty of the science, and its usefulness, not for buying and selling and trading, but for assisting
the 'conversion' of the soul to transcendental reality. Plato
holds that the influence of arithmetic is to make a man who has
a gift for it able to understand all branches of science; while
a slow learner who has some training and practice in it, even if
he gets nothing else out of it, will have his apprehension sharp-
ened at least.[118] Mathematics is a difficult subject, and that
qualifies it to be studied by the intellectual élite.

Besides arithmetic and geometry, the mathematical branch of
the sophists' system included astronomy and music. The entire

group was later called the Quadrivium.[119] It is not clear whether Plato took the scheme over from sophistic tradition or from other sources. In *The Republic*, when he passes from astronomy to music, he mentions the Pythagoreans as believing that astronomy and music were sister sciences.[120] We might infer from this that the connexion of these two subjects with arithmetic and geometry was also Pythagorean, or at least known to the Pythagoreans. Whether we can go so far as to credit the Pythagorean school, centring on Archytas, with creating all the exact sciences known to the Greeks, is another question. Probably not; but at least they greatly encouraged the study of these 'mathemata', and Plato had close associations with them.[121] In discussing the part played by mathematics within his philosophical paideia, Plato speaks very respectfully of the Pythagoreans, calling them the greatest authority in this branch of knowledge. Still, he criticizes them for clinging to sense-perception instead of pressing onwards to pure thought.[121a] They were specialists, therefore, and although he owed them much, it was left to him to bring out the point of view which dominated his own thought. He states this expressly in discussing music—by which he means not the teaching of instrumental music, but the theory of harmony. The Pythagoreans, he says, measure audible harmonies and sounds against one another, and try to discover the numbers in them;[122] but they stop at the beginning of the 'problems'[123] which, not only in music but in geometry and astronomy, Plato believes his system of education is intended to study.[124] By 'problems' in this sense, he means the questions which lead straight to the contemplation of things in themselves, of bodiless Being. The Pythagoreans do not ask 'which numbers are harmonious and which are not, and why they are as they are'.[125] They do not study, from the new point of view recommended by Plato, the mutual relationship of all objects of mathematics; they do not go back to the common basis of them all[126]; they merely work out scattered observations of numbers, lines and surfaces, the visible phenomena of the sky, and audible sounds and concords. Therefore it is Pythagorean astronomy he is reproaching when he says it would be difficult to believe that the phenomena of the skies are eternal, and always follow the same laws, if we thought only about the movement of physical and visible quantities.[127] These criticisms, which imply that Plato is

saving the positive exposition of his own theories for a special
book, lead to the logical conclusion which we meet again in
Timaeus and *The Laws*: that the mathematical regularity of
celestial phenomena presupposes the existence of intelligent and
conscious beings to conduct them in heaven.[128] But because he
is concentrating on paideia, he refrains from going into these
scientific details here—he always keeps to the broad outlines
even in discussing his own philosophy.[129]

Plato finds no difficulty in crediting Socrates with knowledge
of all these special sciences which he adumbrates rather than
explains. Socrates always appears as the man who knows every
subject that comes up; and, although he seems to be concentrating on the central subject, he reveals from time to time an
astonishing familiarity with subjects about which we should expect him to know very little. There must be some historical
foundation for this omniscience; and yet one fact is very well
established. The real Socrates did not think so highly of the
various mathematical disciplines which Plato here makes out to
be *the* way to knowledge of the Good. This is a fine test-case
to prove the complete freedom with which Plato, in writing his
dialogues, puts his own thoughts in Socrates' mouth. Xenophon
is obviously pointing to Plato's unhistorical treatment of facts
when he says that Socrates knew something about mathematics,
but thought its educational value was strictly limited by its practical usefulness.[130] This of course is the exact opposite of what
Plato makes him say. The fact that Xenophon deliberately contradicts Plato may be taken to prove that he, and not Plato, is
sticking to facts. The historical Socrates would never have reproached his interlocutors, as the Platonic one does, for justifying astronomy by declaring its usefulness in agriculture, navigation, and strategy.[131] Here Plato's paideia shows the immense
importance he attaches to mathematics, even in the theoretical
elaboration of Socrates' ideas. He is suspicious of any purely
utilitarian foundation for the science, even though he himself
points out that mathematics is indispensable for a strategist. 'To
look upwards' with the soul, as we are taught to do by astronomy
treated mathematically, is very different from turning one's gaze
towards heaven as professional astronomers do.[132] That part of
the soul which is kindled to pure flame by mathematics studied

on the Platonic system is 'more important than ten thousand eyes'.[133]

Plato does not follow the tradition that there are only four branches of mathematics. He introduces what he himself calls a brand-new mathematical science, stereometry.[134] The position of astronomy, after geometry, must have been well-established by his time. As if following regular custom, he mentions it in the third place, and begins to discuss it [135]; but then he corrects himself, saying that the science of bodies in space ought to come in next, since it should follow geometry, the science of lines and surfaces, and precede astronomy, the science of moving bodies in space.[136] The introduction of stereometry is a surprise, by which Plato is enabled to bring in certain variations in this section. Evidently his train of thought here is directly influenced by the educational routine of the Academy. Historians of mathematics in the late classical period, using a tradition which went back to the fundamental book by Aristotle's pupil Eudemus, state that the science of stereometry was introduced by Theaetetus. Theaetetus was a distinguished Athenian mathematician, after whom Plato named a dialogue published a few years after *The Republic*.[137] He died, we now think, in 369 B.C., of epidemic dysentery caught while serving in the army.[138] The ideas on solid geometry in the last (thirteenth) book of Euclid's *Elements*—the imperishable foundation of all Greek mathematics—which was written only a generation later, must have been basically those of Theaetetus.[139] He was a well-known personality in the Academy. Plato draws a very sympathetic portrait of him in *Theaetetus* as an amiable scholar. No doubt it was his personal influence that induced Plato to give such an honourable place in *The Republic* to the science he had founded.

It is vital for us, in studying Plato's paideia, to use this important opportunity of estimating the actual scientific interest which the various precepts for philosophical education in *The Republic* held for Plato himself. More than two thousand years have passed since Euclid gave mathematics its classical form, the scientific form whose outlines have been valid ever since. It is hard for us to think back to the intellectual epoch in which that form was still moving towards finality. If we recollect that it was the work of comparatively few generations, we can realize how the concentrated thinking of a small band of brilliant scientists, vying with one another to advance their subject, created an atmosphere of victorious confidence which was bound to produce reactions on philosophical thought, in the general excitement of the intellectual life of fourth-century Athens. To the philosopher, mathematics looked like an ideal science: a solid and exact structure of logical inference and proof, something undreamed-of in the days of the pre-Socratic natural philosophers. The attention which mathematicians had lately paid to the development of scientific method enhanced the value of mathematics as a model for the new science of dialectic developed by Plato out of Socrates' conversations on virtue. Like all other great philosophers, Plato could not have brought his philosophy into being without the fertilizing influence exercised by contemporary science through its new questions and new solutions. Next to medicine (whose influence on him we have so often pointed out) it was mathematics which stimulated and encouraged him. From medicine he took the analogy between physical and spiritual conditions (condition = *hexis*) and the idea that philosophy ought to be a techné, a skill comparable to medicine, a science of the soul's health. Mathematics showed him how reason could operate with purely intelligible objects, such as the Ideas. On the other hand, Plato himself, with his new logical discoveries, strongly encouraged the mathematicians to build up their science into a systematic structure—so that the benefit was mutual, as indeed ancient tradition tells us.[140]

It was relatively late in Plato's life that Theaetetus became important for him. The latter was still in his prime when he died in 369 B.C.: therefore his discoveries must have been quite new some years earlier, when Plato brought them into *The Republic*.[141] Plato's first contacts with mathematics must have been made even before he met the Pythagoreans, because dialogues like *Protagoras* and *Gorgias,* which betray a marked interest in the subject, were written before his first visit to Sicily. There must have been plenty of opportunity to study mathematics in Athens at that period.[142] Unfortunately we cannot follow up Plato's connexions with Cyrene, which city he is said (though the tradition is not firmly established) to have visited after Socrates' death.[143] Later, when he wrote *Theaetetus,* he contrasted Theaetetus himself, representing the younger generation of mathematicians, who were receptive to philosophical problems, with an older man, Theodorus of Cyrene, who was a famous scientist but had no interest in philosophical problems. This seems to presuppose some personal knowledge of Theodorus too.[144] On his journey to southern Italy in 388, Plato met the leading Pythagorean scholars of the day. Probably one of them was Archytas of Tarentum, statesman, mathematician, 'and the most distinguished scientist among the Pythagoreans. Plato stayed with him for some time, and became his lifelong friend.[145] Indeed, he was the living prototype on which Plato based his ideal of the philosopher's education. Aristotle's remarkable statement that Plato's system of research and teaching was essentially modelled on that of the Pythagoreans, although it contained something of his own too, must have referred chiefly to the mathematical side of his teaching—which is not very prominent in the dialogues, but played a very important part in the Academy.[146] The remark of Aristotle's Greek biographer that he entered Plato's school 'under Eudoxus' permits us to draw an inference. The great mathematician Eudoxus is very often mentioned in connexion with the Academy; and Aristotle in the *Ethics* says he knew him personally. Therefore he must have been attending Plato's school for some time, at the period when Aristotle himself entered it (367).[147] Eudoxus' own school was in Cyzicus, and the connexion between it and Plato's Academy survived into the next generation.[148] That is the palpable proof of the active part taken by Plato's school in the progress of mathematical science. Plato's secretary and closest assistant in his later years was Philip of Opus, whom we have already mentioned as editor of his posthumous work, *The Laws*. He too was famous in antiquity as a mathematician and astronomer, and wrote numerous books.[149] He was, it appears, one of the leading authorities on that subject in the school, along with Hermodorus and Heracleides. While Heracleides seems rather to have represented astronomical speculation, Philip was the typical research-student, although in the *Epinomis* (like all Platonists) he treats astronomy as the foundation of theology.

These facts should be a warning to us to remember that Plato's books are only the reflection of the scientific research and teaching of the Academy, whose internal structure they reveal. The rules given in *The Republic* for instruction in

mathematics show exactly what was the position of mathematics in the philosophical course given by the Academy. Evidently Plato made no distinction between research and teaching. The field was still clear and within view, so that he simply
directed his future rulers to study the entire subject,[150] without
making any selection, and he even welcomed newly developed
branches like stereometry (the science of solid geometry) to
extend the programme. It is easy to imagine that other schools
had a different idea of the right paideia for a statesman.
Wherever it was held to have a practical end in view, namely
rhetoric, as in Isocrates' school, Plato's estimate of the value
of exact mathematical knowledge in political education must
have seemed exaggerated and greater emphasis must have been
put on experience.[151] But the fact that Plato was criticized for
developing mathematics too strongly shows that it was held to
be the keystone of his educational system.

Neither in the simpler education of the guards, nor in this
higher form of education, is Plato's paideia based on pure
theory. In the former, he took over as its chief material all the
traditional culture (by which he means Greek culture) in existence, all the poetry and music of his nation; only he compelled
it to purify itself and prepare to fulfil its highest duty. In the
latter, he guided the living stream of contemporary science into
the channel of his own philosophical paideia; only he sought out
everything which could serve his philosophical purpose directly,
and subordinated it to that purpose. This suggests another question: what was his attitude to those other sciences which he does
not mention in his programme? Nowadays we believe that
science has no frontiers narrower than those of human experience. This might make us think that the great prestige given
to mathematics in Plato's paideia was (however noble) a serious
distortion of emphasis, or perhaps that it was due to the temporary predominance of mathematics in his time. But although
it must have owed its pride of place in the Academy to the great
specialists who were working in it and the feeling of confidence
and progress they inspired, its importance was ultimately based
on the character of Plato's philosophy and his conception of
knowledge. He excluded all empirical knowledge from education. The attempts made by the sophists to cultivate encyclopaedic 'scholarship' were carried no further in Plato's school.

In fragments of contemporary Attic comedy we find jokes about the long-winded arguments between Plato and his pupils, as they discussed how to define and classify plants and animals. These allusions confirm the impression we derive from Plato's dialogues. It was the comedian Epicrates whose jokes cast a harsh side-light on the esoteric secrets of Academic teaching; and, despite his exaggerations, he brought out the right point. Philosophers in fact did not know very much about plants, and made themselves rather silly in their attempts to classify them— silly enough to amuse the theatre-audiences.[152] Epicrates makes a famous Sicilian doctor (therefore a representative of empirical knowledge), who happens to attend these discussions, express his boredom wordlessly but impolitely, in the manner appropriate to an 'uncultured naturalist'. Since the researches he attended were zoological and botanical, some readers have wrongly inferred that the teaching given in the Academy must have been materially different from that described in *The Republic,* with a great deal more attention paid to empirical science.[153] But even though research into the classification of plants and animals cannot be done without observation (particularly if it aims at systematic completeness), the scientists of the Academy were not trying to collect everything known about the various types of flora and fauna, but to distinguish the types from one another, and assign them their correct place in a great scheme of logical division covering 'all existence'—as is done with other subjects in Plato's later dialogues. The real aim of these researches on concrete subjects was dialectic. If Plato's account of educational method in *The Republic* does not give us the same impression, that is because (as we have pointed out above) he is merely giving outlines of the various stages in his paideia. Therefore the classifications of plants and animals alluded to by Epicrates should be placed in the second part of the educational programme of *The Republic,* the part which follows mathematics, and deals with dialectic.

EDUCATION IN DIALECTIC

Socrates' interlocutors tell him that the curriculum he has mapped out so far is extremely difficult and arduous. In reply, Plato makes him compare it with the prelude to a nomos (a vocal solo), thus showing the point he has reached, and the transition to the highest stage.[154] Mathematics was only the prelude to the song which is now to be learnt. Even an expert in it is not a dialectician. Plato hints that he has met very few mathematicians in his lifetime who were dialecticians too. But one of them was certainly Theaetetus. In the dialogue named after him, Plato portrays the new type of philosophical mathematician (as we have said above); but also, by discussing the great problem of knowledge which is common to both mathematics and philosophy, he shows how a trained mathematician is led through dialectical contradictions to philosophical knowledge. It is not a mere coincidence that Socrates' chief interlocutor is an eager and gifted young mathematician. He is meant to show the effect of dialectic paideia on the man who is best prepared to receive it. In *Theaetetus*, too, philosophical understanding is shown to be connected with mathematics, and the fruit of long and laborious paideia.[155] The dialogue, which is a few years later than *The Republic*, reads like a continuous illustration of the description given in *The Republic* of philosophical education through dialectic. In laying down the rules for paideia, Plato cannot of course give examples of dialectic, any more than he could for earlier stages of education. Instead, there are examples of it in all the other Platonic dialogues— they record the dialectical investigation of some special problem, and the nature of the process becomes entirely clear to the reader following it and watching its logical sequence. But what gives special interest and charm to Plato's description of dialectic as the highest stage of paideia in *The Republic* is his attitude to his own invention, and his effort to describe its value and its problems as an instrument of education, on the basis of twenty-five years' experience.

Even here he offers nothing more in the way of definition of dialectic than we already know from earlier dialogues. Right at the beginning of this final stage of education, he defines it as 'the ability to give and take account of something', and thereby he gives its origin.[156] This definition is simply the traditional description of Socrates' old method of coming to an understanding with other men through argument and contradiction, the *elenchos*, out of which Plato's logical theory and art of dialectic grew.[157] Plato clearly thought the great transforming force he had felt in Socrates' conversations still justified the claim of dialectic philosophy to be the real paideia. Seen from this altitude, the first stage, mathematics, sinks away into a mere preliminary training (*propaideia*).[158] But what is the 'song' which is first heard in the 'prelude' of mathematics, and is then completed in dialectic? To understand what it is we must go back to the parable of the cave. It is a visual image of the upward journey of the soul. After the soul's eye has been turned round, and the soul has left the cave and entered the real world, it tries to see, first living animals, then the stars, and finally the sun itself. And so, step by step, it learns to see things themselves, without the shadows it has been accustomed to. In the same way, the man who reaches knowledge through dialectic tries to reach the nature of everything through thought without sense-perception, and does not stop till he thinks through to 'the Good itself, what it really is', and thereby reaches the end of the thinkable—just as the sun, the source of light above, is the end of the visible.[159] This 'journey' (πορεία) is dialectic.[160] The purpose of the study of the sciences already learnt is 'to bring the best part of the soul to see the best thing that exists'.[161] After reaching that point the mind can rest in its journeying.[162] Plato himself feels how forced and summary this short metaphorical description is, but he prefers to put it down simply as an outline, since he is going to return to it often.[163]

The character (τρόπος) of dialectic can be defined only by its relation to the other types of knowledge. There are various methods of apprehending the nature of things. The empirical skills, technai, deal with men's opinions and desires: they are designed either to produce something or to take care (θεραπεία) of things produced by art or nature.[164] The mathematical disciplines are closer to true reality, but touch it only in sleep, as it were—they cannot see it with their eyes wide open. As shown above, they start from hypotheses which they cannot explain. Therefore their 'principle' is something which they do not know; and everything else is 'woven' out of something they do not know. This kind of 'admission' (ὁμολογία) ought not to be called science (ἐπιστήμη), although usage has accustomed us to do so.[165] Dialectic is the science that 'does away with' the assumptions of other sciences, and travels upward to the first principle of all, 'gently turning upward the soul's eye, which had been buried in a bog of savagery', with the assistance of mathematics.[166] We now know the meaning of the ratio between the various stages of reality and of knowledge which Plato earlier gave to illustrate the purpose of his paideia. It is this. Reason is to opinion what being is to becoming. And as thought is to opinion, so true knowledge (ἐπιστήμη) is to the evidence of the senses (πίστις), and so mathematical reason is to the shadows of visible objects.[167] In other words, the knowledge given by dialectic is as superior to mathematical knowledge in the amount of being and reality that it contains, as real objects in the visible world are to their shadows and reflections. So the dialectician is the man who apprehends the true nature of everything and can give account of it.[168] In the same way he must be able to separate (ἀφελεῖν) the Idea of Good from everything else—that is, to distinguish 'good by itself' from the separate things, persons, actions, et cetera, which we call good, and to delimit it by the logos, 'going through all contradictions' as if in battle, and pressing on bravely to the last phase of the fight without letting his thought stumble anywhere.[169] The real strength of this paideia which teaches 'scientific questions and answers' [170] is that it makes the mind fully awake and alert. That is why Plato calls it the education of the guards in the highest sense—i.e. the education of the rulers. 'Guards' is a rather odd name for the ruling class, which he seems to have chosen with an eye on the philosophical virtue of intellectual watchfulness to which they are educated.[171] The name 'guards' is first given to all the soldier class, and as their selection proceeds, it is confined more and more to the rulers,[172] and they are the few who take part in higher education. Anyone who does not enjoy this education, Plato says, is dreaming away his life, and before he can wake up he enters the eternal sleep of death.[173] But in the system of the sciences, dialectic is the coping-stone (θριγκός) in which human knowledge culminates: no other science can be added to it, or come above it.[174] The knowledge of *meaning* is the final aim of the knowledge of *being*.

THE PHILOSOPHER'S CURRICULUM

We now ask who is fit to rise to this height, to wear the crown of culture. When Plato was explaining how the guards were to be trained to have the rulers' virtue, he said that only the most reliable and brave natures were to be chosen to be philosophical rulers, and that they must be as handsome, noble, and proud as possible.[175] But they must combine this *kalokagathia* with the qualities indispensable for higher education—acuteness, quick apprehension, memory, and perseverance. The man who is to take part in the nimble game of dialectic must not be lame of one limb. That is, he must not be a man who enjoys the physical effort of athletics and hunting, and can persevere in them, but easily gives way to intellectual fatigue, and dislikes it. And he must not be only a half-lover of truth—hating deliberate lies, but putting up with unconscious and unintentional falsehoods. He must be annoyed with himself when convicted of ignorance, and not wallow in his own ignorance like a pig in the dirt. No one can be a ruler unless the frame of his soul is as healthy as his body ought to be.[176] So the tests of character already pre-scribed for the future rulers are not enough.[177] They must be supplemented by a very carefully worked out system of intel-lectual selection which will examine and prove those who are fit for dialectic and put them in the right place. In Plato's time, all these ideas were entirely new, and they are a complete contrast to the blind belief in healthy human reason which is character-istic of the man who has learnt nothing but his daily routine. Since Plato's day, a large number of schools and examinations have come into existence, although we cannot be sure that, if he returned to life, he would think they were everything he had hoped for.

In order to discover the few men and women (perhaps only one) who are to govern the Republic, the work of selection must be begun very early in life and on a broad basis. Though Plato had previously opposed the idea of concentrating philosophical study into a few years of early manhood,[178] he did not mean that philosophy should not be studied at all by the young. The pre-liminary work at mathematics, the *propaideia,* is to start in boy-hood.[179] But every attempt to begin education early comes up against one enormous hindrance. Children do not want to study. They must not be compelled to, for it is absolutely contrary to the spirit of free culture to make them learn anything through a slavish fear of punishment. The healthy effects of physical exercise are not diminished if it is made compulsory, but knowl-

edge imposed on the soul by force does not cling to it.[180] Therefore Plato asserts that in this stage of education children should
be introduced to knowledge as if it were a game.[181] This assertion is no doubt based on the bad results which must have been
produced by the increase in 'cramming' during his lifetime, as
soon as the new subjects were not kept for the keenest and most
gifted pupils but were tried on the average boys too. Even Plato
himself does not set the standard too high at this stage: he says
that the games which compose elementary education are to show
which are likely to be the most gifted pupils. He compares this
system of learning by play with the other device which is put into
action at the same period—taking the children out to watch the
spectacle of battle: they are to 'taste blood' like puppies, and
conquer their fear of the terrors of learning.[182] Even at this
stage, they must not learn anything mechanically. Their teachers
are to 'propose' (προβάλλειν) mathematical problems to them
which are suitable for their age. This is the first hint of the
concentration on 'problems' which is to become more and more
pronounced in later and higher stages of Plato's mathematical
curriculum.[183]

The first selection is to be made after the compulsory training in gymnastics is over. Plato says that will last two or three
years. During that period, the mind is not trained at all, for
exhaustion and sleep are enemies to study. Anyhow, perseverance in athletic exercises is itself an important element in the
examinations and the selection based on them.[184] The fact that
intellectual training recommences at the age of twenty shows
that the compulsory athletic training, which is to be distinguished from voluntary athletics at earlier and later stages, falls
in the period between the seventeenth and twentieth years. That
was the age at which eligible young men in Athens were trained
as military cadets, *ephéboi:* their service began at eighteen and
lasted two years. Plato copied its duration, but felt that a third
year might be added.[185]

Thereafter begins another course of education connected with
the mathematical studies which were completed earlier, and designed to reveal and illuminate the connexion between the disciplines previously studied in isolation, and their objects. They
are now to be compared with one another, until the student
arrives at a 'synopsis', a comprehensive view, 'of their mutual

relationships and the nature of being'. Although it starts with mathematics, this stage of knowledge is not mathematical but dialectical, for the dialectician is the 'synoptic' who can see the connexions and relationships of the various realms and objects of knowledge.[186] By stating that the chosen pupils ought above all to 'stand their ground' (μένειν) in study as in war, Plato shows that he is transposing the highest commandment of the old military code of honour into the realm of the intellect, just as he always transposes what he borrows from Sparta to a higher plane of the spirit.[187] After ten years' study of dialectic, another selection is made out of the selected candidates (προκρίνεσθαι ἐκ προκρίτων), and those who are chosen are highly honoured.[188] After that, the five years from the age of thirty to thirty-five are meant to show who is capable of setting himself free from sense-perception, and pressing on to true Being.[189] Plato says these last five years are parallel in intention to the two or three years of compulsory athletics.[190] They are the gymnastics of dialectic; they are to the dialectic contradictions and synopses of the previous ten years what the abstract and systematic dialectic of Plato's *The Statesman* and *The Sophist* are to his more elementary early dialogues.[191]

The training in dialectic has now gone on for fifteen years, and has still not reached its real conclusion. It shows absolutely clearly what Plato's own concept of knowledge was, and reveals the nature of his work as a writer. His writing is simply a reproduction of the dialectic process in its various stages. At first glance, this fifteen years' study looks like the wish-dream of a specialist who has never been able to get enough time to teach his subject as he thinks necessary for full appreciation, and who seizes the chance of an educational Utopia to dedicate as many years to his subject as it usually gets months. But these are not the true reasons for Plato's demand. Long before this, he said with great clarity that he did not expect any good would be done either in teaching philosophy or in educating rulers, by limiting the course of philosophical study to a few years, as schools did in his day and still do.[192] In his seventh Letter, he describes the process by which men come to apprehend good (and that is the intention of *all* education in Plato) as an inward process which comes to completion through long years of life and study in common.[193] It is a gradual transformation of their natures—

what he calls conversion of the soul to reality, in *The Republic*. The same Letter describes what actually happens when two people join in studying philosophy, by saying that each one 'accepts kindly contradiction';[194] and that coheres with the description given in *The Republic* of the student's passage through all degrees of contradiction.[195] Knowledge of the Good as understood by Plato assumes a kinship between the soul and its object. Therefore as the mind moves towards knowledge, the character must develop along the same lines, and the result of both these movements is knowledge of Good.[196] But the student cannot understand this far-reaching process of learning and apprehension all at once. The very nature of it is such that it approaches its goal step by slow step, as *The Symposium* shows with its image of initiation into the lower and the higher mysteries. But in *The Symposium* Plato is giving only a general religious symbol, whereas in *The Republic* he is expounding a concrete method of learning, complicated by the fact that it must include training for the practical task of governing the state. In this plan, the intellectual basis of the ruler's education is instruction in dialectic during the period from the twentieth to the thirty-fifth years. But still it is important to note that it does not finish with the apprehension of the Good, as we should expect. After the conclusion of that fifteen-year period, Plato envisages another fifteen years of learning before the Good can be known. This course stretches from the thirty-fifth to the fiftieth years.[197] During it, the student, now thoroughly educated, will gain the experience without which his culture would be useless to him in government. Its purpose is to school him in action and train his character. That makes fifteen years of theory and fifteen years of practice: a proportion which expresses the ideal of harmony between both sides of the mind and their union in the ruler. It corresponds to the ideal of complete harmony between gymnastics and 'music' in the lower education of the guards.[198]

The second fifteen years of character-training are necessary, not only to the student's education as a ruler, but to the proper use of his intellectual education. Plato knows the danger of dialectic. It may well create a feeling of educated superiority, and lead those who have become experts in it to use their new skill to contradict others, making that sport an end in itself.[199]

This idea often recurs in Plato, but is nowhere so fully developed as here, where the educational value of dialectic is being discussed. His warning against its dangers is made an actual part of his description of it, by revealing a negative aspect and throwing up the positive side concealed by it. For if dialectic seduces young men to practise it as an intellectual sport, that is not only because they are too young to know better, but partly because of the very nature of dialectic and its formal character. In the criticisms levelled at Plato by his contemporaries, especially rival educators, the close resemblance between his dialectic and eristic (or pure disputation) comes out very clearly. Dialectic and eristic are actually put on the same level.[200] For its bad reputation, its own students are responsible. Plato is very anxious to make his readers aware of the distinction between paideia and *paidia,* education and play. In Greek the two words have the same root, because they both originally refer to the activity of the child (*pais*) ; but Plato is the first to deal with the problem of the relation between the two concepts.[201] That was almost inevitable in an epoch when one of the two, paideia, acquired such a comprehensive meaning as to become equivalent to 'culture'. Down to the end of his life, Plato was interested in the subject of play. Nowhere is his interest clearer than in *The Laws,* the work of his old age, where we shall meet the problem in a new guise.[202] It was taken up by Aristotle, and serves to illustrate his ideal of culture—scientific leisure as opposed to pure play.[203] Plato is anxious to include the play-element in his paideia: the guards' children are to learn their lessons through play, which means that paidia helps paideia. Dialectic, however, is a higher stage. It is not play, but earnest, σπουδή.[204] Since many modern languages have taken over this classical contrast of the two concepts, it is difficult for us to realize what an effort of abstract philosophical thinking created it. The idea of 'earnest', or rather 'earnest activity', *spoudé,* does not occur as a philosophical problem until *The Laws;* but Plato obviously has it in mind when he compares beginners in dialectic who misuse their skill in contradicting others for their own amusement, to young puppies who love chasing other dogs and biting them.[205]

But the danger that dialectic will annoy others is not so great as that it may lead the student himself to lose his respect for tradition. The study of dialectic accustoms him to criticize all prevailing opinions, so that he easily falls into anarchy and law-lessness.[206] He is like an adopted child that grows up believing his foster-parents are his father and mother, and one day when he is grown up, discovers his real parents, and despises every-thing he has honoured hitherto. Plato's own discussion of the case of justice is a practical example of what he means. Dia-lectic leads to refutation of the current views about what is 'just and beautiful'—i.e. of the laws and customs by which the stu-dent has been brought up, as if they were his parents.[207] Plato himself has expressed his views about obedience to the laws in *Crito*, which tells how Socrates voluntarily submitted to the state and its authority at the moment when he was about to be put to death by a judgment he felt to be wrong. Plato's pupil Xenocrates held that the essence of philosophy was teaching men to do voluntarily what most men do only because the law makes them.[208] Of course, that definition obliterates the conflict between positive law and absolute justice which is so important in Plato's description of dialectic.[209] But Xenocrates too cer-tainly meant that philosophy was compliance with a higher order of justice which exacted not less but more than the law com-manded. Plato thought the chief safeguard against intellectual and moral anarchy was to postpone the final stage of dialectical education as long as possible (till the age of fifty!) and thus to counteract its disruptive influence by fifteen years of practical work to train the character. When he says the student of dia-lectic may take it as a purely formal tool and misuse it, we re-member Socrates' accusations against students of rhetoric in *Gorgias*.[210] The difference is that rhetoric pays no attention whatever to the problems of good and evil, right and wrong, which are the aim of dialectic. Therefore misuse of dialectic is a denial of its real nature, and, in Plato's view, a proof that the student who does so has not penetrated to real knowledge.

It is only after fifteen years of theory and fifteen of practical work that his students reach the supreme goal, the Idea of Good.[211] They turn the eye of their souls, their intellect, to-wards the source of all light, and after seeing it they 'arrange' the public and private lives of themselves and other men in con-formity with that pattern, that paradeigma. They divide their lives between intellectual culture and service to the community in such a way that they spend most of their lives in study, but are always ready when their time comes to take on the task of ruling—not as an honour, but as a duty.[212] And after training others in the same way to succeed them as guards of the state, they depart to the isles of the blest, this time not metaphorically, but literally. But during their lives, they have inhabited the blessed isles of peaceful study, and their journey to them now means only a passage into the bliss of an eternal *vita contemplativa*. The honours they are to receive after their death are like those paid by Greek states to the heroes of old. The final decision about their canonization as heroes is left to the Delphic oracle.[213]

That is Plato's description of the philosophical ruler, the philosopher-king. The supreme purpose of Plato's paideia is to produce such men. It is only through them that the perfect state can be realized—if it is possible at all, which Plato believes it is, despite difficulties.[214] He conceives that the Republic will be governed by one man or several men of that type, invested with all power—a king, therefore, or an aristocracy. It does not matter whether there is one ruler or several, since the nature of the constitution will not be altered by a variation in their numbers. They can be called an aristocracy in the true sense of the word. Greek culture had started in the aristocracy of blood. Now, at the end of its development, it became in Plato's vision the selective principle of a new aristocracy of intellect—whether it actually ruled or not. Two elements co-operated in the culture of those knights of the spirit. The perfect state contains them, as two complementary stages of education: 'philosophical logos mixed with music'.[215] Together, they are the two supreme forces of the Greek genius.

Plato claimed a great deal for his new paideia. His high conception of its position and function in the world is revealed by his proud assertion that it ought to produce the nation's true leaders. They will despise the honours given out by the contemporary state, for they know only one honour, that of ruling in the true sense, on the basis of justice.[216] If we ask how the rulers who have been formed in this way, through supreme paideia, are to construct and establish the state, the answer is once more 'through paideia'. Their purpose is to give ethical education to the entire population—the process which Plato had described,

just after the close of the first stage, as *education to justice:*
that is, education to have the proper *hexis* of the soul, which
comes from the perfect harmony of all its parts. An action is
just if it tends to create or maintain that harmony, he said, and
wisdom is the science (*epistémé*) which is capable of guiding
such acts.[217] Those who possess that science are now found.
Plato does not waste words explaining how they will carry out
this task, for all details are to be left to their judgment. Note
that Plato does not think they must start by establishing a
brand-new city (as in *The Laws*), but by reforming one which
exists already. If the rulers are to fulfil their educational purpose in this reformed state, they must take the little boys and
girls as material for their reconstruction. All human beings over
ten years of age are to be sent out of the city to the country;
the younger children are to be brought up, not in the customs
of the parents, but in the spirit of the perfect state.[218] Just as
medical books promise that the man who follows their injunctions will eventually be healthy and live long, so Plato promises
that the state which takes his educational system and makes it
universal will very quickly realize the ideal constitution, and its
people will be happy ever after.[219]

TYPES OF CONSTITUTION AND TYPES OF CHARACTER

In the description of the philosopher who is to realize the
perfect state as its ruler and inspire it as its teacher, it would
appear that we have reached the end of the contribution of *The
Republic* to paideia—namely, the transformation of the state
into an educational institution for the development of the best
in human personality (ψυχῆς ἀρετή), which is, both individually
and socially, the highest possible value. But Plato does not think
the subject is exhausted. He had laid down his real aim at the
beginning. It was to define the nature and value of justice in
itself, and thence to compare the just man with the unjust man,
and determine how much happiness each of them has.[220] After
the perfectly just man has been discovered, the character of the
perfectly unjust man must be described.[221] This is not only a
formal fulfilment of the undertaking, which any attentive reader
could fulfil for himself, but the transition to one of the most
interesting parts in the whole book. We move from the state

which is natural and right to that which is wrong and deviates from the standard. If we disagree with Plato's outlook, we might say we were passing from the ideal to the real world of politics. There is only one perfect state; but there are many types of imperfect state.[222] There are as many as the types known to us by actual experience. The only difference between them is the degree of their imperfection. In order to establish their relative rank, Plato picks out the best-known types of constitution, and arranges them in a scale of value according to their distance from the perfect state.[223]

Aristotle too, in his *Politics,* combined a theory of the perfect state with a morphology of bad constitutions. He discusses in great detail why one science should perform these two apparently disparate functions.[224] Both the conjunction of the two subjects and the question why it is justified are taken by him from Plato's writings on political theory. In the final form of his *Politics* (which is the one we have) he begins by examining all existing forms of constitution one by one, pointing out that several of them are right,[225] and then works out the perfect type of state.[226] Plato does exactly the opposite. He begins with the problem of absolute justice and the ideal state which embodies absolute justice,[227] and then describes all other forms of state as departures from the norm, and therefore degenerate types.[228] If we accept his conception of politics as being an accurate science of standards, it is only logical to begin with the standard and then use it to appraise the inadequate reality. The only thing that needs discussion is the question whether the empirical types of constitution ought to be described at all, and whether they really form an organic part of the political science of standards.

Plato's answer to this question is determined by his idea of the meaning and purpose of political science. His science of dialectic in its *logical* aspect is based on mathematics, but in its *political* or *ethical* aspect (as we have observed) it is inspired by medical science.[229] His new techné of politics is first constructively outlined in *Gorgias,* and there Plato explains its method and purpose by parallels with medicine.[230] It makes the philosopher appear not merely a man who discusses abstract values, but an educator, the parallel to a doctor. His interest is the health of the soul, as the physician's is the health of the body. In *The Republic* we see clearly how profoundly important

Plato thought the parallel between medicine and politics was. It is based on the assumption, which is carried all through *The Republic,* that the purpose of every society is to develop the soul of the individual—to educate him until his character is as perfect as possible. Like medicine, politics has human nature (*physis*) for its object. What Plato means by human nature is explained at the end of book 4, where he defines justice as the real physis of the soul. That means that he is giving a normative sense to the concept of nature—just as the doctor does when he takes 'health' to be the normal state. Justice is health. And we must endeavour to attain it, because it is the only state which is natural (κατὰ φύσιν) to the soul. From this point of view it is impossible to ask whether one would be happier if one acted wrongly, any more than one could ask if it would be better to be sick than sound. Evil is unnatural (παρὰ φύσιν).[231] In treating the body, medicine distinguishes between individual and general human nature. As far as the individual is concerned, for example, many things seem all right for a weak constitution which would be not normal but unhealthy for the general average nature.[232] In the same way, if the physician of the soul is studying the individual, he will use the concept of nature to describe variations from the general norm; but Plato will not admit that 'everything is normal' if it corresponds to the nature of *some* individual or other; nor will he agree that the form which is most frequent by statistics is therefore normal. Few men, plants, or animals are perfectly healthy; but that does not make illness into health, it does not make the inadequate average into the standard.

If then the state is normal only when it educates men and women who have normal souls—i.e. who are just—then the types of state which actually exist are departures from the standard. At the end of the fourth book, Plato called them that briefly; having broken off the discussion there just after beginning it, he now takes it up again.[233] All actually existing states are phenomena of disease and degeneration. This is not merely a striking inference which is forced on Plato by his conception of the true meaning of 'standard'. The remarks he makes about his own life in the seventh Letter show that it is his own belief, the fundamental and unshakable principle of his political thought.[234] Still, his conception of politics necessarily includes the degen-

erate forms of state as well as the healthy one—just as medicine is the knowledge not only of health but also of illness: it
is therapy and pathology too.[235] We knew this from *Gorgias*.
The novelty in *The Republic* is Plato's working out of this scientific idea, by which the understanding of anything is linked with
the understanding of its opposite.

The opposite to the one right kind of state is the multiplicity
of wrong states. To study them he has to use another method,
partly constructive, partly based on experience, which later
assisted Aristotle to develop still further the empirical element in
Platonism. The fact that it was Aristotle who elaborated this part
of Plato's political science shows how fertile and suggestive was
Plato's blend of ideal and reality. His theory of the forms of state
is not primarily a theory of constitutional types. It is primarily,
like his theory of the ideal state, a theory of the human soul.
Using as a basis the parallel of state and man which runs all
through his book, he describes and distinguishes the timocratic,
oligarchic, democratic, and tyrannical man, corresponding to
timocracy, oligarchy, democracy, and tyranny; and he sets up a
scale of value for these types, sinking to the tyrant, who is the
most extreme contrast to the just man.[236] But in *The Republic*,
man and state are not merely outward parallels to one another;
the state is the empty frame for the portrait of the just man.
Similarly in the other types of constitution, the state is nothing
without men. We speak of the 'spirit of the constitution' in this
state and that; but the spirit has been created and given its special character by the type of men who have made the state that
suits them.[237] This does not exclude the fact that the type of the
community, once it takes form, usually stamps the individuals
living under it with its own mark. But when the circle is broken
and one form of state changes into a different one, as happens
in reality, the cause is not some external circumstance, but the
spirit of man, whose 'soul-structure' (κατασκευὴ ψυχῆς) is changing.[238] From this point of view Plato's theory of constitutional
types is a pathology of human character. If we believe that the
disposition (*hexis*) corresponding to the norm is created by the
right education,[239] we must hold that degenerates are created by
wrong education. If all the citizens of a state fall short of the
standard in one particular way, the fault must lie with educa-

tion, not with nature, which strives towards the Good. Therefore the theory of constitutional types is also a pathology of
education.[240]

According to Plato, every change in the state begins with the
rulers, not with the subjects: a dissension (στάσις) appears in
the governing class.[241] The entire teaching of Plato and Aristotle about political change is simply a theory of stasis—a word
which has a wider connotation than our 'revolution'. The cause
of deterioration in human nature, and therefore in the nature
of the state, is the same as in plants or animals. It is the incal-
culable factor of *phora* and *aphoria,* good and bad harvests.[242]
The origin of this idea (which we first met in Pindar's observations about areté)[243] is obviously in the old Greek aristocratic
tradition of paideia. The old nobles were good farmers and
good teachers; they must soon have found out that the maintenance of perfection anywhere in nature depends on the same
laws. Plato gave scientific formulation and systematic development to this doctrine, using his favourite analogy of ethics and
medicine. This passage is the first appearance in his work of the
parallel between the pathology of plants and animals and the
degeneration of areté in men. This way of regarding nature does
not come from earlier natural philosophy, although it did study
the problem of coming-to-be and passing-away, and therefore
the causes of the pathé; it is closely connected with the problem
of areté. Farmers and stock-breeders must have known something of·these questions for centuries. To build their knowledge
into the sciences of animal and botanical pathology was the
work of the two generations from Plato to Theophrastus.
Plato's biology of human areté could not have been worked out
unless on the basis of empirical observation as practised by
Aristotle's school. Yet its teleological concept of nature and its
insistence on standards[244] evidently stimulated empirical observation in their turn. In Theophrastus' botanical pathology,
whose classical expression is his book *On the Causes of Plants,*
we may still trace the struggle between the severe Platonic idea
that the norm is the best and most efficient form of the plant,
its areté, and the purely statistical conception of the norm,
which calls even an aberration 'normal' if it occurs frequently.[245]
We have already pointed out that Plato calls for the commu-

nity of women in the ideal state in order to control chance selection—the ordinary kind of marriage, in which so many other
factors intervene—by a deliberate policy of eugenics.[246] Nevertheless, the birth of every living thing is subject to mysterious
and inviolable arithmetical laws, which are almost beyond human
comprehension;[247] and when marital copulation does not fall in
with this hidden harmony, and misses the right kairos, to which
divine chance and its success are bound, then the breed will not
have the best physis, and will lack *eutychia*,[248] good luck and
prosperity. Then gold will not marry gold, but silver or even
iron; metals which have no kinship will be mated, and the results of this anomaly will be civil strife, discord, feuds. And that
is the beginning of *metabasis*, the change from the ideal state
to another less good.[249]

Plato's description of the constitutions is a masterpiece of
psychological insight. It is the first general description of types
of political life as seen from within in world-literature. Plato's
analysis of the democratic type is differentiated from Thucydides' eulogy of Athens in Pericles' funeral speech by its realistic perception of the weaknesses of democracy, and from the
critical pamphlet called *The Constitution of Athens* by its freedom from oligarchic rancour. Plato is not a partisan. He is
equally critical of all constitutions. The nearest to the ideal Republic, he thinks, is Sparta, which like Crete was often eulogized by the sophists as the model of *eunomia*, political order.[250]
To describe it Plato coins a new concept, timocracy, 'the rule
of honour', because it is entirely founded on the standard of
honour;[251] and his account of it has the charm of historical individuality, whereas the other constitutions are described in
broader outline. Many points of *The Republic* are evidently
borrowed from Sparta, so much so that he has been crudely
called a philolaconian, like the Old Oligarch; but if we compare
his description of Sparta with his own ideal state, we shall see
what Spartan traits he made a point of avoiding.[252] The Spartan
type, full of contradictions, is created by the mixture of inappropriate 'metals'. The iron and brass element in it inclines it
towards making money and gathering landed property; for that
poor element in the soul tries to complete itself by external
riches. The gold and silver elements push it towards areté,

back to its original condition.[253] In this metabasis the original form is the standard of perfection, and this way of looking at the problem replaces the historical approach, which never goes back to the true 'origin' of all such changes. So the elements which make up the Spartan character conflict with one another, and finally meet in a compromise between aristocracy, which is the rule of true areté, and oligarchy.[254] Land and houses become private property, and fall to the ruling class. The members of the lower class, whom they used to protect, and who were their friends and breadwinners, are enslaved and become perioikoi and helots. The rulers change into a class of nobles, and take as much care to control the masses as to defend the state against external dangers.[255]

Because of its intermediate position between the ideal Republic and oligarchy, the Spartan type of state has many features in common with both; and it has some which belong to neither. Respect for authority (a trait which Plato says was missing from democratic Athens), abstention from money-making by the ruling class, meals in public messes, athletics, and military efficiency—both Sparta and the Republic have all these features. That means that Plato thought they were right, and therefore borrowed them from Sparta.[256] But the Spartans were afraid of culture, and avoided putting educated men into positions of authority. There was no pure intellect in that state. Spartans preferred the simple courageous type, more inclined to war than to peace; and they admired any cunning and duplicity which led to military success, since Sparta was in a perpetual state of war.[257] All these features are peculiar to Sparta, but irreconcilable with the perfect state. On the other hand, Sparta resembled the oligarchy in its passion for money. Outwardly there was a great show of plainness and simplicity, but the citizens' homes were treasure-houses, nests of luxury and extravagance. They were mean about spending their own money, and recklessly extravagant in throwing away money stolen from others; and, like runaway children, they flouted the law which the state was supposed to embody, in secret orgies at home.[258]

That sham puritanism is, according to Plato, the product of Spartan education, based as it is not on inward conviction but on outward training. It results from the absence of a true 'musical' education, which always stimulates thought and aspirations to knowledge. The one-sided Spartan character and the one-sided Spartan state are produced by the disturbance of the balance between athletics and 'music' aimed at by Plato in the education of the guards. Therefore it is a mixture of good and bad. The influence which dominates it through and through is ambition.[259] Plato realizes how sketchy his picture is; he means simply to draw the outlines, and makes no claim to completeness. For this whole section of his book, he reminds the reader of the principle by which the philosopher must direct paideia: marking the outlines, bringing out what is typical.[260] For there is infinite variety in the details, which are far less important for the knowledge of the truth than the outlines. So then the 'Spartan character', that type so often cited nowadays and transposed into all backgrounds and all eras, is Plato's invention. To-day most people think of it only as a composite picture: the average representative of Spartan civilization. But that is not what Plato means. By a type he means the embodiment of a standard or a certain degree of value. His 'Spartan man' illustrates the ideal Republic at its first stage of degeneration, being the type of character on which it is based. Plato summarizes the typical Spartan [261] as self-controlled; loving 'music' but himself unmusical; loving to listen but unable to speak; cruel to slaves,[262] friendly to free men; obedient to authority, but eager to be an official and to be distinguished himself; he does not wish to rule by persuasive speech but by military discipline and prowess; he is exceptionally keen on sport and hunting.[262a]

Plato now gives a description of the development of a young Spartan, which illustrates the educational influences that affect him. When he is young he despises money, but as he gets old he yields more and more to avarice, for he lacks the best protection against it, intellectual culture, which is needed to preserve areté and maintain the spiritual level once it has been reached.[263] Perhaps he has a distinguished father who lives in a country which has a bad administration, keeping as far as possible from honours and offices, and hiding his light under a bushel to keep from attracting attention. His mother is ambitious, and discontented with her husband's position in the community. She is upset because he cares little for money, refuses to put himself forward, and is wrapped up in himself; also, he does not idolize her, but gives her just the proper amount of respect. So she tells the boy that his father is only half a man; he is an absolute slacker; and all the usual things that women say about such a husband. And the slaves too pretend to be friendly, by whispering to him that his father is not properly respected because those of his own class think he is a fool. So the boy's soul is pulled in two directions: his father 'waters' and strengthens the reasoning element in it, and other people foster the desiring and the spirited elements. Finally he hands over the government of it to the 'middle' element, which is spirited, and so he becomes a proud and ambitious man.[264]

It is necessary to quote Plato's argument complete in its context, not only to bring out the wealth of interesting detail, but to illustrate how consistently he works out his basic idea, the pathology of education. He starts with an account of Sparta, not so much explaining its institutions as describing its spirit.[265] He assumes that his readers will already know the Spartan ordinances, and analyses them in such a way as to distinguish the conflicting elements in the Spartan state and group them round the two contrasting poles, aristocracy and oligarchy. The Spartan state is held in tension between these poles, which attract it in opposite directions until at last the worse tendency wins. Beside this description of the Spartan state Plato sets a picture of the Spartan man and of his ethos, which corresponds to it line for line. We must, however, be careful to remember that he is not starting with the state because it naturally comes first,[265a] but because it is easier for us to observe. In his examination of justice and the just man, he first of all demonstrated the nature of justice in the state, where it can be read in larger letters, and only after that expounded it in individual character, though it originates there and really exists only there.[266] In the same way here he describes the pathology of soul-sickness in such a way that we read it first writ large in the afflicted state, and then turn to the microscope of psychology to see the symptoms of the disease in the individual's soul. There lies the germ which finally poisons the whole life of the community.[267] So Plato starts from the visible phenomenon and approaches the hidden cause. It is the disturbance of the harmonious balance between the three parts of the soul, the balance which he had previously described as justice, the soul's 'health'.[268] It looks as if he wished, by recalling and emphasizing the image of the three parts of the soul in the last sentence,[269] to draw his readers' particular attention to the logical way in which he reasons from the phenomenon of Spartan timocracy, apparently purely political, back to the pathological process within the Spartan soul. Health as defined by Greek doctors depends on keeping any one of the physical factors which constitute it from becoming dominant.[270] Plato did not take over this idea, because it would not lead to his own 'best constitution'. He thought the essence of health, physical as well as spiritual, was not a negative thing—the absence of domination by one part—but a positive thing, the symmetry of the parts, a condition he thought could easily exist if the better part dominated the worse. He believed the natural condition of the soul was that the best part, i.e. reason, should dominate the others.[271] Therefore disease originates when the part or parts of the soul which are not designed by nature to rule nevertheless come to dominate the soul.

So then Plato, in contrast to the general admiration of his contemporaries for all-powerful Sparta, feels that its weakness is the deficiencies in the famous Spartan education, on which the whole community depended.[272] According to the prevailing theory of chronology, which is probably right, *The Republic* was written between 375 and 370 B.C. His description of Sparta does not look as if it had been written after the striking Spartan defeat at Leuctra in 371. That event revolutionized contemporary thinking about Sparta, as we can see from Aristotle's *Politics,* and from the criticisms of other writers of the time, who are for once unanimous.[273] But both these criticisms and the previous adulation of Sparta spring directly from the inevitable admiration for the success of the state which had conquered powerful Athens. Plato seems to be the one great exception. Probably his analysis of the Spartan type was written before the unexpected collapse of Spartan power. Leuctra was not only a turning-point in the history of Greek power-politics, but also, because Sparta ceased to be a model to be copied and respected, a violent revolution in Greek paideia. The idealization of Sparta which had been so rife in the previous twenty or thirty years was essentially, as we have shown, a reflex of the general admiration of the Spartan system of education.[274] In spite of all Plato's respect for Sparta, and all he borrows from it, his educational state is really not the pinnacle of admiration for Sparta's ideal, but the severest blow that ideal ever suffered. It is a prophetic anticipation of its weakness. Plato took from it what was good and fertile, and left Sparta to sink from the level of an absolute ideal to be merely the best of the states which had something wrong with them.

Plato gives oligarchy the place after timocracy. This is because of his dislike for the degenerate Athenian democracy of his age, which blinded him to the historical achievements of his country.[275] Lowest of all he places tyranny. But although his fundamental hatred for tyranny looks like agreement with classical democratic ideas, it really divides him from them. His sense of meaning, which was too subtle to be blurred by words, had already led him in *Gorgias* to compare the terrorism exercised by the mob to that exercised by the despot.[276] Therefore democracy moves lower in the scale, nearer tyranny. Absolute liberty and absolute tyranny are not merely contrasts. They touch, because one extreme can so easily swing into the other.[277] On the other hand contemporary Sparta had come to put some emphasis on money, and thus revealed its hidden kinship with oligarchy,[278] to which it had originally been directly opposed. It was natural for Plato to treat this transition as natural and inevitable, and therefore to put oligarchy after timocracy and before democracy. For Plato, even before Aristotle, saw that the essence of oligarchy was to think of money as the highest standard of social value for every individual, and to estimate a man's civic rights by his property.[279] Oligarchy is, as it were, an aristocracy based on the materialistic belief that money is the essence of rank. Of course property had been one of the essential assumptions of the early aristocracy,[280] but landed property had developed a different code of ethics from money. When money supplanted land as the basis of economics, or made land dependent on gold, the admiration for wealth, Ploutos, had sunk in the estimation of the nobles to a point from which it had not yet recovered. Plato and Aristotle still thought of noble generosity as the same virtue as it had been in the days of the old Greek nobility.[281] But the art of gaining money was based on a different code from that of giving money away rightly. Plato lays down this principle: where money is prized, virtue is despised.[282] As early as Solon and Theognis, both representatives of the old aristocracy, the connexion between wealth and nobility had been broken, and Solon had cried that he would not sell his areté for gold.[283] The vulgar idea that the power to make money might be a standard of *ability* is so far from Plato's ideal of areté that he does not even mention it—although he does observe that the mob naturally admires successful men.[284] He believes that both profit-making and virtue can be practised with devotion and self-sacrifice. But the necessary worship of Mammon and contempt for poverty appear to him to be symptoms of disease in the social organism.

He believes that there are four characteristics of the oligarchic state:

1. Money is the standard for everything. It is needless to point out that this is a fault, for just as we should not make a man captain of a ship because he was rich, so we ought not to make him ruler of the state for the same reason.[285]

2. The state is not a unity. It is really two states, the rich and the poor, who distrust and hate each other.[286] Therefore it is not able to defend itself. The government is afraid (and rightly afraid) of equipping the poorer citizens with arms, for it is much more nervous of them than of the enemy. It is equally afraid of showing its fear and exposing the unwillingness of the rich to bear the burdens of war.

3. There is another feature in which the oligarchy is in conflict with Plato's political principles. That is the versatility which it forces on the citizens. Farming, making money, and fighting wars must all be done by the same people instead of everyone's doing his own job.[287]

4. Everyone in an oligarchy can sell his possessions, and anyone else can buy them; but even a man who has sold everything, and is really not a member of the state at all, being neither businessman nor artisan nor knight nor infantryman, still has the right to live destitute in the state.[288]

Here is evidence of some very concrete thinking about economic problems, much more so than in the discussion of the ideal state, which was concentrated upon its educational function to the neglect of other topics. The ideas here put forward as criticisms and sometimes as general principles are later given positive form in *The Laws*. There he tries to abolish the dan-

gerous conflict between excessive wealth and bitter poverty by
restricting the extent of any one man's landed property and
making it inalienable;[289] but in principle he had evidently held
these ideas since his youth.[290] To continue: the unhealthiest
factor in the oligarchy is the existence of many 'drones', some
poor, some professional thieves, burglars, and pickpockets.[291]
Plato holds that this phenomenon is due to bad education.[292]

The timocratic man turns into the oligarchic man, when he
realizes that ambition, which dominates everything in the Spartan state, demands too many sacrifices to the common weal,
which 'do not pay'. Since Plato treats every political change as
a phenomenon of education, he begins here too with the development of the oligarchic man while he is still young. He is the
son of a father who has embodied the ambitious type characteristic of timocracy, and has given everything to his country,
as a general or statesman. But instead of honour and distinction, he is rewarded by loss and damage: his office is taken
away, he is slandered by professional informers, he is brought
to trial, his property is taken away, he is dishonoured, banished,
or put to death. The son watches all this with horror, and
swears he will never suffer the same fate.[293] He pushes the ambition in which his father trained him out of the throne of his
heart, and along with it rejects the high-spirited part of his
soul which is the source of all ambition. Humbled by his poverty, he goes in for hard work and saving money, and gradually
collects cash. The desirous, money-loving part of his soul now
ascends the throne and becomes its maharajah, decked with
gold tiaras and torques and scimitars.[294] Here we see the transformation as a visible political picture; but the dynastic change
which dethrones self-sacrificing Spartan ambition in favour of
the purse-proud oriental despot, avarice, takes place within the
soul.[295] It is actually a pathological process in the soul, a disturbance of the healthy harmony of its parts. The new sultan, Desire, degrades the reasoning part and the fiery honour-loving
part of the soul to be slaves crouching at the foot of his throne.
He allows Thought to think of nothing except how to get more
money, and Spirit to admire and honour nothing but wealth and
rich men.[296] Plato shows amazing skill in avoiding the pedantic
repetition of the same fundamental ideas at every change, and
concealing them in images which make the three parts of the

soul and the disturbance of their normal relation ever more vividly present to us. The displacement of the three parts had already caused the best state to decay into the timocratic state.[297] We now see that the first change inevitably brings the second after it. The portrait of the oligarchic man stands finished before us: thrifty, hard-working, temperate, subordinating all his desires to the one desire for money in cool self-discipline, despising good style, impervious to culture or paideia—as is shown by the fact that he makes a blind man (Ploutos is blind) the leader of the chorus.[298] His unculture (*apaideusia*) fosters the crowd of drone-lusts within him, the instincts of the poor man and the criminal which spring from the same root, greed.[299] The true character of the oligarchic man appears wherever he has the power to get hold of someone else's money without risk. He takes possession of the property of the orphan whose guardian he was made: but in normal business, where the appearance of honesty pays, he controls himself, not because he is softened by knowledge of the Good, but because he is afraid of losing his property.[300] So, from outside, the money-man looks like an unusually respectable and decent person, but he is pretty much of a Pharisee, and does not possess true virtue and inward harmony.[301] The great gifts to the state for public shows, which the democracies demand of their rich citizens, upset him, and he does not mind being surpassed by others in them.[302] He has none of the spirit of competition for noble ends which had become so natural to citizens of Athens that Plato actually forgets to count it as an achievement of his own nation.

Just as the excesses of Spartan ambition had led to the replacement of timocracy by oligarchy, so insatiable greed for money produces democracy out of oligarchy.[303] Once again it is medical thought that enables Plato to understand the causes for the transformations that take place in human character. Medical language uses the concepts of isomoiria and symmetry—[304] two ideal conditions which can be maintained chiefly by the avoidance of excess.[305] They are simple enough to understand: after all, changes in substances are a regular succession of filling and emptying.[306] The secret of health is that mysterious measure or balance which is so easy to miss. Now, the Greeks had long believed that the real social problem of wealth was that 'even

the richest strive to double their riches' (Solon), because wealth
has no limits in itself.[307] This impulse uses every human weakness as a means to enrich itself—particularly the tendency of
young men to give money away freely: and therefore in oligarchic states that tendency is not limited by any law, because
the citizens' only interest is to acquire more property.[308] More
and more people become poor and are exploited by the rich.
Luxury and usury become dominant. Eventually these conditions
produce unrest and revolution.[309] Since there is a growing number of the better type of citizen among the destitute, and since
money-men naturally tend to neglect all their abilities except the
power of making money, the rich are bound to gain more and
more power. Communal life gives both classes a chance to become acquainted with one another. Plato's realism is more effective than ever in his description of the plain man, lean and sun-
burnt, who finds himself fighting in a battle next to one of those
spoiled rich men, and sees him puffing helpless in his superfluous
fat, until at last he tells himself that the rich owe their domination only to the cowardice of the poor. Plato lets us overhear
how the new conviction spreads gradually through the poor and
oppressed, as they say to one another, 'We've got these fellows.
They're no good!' [310]

In a sickly body a small external factor is enough to give
illness a hold it is hard to loose. Similarly, in such a state,
on the slightest occasion the latent discord breaks out—for
instance, when the rich sympathize with some external power
which oppresses the people in its own country, or when the
poor try to get support from a democracy elsewhere.[311] In the
twinkling of an eye, the oligarchy is displaced by a democracy. The opponents of democracy are either killed or exiled.
Every citizen now gets the same rights. Offices are distributed
by drawing lots for them. Drawing lots for official posts is, in
Plato's eyes, the peculiar characteristic of democracy. He saw
it constantly in his native city. Since he prized exact knowledge
above everything else, he was bound to think the lot was symbolic of a constitution which held one citizen's judgment was
as good as another's in deciding the most important political
problems.[312] Historically speaking, he is taking a phenomenon
of degeneration for the essential character of democracy: for
those who had created Athenian democracy would have agreed

with him in condemning the ideal of mechanical equality expressed in distributing offices by lot.[313] As we know, Aristotle criticized his master for being too summary on this point. He held that there were a right and a wrong form for every constitution. Indeed, he even subdivided these forms further, and in his *Politics* he distinguished between a number of different stages in the historical development of democracy and other types of constitution.[314] No doubt that was closer to the truth. But Plato is not concerned with preserving every detail of actuality. His first interest is not in constitutions at all: he uses them merely to illustrate, by describing the state it fashions, the particular type of diseased soul he is discussing—in this case, the democratic man.

To prove his point that all forms of state except the educational one are pathological degenerations, he emphasizes all their unfavourable aspects. For instance, in his Letters he seems to understand something of the national function performed by the Syracusan tyrants in uniting the Greek cities of Sicily against the Carthaginian danger, provided it was not done by force, and provided the tyrant granted full freedom to the cities with regard to their internal constitution.[315] But nothing of that can be seen in *The Republic,* where tyranny is described without qualification as disease. The same applies to democracy. Its services in saving Athens during the Persian wars are eulogized in Plato's *Menexenus,* as was the custom in a funeral speech over the dead soldiers,[316] but nothing is said of that in *The Republic.* Nor does Plato mention the historical fact (which must have pleased him) that democracy had begun by being the rule of law, and thereby ended the general anarchy that preceded it. He does not take its essential nature to be either education of the citizens to act on their own responsibility, under the protection and guidance of law, or the duty of all officials to give account of their stewardship, by which Aeschylus in *The Persians* distinguishes the Athenian form of state from Asiatic despotism. Instead, he shows us a gloomy picture of the democracy of his own time, gradually coming to pieces. 'Now the state is full of freedom', he writes, 'and everyone in it may do just what he wants'.[317] Freedom therefore means being free from duties, not being bound by one's own spiritual standards. 'Everyone arranges his own life exactly as he pleases'.[318] The individual is triumphant, with all his purely contingent nature; but therefore man, and his true nature, are neglected. This system distorts humanity as much as the system of compulsion and extreme discipline, which oppresses the individual. What Plato calls the democratic man we should call the typical individualist, which, like the ambitious, the avaricious, and the tyrannical type, occurs in all states, but which is the particular danger of democracies. Individualism is therefore a new disease of personality. Personality, remember, is not merely individuality. Man as representative of areté is human nature educated by reason; and Plato has shown by means of the paideia of his ideal state what he thinks that means. In comparison with this lofty conception of freedom as inner discipline, a conception most nobly expressed in the fact that all laws in his Republic are omitted except those dealing with paideia, our average conception of freedom is merely a cliché which covers up much that would be better abolished or prohibited.

Of course Plato tacitly assumes that his own sharp criticisms of his state and the 'revolutionary' teachings of his philosophy would have been impossible anywhere except in Athens. But he thinks the value of this freedom is dubious because everybody possesses it. He feels that he is in possession of the only true philosophy: how is he to concede the same rights to false ones? Although his dialectic method is named after 'conversation', it is absolutely different from the kind of 'discussion' which ends in nothing, with both parties saying, 'Well, that is your opinion, this is mine, let's each stick to our own'. At this point there is a conflict between the educator who feels helpless in such an atmosphere of irresponsibility, and the politician who believes in tolerance and would rather have a wrong view expressed than crush it out by force. Plato thinks democracy is a state full of all kinds of men, a 'universal store' packed with all kinds of constitution, where everyone takes the one that suits his personal taste.[319] Even a man who does not want to play any part in politics can do that. If you do not wish to join in a war when the rest of the country is fighting, you can be at peace. If you are banned by law or legal judgment from holding office, you can hold office just the same.[320] The courts are full of toleration and leniency.[321] The moral code of society pays no attention to details. No intellectual training is necessary to become a politician, the only qualification demanded is that the speaker must love the masses.[322] This description can be confirmed line for line from the legal orators and the writers of comedy. Patriotic defenders of the Athenian constitution are the loudest to accuse these weaknesses in it, although they will not therefore abandon its advantages. Plato too had considered altering the Athenian constitution by revolution, and had decided against it, although for other motives. He was like a logical doctor, who can only examine the patient and find his state of health alarming, without being able to cure him.[323]

According to Plato, the democratic man, like other types, is produced by faulty education, which takes a type already bad and makes it worse. The money-man of the oligarchic state is thrifty, but profoundly uncultured.[324] Therefore the factor of desire which dominates him soon overthrows the barriers within which his instinct of getting and keeping ought to be confined. He is not capable of distinguishing between the desires which are by nature necessary and those which are not,[325] particularly in his youth, and so his soul becomes a battleground for party-strife and revolt. As in the change from the timocratic to the oligarchic type, Plato describes the alterations which happen in the soul through the imagery of a political disturbance within the soul-state, so as to make their political significance quite clear. The ambitious man was produced by the victory of the spirited part of the soul over the reasoning part, and the oligarchic man by the victory of the desires over the spirited and reasoning parts. So the democratic man is produced by battles within the desirous part of the soul. At first the oligarchic elements in the young man defend themselves by seeking help from kin outside—for instance, from his father who educated him. But in the long run the restraining influence of aidos, respect and shame, is shaken off by the influence of the desires, which become stronger and stronger because the father does not know how to foster (τροφή = paideia) the youth's better impulses. Because of his *anepistemosyné* (scientific ignorance) of right upbringing, the whole work of education collapses.[326] And a plethos, a mob, of unquiet desires grows up secretly within him.[327] One day they assemble and storm the citadel of his soul (= his reason), because they have discovered that its barracks are empty of science and knowledge and intellectual ac-

tivity.[328] Instead, the fortress is now manned by false and narrow ideas, and the youth is entirely dominated by them. They
shut the gates. They allow no help to come in from the other
side, no envoys nor counsel from older friends.[329] They send
honour (*aidos*) into exile, calling it 'stupidity', and begin to
rename all the concepts of good and evil. They call temperance
cowardice, and moderation and reasonable expenditure vulgar
stinginess, and hunt them into banishment.[330] Instead, they bring
in, seductively arrayed and splendidly ornamented, the opposite
qualities, and they call anarchy freedom, licence munificence, and
shamelessness manliness.

It is fairly obvious that Plato is here using the great passage
in which Thucydides explains how the collapse of morality was
reflected in the change in the meanings of words,[331] and adapting it to his own theme. In this invisible shift within the soul,
he sees a symptom of the gravest convulsion in the history of
paideia. Following his first assumption, he takes the fact which
the historian saw as the lamentable result of the Peloponnesian
war throughout Hellas, and interprets it as the fault of the
'democratic man' as such. Here as everywhere, it is obvious that
what was originally a purely political concept has become for
Plato a symbol of a definite psychological type. What he sees
is a man given up to all the impulses of his desires, one after
another, both the necessary instincts and the evil lusts.[332] If he
is lucky enough not to ruin himself by his extravagances, he
might well readmit a number of the better desires when he is
older and has passed the climax of disorder. Then he would
have a period of 'equilibrium' by giving in to the contradictory
inclinations which dominate him from one time to another.
Sometimes he lives amid song and revel, sometimes he signs the
pledge and goes into training; sometimes he is keen on sport,
sometimes he is entirely idle, sometimes he studies philosophy.
He takes part in politics, and jumps up and makes speeches, or
else he goes in for the army out of admiration for a general,
or takes to business and the stock-market. His life has no kind
of order or system, but he calls it delightful and free and heavenly. He is a huge collection of mutually exclusive ideals.[333]

Plato's estimate of the democratic man is qualified by the
close connexion between that type and the origin of tyranny.[334]

Externally, of course, tyranny seems to bear the closest resemblance to Plato's own ideal Republic. Like the kingship of the wise and just man, it is based on the absolute rule of one person. But the resemblance is deceitful. Plato does not think that the existence of absolute monarchy defines the character of the state: it is only the form of the highest unity and concentration of *will*, which can be just, or can be unjust. The principle of tyranny is injustice. Because of its outward resemblance and inward contrast, it is the caricature of the ideal state, and the more any other state resembles it, the worse that state is. A complete lack of freedom is characteristic of it. That is what makes its origin from democracy understandable. Democracy contains the maximum of freedom. When any condition is exaggerated, it tends to swing back into the opposite. Excessive liberty is the shortest way to absolute unfreedom.[335] This medical explanation of a political phenomenon is of course based on the experience of the twenty or thirty years following the Peloponnesian war. The tyranny of an earlier age had been part of the change from aristocracy to democracy. The new tyranny of Plato's own day was the characteristic form of collapse in democracy, after it had become as radical as it possibly could. Therefore Plato's theory is one-sided, since it considers only the existing type of tyranny; but subsequent history seems to justify him. It shows that democracy is usually succeeded by tyranny. The Roman republic attempted to stop this process by the interesting device of making the absolute rule of one man a democratic institution, called into play for a short time at emergencies. This was the office of dictator. But Plato is not simply interpreting history when he connects tyranny with democracy. The connexion is made logically necessary by the psychopathological arguments which come from his theory of paideia. Interesting as his description of tyranny is, it is not what he says about the political pattern that interests us so much as his study of the psychological origin of tyranny as an ethical phenomenon in the widest sense of the word. In his whole gallery of tyrannical types, the political tyrant is only the most extreme, the one which affects society most deeply. This gradation in importance is evident in Plato's methodical transition from describing the political pattern of tyranny to analysing the tyrannical type of man in general.

As we have said, the origin of tyranny is liberty in excess. Plato is not content with the epigram alone. He illustrates it vividly by describing the symptoms of anarchy [336]—a description of the close interrelation of state and soul that is unequalled in world literature. Every line of it tells us that the gloomily realistic and sometimes sarcastically exaggerated colours in which it is drawn come from Plato's own experience in Athens. Sparta and oligarchy really mean much less to him than the situation he depicts here. He was able to describe anarchy so well because it was the phenomenon that had always determined the whole trend of his philosophy. Here we can see how his Republic and his paideia grew out of the anarchy which he saw around him. Therefore everything he says is a warning against what he knew to be the logically inevitable sequel of the present. It is a repetition on a higher plane of Solon's prophecy. For all politics is ultimately prophecy, whether it is based on the observation of recurrent phenomena (the method so despised by Plato),[337] or on knowledge of the profoundest logic of spiritual change. His theory of the passage of one type of constitution into another does not describe a historical sequence; but just as he describes the death-agony of freedom, he had seen the future to which Athens was doomed, during the last years of her apparent recovery. At some time, possibly, history might have taken that course, if the Athenian state could have developed wholly by inner laws. Tyranny, however, was not to grow up within it, but to be imposed on it by a foreign power. Yet the Macedonian invasion of Greece, while it struck across the fever-curve drawn by Plato in its last phase, was to give democracy one more great national duty to fulfil; and only in the weakness with which it faced that task was Plato's diagnosis, in conditions he had not foreseen, to be confirmed.

The symptoms of anarchy are first visible in education, for according to Plato's aetiology, it is in educational disorganization that it originates. The paideia of false equality results in strange unnatural situations. Fathers try to behave like children, and become afraid of their sons; while sons behave as if they were grown up, and stop respecting their parents and behaving properly, so as to feel quite free. Foreigners and resident aliens behave as if they were citizens, and citizens as if they were foreigners. Teachers are afraid of their pupils, and flatter them, while the pupils despise their teachers. In general, young men copy their elders, and older men try to look young, smart, and amusing: anything to avoid being thought unpleasant and tyrannous.[338] There are no more distinctions between master and slave—to say nothing of the emancipation of women. These words read like a running commentary on the lively pictures given in the new Attic comedy, especially the description of the sons and the free behaviour of slaves. Plato's subtle perception of psychical facts enabled him to observe animals as well as men. In a democracy, dogs, horses, and donkeys are perfectly free and unrestrained, walking about full of dignity; when anyone meets them in the street, they seem to say, 'If you don't make way for me, I certainly won't for you'.[339]

Every extreme swings to the opposite pole, by an inevitable law of nature which holds in climate, in the vegetable and animal world, and which must surely hold in the world of politics too.[340] Plato emphasizes the fact that his principles are drawn from experience, by his careful choice of words. For instance, 'it is usual' (φιλεῖ) and 'it is customary' (εἴωθεν) are obvious allusions to the method of medical and biological pathology, in which these words are used to show the relative degree of certainty in our knowledge of any phenomenon.[341] Then follows the description of the disease. Just as phlegm and bile disturb physical health, so these elements in the social organism which do nothing and only spend money are the origin of unhealthy inflammation.[342] The 'drones' whose evil effects we have already seen in the oligarchic state are the cause of dangerous disease in democracy too.[343] A wise bee-keeper cuts them out, combs and all, to preserve the whole hive. The drones are the demagogues who talk and act on the platform, while their supporters sit round humming applause and preventing anyone from contradicting them. The honey is the property of the rich—that is what the drones feed on. The mass of the population, the working class, which is not interested in politics, is not very well off; but when it is collected, it is most powerful of all. The demagogues always give it a little honey as a reward, when they confiscate the rich men's money; but they keep most of it for themselves. Now, the rich enter politics too, to defend themselves with the only weapons which have any effect in such a state.

Their resistance infuriates the other side; and the masses hand over unlimited power to their own champion. And so he becomes a tyrant.[344]

In the remote valleys of Arcadia lives a wild race with many ancient customs. Even in the civilization of the fourth century, they have preserved strange primitive rites. They still offer a human sacrifice once a year to Lycaean Zeus. The heart and entrails of a man are sliced up into the sacrificial meal, which is largely made of the intestines of sacrificed animals. Legend says that anyone who eats a piece of human flesh in his portion changes into a wolf. And so, anyone who has tasted the blood of his fellow-citizens with unholy lips changes into a tyrant. After he has driven out or executed many of his opponents, and embarked on plans of revolutionary social reform, he has no choice except to be killed by his enemies or to rule as a tyrant and become a wolf instead of a man.[345] To protect himself he surrounds his person with a bodyguard granted to him by the mob—which is foolish enough to be more worried about him than about themselves. All the rich get their money out of the country, or else they are caught doing it and are put to death. Meanwhile, he overthrows his last opponents inside the country. Now he is the charioteer of the state, but instead of being its leader, he is its tyrant. He begins by pretending to be a friend of all the citizens, and wins all their affection by his ingratiating ways. He assures them that his leadership has nothing in common with tyranny, makes them huge promises, abolishes debts, and hands out grants of land to his followers and the public.[346] But in order to make himself indispensable as a leader, he has to start war after war. Therefore he gradually becomes hateful to the citizens. Even his most faithful followers and closest advisers, who helped him to gain power and now hold important positions, criticize him severely. He has to do away with them all in order to keep his power.[347] The bravest, noblest, and wisest men are bound to be his enemies, and whether he wants to or not he is forced to 'purge' the state of them. This idea, which Plato has transferred from medicine to politics, has the opposite sense to its usual one: the tyrant is compelled to purge out not the worst but the best elements from the social organism.[348] He must have a stronger bodyguard, and so he uses the worst elements in the nation to rule the best. He cannot maintain this numerous following except by committing further crimes, and confiscating the property of the church. Finally, the people realize what a monster they have produced. In trying to escape from the shadow of slavery, which they feared from free men, they have fallen into a despotism exercised by slaves.[349]

The tyrannical man seems to be the converse of the democratic man; but he originates in the hypertrophied desires to which Plato traces the origin of the democratic man too. The latter comes from the luxuriant growth of *superfluous* desires, and the tyrannical man from *unlawful* desires, a new type not mentioned hitherto.[350] In order to understand their character we must descend into the subconscious. In dreams, says Plato, the soul casts off the restraining bonds put upon it by reason, and the wild and bestial part of man awakens, revealing a part of his nature which he himself did not know. Plato was the father of psychoanalysis. He was the first to disclose that the horrible Oedipus-complex, the lewd desire to have sexual intercourse with one's own mother, was part of the unconscious personality. He disclosed it by analysing the experience of dreaming, and added a number of analogous wish-complexes, similarly suppressed, ranging from sexual intercourse with gods to sodomy and murder.[351] As an excuse for the detail with which he expounds the subject, he pleads its importance in educating the desires—for the tyrannical type does not even try to train and discipline his lusts. The unconscious, he says, thrusts upwards in dreams even with perfectly normal and self-controlled men: which proves that everyone has such wild and horrible desires in his heart.[352]

Plato draws the inference that he must extend paideia to the subliminal life of the soul, in order to bar these subterranean elements from breaking loose into the orderly world of conscious purpose and impulse. He describes a method of taming the abnormal desires which is based on the psychology of the three parts of the soul. The foundation is a healthy and temperate relation of every man to his own self. It has been remarked, correctly enough, that the modern individual concept of the personality, the Ego, does not exist in Plato. That is due to his idea of the structure of the personality. Personality for Plato consists in the right relation of the desirous part of man

to his *real self,* which Plato calls the virtue (i.e. the best form)
of the soul. Therefore the Ego as such has no real value. In
relation to the self, it is only a vague something. Educational
influence on the subconscious life of desire must especially affect
our sleep, the only realm of life not yet covered by paideia.
Plato brings it in exactly as he brought in the pre-natal life in
the mother's womb, and the life of parents before the child's
conception.[353] The rational life, he holds, is previously formed
in the irrational life;[354] and so the irrational life is predeter-
mined by the unconscious. From Plato's revelation of the connexion between the life of dreams and waking experience and
action, Aristotle got valuable suggestions for his own study of
dreams. But Aristotle's work is more in the spirit of abstract
science, while Plato, even in discussing the psychology of dreams,
is always closely concerned with the problem of education. Before a man lies down to sleep (he says) he 'must' awaken the
thinking part of him. He 'must' give it a rich banquet of noble
thoughts and reflections, so that he can come to himself and
concentrate. The régime for the soul's desires is to be based on
the principle 'neither too much nor too little', so that they will
not disturb the better element by movements of joy or pain, but
to leave it pure for quiet study and effort to attain something
hitherto unknown to him, in the past, the present, or the future.
In the same way the spirited part of the soul must be quieted
so that the man may not go to rest with his spirits excited. The
two principal forms of the 'spirited' emotions—anger and excitement—must be lulled. Accordingly, the two lower parts of the
soul must fall asleep first, and the reason must stay awake till
the last possible moment, so that its soothing influence may continue in the unquiet regions of the soul, even when consciousness
is entirely eliminated.[355] This sleep-education had far-reaching
influence in later antiquity. There (for instance, among the Neo-
Pythagoreans) it was connected with a nightly examination of
the conscience,[356] which is not mentioned in Plato. His prescription for the soul is not moral, but dietetic.

The tyrannical type is brought into being by the domination
of abnormal desires in the soul. It is created by a retrogression
to an earlier stage of psychical life, which is usually chained in
the subconscious and lives only a subterranean life in us.[357] It
may not always be observed that, just as in explaining the origin

of the other three pathological types of personality which create
the other three types of state, Plato here finds the first seeds
of decay in the relation of father and son. In all four cases,
he illustrates the increasing degeneration by describing a young
man who holds ideals and opinions directly opposite to his father's.[358] It is impossible not to admire his educational and psychological insight: in speaking of the degeneration of the soul
through bad education, he does *not* begin by discussing the boy's
school and the teaching he gets there. He begins by discussing
the educational relationship of father and son. All through
Greek tradition, the father is shown as the natural model for
the son to imitate. Paideia, in its simplest and clearest form, is
the transmission of the areté embodied in the father to his own
children.[359] Later, a higher stage, or rather system, of education
emerges, in which the father is given a more elementary function or dispensed with altogether, and the teacher is introduced
in his place. But in one way, the father is the prototype of all
teachers, because he is at once the living ideal to be copied and
the proof of its value. Now, the father pushes those impulses
which, within limits, would have been justified, too far in one
direction towards his own exaggerated ideal. The youth is
moved by the natural opposition of youth and age, and so he
refuses to copy his father's type of areté. Thus, timocracy begins with the son's objection to the unambitious life of his father
who is entirely devoted to his work.[360] Here the father's conduct is in perfect conformity with the norm. So the bad character of the son does not come from reaction against his father's
one-sided ideal, but rather from the fact that the physis of the
younger generation grows progressively worse. So, when each
generation become fathers, their areté grows more and more
one-sided, and so progressively degenerate; and every father
hands on a faultier inheritance to his sons. The young timocrat
despises his quiet retiring father for avoiding *philopragmosyné,*
'being careful and troubled about many things'.[361] He prefers ambition. His son in turn thinks that this is too unselfish, and prefers to be a money-grubber.[362] Next, *his* son despises the money-
grubber for rejecting so many pleasures and desires—all except
those connected with making money—and so he becomes a
'democrat'.[363] He thinks it a sign of true freedom and manliness

to satisfy all his superfluous desires. His son again goes beyond them, and ventures out on the wild sea of abnormal desires.[364]

Plato illustrates this latter process and demonstrates its parallelism with the earlier stages of human degeneration, by showing how the typical phenomena that occur during the incidence of political tyranny are reflected in the state of the soul. But although he takes the description of anarchy from the world of politics, he has already laid down the principle that events in the soul are the invisible prototype of the analogous political processes. Tyranny comes into being in the soul of a young man when he himself becomes the plaything of his own lusts. His father and any other teacher he has do their best to turn his desires into less dangerous channels, away from the unlawful course they are taking. But the clever magicians and tyrant-makers try to seduce him by creating a great dominating passion (ἔρως) to be leader (προστάτης) of the desires that are unemployed and merely consuming his substance.[365] Notice that both in the soul and in the state, tyranny begins with the problem of unemployment. And so, with the other desires humming around it and goading it on, the passion surrounds itself with a body-guard of madness, and if there are any other desires in the soul with some power to resist, it purges the soul of them and of the last traces of self-control remaining.[366] In actual experience we find that what may be called a tyrannical nature is chiefly associated with three forms of psychical disorder—alcoholism, sexual excess, or manic depression. The tyrannical soul appears when a man, by nature or habit, or both, becomes an alcoholic, a melancholiac, or a sex-maniac.[367] He usually starts by rebellion against his own parents. Then he becomes violent to others.[368] The democracy of his soul is destroyed. Eros, Passion, the great despot, draws him on like a subservient mob to every daring excess.[369] By 'tyrant' Plato does not mean only the political despot, but all sorts and conditions of men from the petty thief and burglar to the man whom smaller tyrant-souls finally raise to the highest position in the state, because they feel that he has within him the greatest tyrant, the wildest passion.[370] And now on a higher plane, the violence done by the tyrant towards his parents is repeated, and the great tyrant attacks the country which is his father and his mother.[371]

The tyrannical man has no real friendships, and no freedom.

He is full of mistrust, and his essential nature is injustice. He and his rule are the extreme opposite to the just man and the just state.[372] The just man is happy because justice is simply the health of the soul.[373] The tyrant is miserable, because the natural order within him is disturbed. No one can really judge that fact except the man who is able to penetrate another man's character, and who is not blinded by any great display like a child who sees only externals.[374] Here, at the end of his pathological analysis of political and individual types, Plato depicts Socrates as both a psychologist and a philosophical student of values—in fact, as the ideal educator whom he has been describing throughout the book. He makes him say, in a charming ironical way, 'Come, let us pretend to be students of the soul.'[375] Is not the tyrant's soul like the country ruled by a tyrant? does it not suffer from the same diseases? Of all kinds of soul, it is the most slavish. There is no freedom anywhere in it: it is dominated by mad lust. Not the best, but the worst, rules it. It is constantly oppressed by anxiety and remorse. It is poor, insatiable, full of fear, mourning, depression, and grief.[376] But the greatest misery of all is that of the tyrannical man who is kept from spending his life as a private person and is raised to the absolute power which 'corrupts absolutely'.[377] In *Gorgias*, Socrates said that despite all the tyrant's authority he had no real power. It is not possible for him to do good, which is the natural aim of the human will.[378] In Plato's account of the tyrannical state we notice that he does not describe the tyrant as a man who acts freely; but he constantly emphasizes the fact that he 'must' drive out the best men, and 'must' do away with even his own comrades.[379] Everything he does is done on compulsion. He is the greatest slave of all.[380] His universal distrust makes him lonely, makes him far more confined in his movements than the ordinary man who can travel about and see the world.[381] So he is, to the eye of the philosophical doctor, the embodiment of utter unhappiness and misery.

THE STATE WITHIN US

As his motive for describing the various forms of state and the types of character corresponding to them Plato stated that the real aim of the discussion was to find out whether justice in itself were a good and injustice an evil.[382] He intends to prove that the completely just man (who, according to the previous definition of justice, is the man of perfect areté)[383] possesses true happiness; and that the unjust man is unhappy. For that, he believes, is the real meaning of *eudaimonia*. The man who has it is not *externally* happy: as the word says, he 'has a good daemon'.

This religious idea could be endlessly varied and deepened. Daemon mostly means God not in his absolute being but in his active relation to man. The man who has a good daemon is (in the mind of most Greeks) blessed with this world's goods, and therefore happy. In Aeschylus' tragedy, the king of Persia lightly risks his old daemon to win new power and greater wealth. That shows very clearly what the usual Greek interpretation of the word was:[384] for it connotes both material possessions and (its real original sense) divine favour. In the fourth century its material significance becomes dominant, even to the exclusion of the other.[385] Still, the word never loses its religious root-meaning, connexion with a daemon: and the root-meaning can be revived, as here by Plato. The word *daemon* itself had acquired more and more spiritual significance, apart from its employment in the common word eudaimonia. It is best known to us from Heraclitus' epigram, 'Character is a man's daemon'. Here the daemon is not something outside man, but absolutely one and the same as his individual nature, because it implies a close relation of divine power to the individual and his destiny. It is not far from that to the Platonic idea that a man's goodness, his areté (what we call his 'personality'), is the only source of his eudaimonia. Or, as Aristotle says in his altar-poem, summarizing Plato's teaching in one phrase, man is happy through areté alone—through his own spiritual worth.[386] We have already seen that this is the meaning of the closing myth in *Gorgias,* when the judge of the underworld gives final judgment on men by examining 'the soul itself' with his own 'soul itself'.[387] In the first part of *The Republic* Plato defined justice as the health of the soul—and thereby showed it was meaningless to ask if it were worth having.[388] Now that we have recognized the utter misery in which the tyrant lives, justice in this sense is revealed as the one source of true happiness and genuine content. Thus Plato has transferred eudaimonia to the inner nature and health of the soul itself, which makes it as completely objective and independent as it can be. If we accept his arrangement of types of constitution and types of character, the question whether the just man is happier than the unjust man is already answered. The tyrant is the greatest of slaves, and the 'kingly' man, corresponding to the perfect state, is the only free man. This is expressly stated to be the final result of the whole discussion, and is formally announced as the judge's verdict—as if proclaimed by the herald after a contest.[389]

Plato strengthens his position by another proof, relating to the factor of pleasure in the lives of the just and the unjust man. Taking the three classes in the state and the three parts of the soul, whose existence he had already assumed, he distinguishes three types of desire and pleasure, and three corresponding types of governing principle. Each part of the soul has a different desire, set on a different object. The desirous part loves profit in the broadest sense of the term. The spirited part loves honour. The reasoning part loves knowledge: it is φιλόσοφος. To parallel these three fundamental desires, he distinguishes three types of man, and three forms of life. Then he asks which of them brings most pleasure?[390] In Greek there are several words for our word *life*. *Aion* means 'lifetime'. *Zoé* is the natural process of living. *Bios* is the unity of an individual life ended by death, but it is also the way of passing one's life, namely, life in so far as it can be qualitatively distinguished from the life of other men. This is the aspect of life expressed in the word *bios* which makes it most suitable to denote the new concept of life as the expression of a particular ethos, a 'way of life'. Plato, with his peculiar ability to distinguish *types*, always saw man as a whole, not as a series of acts or a collection of qualities. By forming the concept of *bios*, he gave a powerful stimulus to Greek philosophical thought, which had long repercussions in philosophy, and in religion and ethics throughout the succeeding centuries, until at last it merged into the Christian idea of the Saint's Life and various other forms and degrees of the Christian life. Now, every one of the forms of life previously described is capable of a different kind of pleasure and eudaimonia. Is there any way to compare the amounts of happiness and pleasure inherent in each one? Plato believes the only way to do so is to experience each of them personally.[391]

The difficulty is that everyone enjoys his own life without knowing the life of others. Plato gets over this by pointing out that
the man representing the philosophical idea is the only one who
has actually experienced all three forms of pleasure. For obviously he has felt both sensual desire and the ambitious craving
for honour. The other two cannot think beyond their own
spheres; but his mode of life, dedicated to knowledge, is fundamentally superior to them both.[392] Here again Plato is talking
about ideals, not about real men. Therefore he feels justified in
holding that his 'philosophical man' fulfils the conditions which
must be satisfied before any objective comparison of the three
lives can be made—namely, that he has actually experienced all
three ways of life. The moral worth of these three experiences
must be judged by reason, the organ of the philosopher.[393]
Therefore only that which the philosopher loves is true happiness. His judgment is valid for other lives too.[394] Therefore the
philosophical ideal of life is the highest human ideal. In his
Ethics Aristotle mitigated the boldness of this conclusion by
stating that the philosophical life was the highest type of human
eudaimonia, but admitting that there was another form of it,
moral excellence, founded on active life instead of pure knowledge.[395] He distinguished the two different stages as sophia and
phronésis; but in Plato they are united in the philosophical
ideal, as we have shown in describing the paideia of the rulers.
Instead of the eccentric philosopher of pre-Socratic tradition,
who lived such an unworldly life and behaved so strangely,
Plato makes the philosopher the epitome of all the best in humanity. That is not simply because he himself estimates him differently. The philosopher's own nature has undergone a transformation. Purged by the acid of Socratic enquiry, the bios of
the philosopher has been revealed as the purpose of all education and culture, the ideal of human character.[396]

But it might be objected that, although Plato takes the philosopher's judgment as the sole criterion for comparing the
pleasure inherent in the three lives, it is really a one-sided judgment. Therefore he tries to give weight to his findings in another
way, by examining the nature of pleasure itself.[397] He is trying
to find a central point from which he can compare and evaluate
the three different types of pleasure. This problem seems to be
almost impossible of solution by rational thought and measure-

ment; and his study of it, both here and in *Philebus,* culminates
in asking whether all pleasures are the same in nature, or there
are false and true pleasures; and, if the latter be true, whether
they can be distinguished. We need not give the details of his
proof. The main argument is that most of what we call pleasures
are nothing more than the feeling of getting rid of pain—that
is, they are negative.[398] Even the 'greatest' pleasures we experience originate, if closely examined, in a change of that kind.
They are feelings of satisfaction after the oppression of some
kind of painful or uncomfortable want has been dissipated by
fulfilment.[399] We feel the repose of satisfaction (which really
lies between pleasure and pain) to be positively pleasant. Plato
compares that mistake with the error experienced when we are
climbing, and look down halfway, and believe we have already
reached the top.[400] We have a similar experience if we look at
a sliding scale of colour ranging from black to white—we feel
we are looking at white when we have only got to grey.[401]
Therefore all feelings of pleasure and pain are relative. As
Plato shows in *Philebus,*[402] they depend on the More and Less
which we desire. Suppose we assume that all pleasure and pain
are accompaniments of being filled and being emptied—a very
common conception in the medical science of Plato's day—then
hunger and thirst are physical emptiness, while ignorance and
folly are emptiness of the soul. Satiation fills the body's lack,
and learning and knowledge fill the wants of the soul.[403]

At first sight it scarcely seems possible to compare the two
conditions and the two types of satisfaction. Yet we can understand the comparison if we measure the two processes with the
accompanying pleasures by the metaphysical standard, and ask
which of them fills the man experiencing it with truer Being and
reality. Whichever does must be truly more filling and satisfying. Now no satisfaction of the body's needs can ever be as filling as the nourishment and satisfaction which knowledge gives
the soul: for the things which nourish the body are not so truly
real as the knowledge of truth which nourishes the soul.[404] If
true pleasure is being filled with things which are appropriate
to one's nature, then it must be more truly and essentially
pleasant to be filled with higher than with lower reality.[405] So
those who enjoy mere sensual desires do not really know what
is 'above' (to continue the metaphor) : they do not even lift

their eyes to it. They have never experienced a pure and lasting pleasure. They look 'downwards' like animals. Stooping
towards the ground, crouched over their dining-tables, they glut
themselves on their own pleasures, and each tries to get more
by butting at the others with horns and hooves of iron, killing
them and getting killed, unsatisfied and insatiable because he is
not satisfying himself with that which really 'is'. They know
only the shadows and phantoms of pleasure, and are ignorant
of the true pleasure which is akin to the spiritual part of man,
his phronésis, so that they actually think reason is opposite to
pleasure. They are like the Greeks who fought at Troy to win
Helen back, although the Helen in Troy was only a deceitful
ghost, and the real one was in Egypt, as Stesichorus writes.[406]
So, even from the point of view of the reality of pleasure, the
philosopher is the only man who has true pleasure.[407] Furthest
of all from it is the tyrannical man, and nearest to it is the
kingly man, the 'just man' of the Republic. Plato actually makes
an ironic joke about the difference between the happiness of the
types of men corresponding to various states: he calculates that
the tyrant has 729 times less pleasure than the philosophical
man. And if the good and just man surpasses him so far in
pleasure, how immeasurably inferior must his life be in value,
beauty, and human perfection![408]

Not only is the life of the just man *happier* than that of the
unjust man. It is not even more *profitable* to be bad than good—
which Glaucon and Adeimantus said was the view of many
people.[409] Plato had already come to this conclusion by defining
justice as the health and harmony of the soul.[410] Now at the end
of the discussion he corroborates it [411] by introducing an image,
as he so often does at decisive points. He proposes an allegory
to illustrate the complex inner structure of human nature. It is
a picture of man—or rather of the soul; and it shows the soul
(in conformity with Plato's theory) as a composite of three
things: a many-headed monster, a lion, and a man. What we
usually call man is only an outward covering that encloses those
three dissimilar and independent things, and makes the trinity
look like a smooth unity with no conflicts involved.[412] The
monster, surrounded by all sorts of heads, wild and tame, is
man as a creature of desire. It is like the desirous part of the
soul which Plato distinguishes from the courageous and the

reasoning parts. Lion is man as an emotional being, feeling anger, shame, courage, excitement. The true man, the 'man in man', as Plato beautifully expresses the new idea, is the intellectual part of the soul.[413]

It is unnecessary to explain the significance of this image in the history of humanism. At one stroke, it makes plain the trend and the meaning of Plato's paideia, as far as it is based on a new evaluation of man and his nature. Plato's paideia is intended to develop the man in man. By strictly subordinating everything else to this intellectual purpose, it produced an entirely different picture of life and of true human perfection. It is clear once more that the whole complex structure of the Republic was meant only to serve as a background against which to work out this picture of the human soul. Similarly, the list of the various forms of degenerate state is only an illuminated background against which the soul in its various degenerations may be displayed. Therefore anyone who praises injustice is giving free rein to the wild beast with many heads. Only the philosopher, who strengthens the tame part of us and makes it dominant, subordinates everything in us to the divine. It can never be profitable to make the better element in us serve the worse, for that is against nature. The image also tells us why there are two kinds of paideia in *The Republic,* a philosophical one for the rulers and a military one for the guards. If the lion is properly tamed, he will not side with the other beast, but obey the man in us and help him to win in his fight with the many-headed monster.[414] The function of education is to train our nobler irrational impulses to harmonize with the intellect so that the weak human element in us may be supported by them, and keep the sub-human part in check.

That is the Republic which Plato's paideia is intended to produce. Young men are not to be let free from their training until *that* state has been constructed inside them and become permanent: the rule of the divine in man over the bestial.[415] The man that Plato calls just, who is of the same nature as the truly just Republic, has nothing to back up his education and his activity in the real contemporary state, which is only a darker copy of the higher human nature. As Plato says in another passage, he will, for lack of a perfect state in which he can be active, *mould himself* (ἑαυτὸν πλάττειν).[416] But he carries the true state in his soul, and acts and lives with his gaze fixed on it, although he cannot live within it. He will take care that nothing in it is altered; and his attitude to the good things of this earthly life—money, property, honour, and so on—will depend on the possibility of acquiring them without contravening the law of the state within him.[417] Is he to take part in politics? All the previous argument debars him from doing so; and Socrates' young interlocutor correctly concludes that he will not. But Socrates says he will. In *his* state, he will certainly take part in politics with all his energy, but perhaps not in the country in which he happens to live, unless a divine tyché makes it possible for him to act according to his own lights.[418] *His* state, the Republic, lies in the world of Ideas, for it does not exist anywhere on earth. But—and with this Plato concludes his enquiry—it makes no difference whether it exists or not. Perhaps it exists in heaven, an eternal pattern for the man who can see it, and, by looking at it, build himself into the true state.[419]

We started out with Plato to find a state. Instead, we have found a man. And in Plato's sense we may feel that we are like Saul, who set out in search of his father's asses, and found a kingdom. Whether the ideal Republic ever comes into being in the future or not, we can and must incessantly strive to build that 'state within us'. We are quite accustomed to finding that, as Plato gives greater metaphysical meaning to his interpretation of the nature of man, he begins to speak the language of paradox and metaphor; but this is the greatest paradox he has produced. From the earliest of Plato's books we have watched the development of a new purposeful attitude to the state. We have several times found it necessary to ask whether it would really lead to the aim it was supposed to be trying to achieve, because Plato is in opposition to everything that is usually thought indispensable for the external existence of a state.[420] Now that we have reached our destination, we can see that (in harmony with the best traditions of Greek thought) he holds the state to be one of the prime conditions of human life; but that he is judging the state exclusively by its moral and educational function. In the history of Thucydides we have already seen that function in conflict with the state's existence as an organization for gaining and keeping power, although he tried, in his idealized picture of Athens, to balance the two functions once again.[421] But there are many other signs that the original harmony had been disturbed in Plato's age. They make it easy to understand how the state had been split into two parts—the gulf which is irresistibly opening both in the actual political life of the age and in Plato's philosophical thinking about the state. Throughout those years we observe the growth of pure power-states, often under the leadership of big politicians and tyrants relentlessly upholding the view that the state's might is right; and, on the other hand, the philosophers' emphasis on the educational character of the state manifests an ethical intention to create a new kind of society. In the new state, power is not the sole standard—as *Gorgias* proved. The standard is man; spiritual value; the soul.[422] By using that criterion with strict logic to purify the existing state of all its dross, Plato has left at last nothing but the 'inner state within the soul'. In the effort to reform the polis, he originally held that this self-reformation of the individual must be the starting-point of a comprehensive new order. But ultimately he realized that the inner depths of the soul were the last refuge of the irresistible will to *law* which had founded the city-states of early Greece, and now had no home anywhere in the world.

So at last, Plato puts forward, as his answer to the question whether his ideal state can be 'realized', a startling principle, worthy of the greatest of all educators. It is this: realize the true state in your own soul. Ancient and modern interpreters who expect to find in *The Republic* a handbook of political science, dealing with the various existing forms of constitution, have tried again and again to find the Platonic state somewhere on this earth, and identified it with some real form of state which seemed to resemble it in its political structure. But the essence of Plato's state is not its external structure (if it has any) but its metaphysical nucleus, the idea of absolute reality and value round which it is built. It is not possible to realize Plato's Republic by imitating its external organization, but only by fulfilling the law of absolute good which is the soul of it. Therefore he who succeeds in realizing that divine order in his individual soul has made a greater contribution to the realization of Plato's state than he who constructs an entire city which externally resembles Plato's political scheme but is deprived of its divine essence, the Idea of the Good, the source of its perfection and happiness.

The just man of Plato's Republic is not the ideal citizen of any real state—whatever its constitution may be. In it, he is necessarily a stranger, as Plato himself has shown. Always ready to work with all his heart in his counterpart, the ideal state which harmonizes with his own moral ideals, he lives in retirement in the actual contemporary state. That does not imply that he evades his duties as a member of society. On the contrary, he takes care to fulfil them punctiliously, for he 'does his own work' in the full sense. That is demanded by the Platonic conception of justice, and it can serve as a standard in every state and every situation. But he is not fully a citizen of any state except the one he carries in his soul, whose law he is striving to obey when he does his own job.[423] Ever since Plato laid down this principle, every man with a lofty moral conscience has inevitably felt himself to be a citizen of two worlds.[424] In Christendom this situation continues. The Christian lives both in the temporal state of this world, and in the eternal invisible kingdom of heaven of which he is a member. It follows from the 'conversion' to true being which Plato says is the essence of his paideia. But this breach of the old harmony of Greek life is not due to the invasion of an other-worldly religion from without. It is the product of the inner dissolution of the Greek unity of man and polis. At bottom, what Plato is doing is simply to explain the real situation of the philosophical man in the polis of his time, as manifested in the representative life and death of Socrates. It was not chance, but a profound historical necessity that character and personality should have been thus refounded on 'the state within' at the very height of Greek culture. In archaic and classical Greece the relation of the individual to the community had been taken very seriously, so seriously that every citizen had for centuries been deeply penetrated by the spirit of the polis. 'The state educates man', πόλις ἄνδρα διδάσκει, was a famous epigram, not of Plato, but of the great old Greek poet Simonides, who expressed in it the original Greek ideal. But Plato transcends it. From his standpoint we can see that the logical consequence of that total penetration was the Socratic conflict. Through it the individual should rise above earthly principalities to the only realm in which he can be truly and wholly one with the 'state'—the realm of the divine. By conscious, deliberate obedience to the law of the state within himself, the individual at last finds true freedom. Thus Greek political thought attained its climax in creating the European idea of free human personality, based not on any man-made law but on knowledge of the eternal standards. In the image of the cave Plato had shown that that eternal 'measure' was the knowledge of God. It is now clear that the purpose of the laborious ascent towards knowledge of that 'measure'—the ascent which Plato in his metaphor described as the purpose of paideia—is to find 'the state within us' in the 'imitation of God'.

THE REPUBLIC

PART III

THE EDUCATIONAL VALUE OF POETRY

The tenth and last book of *The Republic* once again takes up the problem of the educational value of poetry. At first we are apt to ask why Plato, after reaching a height so sublime that his readers could look back from it on all the road they had traversed, should apparently turn back to a subject he had dealt with already: for in that case he would certainly be weakening his effect. But here, as often in Plato, a structural difficulty leads us to a profound philosophical problem. Therefore we must try to be clear about his reasons for arranging his material like this. It is easy to see that the earlier criticisms of poetry, which were brought in apropos of the education of the guards, and which were attacks on the low religious and moral tone of most Greek poetry, were in the dogmatic form which Plato cultivated at that stage. They had to address the reader's 'right opinion' without giving him any real knowledge of the principle involved.[1] The education of the rulers, which comes later, is founded entirely on pure philosophical knowledge. There is no place in it for poetry and music, so that Plato cannot say anything definite about the educational function of poetry from the standpoint of philosophy—that is, of pure knowledge. Before he could do that, he had to expound the theory of Ideas, which was brought into the discussion as the chief subject to be studied by the future statesmen. Therefore it is entirely logical that the question of poetry should be discussed once again on this higher plane.

But the important thing is to decide why Plato chooses just this spot as the battlefield for the last decisive struggle between philosophy and poetry. We are helped in understanding it by observing that the whole discussion of the ideal Republic, including the far-reaching discussion of degenerate types of state,

358

is only a means to expose more clearly the moral structure of the soul and the collaboration of its parts in the larger image of the state.[2] The books dealing with the various types of constitution and the types of character corresponding to them are also part of the long progressive description of paideia. Only if we realize that can we understand why the analysis of states and men culminates in the foundation of 'the state within us', of the noblest human character as the climax and purpose of the whole book.[3] We have made our way from the education of guards and soldiers, which included the traditional 'musical' paideia, to the philosophical education which is intended to mould the minds of the rulers by leading them to knowledge of truth and of the supreme standard. Through that education the soul is to be founded on the order and the law which lie within it—namely, on the state-like quality in its structure and actions. There is a close relation between this conception of the function of education and the philosophical logos, which Plato here describes as the highest form of culture. From this point of view, the opposition between poetry and philosophy, which was only relative on the lower plane of the guards' education, becomes absolute. Those forces in the soul which create law and order, and are embodied in philosophy, are unquestionably superior to those that represent and imitate, from which poetry originates; and they demand that the latter pay homage to them and subordinate themselves to the logos. To-day we think poetry is merely a branch of literature. It is difficult for us to understand this ruling of Plato's, which looks just like tyranny, like the intrusion of philosophy into realms where it has no business. But the Greeks held that poetry was the chief vehicle of paideia, so that the dispute between philosophy and poetry was bound to become acute as soon as philosophy began to claim to be paideia, and to hold the leading place in education.

The problem becomes urgent with the attack on Homer, first of all because everyone loves him, and so feels the gravity of the problem most quickly when the perfect poet is impugned. Plato's Socrates excuses himself for exposing his secret ideas about poetry to criticism in this way.[4] Ever since his childhood, he says, he has been held back by holy shame and respect towards the poet from openly stating his views. That is a warning to all those who might complain about his being disloyal, or impious, or uncomprehending. But he is not attacking Homer simply to make the contrast of philosophy and poetry sharper. There are two other reasons. Plato tells us one of them at the beginning of the discussion, when he calls Homer the master and leader of tragedy.[5] It is on tragedy that the full weight of the objection falls—for it is tragedy which reveals most plainly the emotional or 'pathetic' influence of poetry on the soul.[6] The second reason is that whenever the educational pretensions of poetry are being challenged Homer must occupy the centre of the discussion. He was believed to be the embodiment of paideia in the traditional sense.[7] And, as we have shown, that belief goes back to early times. (In the sixth century Homer's critic Xenophanes called him the source from which all had taken their wisdom since the beginning of time.[8]) It had been fostered by the sophists, who tried to bring out the educational elements in every poet and in every subject they studied.[9] Towards the end of Plato's polemic, we begin to realize that he is attacking one particular essay or speech by a sophist maintaining the thesis that Homer was the educator of all Greece.[10] It evidently supported this view by making Homer a sort of encyclopaedic teacher understanding all arts (τέχναι).[11] This kind of attitude must have been fairly common, as Plato's *Ion* shows; it reappears in the interpretation of Homer given by the rhapsodes who praised and explained their poet.[12] Even 'Plutarch', in his essay *Life and Poems of Homer,* written centuries later, treats Homer's poetry in the same practical and pedagogical way, as a reservoir of knowledge.[13] Therefore Plato is attacking the general Greek view of the paideutic value of poetry in general, and of Homer in particular.

This is a turning-point in the history of Greek paideia. The contrast between philosophy and poetry is, Plato says, a battle of truth against sham. He refers briefly to the rule that imitative poetry is to be banished from the ideal Republic.[14] Since the Republic can perhaps never be realized (as Plato himself has admitted [15]), this condemnation of poetry does not imply its absolute banishment from all human life so much as a sharp definition of its intellectual influence, for the behoof of all those who follow Plato's arguments. Poetry injures the intellect of its readers and hearers if they do not possess knowledge of the truth as a remedy.[16] That means that poetry must move down to a lower plane. As it was before, it will remain a source of aesthetic pleasure, but it is debarred from attaining the highest rank and being the teacher of mankind. The question of its value is concentrated on the point which Plato must hold to be decisive, the relation of poetry to absolute reality, to true Being.

Plato's main attack is directed against imitative poetry. But what is imitation? He explains in his usual way, by starting from the Ideas.[17] Ideas are the unity which thought perceives in diversity. Things perceived by sense are the copies of the Ideas: for instance, the many visible chairs and tables are copies and imitations of the Idea of a chair or the Idea of a table. There is only one such Idea of chair or table. The carpenter makes his furniture by copying the Idea, which is his pattern. What he produces is a table or a chair, not an Idea.[18] But as well as the Idea and the thing perceived by sense there is a third stage of reality. To it belongs what the painter produces when he represents any object.[19] It is with that stage that Plato compares the relation of poetry to truth and reality. The painter takes the chairs and tables made by the carpenter, which are perceptible to sense, and, using them as models, imitates them. As if setting out to create a second world by reflecting the real one in a mirror, the painter is content with the image of things, a sham reality.[20] Therefore as far as making chairs and tables goes, he is inferior to the carpenter, who can make real ones. The carpenter, again, is inferior to him who made the eternal Idea of a chair, in imitation of which all earthly chairs are constructed. The original creator of the Idea is God.[21] The artisan makes a copy of the Idea. The painter copies the copy made by the carpenter, and his copy is therefore two degrees removed from reality. Poets are on the same plane. They make a world which is nothing but appearance.[22]

Of all the arts attributed to Homer by his interpreters, there is only one that interests Plato in this connexion, and which he chooses, in order to test whether Homer really possesses it or not. He does not ask whether Homer was a great doctor, as people say he was, or had any of the other skills they praise him for. He merely asks whether he knew the art of politics and understood how to teach people.[23] As if in a regular examination, he asks the poet if he ever made a city-state better and improved its institutions, like the great old lawgivers of Greece;

or won a war; or, in private, like Pythagoras and his pupils, showed men the pattern of a new life (βίος). Of course he never gathered round him a band of pupils and adherents to praise his achievements, like the sophists, the contemporary virtuosi of education.[24] (This is obviously a sneer at the sophists who thought themselves equal to Homer and the ancient poets, as Protagoras claims to be in the dialogue named after him.[25]) All the poets since Homer have merely produced copies (εἴδωλα) of areté without touching the truth, so that they cannot really be educators of mankind.[26]

Poetry is like the bloom on a young face, which is not beautiful in itself and whose charm perishes when youth goes.[27] This idea casts a flash of light on the situation of poetry as Plato sees it. Youth is the first unfolding of charm and grace which occupies a definite period in the individual's life, and which, purely for its own sake, is a source of pleasure to others. But when it is over, it must be replaced by other good qualities, and often its passing shows that the charming girl or boy had no real fundamental beauty. Here for the first time in Greek thought appears the profound idea that poetry is a thing that does not exist in every epoch. Nations have their youth as well as men, and poetic imagination is the delightful companion of their youth. If we take Plato's views of the relation between poetry and philosophy too much in the abstract, they strike us as rather shocking, even if we accept them as true in every detail. But every truth Plato utters surprises us by his astonishing, often prophetic powers of anticipation. In the form of universal concepts, he prefigures the destiny of the Greek spirit. The exaltation of the moral personality above the degenerate state, the release of the creative spirit from the forms of poetry, the soul's return into itself—all these are points which only a supreme genius like Plato could have picked out and made into a vision of a new age, which was yet to be born. He was of course consoled by the breadth of the thought that poetry did not have the true imperishable beauty possessed by truth alone. According to Plato, poets have neither knowledge in the philosophical sense nor true opinion like the non-philosophical practical man. They merely imitate life as it seems good and beautiful to the masses.[28] Their work reflects current standards and ideals, but it lacks the true art of measurement, by which error and appearance may be avoided.[29] Throughout the dialogue it is worth noting the irony with which Socrates disguises his profound thoughts in the familiar pedantic form, and chooses examples (such as chairs and tables) which leave it to the reader to do the thinking.

But from the educational point of view, the chief objection to poetry is something else again. It is that poetry is not directed to the best part of the soul—reason—but to the emotions and passions which it stimulates unduly.[30] A man of high moral character can master his emotions, and if exposed to strong stimuli he takes care to moderate the effects.[31] Law and reason enjoin him to curb his passions, and his passion urges him to give way to grief. Passion ($\pi\acute{\alpha}\vartheta o\varsigma$) and law are opposing forces. The command of law supports the thinking part of the soul in resisting lust.[32] But poetry appeals to the childish part. Just as a little boy who gets hurt holds the sore place and cries, so poetry exaggerates the feeling of grief which it evokes by imitation. Therefore it leads people to surrender entirely to these emotions, instead of accustoming their souls to recover as quickly as possible from the sympathetic emotion they have felt, and replace the dirge by recovery.[33] The opposition between the spirit of tragic poetry and Plato's philosophy could not be more trenchantly characterized. He explains the poets' tendency to play heavily on feelings of grief and tenderness by their natural interest in the passionate aspect of the soul's life. It offers far greater opportunities to the imitator, who is trying for both vivid representation and interesting variation, than the thinking part of the soul, with its calm, rational, and consistent ethos. This applies particularly to performances given to a large holiday audience. The emotional part of the soul is always excited, and assumes manifold shapes, so it is easier to imitate.[34]

From this Plato concludes that imitative poets have a bad influence on the soul by arousing, fostering, and strengthening bad forces in it, and killing thought and reason—as when a ruler strengthens the bad elements in a state.[35] He reminds us once again that that is why he kept imitative poets out of his ideal Republic; but he does not spend much time discussing this ruling (which was merely a police regulation), although we naturally think of it first if we take his Republic to be the blue-

print for a real constitution. Instead, he says the important
thing about this prohibition is its effect on the education of the
individual. That was the only ideal he had preserved at the end
of the ninth book, while he pushed aside the question of the
realization of the ideal state as merely incidental.[36] His charge
against the imitative poet is that he 'makes a bad state in the
soul of every individual', by trying to gratify the unreasoning
element in it.[37] The image is taken from the habit of flattering
their audiences for which demagogues were often criticized. The
poet makes the soul incapable of distinguishing between important and unimportant, for he presents the same things as great
or small, according to his purpose. But it is precisely that relativism which shows he only makes idols and does not know the
truth.[38]

The gravest charge is that poetry corrupts our sense of values.
While we drink in the words of the tragic hero lamenting his
woes and showing his passionate grief, we feel pleasure, and we
surrender to the power of the poet. Our own emotion wells up
in sympathy, and we admire the poet most who is best able to
put us in this condition. Sympathy is the essence of all poetic
effect.[39] But in our private life we behave in just the opposite
way. We are careful not to give way to grief and lamentation
when we suffer any hardship. We despise the conduct that we
praise on the stage, and we even call it unmanly. Hence the
anomaly that in poetry we enjoy watching a man we should not
like to be, and indeed would be ashamed to copy.[40] In other
words, our ethical ideal is in sharp contrast to our poetic sensi-
bility. The natural yearning to weep and complain which is forcibly suppressed in life is encouraged by the poet, and we enjoy
the process. In that case, if the truly best part of our nature
has been badly trained by reason and habit, it drops its watchful
opposition and gives free rein to the passion for weeping and
wailing.[41] It feels quite justified in doing so because the tears are
not for our own grief, but for that of other men; and at last it
thinks the pleasures of sympathy are really valuable. In tragedy
the audience is affected by sympathy, in comedy by the sense of
the ridiculous. All of us are subject to these feelings, but few
of us realize the invisible transformation in our own nature
which is effected when poetry strengthens these emotions.[42]

Therefore Plato refuses to admit that Homer is what every-

one calls him, the teacher of the Greek people. He is indeed
its greatest poetic genius, and its first tragedian, but we must
not love and honour him beyond his terms of reference. The
only poetry suitable for the ideal state consists of hymns to
gods and poems in praise of distinguished men. Plato does not
want to be thought pedantic.[43] He points out that the opposition
between poetry and philosophy is very ancient. He knows the
magic of poetry by personal experience. He offers to give it and
its advocates a chance to defend themselves by proving that it
is not only *pleasant* but also *useful* in life and in the state. He
promises to listen willingly to their defence of it.[44] No doubt the
sophists had already composed a prose *Apology for Poesy,* and
a defence of Homer, along these lines. Plato was probably
thinking of the same treatise whose existence we have already
inferred,[45] the first to describe Homer as combining pleasure
with profit, on Horace's standard:[46]

> omne tulit punctum qui miscuit utile dulci.

He compares poetry to an old love which we still cling to although we know it is bad for us, and which we are finally forced
unwillingly to put away. We try our best to be kind to it, and
hope it will prove to be as good and true as possible when it is
examined. But if it cannot really justify itself, we defend ourselves with a new sober realization of the facts, and use it as
a countercharm against the old magic. We say that we need not
take all poetry of this kind seriously, and that we must shun it
for fear of disturbing 'the state within us.' The only way to
judge its educational value is to see how near it brings the soul
to that inner order and harmony.[47]

PAIDEIA AND ESCHATOLOGY

It is now proved that education through philosophy is the
only valuable education. It is the only way to realize 'the state
within us'. But we have already admitted that that is the only
possible purpose of education in a world which cannot admit
any decisive political reformation. We might think at first that
Plato was mainly interested in making an ideal state ruled by
a small élite, and was subordinating ethics and education to that
end. But as we study the book, it becomes crystal-clear that he

is doing the opposite. He is founding politics upon ethics, not only because he must begin political reform with teaching people how to behave, but because, in his belief, the principle of action which guides society and the state is the same as that which guides the moral conduct of the individual. For Plato the perfect state is only the ideal frame for a good life, constituted so that human character can develop unrestrained within it according to its own innate moral laws, in the certainty that it is thereby fulfilling the purpose of the state within itself.[48] In his view, that is impossible in any existing state. In every one of them there are inevitable conflicts between the spirit of the state and the ethos of the man who has the 'best state' in his own soul and tries to live up to it—the perfectly just man.[49] Looked at from this point of view, Plato's *Republic* is not so much a plan for the practical reform of the state as an artificial society in which all interests are subordinated to the education of the moral and intellectual personality, which is paideia. Everything in it is aimed at making men happy, not by satisfying the individual's will or judgment, but by assisting him to maintain the health of the soul, which is justice. At the end of the ninth book, where Plato draws distinctions between the various types of soul and ways of life, he says the only truly happy man is the just man. This was the answer to Glaucon's question, which started the main discussion: whether justice could make a man happy in itself without any social recognition.[50] But that was not his last word about the value of justice, and about the paideia leading to it. The prize of justice is greater, and the value at stake is higher than anything that can be realized in the brief span of human life.[51] The frame in which we must study the soul's existence is not time but eternity. What we are trying to do is to ensure its lasting safety in both this world and the next. The just man's life on earth is a constant education for the true state which, like the Ideas, is in heaven;[52] and so all education is preparation for a higher life in which the soul will not exist as a composite of the many-headed beast, the lion, and the man, but in its pure form.

It is not necessary here to go into the proofs of immortality which Plato advances.[53] Their general trend is that if the soul cannot be destroyed by its own illness, which is vice, then it cannot be destroyed at all. He does not even consider that the life of the soul might depend on the life of the body. He is not really interested in the psycho-physical aspect of the soul, but in the soul as a repository of moral values. In *The Republic,* as in the concluding myths of *Gorgias* and *Phaedo,* he shows the soul to us in the supernal light which falls on its earthly destiny from the world beyond. The mythical form, in which he has shrouded the secret of the soul's connexion with the divine which is above this life, forbids us to examine the physical structure of that other world too closely. Here, as everywhere in Plato, it is very difficult to separate the body of poetic fantasy from the profound religious conviction which ensouls it. Neither state nor the human soul can appear in its perfect form in this world. We always see the soul like the old god Glaucus, emerging from the tides of life covered with weed and shells, scarred and maimed and hurt by the waves, liker to an animal than to its true self.[54] We cannot apprehend its true nature unless we contemplate its love of knowledge, and its high endeavour to soar aloft in the knowledge of its own divinity and immortality. Its nature is simple, not manifold, unlike the sufferings and distortions we have described, and their forms.[55]

Plato's catalogue of the glories possessed by the just man is like the eulogies of heroes in old Greek poetry, and the descriptions of the honour paid them by their fellow-citizens.[56] Just as the ancient poets divide the rewards into those which he receives during his life and those he enjoys after death,[57] so the philosopher begins by describing the honour given to the just man here on earth in his own polis (a description which inevitably has some conventional features, and is meant to have, in order to remind readers of the old models Plato is copying) and then goes on to give a more detailed account of the destiny of the just man's soul after death.[58] The ethical code of the ancient city-state could promise its dead heroes nothing more than the immortality of their names carved upon their tombs and commemorated with their deeds.[59] In Plato's Republic they are guaranteed the immortality of the soul, which is incomparably worthier than all the honours the polis could give. The Platonic man is inspired not by the hope of winning glory from his fellow-citizens, as the great men of the old city-state had been, but by the hope of earning glory from God. This is true even of his life on earth, where Plato puts his title 'beloved of God' above all human distinctions.[60] But it is even more true of the after-life of his soul in the thousand years of wandering which it enters after its separation from the body.

The myth of *The Republic*, like those in *Gorgias* and *Phaedo*, contains a description of the judgment after death; but here the emphasis is neither on the judge's method of determining the worth of the soul, nor on its punishment. These things are mentioned at the beginning, to show that the just man has a happy fate awaiting him, and the unjust man a long term of suffering.[61] The decisive factor in the eschatology of *The Republic* is the *choice of lives* (βίων αἵρεσις) which the souls make after the thousand years' wandering.[62] There is only a limited number of souls, and after their sojourn beyond they must return to earth and start a new existence. The doctrine of the soul's wanderings (taken over here from Orphic tradition) enables Plato to give a more profound significance to the supreme assumption of all education, the moral responsibility of man. That is the meaning of the change he makes in the theory of metempsychosis. It is a bold attempt to reconcile the sense of moral obligation within us with an opposing idea, the old Greek belief in the daemon which magically controls all the individual's actions from the beginning of his life to the end.

The ideal of paideia assumes that men can make a free choice.[63] The power of the daemon assumes that they are bound by ananké, necessity.[64] Both conceptions of human life are, within their limits, justified. The ancient Greek belief was that the gods sent blindness which drove men unawares into evil doom; but by degrees another tradition had developed according to which men suffered from an até for which they were themselves responsible, and which they had knowingly incurred. This gave birth to a new concept of responsibility, expressed in Solon's poetry, and it created the entire system of thought that lies behind Greek tragedy.[65] But the tragedians' conception of guilt and sin always suffered from the uncertainty implicit in the double aspect of até, which was never completely resolved. As long as the conscience of men was burdened with this uncertainty, Plato's powerful belief in the force of education, the conviction which at last takes shape in *The Republic*, could not properly envisage its ultimate aim. But not by cool psychological analysis, not even by his ethical 'art of measurement', could Plato master that supreme problem. The only way he finds open is to project the solution he sees darkly in his soul onto the diviner world beyond this life, just as the ancient poets, above their picture of human life, raised a nobler stage whereon the gods lived and acted, and all human questions were finally solved. Only its broadest outlines can be seen by human eyes, so that our reason is unable to understand it in detail.

In his first attack on 'musical' paideia as represented by classical poetry, Plato had criticized the idea that the gods are responsible for the tragic errors of men, and hurl whole families into ruin.[66] Every paideia must oppose that belief, because it assumes that man is a responsible being. Therefore the climax of Plato's *Republic* is that passage of the concluding myth in which, after poetry has been dethroned, the logos of Lachesis, daughter of Ananké, is glorified.[67] A prophet takes the lots and paradeigmata symbolizing the various forms of life (βίος) from her knees, the 'knees of the gods', where Homer had laid them. But the prophet does not hand them out to mortals by the command of inevitable necessity. As the souls wait for their new bodies, he calls to them: 'Luck will not bring you your daemon, you must choose him'. Once a soul chooses a life, it must keep it and be chained to it. 'Areté is no one's property. As you honour or dishonour it, it comes to you or shuns you. The chooser is responsible; Heaven is guiltless'. And so we watch the souls choose their next earthly lives by picking one of Lachesis' lots, confirmed by the other two Fates, Clotho and Atropos. The choice once made is irrevocable.

As we watch this scene and hear the prophet's warning, we see the first soul advance to make its choice. It selects the life of the most powerful tyrant; but its woeful complaints against fate fill the air as soon as it sees the burden of guilt and unhappiness it has taken on itself.[68] The injustice of its complaints is plain to see. It is the old problem of the theodicy, justifying God's ways to man, which runs throughout Greek poetry from Homer to Solon and Aeschylus.[69] Now, as ethical feeling reaches a new height in Plato's *Republic,* the problem appears once more. Plato keeps the characteristic Homeric idea that men sin in spite of previous warnings from God.[70] The warning, like the choice itself, is pushed back to one decisive instant of the soul's pre-natal life; but the soul which makes the choice is not a *tabula rasa,* a white sheet of paper. It has gone through the cycle of births, and its choice is conditioned by its previous life. Plato makes this point clear by many examples. Men, he says, choose the lives of animals that are sympathetic to the tone and spirit of their earlier lives.[71] The singer picks the life of a swan, the hero that of a lion; Thersites becomes an ape and Agamemnon an eagle. Only Odysseus, after his manifold experience, chooses not a life of glory and action and suffering, but a new little life which is lying about without being noticed, that of a man living quietly in retirement. He spends a long time searching for it, and at last finds it with delight. He has learnt that wealth, glory, fame, and power do not mean happiness any more than their opposites. The middle life is best.[72]

The only science which is valuable is the science of choice, which enables us to make the right decision. That is the meaning of the myth, as explained by Plato himself. The greatest danger for each of us is that he may choose the wrong life—or, as the philosopher would explain it, the wrong pattern of life, the wrong ideal. Therefore he must seek out the knowledge which enables him to choose the right life, and neglect all others.[73] This is the final explanation and transcendental justification of paideia. Plato thinks of it as a grave and important task, the one supreme duty in human life. His profound conviction is inspired by his belief that everyone should give all his energy in this world to preparing for the great choice he will have to make in the next life, when he will proceed, after a thousand years of wandering, to put on a new life for better or worse and return to earth.[74] He is not free, in the full sense, especially as he is hampered in his progress by ancient guilt. But he will be able to assist in freeing himself if he perseveres in his journey upward.[75] In another life, he will find perfection.

NOTES

CHAPTER 2

THE MEMORY OF SOCRATES

1. To write a history of Socrates' influence would be a gigantic task. The best chance of succeeding would be to break it up into separate periods and deal with them individually. One such separate treatment is B. Boehm's *Sokrates im achtzehnten Jahrhundert: Studien zum Werdegang des modernen Persönlichkeitsbewusstseins* (Leipzig 1929).

2. Nietzsche's hatred of Socrates appears even in his first book, *Die Geburt der Tragödie aus dem Geist der Musik,* where he treats him as the symbol of pure 'reason and science'. The original printer's MS. of this work (lately published by H. Mette, Munich 1933), which does not contain the passages dealing with Wagner and modern opera, shows in its very title, *Sokrates und die griechische Tragödie,* that Nietzsche was thinking of a profound contrast between Socrates' rational spirit and the tragic world-view of the Greeks. His preoccupation with this subject cannot be appreciated without reference to his lifelong struggle to understand and master the Greek spirit. See E. Spranger's *Nietzsche über Sokrates,* in *40 Jahrfeier Theophil Boreas* (Athens 1939).

3. This new conception of the earlier Greek philosophers (characteristically expressed in Nietzsche's youthful essay, *Die Philosophie im tragischen Zeitalter der Griechen*) was not introduced by Zeller's historical account of the pre-Socratics in the first volume of his *Philosophie der Griechen,* so much as by the philosophies of Hegel and Schopenhauer. Hegel's theory of contradictions constantly resolved leads back to Heraclitus, and Schopenhauer's doctrine of will in nature closely resembles pre-Socratic patterns of thought.

4. With those beliefs, Nietzsche firmly took the side of Aristophanes in the criticisms he had levelled against Socrates 'the sophist'. Cf. *Paideia* I, 370 f.

5. Two of the most distinguished modern scholars who believe that the Socratic dialogue, as a literary form, appeared during Socrates' lifetime, are C. Ritter (*Platon* [Munich 1910] I, 202) and Wilamowitz (*Platon* [Berlin 1919] I, 150). Their early dating of Plato's first dialogues is part of their general conception of the nature and philosophical content of these works. See p. 88 f.

6. Detailed grounds in support of this theory, as against Ritter, have been given by H. Maier, on p. 106 f. of his *Sokrates* (Tübingen 1913). A. E. Taylor accepts it too, in his *Socrates* (Edinburgh 1932) p. 11.

7. Plato, *Apol.* 39c.

8. This has been shown by Maier, *Sokrates* 106.

9. Cf. I. Bruns, *Das literarische Porträt der Griechen* (Berlin 1896) p. 231 f., and R. Hirzel, *Der Dialog* I (Leipzig 1895) p. 86.

10. See Hirzel, *Der Dialog* I, 2 f. on the earlier development of the dialogue, and p. 83 f. on the forms it took and the principal authors who wrote Socratic dialogues.

11. Aristotle in Diogenes Laertius 3.37 (Rose, Arist. frg. 73).

12. This view was held as early as the Hellenistic philosophers, who are followed by Cicero, *De rep.* 1.10.16. [*Wahrheit und Dichtung,* literally *Truth and Fiction* or *Poetry,* is the title of Goethe's famous autobiography.—Translator.]

13. I think that K. von Fritz (*Rheinisches Museum* N.F. 80, pp. 36-68) has given new reasons for believing Xenophon's *Apology* to be spurious.

14. Maier, *Sokrates* 20-77.

374 THE MEMORY OF SOCRATES

15. I follow Maier, *Sokrates* 22 f., and others in using this name for the first two chapters of Xenophon's *Memorabilia* (1.1-2).

16. In *Mem.* 1.1-2 Xenophon speaks only of 'the accuser' (ὁ κατήγορος) in the singular, while Plato in the *Apology* speaks of 'accusers' in the plural, which corresponds to the facts of the case. Although Xenophon begins by answering the legal indictment too, he is principally engaged in combating charges which (as we learn from other sources) had been levelled at the dead Socrates in Polycrates' pamphlet.

17. See the convincing arguments of Maier, *Sokrates* 22 f.; he also examines the relation of Xenophon's 'Defence' to his *Apology*. One example to show how Xenophon could incorporate an originally independent work into a larger whole is the beginning of his *Hellenica* (1.1-2.2). This part was originally meant to complete Thucydides' history, and naturally ends with the close of the Peloponnesian war. Later he attached to it his history of Greece from 404 to 362.

18. The dependence of Xenophon's description of Socrates upon Antisthenes has been examined, first by F. Dümmler in his two essays *Antisthenica* and *Academica,* and then by K. Joël in his long and learned work, *Der echte und der xenophontische Sokrates* (Berlin 1893-1901). But Joël's conclusions are too heavily weighted with hypotheses to be convincing. Maier (*Sokrates* 62-68) has tried to sift out the author's exaggerations and show what really acceptable results he has achieved.

19. F. Schleiermacher, *Ueber den Wert des Sokrates als Philosophen* (1815), in his *Sämtliche Werke* III, 2, p. 297-298.

20. This was the view held by Zeller in his treatment of the Socratic problem: *Die Philosophie der Griechen* II, 1⁵, pp. 107 and 126.

21. Aristotle's remarks on the subject, which sometimes repeat and sometimes supplement one another, are in *Met.* A.6.987a32-b10; M.4.1078b17-32; M.9.1086b2-7; and *de part. an.* 1.1.642a28. In conformity with his conception of the relation between Plato and Socrates, A. E. Taylor has tried to minimize the differences between them which Aristotle brings out. Against him, see Ross's new and careful examination of the meaning of Aristotle's evidence, which corroborates its value: *Aristotle's Metaphysics* (Oxford 1924) I, p. xxxiii f., and *The Problem of Socrates* (*Presidential Address delivered to the Classical Association,* London 1933).

22. Xen. *Mem.* 4.6.

23. E. Zeller, *Philosophie der Griechen* II, 1⁵, pp. 107 and 126. Zeller's confidence in Aristotle's evidence is shared, in principle, by Joël (note 18) p. 203, and T. Gomperz, *Griechische Denker* II (4th ed.) p. 42 f.

24. See especially the criticisms of Maier, *Sokrates* 77-102, and Taylor, *Varia Socratica* (Oxford 1911) 40.

25. See Maier, *Sokrates,* and A. E. Taylor—who is diametrically opposed to him—in *Varia Socratica* and *Socrates* (Edinburgh 1932). Taylor is in general agreement with the views of Burnet, which he has developed and elaborated. See Burnet's *Greek Philosophy* (London 1924) and his article *Socrates,* in Hastings' *Encyclopaedia of Religion and Ethics,* vol. XI. C. Ritter, *Sokrates* (Tübingen 1931), is another who denies the value of Aristotle's evidence.

26. Maier, *Sokrates* 104 f., thinks the chief evidence on the real character of Socrates is given by Plato's 'personal' writings (*Apology* and *Crito*); after them, he believes, come the smaller dialogues like *Laches, Charmides, Lysis, Ion, Euthyphro,* and the two called *Hippias*—which he holds to be invented, but true in essence.

27. See the works by Taylor and Burnet cited in note 25.

28. Thuc. 2.37.1.

29. Diog. Laert. 2.23.

30. Plutarch, *Cimon* 4 *init.* and *ad fin.*, mentions poems addressed by Archelaus to Cimon, who probably stood in the same relation to him as C. Memmius to Lucretius.

31. Plato, *Apol.* 28e.

31a. On Socrates' love for the common people, see Xen. *Mem.* 1.2.60.

32. Cf. Socrates' own words, in Plato, *Apol.* 31e: 'No one can escape death who energetically opposes you or any other mob, and tries to stop great wrong and injustice from being done in the state. No, anyone who wishes to fight for justice must, if he wants to live even a short time, lead a private life and not enter politics.' The passionate emotion in these words is Plato's own: it comes from his knowledge of Socrates' death and presupposes it. But of course they are meant to explain Socrates' actual conduct.

33. Plato, *Apol.* 32a; Xen. *Mem.* 1.1.18.

34. Plato, *Gorg.* 454e f., 459c f., and passim.

35. Cf. Xen. *Mem.* 3.5.7 and 14, where Socrates speaks of the collapse of the 'old decency' (ἀρχαία ἀρετή) of the Athenians. See also Plato, *Gorg.* 517b f.

36. Plato, *Phaedo* 96a-99d.

37. Plato, *Apol.* 19c.

38. Plato, *Apol.* 26d.

39. Xen. *Mem.* 1.6.14. What Xenophon means by the works of the sages of old is shown by his words in 4.2.8 f.: books by doctors, mathematicians, physicists, and poets. From the latter passage one might conclude that Socrates despised all book-learning, but that is contradicted by *Mem.* 1.6.14. All Socrates does in 4.2.11 is to blame the omnivorous reader for neglecting the most important of all arts, the art of politics, which contains and implies all the rest.

40. Plato, *Phaedo* 97b f.

41. Xen. *Mem.* 1.4 and 4.3.

42. Xen. *Mem.* 1.4.5 f. On the origins of this theory, see W. Theiler's penetrating book, which analyses the work of his predecessors: *Geschichte der teleologischen Naturbetrachtung bis auf Aristoteles* (Zurich 1925).

43. Plato, *Phaedo* 98b.

44. At every new stage in the development of the Greek spirit, I have empha-sized this co-ordination of the ethical and social structure with the cosmic order, which is so characteristic of Greek thought: see *Paideia* I, 5-7; 49-51; 54; 152; 160 f.; 182 f.; 266-267; 323 f.

45. Hipp. *On ancient medicine* 12 and 20.

46. This is emphasized by Xen. *Mem.* 1.1.12; 16 and Aristotle (see note 21). Cf. Cicero, *De rep.* 1.10.15-16.

47. Cic. *Tusc. disp.* 5.4.10.

48. Plato, *Apol.* 18b, 23d.

49. Plato, *Apol.* 19c.

50. See note 21.

51. Xen. *Mem.* 4.2.11, Plato *Gorg.* 465a, and many other passages.

52. Xen. *Mem.* 1.2.4, and 4.7.9.

52a. Cf. also Xen. *Mem.* 1.1.10, on Socrates' daily routine.

53. Plato, *Charm.* 154d-e, *Gorg.* 523e.

54. See the medical literature dealing with daily regimen, for the extent of time given to exercises every day (*Paideia* III, 42 f.).

55. E. N. Gardiner, *Greek Athletic Sports and Festivals* (London 1910) 469 f.

56. On the symposium as an intellectual focus, see p. 176 f.

57. Plato, *Apol.* 29d.

58. Among those who believe the *Apology* is a carefully constructed work of art, E. Wolf deserves special mention. His book, *Platos Apologie* (*Neue Philolo-*

gische Untersuchungen, ed. W. Jaeger, vol. VI), gives a detailed analysis of the artistic form of the work, which demonstrates very convincingly that it is a free-hand portrait, by Plato, of Socrates himself; Plato has made his master describe himself.

59. Euripides, *Her.* 673 f.:

οὐ παύσομαι τὰς χάριτας
Μούσαις συγκαταμειγνύς
ἁδίσταν συζυγίαν.

Cf. Plato, *Apol.* 29d: ἕωσπερ ἂν ἐμπνέω καὶ οἷός τε ὦ, οὐ μὴ παύσωμαι φιλοσοφῶν.

60. In *Prot.* 311b f., we have, first, a dialogue in which Socrates cross-examines young Hippocrates, and then a protreptic address, 313a f.

61. Plato, *Apol.* 29d f.

62. Cf. Plato, *Apol.* 29d, and 30b.

63. Plato, *Prot.* 313a.

64. This concept, 'the service of God', appeared early in Greek literature; but it was Plato who gave it the sense discussed here. In *Apol.* 30a Socrates speaks of ἡ ἐμὴ τῷ θεῷ ὑπηρεσία. The word ὑπηρεσία is synonymous with θεραπεία, and θεραπεύειν θεούς is *deos colere.* It always has a religious sense; Socrates' activity as a teacher was, for him, a sort of worship.

65. Cf. note 62. The phrase 'care for the soul' has a specifically Christian sound to our ears, because the idea has become part of the Christian religion. But its incorporation in Christianity is due to the fact that Christians have the same belief as Socrates: that paideia is the true service of God and that care for the soul is true paideia. In formulating that idea, Christianity was directly influenced by Plato's presentation of Socrates' thought.

66. Plato, *Apol.* 29e.

67. Scol. Anon. 7 (Anth. Lyr. Gr. ed. Diehl), and see Bowra, *Greek Lyric Poetry,* 394.

68. Rohde mentions Socrates only once in *Psyche* (II, 263, 8th ed.). The only thing he has to say about him is that he did not believe in the immortality of the soul.

69. J. Burnet, *The Socratic Doctrine of the Soul,* in *Proceedings of the British Academy* 1915-1916, p. 235 f. I need hardly say that I do not follow Burnet in describing Socrates' idea of the soul as a 'doctrine', so much as in emphasizing the importance of the soul, as he does in his portrait of Socrates.

70. The moral sermon, or diatribe, originated at a very early date. But the educational and moral form of the sermon which dominates Christian preaching (along with the dogmatic and exegetic form) took its shape from the Socratic writings, and they in turn took theirs from the master's own teaching.

71. *Wesen des Christentums,* Dritte Vorlesung, p. 33.

72. Cf. Plato, *Prot.* 356d-357a. The passage is of course a characteristic Socratic parody on the life-saving (βίου σωτηρία) which consists in the proper choice (αἵρεσις) of goods. In *The Laws* 10.909a, Plato speaks, again in a Socratic tone, of 'saving the soul'. But the means he recommends to save souls (an inquisition against atheists) is anything but Socratic!

73. Burnet, *Greek Philosophy* 156; A. E. Taylor, *Socrates* 138.

74. Plato, *Apol.* 40c-41c.

75. One piece of evidence is particularly important in deciding whether Socrates thought the soul to be immortal. That is the fact that in Plato's *Phaedo* (which Burnet and Taylor consider a true account of the facts) he deduces the pre-

existence and the immortality of the soul from the theory of Ideas. Plato says there that the theory of Ideas and the belief in immortality must stand or fall together (*Phaedo* 76e). But if we accept Aristotle's statement that the theory of Ideas is not Socrates' but Plato's, then the doctrine of immortality in *Phaedo* must also be Plato's, since one is based on the other.

76. Aristotle (frg. 15 Rose) describes the typical religious experience of a believer in the mysteries as παθεῖν (see my *Aristotle*, p. 160). In contrast to the official religion, it affected the character, and produced a certain disposition (διάθεσις) in the soul.

77. The connexion between the language of philosophy and that of religion, and the adoption of religious terms and concepts by philosophical writers, would be an interesting subject for a book.

78. Xen. *Mem.* 1.4.8.

78a. Xen. *Mem.* 3.10.1-5.

79. See p. 38.

80. Xen. *Mem.* 1.2.4, and 4.7.9.

81. On what follows see Xen. *Mem.* 4.7.

82. See Xen. *Mem.* 1.1.16 and Plato *Apol.* 20d.

83. Plato, *Apol.* 20e; Xen. *Mem.* 4.7.6; Arist. *Met.* A 2, 982b28.

84. Xen. *Mem.* 4.7: ἐδίδασκε δὲ καὶ μέχρι ὅτου δέοι ἔμπειρον εἶναι ἑκάστου πράγματος τὸν ὀρθῶς πεπαιδευμένον. On the study of geometry see 4.7.2, on astronomy 4.7.4, on arithmetic 4.7.8, and on dietetics 4.7.9.

85. Plato, *Rep.* 522c f.

86. Plato, *The Laws* 818a: ταῦτα δὲ σύμπαντα οὐχ ὡς ἀκριβείας ἐχόμενα δεῖ διαπονεῖν τοὺς πολλοὺς ἀλλά τινας ὀλίγους.

87. See *Paideia* I, 287 f.

88. This fundamental idea runs through the description of Socrates given by both Plato and Xenophon. On Plato, see p. 95 f. Xenophon recognizes political culture as the aim of Socrates in *Mem.* 1.1.16, 2.1, and 4.2.11. Even his opponents assumed that his teaching was political by declaring that Alcibiades and Critias were his pupils (cf. Xen. *Mem.* 1.2.47 and all chapter 1.2). Even Xenophon does not dispute this, but tries to show that Socrates' idea of πολιτικά was something different from the average man's. During the regime of the Thirty tyrants, it was the political aspect of his teaching which allowed them to extend to him the general prohibition λόγων τέχνην μὴ διδάσκειν, although strictly speaking he did not teach rhetoric (Xen. *Mem.* 1.2.31).

89. The chief passage showing that the 'human things' (ἀνθρώπινα) taught by Socrates were the same as 'political things' (πολιτικά) is Xen. *Mem.* 1.1.16. It proves that what we call 'ethics' and set apart in a world of its own was indissolubly connected with politics; and that is true not only for Xenophon but for Plato and Aristotle.

90. Xen. *Mem.* 1.2.47 makes this quite clear.

91. Socrates' political teaching was aimed at leading young men to *kalokagathia:* gentlemanliness; see Xen. *Mem.* 1.1.48.

92. The finest evidence for this is the confession of Alcibiades in Plato, *Symp.* 215e f.

93. Plato, *Gorg.* 521d.

93a. Xen. *Mem.* 1.6.15 (the charge made by the sophist Antiphon against Socrates).

94. Xen. *Mem.* 4.6.12. See also 1.1.16, where the main subjects of Socrates' conversations are said to be the ἀρεταί (which means civic virtues, πολιτικαὶ ἀρεταί) and questions such as these: what is the state? what is a statesman? what is rule

over men? who is the right ruler? Cf. 4.2.37: what is a demos? and 4.6.14: what is the duty of a good citizen?

95. Xen. *Mem.* 1.2.40 f.

96. Xen. *Mem.* 4.2.11 f., cf. 3.9.10.

97. Xen. *Mem.* 4.4.16 f.

98. Xen. *Mem.* 4.4.14 f. And see the conversation between Alcibiades and Pericles about law and government in *Mem.* 1.2.40 f. Discussion of the unwritten law, 4.4.19.

98a. Cf. Plato, *Ion* 536d, *Rep.* 606e. In *Prot.* 309a it means one who knows Homer, not one who teaches him.

99. Xen. *Mem.* 1.2.56 f.

100. See p. 29. Election by lot criticized, Xen. *Mem.* 1.2.9.

101. Xen. *Mem.* 1.2.31-38.

102. Of course the details of the proposals which Plato puts in Socrates' mouth in *The Republic,* during the discussion of this matter, are Plato's own. See my analysis of the subject on p. 251 f.

103. Cf. Xen. *Mem.* 3.1-5.

104. Xen. *Mem.* 3.1.1 f.

105. Xen. *Mem.* 3.3.

106. Xen. *Mem.* 3.3.11.

107. Xen. *Mem.* 3.4. And see 3.2 on the areté of the good leader.

108. Xen. *Mem.* 3.5.

108a. Xen. *Mem.* 3.5.7 and 3.5.14.

109. Plato, *Menex.* 238b, cf. 239a and 241c.

110. Xen. *Mem.* 3.5.14 and 15.

111. On the role of the Areopagus, see Xen. *Mem.* 3.5.20. Compare Isocrates' claim that the Areopagus should be given back its educational authority; *Paideia* III, 119. The festival chorus is used as a pattern of order and discipline in Xen. *Mem.* 3.5.18; similarly, Demosthenes, *Phil.* 1.35 praises the sound order kept at the Dionysia and the Panathenaea and during the preparations for these festivals.

112. Probably Xenophon got the rudiments of these criticisms from Socrates, and adapted them to his own mind. Some things in the conversation with the young Pericles really belong to the decline of the second Athenian naval league; on that fact, and on the educational aim of the *Memorabilia,* see *Paideia* III, 172.

113. Xen. *Mem.* 2.1.

114. Xen. *Mem.* 2.1.6.

115. Xen. *Mem.* 2.1.8 and 2.1.11.

116. Xen. *Mem.* 2.1.13.

117. Xen. *Mem.* 2.1.17: οἱ εἰς τὴν βασιλικὴν τέχνην παιδευόμενοι, ἣν δοκεῖς μοι σὺ (Socrates) νομίζειν εὐδαιμονίαν εἶναι. The 'kingly art' appears as the aim of Socrates' paideia elsewhere too—in the conversation with Euthydemus 4.2.11.

118. This was an epideictic speech of Prodicus, published as a book (σύγγραμμα); it treated Heracles as the embodiment of the struggle to achieve areté. The allegorical story of his education ('Ηρακλέους παίδευσις) by Lady Areté was an important stage in the hero's advance towards greatness; cf. Xen. *Mem.* 2.1.21 f. On the title and form of the speech, see Xen. *Mem.* 2.1.34. Despite the dry moralistic and rationalistic tone of the allegory, it still had some feeling for the true character of the myth of Heracles: cf. Wilamowitz, *Herakles* I, 101, who compares it with the story about Heracles' education in the contemporary romance about him by Herodorus.

119. See *Paideia* I, 321 f. on the collapse of the authority of law. On p. 330 of that volume I have mentioned a change parallel to Socrates' turning away from the outer to the inner world. It was Democritus' substitution for the old social

meaning of αἰδώς (shame before one's fellow-men) of a new sense, the shame which a man can feel for himself (αἰδεῖσθαι ἑαυτόν). This creation of a new concept was highly important in the development of the ethical consciousness.

120. The relevant passages are collected in F. Sturz, *Lexicon Xenophonteum* II, p. 14, and F. Ast, *Lexicon Platonicum* I, p. 590. See Isocrates, *Nic.* 44 (and cf. c.39): the ideal of self-mastery, put in the mouth of a ruler, is Socratic. The concept of *enkrateia* plays a most important part in Aristotle's thought.

121. Xen. *Mem.* 1.5.4.

122. Xen. *Mem.* 1.5.5-6.

123. See p. 241 f.

124. See Benedetto Croce's *Geschichte Europas im neunzehnten Jahrhundert* (Zurich 1935), chap. I: *Die Religion der Freiheit.*

125. On the origin and development of this ideal in Greek philosophy after Socrates, see H. Gomperz, *Die Lebensauffassung der griechischen Philosophen und das Ideal der inneren Freiheit* (Jena 1904). By treating the whole development of Greek philosophical morality from this point of view, Gomperz demonstrates the vast historical importance of the ideal of spiritual freedom, and makes a valuable contribution to our understanding of Socrates. But from that point of view we cannot understand *all* of Socrates. Firstly, we cannot understand the logical and scientific development which his thought underwent in Plato's hands; and secondly, Gomperz' approach would make the morality of the Cynics, Cyrenaics, and Stoics (where the problem of ethical independence is central) into the real culmination and zenith of Greek philosophy. His book anticipates Maier's conception of Socrates in many important features: for Maier's last chapter alters the perspective of the history of philosophy in a very similar way. For him too Socrates was the prophet of moral freedom.

126. Cf. Xen. *Mem.* 1.5.5-6 and 4.5.2-5. The connexion of this new conception of freedom with the Socratic ideal of self-mastery is made quite clear in both passages.

127. Xenophon does not use the noun αὐτάρκεια. The adjective αὐτάρκης appears in one passage of the *Cyropaedia* and four passages of the *Memorabilia,* but only in *Mem.* 1.2.14 with the philosophical sense of 'independence of external things'. But there it is used of Socrates himself.

128. In *Timaeus* 68e (cf. 34b) Plato says *autarkeia* is part of the perfection and blessedness of the cosmos, and in *Phileb.* 67a a fundamental quality of the good man. In *Rep.* 387d the admirable man, ὁ ἐπιεικής, is called 'the independent man'. Aristotle too uses 'independent' and 'perfect' as synonyms. For the *autarkeia* of the wise man, see *Eth. Nic.* 10.7.1177b1. Zeller describes how the Cynics and Cyrenaics imitated and exaggerated·the independence of Socrates (*Philosophie der Griechen* II, 1⁵.316; and see H. Gomperz, cited in note 125, p. 112 f.).

129. See the remarks in Wilamowitz, *Euripides' Herakles* I², pp. 41 and 102.

130. See Socrates' remark about the independence of God in Xen. *Mem.* 1.6.10. The idea appears in Euripides too (*Her.* 1345) and obviously goes back to the philosophical attacks on anthropomorphic deities wᵢich we find first of all in Xenophanes (see *Paideia* I, 170 f.). The humour of Socrates' remark in Xenophon lies in the fact that it is made to Antiphon, who has been twitting him with his independence of external things: for Antiphon had himself praised the independence of God in almost identical words (see frg. 10 Diels).

131. Concord (ὁμόνοια) as a political ideal, Xen. *Mem.* 4.4.16; see also 3.5.16. Co-operation between the various members of one family, ib. 2.3; the various parts of the organism as an example of co-operation, ib. 2.3.18.

132. Xen. *Mem.* 1.2.49.

133. Xen. *Mem.* 2.2.

134. Xen. *Mem.* 2.3.4.
135. Xen. *Mem.* 2.3.14.
136. Xen. *Mem.* 2.5.
137. *Paideia* I, 199 f.
138. Xen. *Mem.* 2.9.
139. On what follows see Xen. *Mem.* 2.6.14.
140. Xen. *Mem.* 2.6.28.
141. Socrates does not speak of his 'pupils', and refuses to be called anyone's 'teacher' (Plato, *Apol.* 33a). He has only an 'association' (συνουσία, cf. οἱ συνόντες) with other men, of whatever age, and 'converses' with them (διαλέγεσθαι). Therefore also he does not take money, as the sophists do: *Apol.* 33b; his poverty, ib. 23c.
142. The phrase 'registered friends' is used to mean 'registered students' in the will of Theophrastus (Diog. Laert. 5.52): οἱ γεγραμμένοι φίλοι. Similarly, after Socrates' death other such words became regular parts of academic terminology: e.g. the *association* of teacher and pupil (συνουσία), *conversation* = teaching (διαλέγεσθαι), school = *leisure* (σχολή) and *pastime* = lecture (διατριβή). They were transferred to the world of professional teaching, from which Socrates had tried to dissociate himself by using them. Thus, the educational technique so carefully developed by the sophists conquered the personality and spirit which were the basis of Socrates' teaching.
143. He thought Gorgias, Prodicus, and Hippias were typical representatives of contemporary paideia: Plato, *Apol.* 19e.
144. Plato, *Apol.* 19d-e: οὐδέ γε εἰ τινος ἀκηκόατε ὡς ἐγὼ παιδεύειν ἐπιχειρῶ ἀνθρώπους, . . . οὐδὲ τοῦτο ἀληθές.
145. Xen. *Mem.* 4.7.1, 3.1.1-3.
146. Plato, *Apol.* 25a, *Meno* 92e.
147. See Plato, *Apol.* 19c. There he says it would be admirable if anyone were really able 'to teach men', but when he adds 'like Gorgias, Prodicus, and Hippias' that is Socratic irony, as is clear from the description which follows.
148. Xen. *Mem.* 4.1.2.
149. Xen. *Mem.* 4.1.3-4.
150. Xen. *Mem.* 4.1.5.
151. Xen. *Mem.* 4.2.
152. Xen. *Mem.* 4.2.4.
153. Xen. *Mem.* 4.2.11 (cf. 2.1.17 and 3.9.10).
154. Arist. *Met.* A 6.987b1.
155. Cf. Arist. *Eth. Nic.* 1.1.1094a27 and 10.10, especially the end.
156. See *Paideia* I, 106, note 27.
157. Arist. *Met.* A 6.987b1, and M 3.1078b18 and 27.
158. Xen. *Mem.* 4.6.1.
159. Maier, *Sokrates* 98 f., believes Aristotle's statements that Socrates discovered universals and tried to define concepts derive from Xen. *Mem.* 4.6.1; Xenophon, he thinks, got this from Plato's later dialectic dialogues, *Phaedrus, The Sophist,* and *The Statesman* (cf. his p. 271).
160. That is the view of Burnet and Taylor: see p. 25 f.
161. See my criticism of Maier's hypothesis about the transmission of the evidence, and his denial of the logical side of Socrates' philosophy, in my review of his book, *Deutsche Literaturzeitung* 1915, pp. 333-340 and 381-389. The criticisms of E. Hoffmann and K. Praechter attacked the same points.
162. Xen. *Mem.* 4.6.
163. See *Paideia* III, 56.
164. This is admirably put by Plato in *Prot.* 355a-b.

165. In Greek it is called 'giving way to pleasure', ἡττᾶσθαι τῆς ἡδονῆς: see *Prot.* 352e. In *Prot.* 353c Socrates' attention is directed to this very point: i.e. to finding out the true nature of this weakness.

166. Cf. Aristotle, *Eth. Nic.* 6.13.1144b17 f. 'Ethical virtue' is chiefly concerned with pleasure and pain: 2.2.1104b8.

167. Knowledge as conceived by Plato (phronésis) means the understanding of good together with the mastery exercised by that understanding over the soul. (See my *Aristotle*, p. 83.) It is an attempt to realize all Socrates meant by saying 'virtue is knowledge'. Evidently Socrates did use the word phronésis: it is not only in Plato, where it appears in passages with what seems to be Socratic colouring, but also in the other Socratics, Xenophon and Aeschines.

168. This is proved in Plato, *Laches* 199c f., and it is the point Socrates is trying to make in *Protagoras* 331b, 349d, 359a–360e, when he sets out to prove that all the virtues are essentially the same—i.e. a knowledge of the good.

169. This is the objection Protagoras raises against Socrates in Plato, *Prot.* 329d, 330e, 331e, 349d, and elsewhere. It is the attitude of the man in the street, and makes Socrates seem to be flying in the face of common sense.

170. Several times Plato depicts Socrates as trying to discover the true relation between the parts of virtue. Obviously that trait comes from the character of the historical Socrates. It was inevitable for him to emphasize the unity of virtue, since he was the first to ask 'what is areté in itself?'

171. Plato's *Laches* casts doubt on the traditional idea of courage as a purely military virtue, by showing that inward courage is just as important (191d). He criticizes the conventional idea of piety in the same way, in *Euthyphro*.

172. Plato, *Rep.* 500d, *Phaedo* 82a, *Laws* 710a.

173. See p. 49 f.

174. Plato's Socrates says that again and again. It is now generally understood to be one of those elements in the earliest Platonic dialectic which go back to the historical Socrates. See Plato, *Prot.* 345d, 358c; *Hipp. min.* 373c, 375a-b.

175. Aristotle (*Eth. Nic.* 3.2-3) takes the view held by Greek legislators. He gives voluntary action (ἑκούσιον) the broad definition accepted by common law: action initiated by the agent himself, with awareness of the facts (τὰ καθ' ἕκαστα ἐν οἷς ἡ πρᾶξις). Therefore no act is involuntary except one done under compulsion (βία) or through ignorance (δι' ἄγνοιαν).

176. On the distinction of will and desire, see (e.g.) Plato, *Gorg.* 467c. The object of will is not what we do, but that for which we do it (οὗ ἕνεκα).

177. The aim (τέλος) is the natural end of an action, towards which the agent looks (ἀποβλέπει). The idea first appears in Plato's *Prot.* 354a and 354c-e; cf. *Gorg.* 499e.

178. See O. Becker's original but sometimes arbitrary book *Das Bild des Weges und verwandte Vorstellungen im griechischen Denken* (*Hermes* Beiheft IV, Berlin 1937).

179. The notion of *telos*, the ideal end, appears first in Plato, *Prot.* 354a-b. There it is explained with reference to the view held by most people, that pleasure is the telos of all effort, and is therefore 'the good', because all effort ends in it (ἀποτελευτᾷ). The misunderstanding that this is Plato's own belief is dealt with on p. 142 f. of this book. In *Gorg.* 499e he says the 'end of all actions' is the good; that is his own view. Elsewhere the word is accompanied by genitives, in phrases like 'the end of areté', 'the end of happiness', 'the end of life': meaning not the time when these things end, but the ideal end contemplated in action. This was a brand-new idea, and changed the history of the human spirit.

180. Plato, *Gorg.* 507d, says the new realization that happiness consists in justice and self-control is the aim (σκοπός) and we ought to live with it in

view. The image of aiming (στοχάζεσθαι), borrowed from shooting, becomes a symbol of right living: see the other passages collected in Ast's *Lexicon Platonicum* III, 278.

181. Diog. Laert. 2.116.

182. Read R. Harder's fine appreciation of that dialogue, *Platos Kriton* (Berlin 1934).

183. That is the real meaning of the belief in his divine mission which Plato ascribes to Socrates in *Apol.* 20d f., 30a and 31a.

184. Plato, *Apol.* 30a.

185. In particular see the summing-up at the end of the 'Defence': Xen. *Mem.* 1.2.62-64.

186. Cf. Xen. *Mem.* 2.1.

187. Xen. *Mem.* 2.1.11-13. Cf. Aristippus' last words: 'In order to avoid all that, I do not allow myself to be harnessed to any state, but remain everywhere a foreigner' (ξένος πανταχοῦ εἰμι). That is why Aristotle (*Pol.* 7.2.1324a16) calls this non-political ideal 'a foreigner's life' (βίος ξενικός): the phrase is aimed at philosophers like Aristippus. In his *Politics* the difference between these attitudes to the state is a recognized problem: 'which is better, active civic life within a polis, or the foreigner's life, free from all political bonds?'

188. Plato, *Apol.* 29d.

189. Plato, *Gorg.* 511b.

190. Plato, *Gorg.* 519a.

191. Plato, *Gorg.* 517a f.

192. Plato, *Crito* 52b.

193. Plato, *Phaedr.* 230d.

194. Plato, *Apol.* 30a.

195. Plato, *Phaedo* 99a.

196. Plato, *Crito* 50a.

197. Diog. Laert. 3.6.

198. See p. 27. Socrates was very much a part of Athens, and was deeply attached to his fellow-Athenians. It was to them primarily that his message was directed (p. 38). Yet he was forced to ask the jury which tried him (Plato, *Apol.* 17d) for permission to speak to them in *his* language instead of theirs. He meant he was like a foreigner, who would have been allowed to use his own language if defending himself before an Athenian court.

199. Cf. Plato, *Apol.* 24b, and Xen. *Mem.* 1.1.

200. Xen. *Mem.* 1.1.2.

201. Plato, *Apol.* 29d; and cf. 29a, 37e.

202. See p. 40 f.

203. Plato's Socrates himself compares his own disregard of death with Achilles, *Apol.* 28b-d. Similarly Aristotle ranks his friend Hermias' death for his philosophical ideals along with the death of Homeric heroes: see his hymn to Areté, frg. 675, and my *Aristotle*, p. 118 f. On the high-mindedness of the Homeric hero, *Paideia* I, 11 f. Aristotle in *An. Post.* 2.13.97b16-25 mentions Socrates as the embodied *megalopsychos* or high-minded man, along with Achilles, Ajax, and Lysander.

Chapter 4

PLATO'S SMALLER SOCRATIC DIALOGUES

1. The importance of form in Plato is dealt with by J. Stenzel, in his *Plato's Method of Dialectic* (translated by D. J. Allan, Oxford 1940).

2. This point of view has been put most tellingly by Wilamowitz, on p. 123 f. of vol. I of his *Platon*.

3. For instance, Wilamowitz (*Platon* I, p. 150) dates *Ion*, the smaller *Hippias*, and *Protagoras* to the years 403-400, which he calls 'the time when Plato was being formed by his contact with Socrates, without knowing the direction in which his life was to move'.

4. Wilamowitz (*Platon* I, p. 122) heads his description of these gay works (which he thinks are the earliest) with the general phrase 'Rollicking Youth'.

5. H. von Arnim, in *Platos Jugenddialoge und die Entstehungszeit des Phaidros* (Leipzig 1914) p. 34, went even further than Wilamowitz was to do: he tried to make *Protagoras* the earliest of Plato's writings, though his reasons were different from Wilamowitz's. (See p. 385, n. 2.)

6. Even in old age, Plato wrote a dialogue in which Socrates was the principal figure (*Philebus*)—although in other works of his old age he made Socrates a subordinate figure: for instance in what are called the dialectic dialogues, *Parmenides, The Sophist*, and *The Statesman*, and in the dialogue on natural philosophy, *Timaeus;* while in *The Laws* Socrates does not appear at all, and is replaced by the figure of the Athenian Stranger. Plato allowed himself to make that departure from his custom, because the ethical theme of *Philebus* was Socratic, though its treatment was far different from Socrates' dialectic. The same applies to *Phaedrus:* on its date, see *Paideia* III, 182 f.

7. Arist. *Met.* A 6.987a32.

8. The founder of modern Platonic scholarship, Schleiermacher, based his understanding of Plato's works on the conviction that in them the inner unity of Plato's thought was manifested. After him the development-theory was started by C. F. Hermann, with his *Geschichte und System der platonischen Philosophie* (Heidelberg 1839). On the history of Platonic scholarship and interpretation in modern times, see the useful but now antiquated book by F. Ueberweg, *Untersuchungen über die Echtheit und Zeitfolge platonischer Schriften*, etc. (Vienna 1861), part I; the introductory lecture in my *Platos Stellung im Aufbau der griechischen Bildung* —its name is *Der Wandel des Platobildes im 19. Jahrhundert*, first published in *Die Antike*, vol. 4, p. 85 f., and then as a separate work at Berlin in 1928; and finally H. Leisegang, *Die Platondeutung der Gegenwart* (Karlsruhe 1929).

9. The chief representative of this school is Wilamowitz: see p. 88.

10. Three scholars holding this opinion are H. Raeder, *Platons philosophische Entwicklung* (Leipzig 1905), H. Maier, *Sokrates* (Tübingen 1913), and M. Pohlenz, *Aus Platos Werdezeit* (Berlin 1913).

11. See p. 89 f.

12. See p. 93.

13. See *Paideia* I, 106.

14. Cf. *Apol.* 36c, where Socrates sums up his whole influence in a final, brief, exhaustive formula. He says that he has tried to convince every man not to attend to his business before taking care of himself, to make himself as good and wise as possible, and not to take care of state-business before taking care of 'the polis itself' (αὐτῆς τῆς πόλεως). Note this distinction between care for state-business and care for the polis itself, to make it as good and wise as possible: it is the fundamental distinction between politics as understood by Socrates and politics in the usual sense. Other references to Socrates' mission to the polis are found in *Apol.* 30e, 31a, etc. See p. 48 f.

15. *Crito* 50a.

16. *Laches* 179c f.

17. *Charm.* 161b; cf. 161c.

18. *Rep.* IV, 433b (see p. 240).

19. *Charm.* 171d-e; cf. 175b.

20. *Charm.* 170b, 173b, 174c, where the art of medicine and the art of piloting are mentioned together, as in *Gorgias, Republic,* and *The Statesman,* and compared to 'the knowledge of good' (ἡ περὶ τὸ ἀγαθὸν ἐπιστήμη) although subordinate to it.

21. *Prot.* 319a. As soon as 'the political art' is mentioned in *Protagoras,* the discussion moves to an enquiry into the four civic virtues.

22. This point is neglected by Wilamowitz in his remarks about Plato as a poet (*Platon* I, 122 f.).

23. See my arguments in *Platos Stellung im Aufbau der griechischen Bildung* (*Die Antike,* vol. 4, p. 92).

24. See above, p. 382, n. 198.

25. *Gorg.* 517c, 519a, 521d.

26. *Ep.* 7.326a-b.

27. *Ep.* 7.325d.

28. *Ep.* 7.324d-e; and a full account of the matter in Xen. *Mem.* 1.2.31-37.

29. *Ep.* 7.325a.

30. *Ep.* 7.325e-326b, and see the well-known parallel passage, *Rep.* 473d. This view was not the outgrowth of Plato's later development, but was active in him from an early period, as is shown by *Apol.* 31e and the recapitulation of the same points in *Apol.* 36b.

31. *Apol.* 36c.

32. *Apol.* 36b.

33. *Ep.* 7.325e f.

34. *Ep.* 7.325e-326a. In *Rep.* 499c he uses similar expressions about the possibility of creating the best state, although the *kairos,* the right moment for it, was not at hand.

35. *Ep.* 7.326b.

36. *Ep.* 7.325c-e.

37. This is A. E. Taylor's argument in his *Plato,* p. 20.

38. M. Pohlenz, *Aus Platos Werdezeit,* p. 227.

39. The words in *ep.* 7.326a, λέγειν τε ἠναγκάσθην κτλ, which Taylor, *Plato* 20, refers to *The Republic* as we have it, should be taken as an allusion to Plato's lecturing and teaching. I have shown this in my review of Taylor's book, in *Gnomon,* vol. 4, p. 9. This also explains the coincidences between Aristophanes' *Women in Parliament* and Plato's *Republic.*

40. There is a formal promise to continue them in *Apol.* 39c-d.

41. See A. Diès, *Autour de Platon* (Paris 1927) p. 156 f.

42. This is especially true of H. Maier, *Sokrates,* p. 264. Burnet and Taylor are amply justified in rejecting such attempts to deny Socrates his logic; but they go too far in the other direction and over-simplify the problem by ascribing everything Plato says of Socrates to the *real* Socrates.

43. Xen. *Mem.* 4.6.1.

44. See H. Raeder, Wilamowitz, Pohlenz, etc. (Cf. notes 2 and 10).

45. For instance, Ritter (*Platon* I, p. 577) says he cannot understand how anyone can find anything in Plato remotely like Aristotle's account of the Ideas as independent truths. J. Stenzel (see note 1) has given the final explanation of this difficulty.

46. Arist. *Met.* A 6.987a32 f.

47. See *Paideia* III, 20, 24.

48. *Rep.* 2.537c: the true dialectician is the synoptic, who can see things all together. The same description is in *Phaedrus* 265d.

49. No investigation of the occurrence of the words *eidos* and *idea* in Plato's

dialogue would be complete unless it treated other descriptions for the concept of One in Many, such as ὁπότε ἐστίν, αὐτὸ ὅ ἐστιν, etc.

50. Arist. *Met.* M and N.

51. *Euthyphro* 6e. See the examples of his use of *eidos* and *idea,* collected in Ritter's *Neue Untersuchungen über Platon* (Munich 1910) pp. 228-326.

52. That is how Schleiermacher's interpretation of Plato still remains true, despite his many successors. Paul Shorey's book *The Unity of Plato's Thought* (Chicago 1904) stoutly maintained this view when it was out of fashion. He himself (p. 88) points out that *unity does not preclude development.*

CHAPTER 5

PROTAGORAS

1. For the sake of simplicity, we shall use the conventional translation of areté and epistémé as 'virtue' and 'knowledge'—although both are open to misunderstandings because they carry modern overtones which are lacking in the Greek. After all that has been said since the beginning of Volume I of this work on the nature of Greek areté, a reader who did not have sufficient intellectual independence to read the Greek implications into the word 'virtue' whenever it is used here, and to put aside the connotations of modern science when he read 'knowledge', in favour of the sense of values which the Greeks called phronésis, would not be much helped if we were to use the Greek words throughout instead of the English ones.

2. The view put forward here—that *Protagoras* assumes the pre-existence of the smaller dialogues—will find confirmation in the course of the argument. Wilamowitz thinks it is one of Plato's earliest works, and von Arnim thought it was his very first. Wilamowitz's reason was that the earliest Socratic dialogues, including *Protagoras,* were 'unphilosophical' (see p. 88 f.). Von Arnim, on pp. 24-35 of his *Platos Jugenddialogen und der Phaidros,* tried to prove that *Laches* presupposed *Protagoras;* hence his conclusion. I think neither of these views is tenable.

3. *Prot.* 310a f.

4. *Prot.* 311a f.

5. *Prot.* 312a.

6. Studying for one's profession is called ἐπὶ τέχνῃ μανθάνειν; the καλοὶ κἀγαθοί study with Protagoras merely ἐπὶ παιδείᾳ (312b).

7. See pp. 38-9.

8. *Prot.* 313a. The emphasis on the soul and its danger is truly Socratic; cf. also 314a1-2, 314b1.

9. On this aspect of the new culture, see p. 111.

10. *Prot.* 313a-314b.

11. The need for a physician of the soul is mentioned in *Prot.* 313d-e; knowledge is called 'the food of the soul' in 313c6; the idea that the soul could be cared for as if by a doctor (ψυχῆς θεραπεία) is systematically worked out in *Gorgias* (see p. 131).

12. *Prot.* 313d2, 313d8, 313e3, 314b3.

13. *Prot.* 314c f.

14. *Prot.* 314e-315b.

15. *Prot.* 315c.

16. *Prot.* 315d.

17. *Prot.* 319a.

18. In *Prot.* 319a, ἐπάγγελμα is the 'promise' which the teacher makes to teach something to the pupil. The verb is ἐπαγγέλλεσθαι and ὑπισχνεῖσθαι (cf. note 22), which means the same as 'announce'. In Latin, ἐπαγγέλλεσθαι became *profiteri*, whence came the professional description of teaching sophists as *professores:* this began during the Empire.

19. *Prot.* 316d.
20. *Prot.* 316d-e.
21. *Prot.* 316d.
22. *Prot.* 317b: ὁμολογῶ τε σοφιστὴς εἶναι καὶ παιδεύειν ἀνθρώπους. Cf. the word ὁμολογεῖν in 317b6 and 317c1.
23. *Prot.* 317c-d.
24. *Prot.* 318a.
25. *Prot.* 312e.
26. *Prot.* 318c.
27. *Prot.* 318e. This is a passing hit at sophists like Hippias, teachers of the 'liberal arts'; he says they 'corrupt the young' (λωβῶνται τοὺς νέους).
28. *Prot.* 318e5-319a2.
29. *Prot.* 319a.
30. *Prot.* 319b-c.
31. *Prot.* 319d.
32. *Prot.* 319e.
33. *Prot.* 320a.
34. *Prot.* 320b.
35. See *Paideia* I, 215, 220, 287.
36. See *Paideia* I, 307.
37. See *Paideia* I, 321 f.
38. Distrust of the power of education appears as early as Homer; see *Paideia* I, 28 f.
39. In *Prot.* 319c7 Socrates describes the things which can be taught through intellectual culture as τὰ ἐν τέχνῃ ὄντα. Cf. *Gorg.* 455b, *Lach.* 185b. The distinguishing mark of this kind of knowledge and culture is the existence of teachers and examinations: *Gorg.* 313e f.
40. This is Socrates' chief objection, and he makes it both before and after Protagoras' speech: *Prot.* 319b2 and 328e.
41. *Paideia* I, 308 f.
42. *Prot.* 328d-e.
43. *Prot.* 329b.
44. *Prot.* 329c; cf. 322b-323a.
45. See p. 91 f.
46. *Prot.* 329c6.
47. Note this, which is a characteristic sign of the relation between *Protagoras* and the smaller dialogues: *Protagoras* goes back to take up their points, and carry them further.
48. *Prot.* 329d.
49. *Prot.* 329e.
50. For instance, the next passage, *Prot.* 349d f., is obviously reminiscent of *Laches*, with its attempts to define the nature of courage. If the discussion in *Laches* is not repeated with a pedantic insistence on exactitude in every detail, that does not prove that *Laches* is a later stage of the dialectic investigation, and therefore later than *Protagoras* (as von Arnim thought, see p. 24 of his book cited in note 2).
51. *Prot.* 330c f., 332a f., 333d f.
52. *Prot.* 331b8, 332a1, 333e, 350c-351b.

53. See p. 103.

54. *Prot.* 335b-c.

55. *Prot.* 338e. Protagoras says that knowledge of poetry (περὶ ἐπῶν δεινὸν εἶναι) is 'the greatest part of culture'.

56. Protagoras chose the poem because it treated of the nature of areté, although it had nothing to do with Socrates' question about the relation of part to whole. Plato here establishes a direct connexion between the paideia of the sophists and that side of early Greek poetry which was concerned with serious reflection about areté and accordingly about education. Simonides was a particularly suitable poet for such meditations.

57. *Prot.* 345e. The interpretation which Socrates elicits from the poem is historically false; and he gets it, not so much by following the sense of Simonides' words as by making logical deductions from them. Even in interpreting poetry, Socrates tries to get at the absolute truth as he sees it.

58. *Prot.* 349d f. Socrates is forced to appeal to Protagoras' reputation as a distinguished practitioner of paideia, in order to make him take further part in the discussion.

59. *Prot.* 350c f.

60. *Prot.* 351b f.

61. *Prot.* 351d.

62. *Prot.* 352b.

63. *Prot.* 352c3-7.

64. *Prot.* 352d. Protagoras actually says 'It is disgraceful (αἰσχρόν) for me, if anyone, not to say that wisdom and knowledge are the greatest of human powers.' Still, we feel quite plainly that it is not so much his own deep conviction which makes him assent to Socrates' proposition as his fear of the disgrace which he, the representative of paideia, would incur by doubting the power of knowledge. Socrates sees through him, and uses this to make him contradict himself. He several times uses his opponent's fear of giving social offence (αἰσχρόν) to make him admit contradiction: see *Prot.* 331a9, 333c, *Gorg.* 461b, and especially *Gorg.* 482d f., where Callicles attacks and reveals this 'trick' of Socrates.

65. *Prot.* 352d-e.

66. *Prot.* 353a.

67. *Prot.* 353a.

68. It is clear why Plato makes Socrates use the device of disputing with 'most people' instead of Protagoras. It makes it easier for Protagoras to admit what social scruples might make him afraid to admit in his own name. See note 64.

69. *Prot.* 353c f.

70. *Prot.* 353d-e, 354b.

71. This is the first appearance in Plato of the fundamental concept of 'end' (τέλος). See 354b7, 354d2, 354d8, and the kindred verbs ἀποτελευτᾶν (εἰς ἡδονάς) in 354b6 and τελευτᾶν in 355a5. In 355a1 'the good' (ἀγαθόν) is synonymous with τέλος. In *Gorg.* 499e the same idea is expressed by 'the reason why', οὗ ἕνεκα, which is there synonymous with 'the good'.

72. *Prot.* 356a.

73. *Prot.* 356b.

74. *Prot.* 356c-e.

75. *Prot.* 356e-357a.

76. *Prot.* 357a-b.

77. *Prot.* 357b. This concept of measuring and of the art of mensuration, which is here emphasized several times (356d8, 356e4, 357a1, 357b2 and 357b4) is extremely important for Plato's conception of knowledge and paideia. Here it appears for the first time, merely as a desirable ideal, and connected with the idea

of defining the highest good, but it is not a reality to Socrates as yet. But in later works of Plato its full force and meaning are revealed.

78. *Prot.* 357c-d.
79. *Prot.* 358a.
80. *Qui tacet, consentire uidetur.*
81. *Prot.* 358b6.
82. *Prot.* 358d.
83. See p. 118, and note 57.
84. *Prot.* 349d.
85. *Prot.* 349e.
86. *Prot.* 358d6.
87. *Prot.* 358e.
88. *Prot.* 359d.
89. *Prot.* 360b-c.
90. *Prot.* 360d5.
91. *Prot.* 360e6.
92. *Prot.* 361a; see p. 114 f., and *Paideia* I, 308.
92a. Cf. *Theaet.* 155a.
93. *Prot.* 361b2; cf. 358c5, where Socrates defines 'ignorance' as being mistaken about true values (ἐψεῦσθαι περὶ τῶν πραγμάτων τῶν πολλοῦ ἀξίων).
94. This is the definition of the sophist in Plato (see *Prot.* 349a: παιδεύσεως καὶ ἀρετῆς διδάσκαλος). The sophists undertook 'to teach men' (παιδεύειν ἀνθρώπους, *Apol.* 19e, *Prot.* 317b), which in *Apol.* 20b is taken as synonymous with 'possessing knowledge of human and political areté'.
95. *Apol.* 19e-20c; Xen. *Mem.* 1.2.2; p. 59.
96. *Prot.* 361c. We can see how this question exercised Socrates' contemporaries, not only from the writings of a contemporary sophist (see chapter 6 of the *Dialexeis*, in Diels, *Vorsokratiker* II[5], 405 f.), but also from an argument like that in Euripides' *The Suppliants* 911-917, proving that courage can be taught just as a child can be taught to hear and say what he does not know. Euripides goes on to declare that everything depends on the right paideia.
97. At the end of *Protagoras* (357b) Socrates puts off the exact discussion of the type of art and knowledge (τέχνη καὶ ἐπιστήμη) which this art of mensuration is.
98. See p. 120 f.

CHAPTER 6

GORGIAS

1. This view is seen in its extreme form in Wilamowitz's discussion of the separate dialogues (*Platon*, vol. 1). For instance, he heads his chapter on *Phaedrus* (which is a serious discussion of the relation between rhetoric and dialectic) with the lyrical title 'A Happy Summer Day'.
2. That is Wordsworth's phrase. W. Dilthey's book *Erlebnis und Dichtung* ('Experience and Fiction') obviously influenced Wilamowitz in his attitude to Plato.
3. John Finley (Harvard Classical Studies, 1939) shows that Gorgias cannot be regarded as the sole creator of rhetoric, or its only representative in Athens.
4. *Prot.* 319a-d.
5. *Gorg.* 449d, 451a.
6. *Gorg.* 450a, 451d, 454b.
7. *Gorg.* 456a f.

8. *Gorg.* 456b.

9. *Gorg.* 456b6-c.

10. *Gorg.* 455d-e (cf. 455b).

11. *Gorg.* 454e-455a.

12. *Gorg.* 456d-457c.

13. *Gorg.* 456e, 457c.

14. *Gorg.* 459d-e.

15. *Gorg.* 460a. On Protagoras' bourgeois caution, see page 387, note 64.

16. *Gorg.* 460d.

17. *Gorg.* 461b-c; cf. p. 387, note 64.

18. *Gorg.* 481b f.

19. *Gorg.* 462b.

20. Aristotle (*Met.* A 1.981a5) takes *techné* to signify a general assumption (ὑπόληψις) about similar cases, made after numerous observations and much experience.

21. *Techné* resembles *empeiria* ('experience') in having a practical character: see Arist. loc. cit. 981a12.

22. The 'art of measurement' is in *Prot.* 356d-357b. This passage kills the claim made in *Prot.* 319a that Protagoras' paideia is 'political techné'.

23. Cf. F. Jeffré's dissertation, undertaken on my suggestion, *Der Begriff der Techne bei Plato* (Kiel 1922): it is unprinted, but the MS. is in the library of Kiel University.

24. *Gorg.* 462b-d.

25. *Gorg.* 463b.

26. *Gorg.* 463d.

27. *Gorg.* 464a-c5.

28. *Gorg.* 464c5-d.

29. *Gorg.* 464d, 465b-d.

30. *Gorg.* 465a. In this passage Plato briefly sums up his whole analysis of the concept *techné*. No ἄλογον πρᾶγμα deserves to be called a techné. It is important for us not to forget one of its characteristics in particular: it is directed towards the best—in other words it relates to a value, and ultimately to the highest of all values. It works for the realization of that value in the sphere of reality with which its activity is concerned. In this analysis of the nature of a true techné, Plato's model is *medicine:* see 464a, 464d. It is from medicine that he takes the idea of therapy, or 'care' for soul and body, the image of 'aiming' (στοχάζεσθαι) at the best, and the description of that best as welfare or good condition (εὐεξία). See p. 131. The 'political art', which is the aim of the philosophy and culture that are to be newly established, is thought of as the physicianship of the soul.

31. Paradox is Plato's characteristic form of philosophical statement. His contemporary Isocrates, who was an enthusiastic and subtle stylist, knew that well. For chaps. 1-3 of his *Helen* are chiefly aimed at Plato, as I think I have shown in *Paideia* III, 68, and as others before me have suggested. It is interesting to see how Isocrates tries to interpret this fact against the background of early Greek philosophy, and to prove it is the general weakness of *all* philosophy. Clearly he did not grasp the truth of the matter.

32. *Gorg.* 465c.

33. See p. 38 f.

34. *Gorg.* 481c: 'If you [Socrates] are serious, and what you say is really true, surely human life is turned upside down, and we are doing what seems to be the very opposite of what we should!'

35. *Gorg.* 466b f. Gorgias' speech too had emphasized the fact that rhetoric can give power to those who practise it: 451d, 452d, 456a f.

36. See p. 123.

37. In *Gorg.* 466b11 f. this definition of power is offered by Polus and controverted by Socrates. The Greek word for 'power' in that sense was δύναμις, μέγα δύνασθαι—see 466b4, 466d6, 467a8, 469d2. In *The Republic* Plato opposes Power and Reason, *dynamis* and *phronésis*, to each other. *Dynamis* is power in the physical, and *kratos* in the legal, constitutional sense.

38. Plato often points this out: see *Gorg.* 466b11, 466d7, 467a8, 469c3, 469d2, etc.

39. Archilochus frg. 22 Diehl; *Paideia* I, 125.

40. Solon frg. 23 Diehl.

41. *Gorg.* 469c.

42. *Gorg.* 470e.

43. This is specially emphasized in *Rep.* 498a1 f.

44. This is explained with brutal frankness in the speeches of the Athenian negotiators engaged in treating with the little island of Melos, to make it abandon its neutrality. See Thuc. 5.104-5; *Paideia* I, 400-402. The idea recurs in the speech of the Athenian envoys in Sparta, Thuc. 1.75-76; *Paideia* I, 396.

45. *Gorg.* 470e9.

46. It would be historically false to identify the Christian standpoint, which takes so many different forms, with this low estimate of human nature.

47. Cf. *Paideia* I, 306 f.

48. It would take too much space to quote all the passages bearing on this. The chief passage showing Plato's identification of areté with that which is in accordance with human nature (κατὰ φύσιν) and of wickedness with the unnatural (παρὰ φύσιν) is *Rep.* 444c-e. Areté is the soul's health: so it is man's *normal state,* his true nature. Plato was confirmed in this opinion by his medical conception of nature as being a reality which embodies its own standard.

49. *Gorg.* 466c.

50. On what follows see *Gorg.* 466b f., especially 467a.

51. *Gorg.* 467c5-468c.

51a. In Isocrates' speech *On peace* there is a similar transformation of the concept of power and the greed for power (πλεονεξία) into a moral force. See *Paideia* III, 151. Like the whole argument of c.31-35, Isocrates borrowed it from Plato's *Gorgias* and *The Republic.*

52. *Gorg.* 472e.

53. See *Protagoras* 324a-b, where it appears that by the age of the sophists the old conception of punishment as retribution (τὸν δράσαντα παθεῖν) had been abandoned; it was now thought to be a means of education—this is the teleological rather than the causal conception of punishment. Plato, still inspired by medicine, changes this; he thinks of punishment as a cure for the sick soul.

54. *Gorg.* 477a f.

55. *Gorg.* 471d4.

56. *Gorg.* 481b-c.

57. *Gorg.* 485d-e.

58. The dislike felt for sophistic culture by the old-fashioned Athenians often appears in Attic comedy; and it is embodied in Anytus, in the last part of Plato's *Meno.* He was one of Socrates' accusers; and in the *Apology* Socrates defends himself against their efforts to treat him as just another sophist.

59. *Gorg.* 484e, 485e-486c.

60. *Gorg.* 487c. Socrates localizes this political discussion of paideia in a group which he describes more precisely by naming three well-known Athenian citizens who belonged to it. Andron, son of Androtion, was a member of the Four Hundred who carried out the oligarchic *coup d'état* in 411. Plato mentions him as a member of Protagoras' audience in *Prot.* 315c. His son Androtion was the distinguished

oligarchic statesman and historian against whom Demosthenes delivered a famous speech. We know nothing of the other two, Nausicydes of Cholargus and Tisander of Aphidna; but the descendants of the former appear to have been wealthy burghers of Athens: see Kirchner-Klebs, *Prosop. Att.* 2.113-4.

61. Thuc. 2.40.1; *Paideia* I, 319.

62. On his 'prospectus', *Against the sophists,* see *Paideia* III, 55.

63. Plato took great care to make Callicles look like a real man, not only by his realistic portraiture, but also by making him a member of an actual group of well-born Athenian citizens. See note 60. Certainly he is quite as historically real as Anytus, the enemy of Socrates and the hater of sophists, in *Meno*—whether Callicles is an authentic name or a pseudonym.

64. See p. 134.

65. This attitude substituted nature and her laws for the Divinity, which had formerly been the source of human power and human laws. See *Paideia* I, 323 f.

66. *Gorg.* 482e.

67. The man who cannot help himself (αὐτὸς αὑτῷ βοηθεῖν) when he is wronged would be better dead: cf. *Gorg.* 483b. Later, in 485c5, it appears that the strong man's self-help is for Callicles the essence of freedom (see n. 77).

68. *Gorg.* 483b-c.

69. *Gorg.* 483c8-d. The age of reason used examples from experience, instead of the mythical *paradeigma* of early didactic poetry.

70. *Gorg.* 483e-484c. On the sophistic theory of the right of the stronger, see A. Menzel, *Kallikles* (1923).

71. *Gorg.* 470e, cf. p. 133.

72. In viewing law as an unnatural fetter (δεσμός), Callicles is at one with the sophist Antiphon and his theory of nomos and physis. Similarly the sophist Hippias, in *Prot.* 337c, calls law the despot of mankind. But the two sophists do not conclude, like Callicles, that the strong man should rule; they make the opposite inference. See *Paideia* I, 327 f.

73. *Gorg.* 484c.

74. *Gorg.* 484c4-485a.

75. *Gorg.* 485a.

76. Cf. the charge which Callicles makes in *Gorg.* 484c: περαιτέρω τοῦ δέοντος ἐνδιατρίβειν and πόρρω τῆς ἡλικίας φιλοσοφεῖν. Cf. *Rep.* 498a-c.

77. In *Gorg.* 485c Callicles infers, from the constant danger that weak men may lose their civic status, that Socrates' pupils are 'unfree'. It is difficult to understand all that this charge implies without remembering that true paideia was always the paideia of free men. He proves that he himself is a cultured man, by elaborate quotations from Euripides and Pindar, which are woven into his argument: 486b-c.

78. *Gorg.* 487b6.

79. Antiphon frg. 44, A.4.1 f., in Diels, *Vorsokratiker* II⁵, 349.

80. Thucydides in 5.105.4 makes the Athenians in their argument with the Melians reduce the egotism natural to every sovereign state to the formula that pleasant things are morally good (τὰ ἡδέα καλά), just like the view of the sophists and 'most people' in Plato's *Protagoras* (see p. 120 f.). They say 'it is not we alone who follow this principle, but the Spartans too'.

81. *Gorg.* 488b3-489a, 491b.

82. *Gorg.* 491d. This is the basic question of all Socrates' 'politics': see p. 54.

83. *Gorg.* 491e-492d.

84. *Prot.* 354d, 355a; see p. 120.

85. *Gorg.* 492e.

86. *Gorg.* 494a.

87. *Gorg.* 494b-499c.
88. *Gorg.* 499d-500a.
89. This assumption is that of Wilamowitz and Pohlenz. The same mistake is not made by Raeder, von Arnim, Shorey, and Taylor.
90. *Phaedo* 68c; cf. *Gorg.* 495a, 499c.
91. Von Arnim too dates *Protagoras* very early, but for different reasons; see p. 386, n. 50.
92. See p. 120 f.
93. *Prot.* 356d-357b.
94. *Prot.* 354b6 f.; 354d1-3; 354d7-e2; 354e8-355a5.
95. *Phaedo* 69a.
96. *Gorg.* 498d.
97. In *Prot.* 349b Plato had raised the question whether the several virtues (ἀρεταί) each possesses a peculiar nature (ἴδιος οὐσία) or all connote a single thing (ἐπὶ ἑνὶ πράγματί ἐστιν). This ἓν πρᾶγμα or common οὐσία is (as *Gorg.* 499a shows) the Good (τὸ ἀγαθόν), which is the telos of all our will and action.
98. *Gorg.* 451d.
99. *Gorg.* 462c, 463b.
100. *Gorg.* 500a.
101. *Gorg.* 500a6.
102. *Gorg.* 500b.
103. Here again Plato drives home the parallel with medicine, which is always present to him when he thinks of his political techné: see p. 131.
104. *Gorg.* 501d-502d. Plato is referring to contemporary choral and dithyrambic poetry; he takes as his example Cinesias, who was laughed at by Aristophanes too. Even Callicles cannot see any educational value in his work. Therefore some of Plato's contempt for the art of his time was due to its degeneration to mere virtuosity.
105. *Gorg.* 502e.
106. *Gorg.* 503b.
107. *Gorg.* 503e-505b. The eidos with reference to which the statesman creates order (τάξις) in his object, the human soul, is the Good, which in 499e is called the telos of all conduct.
108. *Gorg.* 505d.
109. *Gorg.* 513c.
110. *Gorg.* 506d.
111. *Gorg.* 506e.
112. *Gorg.* 506d-507a.
113. *Gorg.* 507a-c.
114. Cf. pp. 103, 115 f.
115. *Gorg.* 507c.
116. *Gorg.* 507d6. In this passage Plato introduces the concept of the 'aim'—the point towards which we should direct our lives: in Greek it is σκοπός. It is identical with the τέλος, the 'end,' which in 499e we learnt was the Good.
117. *Gorg.* 507e f.
118. *Gorg.* 508a.
119. *Gorg.* 483b, 486b.
120. *Gorg.* 509b-d.
121. *Gorg.* 509d7-510a.
122. *Gorg.* 510a.
123. *Gorg.* 510b. In 470e paideia was treated as the criterion of the good and happy ruler.
124. *Gorg.* 510c.

125. *Gorg.* 510d.

126. *Gorg.* 510e-511a. This imitation of the despot will most gravely hinder their education, as Plato explains in more detail in *The Republic*. There he systematically develops the doctrine that education always accommodates itself to the existing political regime.

127. *Gorg.* 511a-b.

128. *Gorg.* 513a-c.

129. *Gorg.* 513d: μὴ καταχαριζόμενον, ἀλλὰ διαμαχόμενον. Cf. 521a, where the word 'fight' recurs in the same significance: διαμάχεσθαι 'Αθηναίοις, ὅπως ὡς βέλτιστοι ἔσονται, ὡς ἰατρόν. Socrates is therefore thinking of the fight which the doctor has to engage in, to control a thoughtless and rebellious patient. The parallel with medicine still holds, even in that small point.

130. *Gorg.* 513e. Here, as in the main passage on this theme, 470e, the possession of paideia is the sole criterion for the value of all wealth and power. For *kalokagathia* in 514a1 means nothing but *paideia,* as is shown by the use of the words as synonyms, in the parallel passage 470e6-9.

130a. This is the concrete usage which we know from so many honorary inscriptions. There is an allusion to it in the word εὐεργεσία in *Gorg.* 513e, where Socrates is talking of the services of the educator to the polis.

131. It was Plato who introduced examinations into higher education, by logically following out Socrates' habit of testing his interlocutors by dialectic. In *The Republic* he trains his rulers entirely on this basis. It was borrowed from the technai of specialists such as the doctor and the architect—as Plato shows through his choice of examples.

132. *Gorg.* 514a-e.

133. *Gorg.* 515a-b.

134. *Gorg.* 515c-516e.

135. *Gorg.* 517a.

136. *Gorg.* 517b.

137. *Gorg.* 517c-518e. Here, for the first time, the medical and educational conception of the state is applied as a critical standard to the historical and contemporary state.

138. *Gorg.* 519a.

139. *Gorg.* 519b-c.

140. *Gorg.* 519e-520b.

141. *Gorg.* 521a. Socrates is here talking of 'the choice of a life' (βίου αἵρεσις), which, according to his philosophy, is the real meaning of human existence and the aim of his search for truth. The pre-natal choice of lives and futures in the other world, described in the closing myth of *The Republic* (617b-620d), provides the transcendental background for this earthly choice. This passage in *Gorgias* is in its turn a development of a theme in the *Apology* (29d), where Socrates firmly maintains his choice of the philosophical *bios,* even in face of the peril of death.

142. *Gorg.* 521c-522a.

143. *Gorg.* 522d. This kind of βοηθεῖν ἑαυτῷ, preservation of the true self, is opposed to what Callicles understands by self-help: the *power* by which the physical ego can be saved: see p. 140. Since Socrates' knowledge (which is identical with areté itself) is self-help in the highest sense, we can now understand why Socrates says in *Prot.* 352c that philosophy is 'capable of helping men'. The meaning of this βοηθεῖν is that which the word has in medicine, to heal men and bring them back to health: see *Paideia* III, 293, n. 11.

144. In *Gorg.* 513c Plato says that is the 'usual effect' (τὸ τῶν πολλῶν πάθος) of Socrates' teaching.

145. See p. 66.

146. *Gorg.* 523a f.

147. This mistake is made by most of those scholars who emphasize the Orphic elements in Plato, from the point of view of the history of religion. The most extreme is Macchioro, who simply says that most of Plato's philosophy is derived from Orphism.

148. *Gorg.* 523e: αὐτῇ τῇ ψυχῇ αὐτὴν τὴν ψυχὴν θεωροῦντα. The deceitful coverings are in 523b-d.

149. *Gorg.* 524b-d.

150. The Isles of the Blest, 523b, 524a, 526c; curable and incurable sinners, 525b-c, 526b7.

151. *Gorg.* 525c-d. Among the incurables are Archelaus, king of Macedonia, and the other absolute rulers, of whom Socrates in 470d-e had said that he did not know whether they were happy or not, for it depended on their paideia and their justice. During the medical examination in the other world it becomes apparent that the souls of those who have been 'brought up without truth' (525a) have nothing straight about them, but are deformed and crippled.

152. *Gorg.* 527e.

153. *Gorg.* 527d7.

154. *Prot.* 358c.

155. *Prot.* 357b5.

156. See pp. 67, 103.

157. *Gorg.* 521d.

158. This criticism of current paideia is elaborated in *The Republic* 492b f., especially in 493a-c. See p. 269 f.

159. Callicles confuses Socrates' criticisms of the Athenian state with the propaganda of the pro-Spartan oligarchic opposition: *Gorg.* 515e. He thinks Socrates gets his ideas from them; but Socrates emphasizes the fact that he is merely stating what everyone can see and hear for himself. Plato is obviously rejecting all party affiliations, and raising his criticisms to a higher level.

160. See p. 72 f.

161. *Ep.* 7.324e; and the end of *Phaedo*.

162. *Ep.* 7.324e, 325b, 325b-326b.

163. *Ep.* 7.325c f.

164. *Ep.* 7.331d.

CHAPTER 7

MENO

1. *Prot.* 357b.

2. *Meno* 70a.

3. *Meno* 71a. From the scientific point of view, this way of attacking the problem is the only logical and sensible one. But the old poets were very far from posing the problem about the nature of areté in that general form, even when they (e.g. Tyrtaeus, Theognis, Xenophanes) believed one areté was superior to all the others. When Socrates makes the acquisition of areté dependent on the answer to the question about its nature—i.e. on a difficult and complex intellectual process —it shows that areté itself had become a problem for him and the men of his time.

4. *Meno* 71d-e.

5. *Meno* 72a.

6. *Meno* 72b says the aim of such an enquiry is to discover the essence (οὐσία) of a thing; but before that see *Prot.* 349b.

7. *Meno* 72c-d.

8. *Meno* 72c; cf. the example given in 72b.

9. *Meno* 72c8.

10. *Meno* 72e.

11. In *Gorg.* 499d and 504b Plato mentions health and strength as examples (though not the only ones, 499d6-7) of the 'virtues of the body' (ἀρεταὶ σώματος). In *Laws* 631c health, beauty, and strength are grouped together, and the same trinity is mentioned by Aristotle (frg. 45 Rose) in his *Eudemus*—written while he was still thinking along Platonic lines, and a good example of accepted Academic doctrine.

12. *Meno* 73c.

13. *Meno* 75a.

14. *Meno* 74a.

15. Cf. *Prot.* 329c-d, 349b.

16. *Meno* 77a.

17. The idea of actual sight contained in the description of this act as 'vision' also appears in expressions such as *eidos* and *idea,* which mean 'visible form' or 'shape'. The root of both words is the same as that of the Latin *uideo.*

18. The concept *eidos* appeared at the very beginning of Plato's career, in *Euthyphro* 5d and 6d-e; in *Gorg.* 503e (cf. 499e) it becomes entirely clear that the eidos of Good is the centre of Plato's thought. In *Meno* 72c-d the logical problem of the 'one eidos' in the manifold phenomena comes to the fore. On *Lysis* see p. 397, n. 5b.

19. Arist. *Met.* A 6.987b1; M 4.1078b17-33; cf. A 9.990b1.

20. The 'Marburg school', which published many books and articles on its new interpretation of Plato's work, violently rejected Aristotle's account of this matter: see especially P. Natorp, *Platos Ideenlehre* (Marburg 1910). This movement went too far in the opposite direction, and therefore the result of its exaggerations was a clearer understanding of the real historical position of Plato and Aristotle. Its representatives actually said that Aristotle had mistakenly changed Plato's Ideas into some sort of 'things'; and they tried to defend Plato, although they were really not defending Platonic doctrine so much as what modern logicians ascribed to Plato, by making his Ideas purely logical concepts. It was J. Stenzel, in his first book *The Method of Plato's Dialectic* (tr. D. J. Allan, Oxford 1940), who turned the mistakes of the Marburg school to his profit and really fathomed the historical truth about Plato's logic of reality.

21. See note 6.

22. The noun *synopsis* appears in *Rep.* 537c; the verb συνορᾶν in *Phaedrus* 265d, where it is accompanied by the word *idea* ('to look at widely scattered things and bring them under one form'). In *Rep.* 537c Plato derives the adjective *synoptic* from that verb, to characterize the nature and the ability of the dialec-tician.

23. *Meno* 75d.

24. See p. 315, and *ep.* 7.341c. The relation of these joint dialectic investigations to the act of intellectual vision at their conclusion is illuminated in the seventh Letter by a comparison between the rubbing of two pieces of wood which at last burst into flames, and the spark that springs from the dialectic discussion and finally lights the soul.

25. See note 13.

26. *Meno* 74b.

27. *Meno* 74d.

28. *Meno* 74e. The curved is 'no more' (οὐδὲν μᾶλλον) a figure than the straight. Cf. *Phaedo* 93b-d.

29. Cf. my *Aristotle* 41-42, where I have shown this of Plato's *Phaedo*.
30. Meno is described as a pupil of Gorgias, who had taught him in Thessaly (70b, 76b f.): he has had a good preliminary training.
31. *Meno* 74b.
32. On the method of hypothesis, see 86e-87a. In the same way Plato showed in *Prot.* that, if areté is knowledge, it must be teachable.
33. *Meno* 82b f.
34. *Meno* 85b-d.
35. Cf. the conception of reminiscence (*anamnésis*) in *Meno* 85d.
36. *Meno* 86b.
37. So in *Phaedo*.
37a. Cf. p. 301 f.
38. *Meno* 80a.
39. *Meno* 80c.
39a. *Meno* 84c.
39b. *Meno* 81c, 81d, 81e, 82b, 82e, 84a, 85d, 86b.
40. *Meno* 85c, 86b.
41. *Meno* 86b-c. Here the search for truth appears as the true essence not only of Socratic 'philosophy', but of human nature in general.
42. *Meno* 84c6.
43. *Meno* 84c11, 84d1, 85d3, 85e6.
44. *Meno* 85d4: ἀναλαβὼν αὐτὸς ἐξ αὐτοῦ τὴν ἐπιστήμην. Plato is interested in the special case of mathematical knowledge, because it shares a common origin with the knowledge of values, and that is his main concern.
45. *Meno* 86b. Courage in enquiry is the mark of true manliness. That is obviously a counterblast to the critics like Callicles who said that long study of philosophy weakened men and made them unmanly. See p. 139.
46. *Meno* 86c5.
47. See p. 161.
48. *Meno* 78b-c.
49. *Meno* 78d f.
50. *Meno* 79a-b.
51. *Meno* 87b.
52. *Meno* 87d f.
53. *Meno* 88c5.
54. *Rep.* 618c. We 'ought to neglect all other kinds of knowledge, and seek this one', which he describes in 618c8-e4 as the knowledge (εἰδέναι) that enables us to make the right choice of good and bad (αἱρεῖσθαι, αἵρεσις).
55. See p. 122.
56. *Meno* 89e-91b, 93a f.
57. *Meno* 97b f.
58. *Meno* 99b f. θεία μοῖρα in 99e and 100b; ἀπὸ τύχης τινός in 99a. On the concept of divine *tyché* or *moira,* see the dissertation of E. G. Berry, *The History and Development of the Concept of* θεία μοῖρα *and* θεία τύχη *down to and including Plato* (Chicago 1940): it gives the earlier literature on the subject. See also p. 268.
59. *Meno* 98a.
60. *Prot.* 361b; see p. 122.
61. See especially Socrates' protreptic speech in *Euthyd.* 278e-282d.
62. *Phaedo* 64b.
63. *Phaedo* 67c, 83a.
64. *Phaedo* 85b.

CHAPTER 8

THE SYMPOSIUM

1. *Rep.* 496c8, *ep.* 7.325d.
2. See p. 57 f.
3. *Lys.* 215a, 215e; cf. Arist. *Eth. Nic.* 8.2.1155a33 f.
4. *Lys.* 219c-d.
5. *Lys.* 219c-d. Plato's way of phrasing this idea here is reminiscent of *Gorg.* 499e, where he describes the Good as the aim (τέλος) of all action, and defines it as that for whose sake we do everything else. It is clear from *Lysis* 220b that he wants to make the same point there; τελευτῶσιν 220b and ἐτελεύτα 220d are close to the idea of τέλος. The supreme φίλον is that towards which all friendships point: their final cause.
   5a. *Gorg.* 507e.
   5b. This is the conclusive proof that the Idea of Good is really implied as the aim of all the discussions carried on in Plato's early dialogues (see p. 96). For the literary form and the philosophical attitude of *Lysis* put it among them; and so do the results of stylistic investigation. The date of the dialogue and its significance in Plato's philosophical development were the subject of an interesting argument between M. Pohlenz (*Göttinger Gelehrte Anzeigen* 1916, no. 5) and H. von Arnim (*Rheinisches Museum*, N.F. vol. 71, 1916, 364). I agree with von Arnim in giving it an early date.
   5c. *Gorg.* 507e-508a: the universe is held together by community and friendship (φιλία); they are based on the rule of Good, the highest standard.
6. *Symp.* 175e.
7. *Od.* 1.338, and elsewhere. The bard at the banquet sings of the glorious areté of heroes.
8. See Xenophanes frg. 1 Diehl, and *Paideia* I, 171-172: the poet says the symposium is the place for μνημοσύνη ἀμφ' ἀρετῆς—for keeping alive the memory of true areté.
9. Theognis 239 speaks of Cyrnus (to whom he addresses his poems) as living on at the banquets of posterity: this means that he would live on in Theognis' poetry.
10. The Greek literature of the symposium and its extant remains are discussed by J. Martin in *Symposion: die Geschichte einer literarischen Form* (Paderborn 1931). Plato's pupil Aristotle also wrote a *Symposium*, and we are told that Speusippus recorded conversations which occurred at symposia (by Plutarch, in the introduction to his *Quaestiones convivales*).
11. See *Laws* 641a. According to Athenaeus 5.186b, Plato's pupil and second successor, Xenocrates, composed *Laws for the symposium* (νόμοι συμποτικοί) for the Academy; and Aristotle did the same for the Peripatetic school. The latter fact is proved by the extant lists of Aristotle's books, which contain one volume of *Laws for dining-clubs* (*syssitia*) or *On syssitia or symposia*, and three volumes of *Problems of dining-clubs*. The *Laws of kingship* (νόμοι βασιλικοί) mentioned by Athenaeus 1.3 f. are clearly the same as the *Laws for the symposium*, since the latter were meant for the use of the 'king' or chairman of the symposium. In the last-mentioned passage, Plato's direct successor Speusippus also is said to have composed rule-books of this kind.
12. See *Paideia* III, 222 f.
13. *Rep.* 416e.
14. *Laws* 637a f., 639d, 641a f.

15. *Areop.* 48-49.
16. *Symp.* 177d. Similarly, Lysias is called 'the father of the speech' in *Phaedrus* 257b.
17. So says his friend Eryximachus in *Symp.* 177a.
18. *Symp.* 178b.
19. *Symp.* 178d.
20. *Symp.* 180d.
21. *Paideia* I, 63-64.
22. *Symp.* 181b f.
23. The motive of shame (αἰσχύνη) occurs in the speech of Phaedrus, *Symp.* 178d.
24. See *Symp.* 184d-e for the concepts of areté and paideusis as the aim of this Eros.
25. *Symp.* 184c: συμβαλεῖν εἰς ταὐτόν; 184e: συμπίπτει.
26. *Symp.* 182a-d.
27. *Laws* 636c f.
28. *Symp.* 186a.
29. See *Paideia* I, 65.
30. *Symp.* 178b. Phaedrus does not name Empedocles, but he does cite the genealogist Acusilaus.
31. *Symp.* 186b; filling and emptying, 186c.
32. *Symp.* 186a-c.
33. *Symp.* 186d-e.
34. For references to medicine and its peculiar approach to problems, see *Symp.* 186a, 186b, 186c, 186d, etc.
35. *Symp.* 187a f.
36. See in particular the Hippocratic treatise *On diet* I.
37. *Symp.* 187c-d.
38. *Symp.* 187d-e.
39. *Symp.* 189c-d.
40. *Symp.* 191a, 192b f.; 192e-193a.
41. *Symp.* 191d f.
42. *Symp.* 192c-d.
43. *Symp.* 194e.
43a. Cf. *Symp.* 204c.
44. *Symp.* 195a f.
45. *Symp.* 196a-197e.
46. *Symp.* 199c.
47. *Symp.* 199d f.
48. *Symp.* 203b.
49. *Symp.* 201b.
50. *Symp.* 201d f.
51. *Symp.* 201e-202b.
52. *Symp.* 202b-c.
53. *Symp.* 202e.
54. *Symp.* 202e. In *Gorg.* 508a Plato says the same of friendship: it holds the universe together.
55. *Symp.* 203b-c.
56. *Symp.* 203c-e.
57. *Symp.* 204a-b.
58. *Symp.* 204c.
59. *Symp.* 204c f.
60. *Symp.* 204d-205a.

61. *Symp.* 205b-c.

62. *Symp.* 205e.

63. *Symp.* 206a: ἔστιν ἄρα ὁ ἔρως τοῦ τὸ ἀγαθὸν αὑτῷ εἶναι ἀεί.

64. Aristotle (*Eth. Nic.* 9.8) describes the man who is truly self-loving (φίλαυτος) as the extreme opposite of the selfish man. He appropriates everything good and noble for himself (1168b27, 1169a21) and his attitude to his true self is the same as his attitude to his best friend. But one's best friend is he who wishes one all possible good (cf. 1166a20, 1168b1). This theorizing about the love of self is one of the genuinely Platonic elements in Aristotle's ethics.

65. *Eth. Nic.* 9.4.1166a1 f.; cf. 1168b1.

66. Cf. p. 186.

67. That is how Plato phrases it in *The Republic;* see pp. 277, 353.

68. *Symp.* 206b.

69. Cf. *Symp.* 206b-c.

70. *Symp.* 207a f.

71. See p. 190.

72. *Symp.* 207d.

73. *Symp.* 207e.

74. *Symp.* 208a-b.

75. *Symp.* 208e-209a.

76. See *Paideia* I, 8 f., and the whole chapter *Nobility and Areté.*

77. *Symp.* 178d.

78. *Symp.* 209a.

79. *Symp.* 209b-e.

80. *Symp.* 210a.

81. *Symp.* 211c.

82. *Symp.* 210e.

83. Cf. the speech of Pausanias, and see Diotima's speech, 209c.

84. *Symp.* 210a.

85. *Symp.* 210b.

86. *Symp.* 210c.

87. *Symp.* 210d.

88. *Symp.* 210d-e.

89. *Symp.* 211c.

90. *Symp.* 211c8.

91. *Symp.* 211d.

92. *Symp.* 211b τέλος, 211d βίος.

93. *Symp.* 206a.

94. *Symp.* 211e.

95. *Symp.* 211c.

96. *Rep.* 505a.

97. *Rep.* 589a; see p. 353.

98. This final step is prepared for by the speech of Diotima, 204a-b.

99. Socrates is the truest illustration of the educational impulse (ἐπιχειρεῖ παιδεύειν *Symp.* 209c), which Diotima describes as the unmistakable symptom of being captivated by a beautiful and noble soul. Also, he is an embodiment of the state of the soul which is between knowledge and ignorance in the eternal search for knowledge. And so, the whole speech of Diotima is a progressive analysis of Socrates' nature. It is wholly impelled by Eros. But because Eros has entered Socrates' noble personality, Socrates himself is changed: he has come under the laws of the god. Plato would say that the true nature of Eros has only now been revealed, in Socrates—as the power which raises the life of man to the level of the gods.

100. *Symp.* 215a-b.
101. *Phaedrus* 279b-c.
102. *Symp.* 215e-216c.
103. *Rep.* 490e f.
104. Isocr. *Bus.* 5 f.
105. Alcibiades personifies the type which is Plato's best illustration of Socrates' real purpose: he is the young genius who 'neglects his own affairs and does the Athenians' business, inadequate as he is' (*Symp.* 216a). This neglect of oneself is directly opposed to the Socratic doctrine that one should 'take care of one's soul' (ἐπιμελεῖσθαι τῆς ψυχῆς: see p. 38 f.). Alcibiades tried to build up a new state before the commonwealth within him was ready: see the end of *Rep.* 9.

CHAPTER 9

THE REPUBLIC

PART I

1. See p. 97.
2. See pp. 113, 120.
3. See p. 98.
3a. Of the innumerable books which deal with Plato's *Republic* the most interesting to the historian of paideia are:
E. Barker, *Greek Political Theory* (London 1925).
R. L. Nettleship, *Lectures on the Republic of Plato* (London 1901).
R. L. Nettleship, *The Theory of Education in the Republic of Plato* (Chicago 1906)
P. Friedländer, *Die platonischen Schriften* (Berlin 1930)
and J. Stenzel, *Platon der Erzieher* (Leipzig 1928), which has many profound analyses of important passages in Plato's works, and sets forth many of the fundamental conceptions of his philosophy of education.
4. The word 'system' (σύστημα) is not used to describe a body of scientific or philosophical doctrine before the Hellenistic age, of which it is a characteristic product. Even Aristotle, whom we think of as the greatest of all systematizers, does not use the word in that sense.
5. This fits in with the elaborate parallel between state and soul. The 'third class' interests Plato only as an antitype of the desiring part of the human soul.
6. Plato is thinking of the different *moral* functions of the soul, the different forms (εἴδη) which its moral activity assumes.
7. The Neo-Platonic interpreter Porphyry rightly remarks that the theory of the parts of the soul in Plato is not psychology in the usual sense, but moral psychology. Aristotle does not adopt it in his work on psychology, but uses it in his ethical works. Its meaning is *pedagogical*. See my *Nemesios von Emesa* (Berlin 1913) 61.
8. We have several times pointed out that the Greek city-state was an educational force: see *Paideia* I, 77, 105 f., and 321. However, Plato is not dealing with the relation between paideia and any one historical state using it as a political instrument, but with paideia as directed towards the divine end, the Idea of the Good, that lies at the centre of the perfect state.
9. This is Theodor Gomperz, *Griechische Denker* II [4]. 372. Gomperz holds that the description of the education of the rulers in *The Republic* (books 6-7) is only a pretext to display Plato's own epistemology and ontology. In the same way Gomperz sees in the education of the guards in books 2-3 only a pretext making it possible for Plato to discuss at length all sorts of problems in the fields of myth-

ology, religion, music, poetics, and gymnastics. In reality this interpretation reverses the true relation. As will be shown by our analysis of *The Republic*, the essence of Plato's paideia requires all the elements enumerated by Gomperz, and it was impossible to make it clear without dealing with them in a philosophical way. Paideia is not a mere external link that keeps the work together; it constitutes its true inner unity.

10. This ideal of what knowledge ought to be had developed in the scientific world, and had been taken over by philology, which thereby completely lost sight of its own true nature.

11. *Gorg.* 521d; see p. 150.

12. See my lecture, *Die griechische Staatsethik im Zeitalter des Plato,* reprinted in *Humanistische Reden und Vorträge* (Berlin 1937), p. 95.

13. Cf. *Paideia* I, 94.

14. See *Paideia* I, 141-144.

15. Ar. *Pol.* 2.7-8.

16. Ar. *Pol.* 2.7.1266b29-33.

17. Anonymus Iamblichi, in Diels, *Vorsokratiker* II[5], 400 f. On this interesting character, so representative of his time, see R. Roller, *Untersuchungen zum Anonymus Iamblichi* (Tübingen 1931).

18. One of the most famous examples of the comparison between different types of constitution is the debate in the royal council of Persia, Herodotus 3.80 f.

19. See *Paideia* I, 106.

20. See *Paideia* I, 106 note 23.

21. Cf. *Paideia* I, 104.

22. A significant example of the increasing relativity in the concept of *nomos* is the well-known antithesis between νόμῳ and φύσει: human law, or convention, and natural right. Cf. *Paideia* I, 326 f.

23. See p. 139.

24. See p. 133.

25. *Rep.* 338c.

26. *Rep.* 357a.

27. *Rep.* 357b-c.

28. *Rep.* 359a.

29. *Rep.* 359d.

30. Cf. *Paideia* I, 328-331.

31. *Rep.* 362e f.

32. *Rep.* 363a-e. See *Paideia* I, 68, 93, and 141 on the catalogue of the rewards of areté and justice and the disadvantages of kakia and hybris, in the poems of Hesiod (*Works & Days* 225), Tyrtaeus (frg. 9.30 Diehl), and Solon (frg. 1.32D).

33. *Rep.* 364a f.

34. *Rep.* 366e, 367b f.

35. Adeimantus insists on disregarding the social benefits of justice in any appraisal of its worth (367b and 367d), just as Glaucon had already suggested (361b). The word for the social prestige of areté is *doxa*. In early Greek ethics, doxa ('good repute') always goes with areté, and indeed is its equivalent (see *Paideia* I, 9: there is a good example of this in Solon frg. 1.4 Diehl). Thus Plato is trying to break the connexion between areté and doxa. His contemporary, the sophist known as Anonymus Iamblichi, was trying to do just the opposite, and restore civic virtue based upon doxa: see Diels *Vorsokratiker* II.[5] 400 f. Plato holds that social doxa has something of the sense of mere *appearance*, which he attaches to the word in his discussions of the theory of knowledge.

36. *Rep.* 365c.

37. See p. 204.

38. See p. 145.

39. *Rep.* 368e.

40. *Rep.* 369a.

41. Right at the beginning, in *Rep.* 371e, the question is asked: where does justice come into the newly created state?—but it cannot be answered at once. Still, there is a hint that it has something to do with the mutual relations of the various individuals who work together in the state.

42. *Rep.* 370a f.

43. *Rep.* 372e f.

44. *Rep.* 373e.

45. The discussion is found in *Laws* 625e-628d, 629a; but of course that does not prove that Plato had planned *The Laws* when he was writing *The Republic*.

46. *Rep.* 374a-d.

47. For criticisms, see Isocrates *On peace* 44-48 and Demosthenes *Phil.* 1.20.47.

48. The word πλάττειν, 'mould', occurs several times in this connexion: see 377b, c.

49. *Rep.* 374e.

50. Cf. *Rep.* 375a-e, and 459a-b.

51. *Rep.* 375e.

52. Their paideia begins in *Rep.* 376c-e.

53. Ar. *Eth. Nic.* 10.10.1180a24.

54. See *Paideia* III, 245.

55. *Rep.* 376e.

56. *Rep.* 376e, 377a.

57. *Rep.* 377a.

58. By introducing the metaphor of 'moulding' or 'forming' (πλάσις, πλάττειν), Plato shows his readers, with the clarity of genius, what is the essential function of education in poetry and music, as practiced in the paideia of earlier Greece. Here as elsewhere, he is not introducing something entirely new, but making his readers fully aware of the importance and meaning of something old and well established.

59. *Rep.* 377c.

60. Cf. *Paideia* I, 170.

61. Cf. *Paideia* I, 350.

62. Cf. *Paideia* I, 53-54.

63. *Rep.* 378c-d, cf. Xenophanes frg. 1.21 Diehl.

64. Xenophanes frg. 9 Diehl.

65. Aesch. *Against Timarchus* 141, Lycurgus *Against Leocrates* 102.

66. Of course the Stoics went furthest of all in using the poets as authorities; and thereby they took up an attitude very different from Plato's to the problem of the value of poetry. They sustained the claim of the poets (especially Homer) to be a part of true paideia, by interpreting them allegorically.

67. See note 64 of this chapter.

68. Cf. *Rep.* 377a: a myth is false, taken as a whole, but it contains elements of truth.

69. See *Paideia* III, 256.

70. *Rep.* 379a: τύποι περὶ θεολογίας; the first appearance of the word 'theology' anywhere.

71. In *Rep.* 377e Plato compares a poet who speaks evil of the gods with a painter whose picture is 'not like' his subject. The words μηδὲν ἐοικότα are well chosen, for they mean both that the poet does not give a true description and that his conception of godhead is inappropriate: Xenophanes (frg. 22 Diehl) said that it 'did not look like God' to move from one place to another. The word πρέπειν,

'to suit' or 'to be appropriate,' originally meant 'to resemble' like the Homeric
ἐοικέναι, and it still has that sense in fifth-century tragedy.

72. *Rep.* 379c.

73. *Rep.* 383c.

74. He begins by criticizing the legends about the gods, and therewith insisting
on true piety or *eusebeia* (377e to the end of book 2). In book 3 he starts by
criticizing those passages in the poets which offend against the true ideal of courage, and in 389d he goes on to speak of self-control in the same way: both these
criticisms are centred on the poets' descriptions of great legendary heroes. It
would seem that he ought to go on to criticize their descriptions of ordinary men,
from the point of view of true justice (392a and c), for justice is the only virtue
left. But he postpones that part of his criticism, because the nature of justice has
not yet been explained.

75. See *Paideia* III, 221.

76. Solon frg. 22 Diehl.

77. I have discussed a number of particularly illuminating examples of this
device of rewriting a famous and authoritative poem in my essay *Tyrtaios über
die wahre Arete* (Sitz. Berl. Akad. 1932), p. 556.

78. On this tradition see E. Norden, *Agnostos Theos,* p. 122 and appendix p. 391.

79. *Laws* 660e f.

80. This passage tells us much of what the Greeks thought about the relation
between artistic enjoyment (as we call it) and the power of poetry to mould the
soul. The two are not mutually exclusive—not at all. The higher the artistic pleasure it gives, the greater is the power which a work of art has to influence the
beholder. This explains how the ideal of the influence of art upon character could
arise among the most artistic people in the world, the Greeks, whose aesthetic sensi-
bility was far greater than that of any other race in history.

81. *Rep.* 387d f, 389e.

82. *Rep.* 390e f.

83. *Rep.* 391d.

84. Plato's discussion of the myths concludes in *Rep.* 392c, and leads into his criticism of style.

85. He mentions this in passing at *Rep.* 373b; cf. also his use of the word 'represent', εἰκάζειν, in 377e to describe the function of both painter and poet.

86. *Rep.* 392d. In this division of the types of poetry Plato uses imitation to
mean, not copying some natural object or other, but the process by which the poet
or actor assimilates himself (ὁμοιοῦν ἑαυτόν) to the person whom he is portraying, and thereby extinguishes his own personality for the time being.

87. *Rep.* 395a.

88. *Rep.* 395b-c.

89. *Rep.* 396b.

90. *Rep.* 395b.

91. Obviously this description does not refer to imitation in the broader sense
(explained above in note 86), but only to the narrower sense: it is the imitation
given by a dramatic poet. Plato thinks the speeches in epic poetry are in the
same class. In this type of imitation, the body, the voice, and the character of the
imitator are necessarily changed, and he takes on the personality of that which
he is imitating (*Rep.* 395d). Plato quite clearly treats it as an ethical category,
whereas ordinary artistic imitation of some real object has no influence on the
imitator's character. Mimesis is a paideutic or educational idea when it means
abandoning one's own character to the imitation; it is a technical idea when it
means simply reproducing an object seen or heard.

92. *Rep.* 395d-397b.

93. *Rep.* 396b-d.

94. See *Rep.* 397a-b, and the description of the two kinds (εἴδη) or types (τύποι) of style (λέξις).

95. *Rep.* 398a.

96. *Rep.* 396e.

97. Cf. *Rep.* 398b-c. Content and form are ἅ τε λεκτέον καὶ ὡς λεκτέον. The former (ἅ) is identical with the detailed discussion of the myths, and the latter (ὡς) with the discussion of style (λέξις). The third part of the discussion of poetry, dealing with music (περὶ ᾠδῆς τρόπου καὶ μελῶν), begins at 398c. This division of poetry into its separate elements partially anticipates the structure of Aristotle's *Poetics*. The normative character of Plato's treatment of the subject is hinted at in the repetition of λεκτέον; his norm is the paideutic, not merely the technical, excellence of a work of poetry.

98. *Rep.* 398d.

99. *Rep.* 398d; cf. also 400a and 400d.

100. *Laws* 701a.

101. Pseudo-Plutarch, *de musica* c. 27; Hor. *Ars Poetica*, 202 f.

102. *Rep.* 400b.

103. *Rep.* 398e f.

104. See p. 228, and cf. Ar. *Met.* A3.995a9 f.

105. *Rep.* 399a-c.

106. *Rep.* 399c-e.

107. Pseudo-Plutarch, *de musica* c. 30; Ath. 636e.

108. *Rep.* 399e.

109. Cf. *Paideia* I, 125-127.

110. Here again (*Rep.* 400a) Socrates gives the young musical expert Glaucon the task of explaining and defining the types of rhythms and their number, as he had done for the modes. But it is significant that for all his technical knowledge Glaucon knows nothing of the ethical content of the various types of rhythm. Evidently Damon was exceptional among musical theorists. That is why Socrates says he will 'consult' him (400b) about which kinds of beat or rhythm (βάσεις) are suitable (πρέπουσαι) for each kind of ethos. That is very instructive, for the treatment of poetic metre in Aristotle's and Horace's discussions of the theory of poetry starts from the same point—that certain metres are appropriate rhythmically for certain types of subject. This continuous tradition evidently goes back beyond Plato, although we should naturally like to make him responsible for this educational attitude to music. Instead of taking it on himself, he makes Socrates appeal to Damon as the great authority on the theory of appropriateness (πρέπον)—and Plato very seldom names names and distinguishes authorities like that. He does so not merely because Socrates was Damon's pupil (and perhaps the tradition that he was may have been invented because of this passage in *The Republic*), but because he felt that Damon was the real originator of the theory of ethos in music on which Plato builds his system of paideia.

111. Ar. *Pol.* 8.5.

112. Ar. *Pol.* 8.5, 1340a18-30.

113. Ar. *Pol.* 8.5. 1340a30f.

114. Ar. *Pol.* 8.5.1340a36.

115. Ar. *de sensu* 1.437a5. Plato's admiration for the eye comes out in the adjective 'sunlike,' which he uses in *Rep.* 508b, and in his metaphor 'the eye of the mind', *Symp.* 219a.

116. Ar. *Pol.* 8.2.1337b25.

117. *Rep.* 401a. Perhaps 'sculpture' is meant by the 'et cetera', 401a1-2.

118. Socrates is inclined to extend the doctrine of ethos in music to other spheres

too—i.e. to go beyond Damon's theory. Damon discovered ethos in the realm of harmony and rhythm; but Socrates asks (400e) whether the young guards ought not to 'pursue' right rhythm 'everywhere' if they are to do their work properly. ('Pursue' is a clever word-play.) The fine arts participate in ethos through εὐαρμοστία, εὐσχημοσύνη, and εὐρυθμία. But see 400d on the ethical superiority of music to the other arts.

119. *Rep.* 401b-d.

120. *Rep.* 401d.

121. See pp. 269, 271 f.

122. Παιδεία and τροφή are at first almost synonymous: Aesch. *Sept.* 18. See *Paideia* I, 5.

123. See n. 121.

124. *Rep.* 401c: ὥσπερ αὔρα φέρουσα ἀπὸ χρηστῶν τόπων ὑγίειαν.

125. *Rep.* 401d: κυριωτάτη ἐν μουσικῇ τροφή. So also, true Being or true Reality is said to be ἡ κυριωτάτη οὐσία, τὸ κυρίως ὄν.

126. *Rep.* 401e.

127. *Rep.* 402a.

128. Ep. 7.343e-344b.

129. *Rep.* 402a.

130. *Rep.* 402c.

131. *Rep.* 403c.

132. *Rep.* 376e, 377a (see p. 211).

133. *Rep.* 403d.

134. *Rep.* 403e: τοὺς τύπους ὑφηγεῖσθαι.

135. *Rep.* 403e.

136. *Rep.* 404b.

137. *Rep.* 404b.

138. Cf. *Rep.* 397b, 399d.

139. Sophrosyné, temperance or moderation, in music, corresponds to health in athletics. See *Rep.* 404e. Both are the result of simplicity.

140. *Rep.* 405a.

141. *Rep.* 405a, *Gorg.* 464b (see p. 131).

142. *Gorg.* 464b.

143. *Rep.* 404e-405a. The ratio μουσική : γυμναστική = δικανική : ἰατρική is not set out in mathematical form in this passage, but is presupposed throughout.

144. *Rep.* 406a.

145. See *Paideia* III, 31-45 on the development of the science of diet in the fourth century.

146. See *Paideia* III, 44.

147. *Rep.* 406d.

148. *Rep.* 407a.

149. *Rep.* 407b-c.

150. *Rep.* 407e f.

151. *Rep.* 408b, 410a.

152. *Rep.* 406a. On Herodicus, see the chapter on Medicine, *Paideia* III, 33, 34 f.

153. *Rep.* 410b.

154. *Rep.* 410c; cf. 376e.

155. *Rep.* 410d.

156. *Rep.* 411a.

157. *Rep.* 411c-d.

158. *Rep.* 411e f. Plato's terms for this blend are συναρμόζειν and κεραννύναι. The latter term is taken from medicine. All health is the result of the right mixture (κρᾶσις), according to Greek medical doctrine; see *Paideia* III, 6. The

harmony of athletic and musical paideia is *healthy* education. See also *Rep.* 444c. But Plato thinks of the health of human nature in its entirety—not of the health of the body alone.

159. At the close of the section dealing with gymnastics (412b), Plato once more reminds us of the principle governing his description of the paideia of the guards. He points out once more that any description of this kind can give only the outlines of education (τύποι τῆς παιδείας), enough to show the spiritual form of the culture he is describing; and he emphatically refuses to enter into details about dancing, sports, horse-racing, hunting, etc.—'why should one go through these topics?' he says, and 'it is fairly clear that all this must correspond with the outlines'. In *The Laws*, the work of his old age, he felt differently about the treatment of these forms of paideia. The position there given to choral dancing is absolutely different, and is in fact extremely important. See *Paideia* III, 228. His treatment of drinking and hunting as forms of education in *The Laws* is equally different from anything in *The Republic*. Both of them receive considerable attention. See *Paideia* III, 222 and 178.

160. *Rep.* 412a.
161. *Rep.* 497d.
162. *Rep.* 412b.
163. *Rep.* 412d-414a.
164. *Rep.* 414b.
165. Cf. *Rep.* 414d-415d.
166. *Rep.* 416a-b. The Greek word for 'guarantee' here is εὐλάβεια. It consists only in their being τῷ ὄντι καλῶς πεπαιδευμένοι, 416b6, or ἡ ὀρθὴ παιδεία, 416c1.
167. *Rep.* 416b.
168. *Rep.* 416c f. These rules are given for the ruler's life, in addition to his 'paideia'.
169. *Rep.* 419a-420b, and 421b.
170. *Rep.* 423b.
171. *Rep.* 423e.
172. *Rep.* 424a.
173. *Rep.* 424b.
174. *Rep.* 424c.
175. *Rep.* 424d.

176. In *Rep.* 424d-e Plato describes, in detail, the evil social effects of changes in paideia, and in 425a-b he contrasts with them the benefits of preserving paideia firm and unaltered. Both these descriptions are pointed by the use of the words παρανομία)(εὐνομία, which recall Solon's elegy (frg. 3 Diehl). Solon makes παρανομία and εὐνομία the ultimate cause of the state's happiness or misery (cf. *Paideia* I, 143 f.); in *The Republic* they are only the effects of change or resistance to change in paideia (cf. *Rep.* 425c).

177. *Rep.* 425c, cf. 427a.
178. Cf. *Paideia* I, 79 f.
179. *Rep.* 376c-d.
180. See p. 209.
181. *Rep.* 423d-425c.
182. *Rep.* 427d, cf. 368e.
183. *Rep.* 433a.
184. *Rep.* 428b-e.
185. *Rep.* 429a-c.
186. *Rep.* 430d-432a.
187. *Rep.* 433a-d, cf. 434c.
188. *Rep.* 434d.

189. *Rep.* 435b-c.

190. *Rep.* 435c-d. This problem is taken up again in 504b. The word Plato uses for the aspects or parts of the soul is εἴδη ψυχῆς, 435c: a concept of medical origin. The corresponding expression θυμοειδές is a new word borrowed from Hippocrates: see *Airs, waters, places* 16, where it is used to describe races in which courage and spirit predominate. Plato seems to refer explicitly to this book in 435e.

191. *Rep.* 435e.

192. *Rep.* 436c f. On the necessity for distinguishing a third element, 'spirit', over and above reason and the desires, see *Rep.* 439e-441a.

193. *Rep.* 441c-e.

194. *Rep.* 441e. See 411e and note 158.

195. *Rep.* 442a-b.

196. *Rep.* 443c. This kind of system in the state is only an εἴδωλον of true justice.

197. *Rep.* 443d-e. Thus areté is the 'harmony' of the various powers of the soul, as in *Phaedo*.

198. See p. 131.

199. *Rep.* 444c-e shows that areté is the health of the soul.

200. *Rep.* 443c-e. The medical conception ἕξις appears throughout the passage dealing with justice.

201. *Rep.* 445a.

202. Cf. the very important and suggestive use of the two medical conceptions, κατὰ φύσιν and παρὰ φύσιν, in *Rep.* 444d. Plato takes over the idea that health is the normal condition (areté) of the body, and so he is enabled to describe the moral quality, justice, as the true nature and the normal condition of the soul. Justice, which might have been a purely subjective idea, is changed to an objective fact by the parallel with the medical conception of 'true nature' or *physis:* to be just is to live according to the right or normal standard.

203. *Rep.* 445a.

204. *Rep.* 445c.

205. *Rep.* 449a.

206. See the reappearance of the problem of the pathology of the state and the soul in books 8-9 (p. 320 f.).

207. *Rep.* 450c, 452a, etc.

208. *Rep.* 451d.

209. In *Rep.* 501e he says he is 'mythologizing' in constructing the Republic. In *Rep.* 450c the question whether his proposals could possibly be fulfilled is mooted, but answered only as far as concerns the gymnastic and musical education of women (cf. 452e-456c). The proposal that the guards should have wives in common is discussed, not so much to determine whether it is possible as to find out if it is desirable or not. The problem of its possibility is pushed aside several times: in 458b and 466d, for instance; and in 471c it looks as if it were to be discussed, but it soon passes over into a discussion of the general possibility of Plato's ideal state.

210. We must not forget that Plato is thinking only of the comparatively few individuals who are destined to rule and to defend the state.

211. Ar. *Pol.* 2.9.1269b12f.

212. Ar. *Pol.* 2.9.1269b37.

213. *Rep.* 416e. The word συσσίτια which Plato uses in this passage for the common meals proves that he is adapting the Spartan custom.

214. *Rep.* 451d.

215. *Rep.* 451d.

216. *Rep.* 452a.
217. Her. 1.8.
218. *Rep.* 452c. The moral feeling of the Greeks of Asia Minor is revealed by their sixth-century art, which in this respect is widely different from Peloponnesian art.
219. The next most important subject of sculpture is the figures of gods. Some writers have wrongly stated that Greek sculptors chose to portray athletes because it was only in the palaestra that they saw men's bodies in all their naked beauty. This mistake is typical of a certain modern idea, that an artist is someone who specializes in portraying nudes: indeed, that idea begins to appear towards the end of classical antiquity. The truth is quite different. The athletes who appear in early Greek sculpture are the embodiments of the noblest gymnastic areté of a young man in the full power of health and training. Plato is merely repeating the general Greek idea when he says that the 'aretai' of the body are health, strength, and beauty.
220. Of course, the figures of naked women in art are not Platonic athletes, but types of the beauty of Aphrodite. That is typical of the later school of sculpture, which was interested in women's bodies for their own sake, rather than in the more masculine figures of women portrayed in the early classical period. Plato's ideal of beauty is something else again: it is ὅτι τὸ ὠφέλιμον καλόν. The female guards are to put on areté as a garment, instead of the *himation:* 457a.
221. *Rep.* 452c f.
222. Thuc. 1.6.5.
223. *Rep.* 453b-d.
224. *Rep.* 454a f.
225. *Rep.* 455c-d.
226. *Rep.* 455e.
227. *Rep.* 456b-c.
228. Cf. Ivo Bruns, *Vorträge und Aufsätze* (Munich 1905) 154: 'Frauenemanzipation in Athen'.
228a. *Rep.* 445d.
229. *Rep.* 457c.
230. Cf. *Paideia* I, 312.
231. Cf. *Paideia* I, 204.
232. Theognis too naturally thought that the ἀγαθοί should be produced by selective breeding, but he was a nobleman-poet, and for him ἀγαθός and κακός always mean 'noble' and 'common': see *Paideia* I, 198.
233. Xen. *Resp. Lac.* 1.
234. Critias frg. 32 Diels.
235. *Rep.* 458d.
236. *Rep.* 458d-e.
237. *Rep.* 458e.
238. *Rep.* 459e.
239. *Rep.* 459c-d.
240. *Rep.* 460a.
241. *Rep.* 460d-e.
241a. *Rep.* 461a. On the other hand, in *Rep.* 461c he allows even members of the governing class to have love affairs freely after passing the age-limit for producing children (40 for women, 55 for men).
242. *Rep.* 459d.
243. *Rep.* 460c.
244. *Rep.* 461d.
245. *Rep.* 462b.

246. *Rep.* 462c.

247. *Rep.* 462c-d.

248. *Rep.* 462b.

249. *Rep.* 463a-b.

250. Plato shows himself particularly aware of the fact that his Republic is a Greek state when giving regulations for war between Greeks, in *Rep.* 469b-c, 470a, 470c, and 471a (cf. p. 255): in 470e he says expressly that the state which Socrates is constructing is to be a Greek one.

251. See the passages quoted in note 250.

252. In *Rep.* 499c he says the Republic might be realized in some other country. The passage shows Plato's respect for the barbarians and the age of their civilization and wisdom.

253. This comes out again and again, cf. *Rep.* 462a-b in particular. The passage is reminiscent of Aesch. *Eum.* 985, where the unity of the citizens in love and hatred is praised as the highest of all good things.

254. Aristotle (*Pol.* 7.5.1327a1) follows Plato in this view.

255. He thinks the happiness of *the entire city* is the highest goal: see 420b. He discusses the happiness of the guards in 419a f., and finally solves the problem in 466a. In the hierarchy of happiness, as in other things, the guards are to stand highest, although their vocation demands most self-sacrifice from them.

256. See below, p. 251, and *Paideia* III, 71 f., on the Panhellenism of the fourth century.

257. See the passages quoted in note 250.

258. *Rep.* 469b.

259. In *Rep.* 403e Plato ironically calls his guards 'athletes in the greatest of all contests'—in war.

260. *Rep.* 466e.

261. In *Rep.* 468a his description of military training in youth leads into general regulations for the ethics of war.

262. The 'musical' and athletic training of the guards is described in books 2 and 3, and their education for war in book 5, 468a-471c.

263. The aim of paideia is to produce the right harmony between 'musical' and gymnastic education: see *Rep.* 410e-412a, and p. 234.

264. Ar. *Pol.* 7.11.1331a1.

265. See p. 226.

266. See p. 212.

267. *Rep.* 466e-467a.

268. *Rep.* 467d.

269. *Rep.* 467c: θεωρεῖν τὰ περὶ τὸν πόλεμον, θεωροὺς πολέμου τοὺς παῖδας ποιεῖν.

270. Tyrt. frg. 7.31, 8.21, 9.16; and see *Paideia* I, 91-92. The line of Tyrtaeus about watching the φόνον αἱματόεντα is quoted twice by Plato in *The Laws,* 629e and 699a. Hence he probably has Tyrtaeus in mind in *Rep.* 467c and e, where the words for 'watch', θεωρεῖν, θέα, θεάσονται, are repeated with great emphasis. Tyrtaeus and Plato are the psychologists of battle, who see the real problem involved in it for a human being.

271. *Rep.* 468a.

272. So also Ar. *Pol.* 3.5.1278a17. He says that they are excluded from citizenship in aristocratic states, and states where areté is the criterion of political rights. In his ideal state, Aristotle distinguishes βάναυσοι and ὁπλῖται, 7.4.1326a23.

273. *Rep.* 468a.

274. *Rep.* 468b-c.

275. *Rep.* 468d.

276. *Rep.* 468e.

277. *Rep.* 469b.
278. Cf. *Paideia* I, 90 f.
279. See *Paideia* III, 220 f.
280. Cf. *Rep.* 469b f.
281. *Rep.* 470c.
282. On Isocrates' Panhellenism, see *Paideia* III, 71. Aristotle's advice is preserved in Plutarch, *de fort. Alex.* 1.6 (Arist. frg. 658 Rose) : evidently the turn of phrase is a reminiscence of Isocrates, *On peace* 134. Aristotle's practical attitude towards Athenian democracy as well as Panhellenic politics follows Isocrates' line, as I hope to demonstrate elsewhere. He shows a moderate Platonism only in the construction of his ideal state.
283. *Rep.* 469b.
284. *Rep.* 469c.
285. *Rep.* 469c.
286. Cf. Isocr. *Paneg.* 3 and 133 f.
287. Ep. 7. 331d f.; 336a; 8. 353a f.
288. *Rep.* 470b, 471a. See the essay of one of my pupils, W. Woessner, *Die synonymische Unterscheidung bei Thukydides und den politischen Rednern der Griechen* (Würzburg 1937).
289. *Rep.* 470d, οὐδέτεροι αὐτῶν φιλοπόλιδες; see 471a.
290. *Rep.* 471a-b.
291. *Rep.* 470b, 470d-e.
292. *Rep.* 470e, 471a.
293. *Rep.* 469c-e.
294. *Rep.* 469e-470a.
295. *Rep.* 471b.
296. *De iure belli ac pacis* 557 (ed. Molhuysen, Leyden 1919). Grotius of course treated Plato's chapter on the rights of war in *The Republic* as a major authority.
297. *Rep.* 471c-e.
298. *Rep.* 472c-d.
299. *Rep.* 472c, 472d.
300. *Rep.* 472d9.
301. *Rep.* 472d5, cf. 472c5.
302. See pp. 61, 131. Socrates' politics are 'looking after one's soul' (ψυχῆς ἐπιμέλεια). Anyone who looks after his soul is thereby looking after 'the polis itself'.
303. *Rep.* 472d, cf. 472e.
304. On the relation between ideal and reality, and the 'approach' to the ideal, see *Rep.* 472c, 473a-b.
305. Cf. *Paideia* I, 40 f.
306. *Rep.* 501e.
307. Cf. Polyclitus A3 (Diels, *Vorsokratiker*).
308. See *Rep.* 472b-c, where justice and the just man appear together. Aristotle's ethics in particular worked out this method of personifying universal ethical concepts: he puts the magnanimous man beside a description of magnanimity, the generous man beside a description of generosity, etc.
309. See p. 133.
310. *Rep.* 473c-d.
311. See pp. 72, 97.
312. See p. 156.
313. See p. 133.
314. See p. 135.
315. Plato's exposition of the nature of philosophy fills the rest of book 5, from 474b onwards.

316. *Rep.* 476a f.

317. *Rep.* 479d.

318. *The Statesman* 300c.

319. *Rep.* 484c. Cf. 540a, where the paradeigma is defined more accurately as the idea of Good.

320. *Rep.* 484d.

321. *Rep.* 493a–c.

322. *Rep.* 493a7 and 493c8.

323. See pp. 129 f., 148.

324. Cf. note 319.

325. In writing the history and explaining the meaning of Plato's theory of paideia, it is not begging the question to assume the truth of its starting-point, and to show how Plato's solution must be built up on that assumption. To test the correctness of the assumption is the task of systematic philosophy.

326. *Rep.* 497b.

327. *Rep.* 487d f.

328. *Gorg.* 485a: οἷον παιδείας χάριν. The charge of ἀνελευθερία, levelled by Callicles against philosophical culture in *Gorgias,* is challenged by Plato in *Rep.* 486a. His defence is also a challenge to Isocrates, whose attitude to Plato's philosophy (considered as paideia) is very like that of Callicles.

329. *Rep.* 488a f.

330. Cf., for instance, *Rep.* 499a, where Socrates says it is characteristic of the philosopher 'to seek truth for the sake of knowledge'.

331. See *Paideia* III, 56 f., 148.

332. *Rep.* 488e.

333. *Rep.* 488b and 488e.

334. *Gorg.* 462b, 464b.

335. *Prot.* 319a8.

336. *Prot.* 361a.

336a. On the origin of general education from political education, see *Paideia* I, 112 f.

337. Plato often anticipates the results of logical analysis by using an image (εἰκών) like this. The most remarkable example is the image of the cave at the beginning of book 7 of *The Republic.* This anticipates the meaning and the general trend of the whole system of paideia worked out in book 7.

338. This happened at the end of book 5.

339. *Rep.* 485e f.; cf. the short recapitulation of the characteristics of the 'philosophical nature' in 487a.

340. *Rep.* 475e; cf. 495c8–d.

341. *Rep.* 487a7. Experience (ἐμπειρία) is strongly emphasized in 484d too, and put on the same level as philosophical training of the intellect.

342. Cf. *Rep.* 500b. The words of Socrates are: 'Don't you agree with me about this too, that most people think badly of philosophy because of those who have shoved their way drunkenly in where they had no business to be, and abuse one another and pick quarrels and keep talking about personalities, which is absolutely unsuitable to philosophy?'

343. *Rep.* 489e. In Aristotle's *Eudemian Ethics* (which in this as in other things is closely connected with Plato) the man of perfect areté, who unites all 'parts of areté' in himself, is characterized by possessing *kalokagathia* (8.3.1248b8). In the *Nicomachean Ethics* Aristotle dropped this, as he dropped other Platonic ideas. It is important, especially for one who, like Plato, is accustomed to regard his philosophy as paideia, to note that the *philosophos* of Plato is simply the

kaloskagathos resurrected and inspired by the spirit of Socrates—the *kaloskagathos* who was the highest cultural ideal of the classical period of Greece.

344. *Rep.* 490d f.
345. *Rep.* 491b; cf. the catalogue of the separate virtues in 487a, and see p. 234.
346. *Rep.* 491c.
347. *Rep.* 491d.
348. *Rep.* 491e.
349. *Rep.* 492a, 492e.
350. See the doctoral dissertation undertaken at my suggestion, E. Berry's *The History of the Concept of* θεία μοῖρα *and* θεία τύχη *down to Plato* (Chicago 1940), and the literature on the subject quoted there.
351. *Ep.* 7.326e.
352. *Rep.* 491e.
353. *Rep.* 492a5-b.
354. *Rep.* 492b-c.
355. *Rep.* 492d-e.
356. *Rep.* 493a.
357. *Rep.* 493a-b.
358. *Rep.* 493c.
359. See note 349.
360. *Rep.* 493b7.
361. *Rep.* 494a.
362. *Rep.* 494c.
363. See pp. 29, 49.
364. Xen. *Mem.* 1.2.
365. *Rep.* 495b.
366. *Rep.* 495c-d.
367. See the catalogue of the types which are saved for philosophy by being isolated and therefore free from corruption, in *Rep.* 496b-c.
368. Theages, a pupil of Socrates who was kept out of politics merely by his weak health, is expressly named. Contemporary readers would know who the others were; but we cannot.
369. *Rep.* 496c5-e2.
370. Cf. *Gorg.* 485d.
371. *Apol.* 31e.
372. *Ep.* 7.325b f.
373. See my *Aristotle*, p. 99. My late friend, J. L. Stocks, tried to prove the genuineness of the tradition in Cicero, *Tusc. Disp.* 5.3.8, according to which Pythagoras used the word 'philosopher' and claimed it for himself. But I have never been able to accept the proofs advanced by that admirable scholar, whose early death was a great loss to the classics.
374. *Ep.* 7.331b-d.
375. *Theaet.* 173c f.
376. *Theaet.* 186c: διὰ πολλῶν πραγμάτων καὶ παιδείας παραγίγνεται.
377. φυτὸν οὐράνιον, *Timaeus* 90a; 'foreign seed', ξενικὸν σπέρμα, *Rep.* 497b.
378. *Rep.* 497b7-c4.
379. See p. 234 f.
380. *Rep.* 498b; and cf. *Rep.* 498a.
381. See p. 140.
382. *Rep.* 498d-499a.
383. *Rep.* 499a-b.
384. *Rep.* 500a-b.
385. *Rep.* 500c.

386. Cf. *Theaet.* 176b: ὁμοίωσις θεῷ κατὰ τὸ δυνατόν.

387. *Rep.* 500d. This is an extremely interesting passage, partly because the idea of self-education appears here for the first time in the history of education, and partly because it illustrates with striking clarity the ideal and the reality of Plato's philosophical paideia. In the difficult circumstances in which Plato lived his philosophy was not education for the community, but only self-education.

388. *Rep.* 500e.

389. *Rep.* 472d; see p. 258.

390. *Rep.* 501b.

391. The relation of philosophy to the state in Greece is parallel to the relation of the prophets to the kings of Israel.

392. *Rep.* 499c-d.

THE REPUBLIC

PART II

1. The selection of the best guards is recommended in *Rep.* 412c; the first hint that they will need a special education is 416c: ὅτι δεῖ αὐτοὺς τῆς ὀρθῆς τυχεῖν παιδείας, ἥτις ποτέ ἐστιν. The last clause anticipates that that education will not be the same as the guards' paideia, described in the preceding pages, and looks forward to the paideia of the rulers, described in books 6 and 7.

2. *Rep.* 449c f.

3. The discussion of the education of the ruling class begins in *Rep.* 502c-d.

4. See p. 211.

5. *Rep.* 484c. Plato has prepared for his use of the concept of paradeigma here by employing it to characterize his description of the ideal state and the perfectly just man in *Rep.* 472c-d. These ideal pictures of state and man can be possessed by no one but the philosopher, for he possesses the knowledge of the Good. The idea of Good as the paradeigma of the ruler, 540a.

6. *Rep.* 503e, 504a, 504d, 504e, 505a.

7. In *Rep.* 503c Plato says that the rulers must be steady and dependable; in 503d that they must be good learners: cf. 504b and 504e, where he speaks of the need for accuracy, *akribeia,* which is the real distinction between the education of the rulers and that of the guards. On *The Laws,* in which he makes the same distinction, see *Paideia* III, 244.

8. *Rep.* 503e.

9. *Rep.* 503e-504b. Plato's reminder refers back to *Rep.* 435d. That was the first mention of a μακροτέρα ὁδός, which is called μακροτέρα περίοδος in 504b. Cf. also 504c9: μακροτέραν (scil. ὁδόν) τοίνυν . . . περιϊτέον τῷ τοιούτῳ.

10. *Rep.* 435d.

11. We must not overlook the fact that the description of dialectic education as a necessary 'detour' which the future statesman must make occurs in *Phaedrus* too. There as here Plato is anxious to prove that dialectic science, which his opponents like Isocrates criticized as useless and remote from life, is indispensable for politicians and rhetors. See *Paideia* III, 193. Isocrates used to describe his own paideia as the true political paideia, in contrast to Plato's intellectual gymnastics. See *Paideia* III, 147 f.

12. *Rep.* 504e.

13. *Rep.* 505a.

14. *Rep.* 505b.

15. *Rep.* 505c. Cf. the distinction of good and bad pleasures in *Gorgias,* p. 145

16. *Rep.* 505b-c.

17. *Phil.* 66b-c. The 'human good' is different from 'Good in itself'.

18. *Phil.* 22b.

19. *Rep.* 505c.

20. *Rep.* 505d.

21. *Rep.* 505e.

22. *Phil.* 65a.

23. *Rep.* 506c.

24. See p. 266.   In the image of the true captain, *Rep.* 488b, and 488e, it is only hoi polloi who think that the art of political navigation cannot be taught.

25. *Rep.* 506d.

26. See p. 241.

27. See pp. 103, 117 f., 165.

28. *Rep.* 507a.

29. *Rep.* 507a; and before that, see 476a f. The words ἄλλοτε ἤδη πολλάκις refer to the dialogues in which Plato had discussed the theory of Ideas more fully, such as *Phaedo, Symposium,* etc. In *The Republic,* where he outlines his paideia as a whole, he has no time for such details.

30. *Rep.* 507c.

31. Cf. *Rep.* 505b.

32. *Rep.* 508a.

33. On what follows cf. *Rep.* 508b f.

34. *Rep.* 508d.

35. *Rep.* 508e.

36. *Rep.* 509a.

37. According to *Rep.* 509b, Good is beyond Reality or Being (ἔτι ἐπέκεινα τῆς οὐσίας). But see 532c, where the vision of the Idea of Good is described as the vision of that which is best in the realm of being (τοῦ ἀρίστου ἐν τοῖς οὖσι θέα): it is therefore the highest Being, and gives reality to everything which we know. Similarly Aristotle, in a fragment of his book on Prayer (Dial. frg. ed. Walzer 100, frg. 49 Rose), says that God is 'either Mind, or even beyond Mind' (ἐπέκεινα τοῦ νοῦ). Therefore the ambiguity in Plato's conception of the relation of Good to Being, shown in both the above-mentioned passages, is not a contradiction for him: either one alternative is true, or else both are true together.

38. *Rep.* 509d.

39. See R. K. Hack, *God in Greek Philosophy to the time of Socrates* (Princeton 1931). I have given a detailed treatment of this aspect of pre-Socratic philosophy in my Gifford Lectures, delivered in 1936 at St. Andrews University, Scotland. They are to be published in book form under the title *The Theology of the Early Greek Philosophers.* Later, I intend to trace this second current in Greek thought (which is so important in discussing the influence of classical culture on later ages) down to Plato, in whose philosophy it joins the stream of paideia at this decisive point. Plato understood that all attempts to form a nobler type of man—that is, all paideia and all culture—merge into the problem of the nature of the divine.

39a. The greatest of western Christian philosophers, Augustine, realized this. There was no one better fitted to appreciate it. In the eighth book of his *City of God* or rather *State of God,* which he deliberately composed as a Christian counterpart of Plato's *Republic,* he puts Plato at the head of all pre-Christian theologians. Christian theology as practised by the fathers of the Church was really the result of treating the problems of Christianity with the concepts and methods of Platonic theology.

39b. On this see the old but still valuable dissertation by the psychologist and philosopher who later taught at Berlin, Karl Stumpf: *Verhältnis des platonischen Gottes zur Idee des Guten* (Halle 1869). It was suggested (as one might have guessed) by Franz Brentano, and accepted as a thesis by Hermann Lotze, father of the modern philosophical theory of 'value'. The history of the problem cannot be written in a footnote; and it will always remain a problem. I shall give my full arguments elsewhere, when I can spare the time to continue my *Theology of the Early Greek Philosophers* (note 39) and pursue the development of the problem in the classical period of Greek thought. In discussing Plato's view, we ought to remember his own words in *Timaeus* 28c: 'It is hard to find the maker and father of this universe, and having found him it is impossible to reveal him to all'. Hence the solemn and mysterious form of all Plato's utterances about God. It is chiefly to this central problem of his thought that we must refer the famous passages in *Phaedrus* and the seventh Letter, which speak of the impossibility of putting the essence of (Platonic) philosophy in written words. Plato approached the problem of God from one side, as has been pointed out, rightly, by F. Solmsen in *Plato's Theology* (Ithaca, New York, 1942). Which are his main lines of approach? The explicit statements in *Timaeus* and *The Laws* about God, partly in the form of myth, partly based on philosophical argument, show Plato increasingly concerned with solving the cosmogonical and physical aspect of the problem. A full discussion of the matter—which of course I cannot give here—would have to take them into account. Solmsen's book is the most recent and careful consideration of the available evidence on this subject. With regard to the problem of the Idea of Good and its divine position in *The Republic,* Solmsen joins those who deny that the 'principle of the universe' (as Plato calls it) is God. See also his predecessor, P. Bovet, *Le dieu de Platon* (a Geneva dissertation, 1902), not to mention many others, among whom are scholars such as Shorey and Gilson. I really find it difficult to believe that Plato originally approached the central problem of his ethical and political philosophy—God—or any other problem, from the standpoint of natural philosophy and physical motion: as he does in *Timaeus* and *The Laws*. True, he gradually came to feel that this aspect was more and more important: God, he thought, was necessary to set the stars in motion. But his *primary* approach to the problem was the Socratic and not the pre-Socratic one. We may see him pursuing that line of thought in his dialogues from *Euthyphro* to *The Republic*. There the Socratic question—what is the nature and unity of areté?—finally reveals itself as the problem of the divine Good, the 'measure of all things' (as God is defined in *The Laws*). There is not only more than one approach to the Divine in Plato; there is more than one aspect of it—God is the absolute good for which everything is striving; God is the world-soul; God is the demiurge or Creator; God is reason, *nous;* and there are the visible gods, the sun, the moon, the planets, et cetera. It was the diversity of aspects and forms of the Divine in Plato's philosophy that bewildered the Hellenistic critics—not only them, but modern scholars even more, who expected to find one God in Plato, and not πάντα πλήρη θεῶν. It was the same with Aristotle's lost dialogue *On Philosophy,* which obviously resembled Plato's theology in this respect: see my *Aristotle* 140, and the criticism of the Epicurean school, frg. 26 Rose (Cicero *N. D.* 1.13.33).

40. The concept of monarchy implies the function of ruling: Plato, *Rep.* 509d, uses the word βασιλεύειν, while the pre-Socratic philosophers often apply the word κυβερνᾶν to the highest principle. The two words are synonyms, both used by the Greeks of the power of Zeus. Many earlier Greek philosophers had avoided the word θεός, or else spoken by preference of 'divinity', τὸ θεῖον, which was quite different from the popular idea that there were a number of individual gods.

41. Plato compares the position of the sun in the visible world with that of the Good in the spiritual world, and says it is the god in heaven who rules

over light and sight. That is not merely a poetic phrase. In others of his books (e.g. *Timaeus* and *The Laws*), and in the *Epinomis* published by his pupil, Philip of Opus, the sun and stars are called 'visible gods' (ὁρατοὶ θεοί), which makes them a parallel and contrast to an invisible divinity. It is important also to notice that in *The Republic* Plato calls the supreme god of the sky, Helios, the son, and Good, the father.

42. The 'outlines of theology' are in *Rep.* 379a: τύποι περὶ θεολογίας. The chief axiom about theology is (379b) that God is good in reality (ἀγαθὸς τῷ ὄντι). The phrase τῷ ὄντι is Plato's way of describing the being of the Idea.

43. Of course, in Greek religion, *God* was a description which could be applied to the supreme, all-controlling Good, with more justice than to any of the many other powers whom the Greeks revered as gods. But the essential point from a philosophical point of view for Plato is the contribution he is making to the knowledge of the divine, by defining the supreme principle of the universe as that which is in itself Good.

44. In *Laws* 716c Plato's remark that God is the measure of all things is of course meant to be a contrast to Protagoras' famous epigram that the measure of all things is man.

45. *Prot.* 356d-357b. The true standard is Good in itself. The idea that there is a supreme art of measurement and that the philosopher's knowledge of values (φρόνησις) is the ability to measure, runs through all Plato's work right down to the end. In *The Statesman, Philebus,* and *The Laws* it appears with a new application to the problem of right action in ethics, politics, and legislation. The climax of its development comes in *The Laws,* where Plato calls God the measure of all things (see note 44). But as early as *Gorgias* (499e) Plato said quite clearly that good was the only true telos, the only aim of action.

46. Arist. *dial.* frg. ed. Walzer 99 (79 Rose).

46a. Aristotle thought that formula was the essence of Platonism: see his altar-poem, and the explanation of it in my *Aristotle* p. 107 f.

47. *Rep.* 526e. Plato says that the soul of the philosopher finally turns towards the region where the 'happiest thing in the realm of being' (τὸ εὐδαιμονέστατον τοῦ ὄντος) is. He means the Idea of Good. Paul Shorey, in his footnote ad loc., minimizes this description as 'rhetoric'; but it strictly corresponds to calling the Good τὸ ἄριστον ἐν τοῖς οὖσι, *Rep.* 532c6; cf. n. 37.

48. *Rep.* 484c. So far Plato has said only that those who lack knowledge of Being, who have no clear paradeigma in their souls, are little better than blind men: because they have no clear point of reference to which they can orient their thoughts and by which they can always steer themselves. The opposite of such people, as we shall soon see, is the philosophical ruler of the Republic, who 'orders' (κοσμεῖ) himself and his polis by turning the bright part of his soul towards that which gives light to everything else, and who looks at Good itself in all its purity in order to use it as a paradeigma (*Rep.* 540a). This supreme paradeigma is the 'measure of everything' which Plato mentions in *The Laws* (716c) and identifies with God.

49. *Theaet.* 176b: ὁμοίωσις θεῷ. Cf. *Rep.* 613b: εἰς ὅσον δυνατὸν ἀνθρώπῳ ὁμοιοῦσθαι θεῷ. If God is Good itself, then ὁμοίωσις θεῷ becomes the formula for attaining virtue.

49a. *Rep.* 511b; see also 508e.

50. *Rep.* 501b: τὸ ἀνδρείκελον; see p. 277.

51. *Rep.* 501b: τὸ θεοειδές τε καὶ θεοείκελον and 501c: εἰς ὅσον ἐνδέχεται θεοφιλῆ ποιεῖν (scil. ἀνθρώπεια ἤθη).

52. See note 44.

53. *Rep.* 509d.

54. In *Rep.* 511c6 the sciences at this stage are called τέχναι.

55. *Rep.* 510b.

56. *Rep.* 510d; cf. 510b.

57. *Rep.* 511c-d.

58. *Rep.* 510b (see note 59).

59. *Rep.* 511b.

60. *Rep.* 510b10 and 511c3.

61. *Rep.* 511d. The basis of the comparison between the four stages described by Plato is the difference in *clearness* (σαφήνεια, sometimes ἀσάφεια) which they represent. Σαφήνεια means not only intelligibility but reality: cf. 510a9: ἀληθείᾳ.

62. Εἰκών means 'copy', not only as a likeness, but as something weaker than the original, as the examples show. Thus in 509e-510a Plato calls shadows and reflections εἰκόνες of sensible things.

63. *Rep.* 510e and 511a.

64. *Rep.* 511b5.

65. *Rep.* 514a. The word 'compare', ἀπείκασον (see also εἰκών at the end of the cave-image, 517a8), puts the whole parable on the same footing as the other 'images', εἰκόνες, used by Plato in this connexion: the image of the sun, and that of the mathematical ratios. Even the latter, the divided line, is a regular εἰκών.

66. *Rep.* 515c.

67. *Rep.* 516c9. Plato is obviously contrasting politics as the apprehension of Ideas culminating in the vision of the divine Idea, with politics as mere experience. It is significant that he uses the word 'accustomed', εἰώθει (516d), to characterize the traditional un-Socratic type of politician. For all judgments based on experience alone could be nothing better than perception of what *usually* happens. The formulæ γίγνεσθαι and συμβαίνειν εἰώθεν are characteristic of the empirical method in medicine: see my *Diokles von Karystos* p. 31; and in politics: see my essay, 'The Date of Isocrates' Areopagiticus and the Athenian Opposition', in *Athenian Studies presented to W. S. Ferguson* (Cambridge 1940) 432.

68. *Rep.* 517b.

69. *Rep.* 517b6.

69a. See the word ἐλπίς *Rep.* 331a in the reflections of old Cephalus about life after death, and Plato's words about the 'good hope' of the man who has lived the life of the philosopher *Rep.* 496e.

70. *Rep.* 517c.

71. *Rep.* 517d.

72. *Rep.* 504e, 505a.

73. *Rep.* 514a: ἀπείκασον τοιούτῳ πάθει τὴν ἡμετέραν φύσιν παιδείας τε πέρι καὶ ἀπαιδευσίας.

74. See p. 165.

75. *Rep.* 518b6 f.

76. *Rep.* 518c.

77. *Rep.* 518c-d. Plato's word in this passage is περιαγωγή, but his terms are not invariable. Μεταστροφή is also used, and so are the verbs περιστρέφεσθαι and μεταστρέφεσθαι. They are all attempts to convey the same visual image, that of the turning of the head and the eyes to the divine Good. See A. D. Nock, *Conversion* (Oxford 1933). He traces the prototypes of the Christian religious phenomenon of conversion in classical Greece, and mentions this passage in Plato among others. If we approach the problem, not from the point of view of the religious *phenomenon* of conversion, but of the origin of the Christian *conception* of conversion, we must acknowledge that Plato was its originator. The word was transferred to Christian experience in the circles of early Christian Platonism.

78. *Ep.* 7. 344a; cf. 341c-e.
78a. See *Rep.* 500d, *Phaed.* 82b.
79. *Rep.* 518d.
80. *Rep.* 518e.
81. See p. 416, note 49. In other words, between God and the human soul there is, according to Plato, a long and laborious process of perfection. Areté is not possible without perfectness. The bridge which Plato sets up between the soul and God is paideia. It is growth towards true Being.
82. *Theaet.* 176e. The passage mentions two contrasting 'paradeigmata which stand in Being', one divine and one not divine (good and bad) : the former is the highest happiness, and the other is complete unhappiness. This reminds us of the passage at *Rep.* 472c, where Plato contrasts the Idea of justice and the perfectly just man, and the Idea of injustice and the completely unjust man as patterns (παραδείγματος ἕνεκα). We have already remarked that the idea of areté as 'becoming like God', which appears in *Theaetetus,* occurs in *The Republic* (613b). See p. 416, note 49.
83. *Rep.* 511b: τὴν τοῦ παντὸς ἀρχήν.
84. *Laws* 716c.
85. *Phaedo* 96a f., 99a f.
86. Cf. Ar. *Met.* A. 3.984b8 f., and A. 6.987b1.
87. See my *Aristotle* 109; and in that connexion compare my essay 'Aristotle's verses in praise of Plato', *Class. Quarterly* 21 (1927) 13 f., where I have shown in greater detail that the position attributed there to Plato by Aristotle is comparable only to that of the founder of a religion.
88. Ar. *Met.* E. 1.1026a19; see my *Aristotle* 138.
89. The *Epinomis* is principally concerned with 'the visible gods' of *Timaeus* and *The Laws,* the deities of the stars. The aspect of God which is the subject of the theology in *Laws* 10 is God as the cause of change and motion.
90. Diog. Laert. 3.37. I cannot here discuss the literature dealing with the authenticity of the *Epinomis:* see *Paideia* III, 337, n. 12.
91. Cf. *Tim.* 40d.
92. *Rep.* 379a.
93. *Epinomis* 988a, Ar. *Met.* A. 2.982b28-983a11, Ar. *Eth. Nic.* 10.7.1177b30-33.
94. *Euthyph.* 11e; and see the sharply phrased dichotomy in 10a: is piety loved by the gods because it is pious, or is it pious simply because the gods love it? The aim of the question is to identify the divine with the good.
95. *Euthyphro* 6d.
96. See p. 219.
97. See page 296, note 80.
98. See page 251.
99. *Rep.* 519c. Plato had already said, in the first book of *The Republic,* 347b-d, that the best men did not want to rule.
100. *Rep.* 516c f., and cf. p. 292.
101. *Rep.* 519b8-c2. From the beginning of the sixth book, where Plato distinguishes the philosopher-kings from 'those who have no clear pattern in their souls' (484c), all his arguments tend to prove that the uneducated man is a man with no single aim (σκοπὸν ἕνα) in his life. Unity cannot exist in anyone's life unless it is directed towards absolute Good, which is the natural aim of all human effort.
102. *Rep.* 519c5. Cf. 540b, where the real death of the philosopher, and his life after death, are described in the phrase 'to depart into the isles of the blest and live there'. That is the life of a hero, enjoying a special paradise. So also *Gorg.* 526c. In *Rep.* 519c5, the religious image of life in the blessed isles means the θεωρητικὸς βίος, the studious life of the philosopher in this life. Aristotle copied

that point: see my *Aristotle* p. 98. The image is still perceptible in his description of the bliss of the contemplative life, *Eth. Nic.* 10.7.

102a. See my *Aristotle* 73.

103. *Rep.* 519d-520a.

104. See my essay *Ueber Ursprung und Kreislauf des philosophischen Lebensideals (Sitzungsber. Berl. Akad.* 1928) 414. There I have attempted to show that some of the Peripatetic historians of philosophy, Dicaearchus in particular, described the earlier thinkers as patterns of the correct combination of thought and action, whereas later philosophers gave themselves up more and more to pure thought.

105. *Rep.* 520b. As we know, the Greek states of the fourth century did little or nothing for higher education. See Aristotle, *Eth. Nic.* 10.10.1180a26: he says that, as far as education went in most cities, people were still at the Cyclopean or cave-man stage, when every man decided what was best for his own family. In Plato's *Crito* Socrates expressed a feeling of deep obligation towards the Athenian state, for the education he had received under the protection of its laws. If this was truly the attitude of the historical Socrates, Plato's judgment in *The Republic,* which is quite opposed to it, becomes even more significant.

106. *Rep.* 519a-d, 521b.

107. *Rep.* 521e-522a.

108. *Rep.* 522b.

109. *Rep.* 522c-d.

110. *Rep.* 522e1-3.

111. That is why mathematics became the favourite science of the Hellenistic generals and monarchs. On Antigonus and Demetrius Poliorcetes, see my *Diokles von Karystos* 81-2. The military angle appears again in *Rep.* 525b-c.

112. *Rep.* 522e4.

113. *Rep.* 523a: ἑλκτικὸν πρὸς οὐσίαν.

114. See *Paideia* I, 317.

114a. There is a tradition that Plato seriously applied this programme when he was asked to educate the tyrant Dionysius II to be a philosophical monarch. Plutarch, *Dion.* 13, says that for some time not only the ruler but the entire Syracusan court was interested in mathematics, and the air was full of dust thrown up by enthusiasts drawing diagrams in the sand.

115. *Rep.* 527a.

116. Cf. *Rep.* 523a2, a6, b1, d8, 524b4, d2, d5, e1, 525a1, 526b2, 527b9.

117. *Rep.* 525c: ἀνθάπτεσθαι αὐτῆς μὴ ἰδιωτικῶς.

118. *Rep.* 526b.

119. Cf. *Paideia* I, 317. Plato too, in *Theaetetus* 145a, lists these four subjects as parts of the paideia received by young Theaetetus in Athens about 400.

120. *Rep.* 530d8.

121. Erich Frank, in his book *Plato und die sogenannten Pythagoreer* (Halle 1923) goes furthest in tracing the exact sciences of Greece back to the Pythagoreans. W. A. Heidel, 'The Pythagoreans and Greek Mathematics', *Am. Journal of Philology* 61 (1940) 1-33, traces the development of mathematical studies in earlier Greece, so far as the evidence allows, in non-Pythagorean circles, especially in Ionia.

121a. *Rep.* 531a5, cf. 530d6.

122. *Rep.* 531a1-3, 531c.

123. *Rep.* 531c.

124. *Rep.* 530b6.

125. *Rep.* 531c3.

126. *Rep.* 531d. About this programme of a philosophical analysis of the mathematical sciences, and how it was put into effect in the Academy, see F. Solmsen,

Die Entwicklung der aristotelischen Logik und Rhetorik (Neue Philol. Unters., ed. W. Jaeger, vol. 4) p. 251 f.

127. *Rep.* 530b.

128. *Tim.* 34c-38c, *Laws* 898d-899b. See also *Epin.* 981e f.

129. A fine example of Plato's habit of cutting out technical details—we have noticed it all through *The Republic*—is *Tim.* 38d. There he refuses to analyse the astronomical details of the theory of spheres, because to do so would make the side-line (πάρεργον) more important than the central aim which it ought to serve. Aristotle (*Met.* Λ. 8) does not follow him. He criticizes the reasons given by astronomers for their account of the exact number of the spheres, but makes a mistake in the number, as ancient experts observed (see W. D. Ross, *Aristotle's Metaphysics,* vol. II, p. 393).

130. Xen. *Mem.* 4.7.2 f.

131. Xen. *Mem.* 4.7.4 says that he justified the study of astronomy by pointing out it was useful in these activities.

132. *Rep.* 529a.

133. *Rep.* 527e.

134. *Rep.* 528b.

135. *Rep.* 527d.

136. *Rep.* 528a-b.

137. Suidas, s.v. Θεαίτητος; Schol. in Eucl. *Elem.* 13 (vol. 5, p. 654, 1-10 Heiberg). Proclus (in his list of geometricians) says that Pythagoras discovered the five regular polyhedra, but that is fiction—as the researches of Junge, Vogt, and Sachs have shown beyond dispute.

138. See Eva Sachs, *De Theaeteto Atheniensi mathematico* (Berlin 1914) 18 f.

139. On Theaetetus as a source for the thirteenth book of Euclid, see Eva Sachs, *Die fünf platonischen Körper (Philol. Unters.* ed. Kiessling and Wilamowitz, vol. 24) 112; and T. L. Heath, *A Manual of Greek Mathematics* (Oxford 1931) 134.

140. See F. Solmsen, *Die Entwicklung der aristotelischen Logik und Rhetorik* 109 f.

141. According to the current view, *The Republic* was written some time between 380 and 370.

142. This is assumed, with historical correctness, by Plato in *Theaet.* 143e f., although he probably made up the meeting between Theaetetus and Socrates, as he did the conversation of Socrates with Parmenides and Zeno in *Parmenides.*

143. Diog. Laert. 3.6.

144. That assumption is probably the basis of the story that Plato went to visit Theodorus in Cyrene, after Socrates' death: see note 143.

145. According to his seventh Letter, 338c, Plato was instrumental in making Archytas and the tyrant Dionysius guest-friends, on his second journey to southern Italy in 368; and both of them therefore encouraged him to make his third trip. Plutarch, *Dion* 11, says that the Pythagoreans (as well as Dion) prompted him to make his second trip—a fact which, if true, he himself does not mention. We might think this was a reduplication of the same fact: but whom would Plato visit on his first stay in Magna Graecia, before he visited Syracuse (388), if not the Pythagoreans? Diogenes Laertius 3.6, speaking of this, mentions only Philolaus and Eurytus on Plato's first journey, and not Archytas.

146. Ar. *Met.* A.6.

147. See my *Aristotle* p. 10 f.

148. Aristotle, Plato's pupil, was a scientific associate of the astronomer Callippus, the pupil of Eudoxus: see *Met.* Λ. 8, 1073b32, and my *Aristotle* 343 f.

149. Cf. Suidas s.v. φιλόσοφος.

150. *Rep.* 525c.
151. See *Paideia* III, 147.
152. Epicrates frg. 287 Kock.
153. On this see my *Diokles von Karystos* 178.
154. *Rep.* 531d.
155. *Theaet.* 186c.
156. *Rep.* 531e.
157. Aristotle, *Met.* M.4. 1078b25, knows that Plato's dialectic originated in Socrates' interrogative discussions, but he makes a clear distinction between its origins and the more highly developed 'dialectic power' (διαλεκτική ἰσχύς) characteristic of Plato's later period, and of his own methods—neither of which existed in the time of Socrates and of Plato's youth.
158. *Rep.* 536d.
159. *Rep.* 532a-b.
160. *Rep.* 532b4.
161. *Rep.* 532c.
162. *Rep.* 532e.
163. *Rep.* 532d.
164. *Rep.* 533b1-6.
165. *Rep.* 533b6-c5; see p. 290.
166. *Rep.* 533c-d.
167. *Rep.* 534a.
168. *Rep.* 534b.
169. *Rep.* 534b8-c.
17c. *Rep.* 534d8-10.
171. *Rep.* 534c6.
172. *Rep.* 413b, cf. 412c.
173. *Rep.* 534c7.
174. *Rep.* 534e.
175. *Rep.* 535a, cf. 412d-e, 485-7, 503c-e.
176. *Rep.* 535a-536b.
177. *Rep.* 412d f.
178. *Rep.* 498a.
179. *Rep.* 536d.
180. *Rep.* 536e.
181. *Rep.* 537a.
182. See pp. 253-4.
183. *Rep.* 536d7, cf. 530b6, 531c2.
184. *Rep.* 537b.
185. *Rep.* 537b3.
186. *Rep.* 537c: ὁ μὲν γὰρ συνοπτικὸς διαλεκτικός.
187. *Rep.* 537d.
188. *Rep.* 537d3.
189. *Rep.* 537d5.
190. *Rep.* 539d8-e2; cf. the gymnasia in *Rep.* 537b3.
191. In *Parmenides* the purpose of the enquiry is expressly described as practice in dialectic, see 135c-d, 136a, 136c.
192. *Rep.* 498a-b.
193. *Ep.* 7.341c.
194. *Ep.* 7.344b.
195. *Rep.* 534c.
196. *Ep.* 7.344a.

197. *Rep.* 539e-540a.
198. See p. 234.
199. *Rep.* 537e-539d.
200. See pp. 56, 147.
201. J. Huizinga, *Homo ludens: Versuch einer Bestimmung des Spielelements der Kultur* (German tr. 1939), has gone into these problems with the subtlety of a philosopher. He treats the Greeks and Plato too; in fact, the questions he asks are really the repetition of a problem which only Plato could have stated, but with the addition of modern material. He goes far further than Plato in tracing all culture to the human instinct of play. It is remarkable that the Greeks were confronted by the problem of play just at the point when they reached the profoundest philosophical understanding of paideia, which they took so seriously. But since the beginning of time it has been natural for play to pass into the deepest earnest.
202. See p. 253.
203. Ar. *Eth. Nic.* 10.6.1176b28 f.
204. Plato, *Rep.* 539b, says that playful use of dialectic skill for the sake of sheer argument (ἀντιλογία) is misuse (καταχρῆσθαι). The logical opposite to play is earnest, σπουδή. See also 539c8.
205. *Rep.* 539b6.
206. *Rep.* 537e.
207. *Rep.* 538c f.
208. Xenocrates, frg. 3 Heinze.
209. *Rep.* 538d.
210. *Gorg.* 460e f.
211. *Rep.* 540a.
212. *Rep.* 540b.
213. *Rep.* 540c.
214. *Rep.* 540d.
215. *Rep.* 549b.
216. *Rep.* 540d.
217. *Rep.* 443e5.
218. *Rep.* 540e5 f.
219. *Rep.* 541a. On the idea that Plato's perfect state is a 'myth', see *Rep.* 376d9, 501e4.
220. *Rep.* 449a: Plato alludes to that passage in *Rep.* 543c9.
221. *Rep.* 544a.
222. *Rep.* 445c5.
223. *Rep.* 544c.
224. Ar. *Pol.* 4.1.
225. Cf. Ar. *Pol.* 3.7.
226. Books 7-8.
227. *Rep.* books 2-7.
228. *Rep.* books 8-9.
229. See p. 242.
230. See pp. 131, 145.
231. Cf. *Rep.* 444c-e.
232. See *Paideia* III, 18, 29.
233. *Rep.* 445c9-d6; cf. 544c f.
234. See especially *Ep.* 7.326a.
235. Aristotle carried the comparison between the methods of philosophy and those of gymnastics and medicine further, at the beginning of the fourth book

of his *Politics,* where he turns from the right to the faulty constitutions. The fundamental idea, however, is Platonic. Faulty constitutions, ἡμαρτημέναι πολιτεῖαι, are described as forms of sickness in *Rep.* 544c, and, before that, in 444d-445c.

236. *Rep.* 544d-545a.

237. *Rep.* 544d.

238. *Rep.* 544e5.

239. *Rep.* 443e6, 444e1.

240. This is the point of view which dominates the following analysis and interpretation; I may observe that commentators usually do it inadequate justice.

241. *Rep.* 545d.

242. *Rep.* 546a.

243. See *Paideia* I, 216.

244. Cf. *Rep.* 444d8-11.

245. Cf. Theophr. *De causis plant.* 5.8 f., especially the double meaning of the concept 'unnatural' (παρὰ φύσιν).

246. See p. 248 f.

247. *Rep.* 546b.

248. *Rep.* 546c.

249. *Rep.* 547c5.

250. Ar. *Pol.* 2.1.1260b names Sparta and Crete as countries whose constitutions are thought admirable (πόλεις εὐνομεῖσθαι λεγόμεναι): for the words at the beginning of the book refer to the description of these two states and of Carthage in chapters 9-11. See also the closing words of chapter 11. On the same problem in the *Protrepticus,* see the argument in my *Aristotle,* p. 77. Plato in *Rep.* 544c calls the Spartan and Cretan constitution 'praised by most people'. So does Isocrates, with regard to Sparta: *Panath.* 41, but see 109, 200, 216.

251. *Rep.* 545b6.

252. Cf. 547d. Even more important in this connexion is the direct criticism of the Spartan state in *The Laws,* books 1-2: see *Paideia* III, 218 f.

253. *Rep.* 547b.

254. *Rep.* 547c.

255. *Rep.* 547b-c.

256. *Rep.* 547d.

257. *Rep.* 547e-548a.

258. *Rep.* 548a-b.

259. *Rep.* 548b-c.

260. *Rep.* 548c9-d.

261. *Rep.* 548e4-549a.

262. *Rep.* 549a2. Between these two opposing ideas, Plato inserts a parenthesis: 'instead of being indifferent to slaves, as the truly cultured man is'. The ἱκανῶς πεπαιδευμένος does not lose his temper at the bad behaviour of slaves, as the Spartan does when he scolds them.

262a. It is easy to recognize this Spartan trait in Xenophon's ideal of culture.

263. *Rep.* 549a9-b7. It is in this context, when he is criticizing the Spartan type, that Plato coins the wonderful phrase λόγος μουσικῇ κεκραμένος ('rational and musical forces rightly harmonized') to illustrate what is lacking in an otherwise admirable character.

264. *Rep.* 549c-550b.

265. This new psychological method of describing types of state is one of Plato's greatest contributions to ethical and political science. It was naturally and logically produced by the shift of his interest from the state as a structure of positive law to its educational function and nature. The point of it is concentration on the

spirit (ἦθος) rather than the institutions of the state, for it is the spirit of the whole community that defines the typical structure of each individual. And in comparing the various constitutions, what chiefly interests Plato is the various types of individual they produce. For there was nothing particularly novel in his day about the difference in constitutions between one city and another. That also is why he could pass over the legal aspects of each constitution so easily.

265a. That is Aristotle's definition of the relation between state and individual, *Pol.* 1.2.1253a19, 1253a25.

266. According to Plato there is justice in the state when every citizen does his own work, performs his social function in the best possible way: but in *Rep.* 443c he says that that would really only be 'a sort of copy of justice', εἴδωλόν τι τῆς δικαιοσύνης—because real justice exists *only* in the internal structure of man, and in the right relation of the parts of his soul to one another, each part doing its own job.

267. *Rep.* 544d6-e2. There are the same number of types of men (εἴδη ἀνθρώπων) corresponding to the types of constitution, 'for constitutions do not spring up of themselves' (or, as Plato puts it, in a reminiscence of Homer, they 'are not born of oak and rock'), 'but grow out of the characters in each city,' which define the tendency of the state to one side or another. By ἐκ τῶν ἠθῶν τῶν ἐν ταῖς πόλεσιν Plato here does not mean the ethos of the constitution, but the characters of the citizens. That is why the five constitutions must correspond to five types of soul-structure (κατασκευαὶ ψυχῆς) which are their cause (544e4).

268. See p. 240.

269. *Rep.* 550b.

270. See *Paideia* III, 6 and 20.

271. *Rep.* 443d-e.

272. One could summarize Plato's judgment about this type of education in his own words in *Rep.* 548b7: it is education 'not by persuasion but by force' (οὐχ ὑπὸ πειθοῦς ἀλλ' ὑπὸ βίας πεπαιδευμένου).

273. Cf. Ar. *Pol.* 2.9.f., where there is an express allusion to the lessons of Leuctra and the period following it. On Isocrates see *Paideia* III, 108, 129.

274. See the section called 'Historical Tradition and the Philosophical Idealization of Sparta', in *Paideia* I, 79 f.

275. His attitude undergoes certain changes in *The Laws*. See *Paideia* III, 237.

276. *Gorg.* 481d. In 510b Socrates says that when a young uneducated tyrant rules the state, everyone who wants to remain alive must copy him and his opinions; and anyone who is better than he fares very badly. Plato is thinking not only of tyranny proper, but of all states with tyrannous rule, and, especially, of what happened to Socrates in Athens.

277. *Rep.* 564a.

278. *Rep.* 548a.

279. *Rep.* 550e-551a.

280. See *Paideia* I, 21 and 144. See also Pindar, *Ol.* 2.53.

281. For Aristotle see the two sections dealing with generosity (ἐλευθεριότης) and munificence (μεγαλοπρέπεια) in *Eth. Nic.* 4.1-3 and 4.4-6.

282. *Rep.* 550e-551a.

283. On Solon's attitude to wealth see *Paideia* I, 144 f., on Theognis *Paideia* I, 201 f.

284. *Rep.* 554a11.

285. *Rep.* 551c.

286. *Rep.* 551d-e.

287. *Rep.* 551e6.

288. *Rep.* 552a.

289. *Laws* 741a f.

290. Cf. *Rep.* 552a.

291. *Rep.* 552c.

292. *Rep.* 552e.

293. *Rep.* 553a-b.

294. *Rep.* 553b-c. What Plato thinks of as characteristic of the man who is turning into an oligarch, 'thrift and work' (553c3), sounds like a political slogan, and obviously is. We find it again in Isocrates' *Areopagiticus* 24, where it is regarded as an admirable utterance, and the principle of the πάτριος πολιτεία. But here Isocrates is speaking as representative of the 'moderate democrats', who were called 'oligarchs' by the radical democrats. The passage in Plato's *Republic* is a new proof of this. See *Paideia* III, 113.

295. Greed for money is always regarded by Plato as un-Greek, more accurately as Oriental. See *Laws* 747c.

296. *Rep.* 533d.

297. *Rep.* 550b.

298. *Rep.* 554b4.

299. *Rep.* 554b8.

300. *Rep.* 554c.

301. *Rep.* 554e.

302. *Rep.* 555a.

303. *Rep.* 555b.

304. See *Paideia* III, 6.

305. *Rep.* 555b9.

306. Κένωσις and πλήρωσις are medical concepts which played a great part in forming Plato's thinking: see *Phil.* 35b, *Symp.* 186c, et cetera. They are very important in the Hippocratic books.

307. See *Paideia* I, 146.

308. *Rep.* 555c.

309. *Rep.* 555d.

310. *Rep.* 556c-d.

311. *Rep.* 556e.

312. *Rep.* 557a. Isocrates takes the same view: see *Paideia* III, 113.

313. This is expressly emphasized by Isocrates (*Areop.* 21-22), whose political ideal was the Solonic form of democracy, 'the constitution of our ancestors': see *Paideia* III, 113-14.

314. Aristotle, *Pol.* 3.7.1279b4-10 distinguishes democracy from a politeia; and in *Pol.* 4.4.1291b15 f. he draws distinctions between several types of democracy.

315. *Ep.* 8.357a; see also 353e and 355d.

316. In *Menex.* 238b, Plato ascribes the virtues of the old Athenians who beat the Persians at Marathon, Salamis, and Plataea not so much to their constitution as to their paideia; see also 238c. In 241c he says the great thing they did was to teach the other Greeks the same spirit of fearlessness as themselves, by making them despise sheer masses of ships and men.

317. *Rep.* 557b.

318. *Rep.* 557b8.

319. *Rep.* 557d.

320. *Rep.* 557e.

321. *Rep.* 558a.

322. *Rep.* 558b.

323. See the whole of the pasage in the seventh Letter about Plato's attitude

to the contemporary state: 330d-331d, and particularly 331c6 on the correct relation of the philosopher to his own country. Here too his ideal of philosophical education is influenced by medicine: 330d.

324. For the part played by paideia as primal cause of this development, see *Rep.* 558d1, 559b9, 559d7, 560b1, 560e5, 561a3.

325. *Rep.* 558d9 f.

326. *Rep.* 559e-560b. Upbringing (τροφή) is here equivalent to paideia, for τρέφειν is a synonym for παιδεύειν.

327. *Rep.* 560b5.

328. *Rep.* 560b7.

329. *Rep.* 560c.

330. *Rep.* 560d. Aidos is evidently thought of as the secret adviser of the part of the soul which has been ruling hitherto: because of her influence on it she is particularly hated by the lusts which head the revolution.

331. Thuc. 3.82.4; see *Paideia* I, 335 f. Not only Plato here, but Isocrates in *Areop.* 20 is obviously influenced by Thucydides' analysis of political crises and their symptoms. This theory of crises was admirably suited to fit into Plato's medical conception of the processes taking place in the state and in the soul of the individual. In *Paideia* I, 392 f. we showed, in discussing Thucydides' treatment of the problem of the origin of the war, how strongly his thought was influenced by the model of medical science. Jakob Burckhardt, with his theory of political crises in world history, is a late representative of this school.

332. *Rep.* 561a.

333. *Rep.* 561c-d.

334. *Rep.* 562a.

335. *Rep.* 546a.

336. *Rep.* 562e.

337. *Rep.* 516c-d.

338. *Rep.* 562e-563a.

339. *Rep.* 563b-c.

340. *Rep.* 563e-564a.

341. Cf. *Rep.* 563e9, 565c9, 565e5.

342. *Rep.* 564b4-c1.

343. *Rep.* 564b6, cf. 552c.

344. *Rep.* 564c6-565d.

345. *Rep.* 565d-566a.

346. *Rep.* 566a-e.

347. *Rep.* 566e6-567b.

348. *Rep.* 567b12-c.

349. *Rep.* 567d-e.

350. *Rep.* 571a-b.

351. *Rep.* 571c-d.

352. *Rep.* 572b, cf. 571b.

353. See p. 248.

354. See p. 229 f. and *Rep.* 401d-402a.

355. *Rep.* 571d6-572a.

356. Iamblichus, *vit. Pyth.* 35.356 (p. 138.3-5 Deubner), where the parallel passages from ancient authors are given.

357. *Rep.* 572b.

358. Plato himself expressly recalls the analogous process in the education of the oligarchic man, which turns him into a democratic man: see *Rep.* 572b10-d3. But in describing earlier stages, he ascribed the change to the same cause. See pp. 327, 332, 340.

359. See *Paideia* I, 32, on Odysseus as a model for Telemachus; I, 217, where Pindar (Pyth. 6.29-30) says Xenocrates is a fine model for his son Thrasybulus; I, 8, on the teaching given by Hippolochus to his son Glaucus and by Peleus to his son Achilles. Socrates sometimes doubted whether fathers were capable of educating their sons properly; see supra p. 113.

360. *Rep.* 549c-e.
361. *Rep.* 549c.
362. *Rep.* 553a9-10.
363. *Rep.* 558c11-d2.
364. *Rep.* 572d8.
365. *Rep.* 572e.
366. *Rep.* 573a-b.
367. *Rep.* 573b-c.
368. *Rep.* 574b-d.
369. *Rep.* 574e-575a.
370. *Rep.* 575b-c.
371. *Rep.* 575d.
372. *Rep.* 575e-576a.
373. See p. 242.
374. *Rep.* 577a.
375. *Rep.* 577b.
376. *Rep.* 577c-578a.
377. *Rep.* 578b6-c.
378. *Gorg.* 466b-468e; see p. 133 f.
379. *Rep.* 567b.
380. *Rep.* 579d-e
381. *Rep.* 578e-579d.
382. *Rep.* 544a.
383. *Rep.* 443c-444a.
384. Aesch. *Pers.* 825; cf. 164.
385. So, for instance, in the phrase frequent in Xenophon and other writers: πόλις μεγάλη καὶ εὐδαίμων.
386. See my *Aristotle* 107.
387. See p. 152.
388. *Rep.* 444c f.
389. *Rep.* 580b-c. The 'kingly man' is here defined once more as the man who 'rules himself' (βασιλεύων αὑτοῦ). Rational knowledge of the Good is dominant in him. The allusion to freedom here is Socratic. The philosopher-king is the Socratic ideal. See p. 55 f.
390. *Rep.* 580d-582a.
391. *Rep.* 582a.
392. *Rep.* 582a-d.
393. *Rep.* 582d11: διὰ λόγων κρίνεσθαι.
394. *Rep.* 582e.
395. Aristotle *Eth. Nic.* 10.7 and 10.8.
396. See my essay *Ueber Ursprung und Kreislauf des philosophischen Lebensideals* (Berichte Berl. Akad. 1928).
397. *Rep.* 583b f.
398. *Rep.* 583c-584a.
399. *Rep.* 584c.
400. *Rep.* 584d-e. Similarly in *Protagoras* 356c and *Philebus* 41e Plato illus-

trates the difficulty of measuring the intensity of feelings of pleasure and pain
by the difficulty of judging distances.

401. *Rep.* 585a.
402. *Phil.* 24a f.
403. *Rep.* 585b. See p. 183.
404. *Rep.* 585b-c.
405. *Rep.* 585c-e.
406. *Rep.* 586a-c.
407. *Rep.* 586e.
408. *Rep.* 587a-e.
409. See p. 203 f.
410. *Rep.* 445a; cf. 444c-e.
411. *Rep.* 588b f.
412. *Rep.* 588c-d.
413. *Rep.* 588e-589b.
414. *Rep.* 589b. The passage also illustrates the difference between any type
of education intended to train men to be *men,* and mere 'lion-taming'. But from
the social standpoint, the latter is not less necessary, since pure humane education cannot be extended to all members of the state; it can exist only as education
for the rulers.
415. *Rep.* 590e; cf. 589d, 590d.
416. *Rep.* 500d.
417. *Rep.* 591e-592a.
418. *Rep.* 592a.
419. *Rep.* 592b.
420. Aristotle, *Pol.* 2, adopts this point of view about Plato's Republic, by
criticizing it chiefly for being impossible to realize. But Plato himself several
times points out that that is irrelevant to his purpose. This is not altered by
the fact that he tried to produce a philosophically educated ruler in Syracuse.
421. See *Paideia* I, 410.
422. See pp. 133, 145.
423. Cf. *Rep.* 592b: 'It is unimportant whether the perfect state exists anywhere,
or will exist in the future: for the just man fulfils the law of that state and of
no other'.
424. Aristotle in his *Politics* (3.4) explains, exactly like Plato, that the perfect
man and the perfect citizen are identical in the perfect state, and nowhere else.
In the real state, the best citizen is he who moulds himself most perfectly to
the spirit of his state (however imperfect that spirit may be in the absolute
sense), while the man who is absolutely best may appear to be a bad citizen
of his country. That is the point which the great Roman historian Niebuhr
raised against Plato: when he called him a bad citizen, he was judging him
by the standard of Demosthenes.

THE REPUBLIC

PART III

1. The education of the guards is based on right opinion (ὀρθὴ δόξα), not
on knowledge (ἐπιστήμη). Plato states this clearly when discussing the virtues
of the soldier class (the auxiliaries) and of the rulers, who are 'guards' in the
narrower sense. Courage, the specific areté of the soldiers, is defined as 'right

opinion about what is and what is not frightening' (*Rep.* 430b); for they have no knowledge of the good, and therefore do not possess the highest Socratic courage which depends on such knowledge. On the other hand, the rulers have knowledge and wisdom, and the state possesses wisdom only because they are part of the state (*Rep.* 428d-e).

2. *Rep.* 368d-e.

3. See p. 354.

4. *Rep.* 595b9.

5. *Rep.* 595c1, cf. 598d8.

6. See the discussion of the concept of artistic imitation (μίμησις) in *Rep.* 595c f.

7. Cf. the criticism of Homer as an educator, in *Rep.* 598e f.

8. Cf. Xenophanes frg. 9 Diehl: ἐξ ἀρχῆς καθ' Ὅμηρον ἐπεὶ μεμαθήκασι πάντες.

9. Cf. *Paideia* I, 295 f.

10. *Rep.* 606e: ὡς τὴν Ἑλλάδα πεπαίδευκεν οὗτος ὁ ποιητής.

11. Cf. *Rep.* 598e.

12. Socrates' description of the wealth of Homer's ideas in *Ion* 531c looks very like the one he gives in *Rep.* 598e. In 533e-534c he argues that Homer's knowledge is not founded on a τέχνη, i.e. specialist knowledge, and that the same applies to his interpreters (535a), who, like the poet himself, speak only from divine inspiration. This is really an attack on the sophists' theory that Homer was an educator because of his universal knowledge: although that theory is not expressly cited in *Ion* as in *The Republic* (598d-e: ἐπειδή τινων ἀκούομεν). It comes up again in Xen. *Symp.* 4.6.

13. Pseudo-Plutarch, *de vit. et poes. Hom.* 1073c f. sets out to prove that Homer did not only possess all the art of rhetoric, but was a master of philosophy and all the other arts too.

14. *Rep.* 595a5.

15. *Rep.* 592a11-b.

16. *Rep.* 595b6.

17. *Rep.* 595c f.

18. *Rep.* 596b.

19. *Rep.* 596e-597b.

20. *Rep.* 596d.

21. *Rep.* 597b-d.

22. *Rep.* 597d-e; cf. 599a, 599d2.

23. *Rep.* 599c.

24. *Rep.* 599d-600e3.

25. *Prot.* 316d f.

26. *Rep.* 600e5.

27. *Rep.* 601b.

28. *Rep.* 602a-b.

29. *Rep.* 602c7-d. On philosophy as the 'art of measurement', see pp. 120, 286.

30. *Rep.* 603c.

31. *Rep.* 603d-e.

32. *Rep.* 604b.

33. *Rep.* 604c-d.

34. *Rep.* 604d-605a.

35. *Rep.* 605b. The metaphor of feeding or nourishing (τρέφειν) here and in 606d4 shows the immediate influence of poetry on education; for, according to Plato (pp. 110, 268) all paideia is nourishment of the mind.

36. See p. 355.
37. *Rep.* 605b7.
38. *Rep.* 605c.
39. *Rep.* 605c10-d.
40. *Rep.* 605e.
41. *Rep.* 606a.
42. *Rep.* 606b-d.
43. *Rep.* 606e-607a.
44. *Rep.* 607b-c.
45. See p. 360.
46. *Rep.* 607d.
47. Cf. *Rep.* 607e-608b. Note the repetition of ἡ τοιαύτη ποίησις—i.e. 'all poetry of this type', all representative or imitative poetry. The phrase leaves the door open for other types of poetry. Cf. 607a4. In 608b1, and even before that in 605b7, there is another allusion to the 'state within us' as the aim and standard by which the limitations to be placed on poetry are defined.
48. See pp. 353-4.
49. Cf. *Rep.* 591e-592b.
50. *Rep.* 488b f.
51. *Rep.* 608c.
52. *Rep.* 592b: the true state exists as a paradeigma in heaven.
53. *Rep.* 608d-610e.
54. *Rep.* 611c-d.
55. *Rep.* 611e-612a.
56. *Rep.* 612d; and in this connexion see my discussion of the promise of praise for true areté in Tyrtaeus: *Paideia* I, 92 f.
57. See my analysis of the poem in *Tyrtaios über die wahre Arete* (Sitz. Berl. Akad. 1932) p. 537 f.
58. Plato's account of the honours paid to areté is in two parts: those paid to the just man in life (612d f.) and those paid to him in death (614a f.). The real novelty in this is the shift of emphasis from the honours given by society in this world, which are treated as rather unimportant, to those which he receives not as a social being, but as a free personality with an immortal soul. But earthly praise must not be entirely omitted. Apart from everything else, it must be brought in to continue the old tradition of city-state ethics, which had been finely expressed in poetry. Therefore all Plato says about the just man's place in society in this world is in the pattern set by ancient poetry. But it is all a little ironical.
59. Cf. Tyrtaeus frg. 9.31-32.
60. The passage treating of the praises given to the just man in this life deals with (a) the honours he receives from the gods (612e-613b) and (b) the honours he receives from men (613b9-614a).
61. *Rep.* 614e-615a.
62. *Rep.* 617d f.
63. Cf. *Rep.* 617e. The idea of ethical *choice* (αἱρεῖσθαι, αἵρεσις) appears at an early point in Plato's work, in connection with the problem of right *action* (πράττειν, πρᾶξις). This is a quite different conception from political election. Plato uses it first in *Apol.* 39a and *Crit.* 52c, where he is talking of Socrates as a perfect example of making a choice that affects one's whole life. In *Prot.* 356e and *Gorg.* 499e it appears for the first time as a general philosophical problem. In the *Gorgias* passage it is connected explicitly with 'action' in the pregnant sense; and in *Gorg.* 500a it is paraphrased by 'selection' (ἐκλέγεσθαι).

Both in *Protagoras* and in *Gorgias*, Plato means the choice of a means to attain an end (τέλος). He coins these concepts by hammering them out of the Greek language through dialectic. Aristotle took the same ideas and built his doctrine of the will (in the *Ethics*) upon them.

64. In *Rep.* 617c the three Moirai, the Fates, are called the daughters of Necessity, Ananké: this is brought out again in the interpreter's proclamation made for Lachesis in 617d6. The daemon is at first presented as the supreme power, which seems to exclude any possibility of free choice.

65. These arguments have been worked out more fully in my *Solons Eunomie* (Sitz. Berl. Akad. 1926): see also *Paideia* I, 144-145.

66. *Rep.* 380a-c.

67. *Rep.* 617d-e.

68. *Rep.* 619b.

69. See *Solons Eunomie* 73, and *Paideia* I, 142. Plato states the old theme that men think they are innocent and accuse tyché and the daemon: *Rep.* 619c: οὐ γὰρ ἑαυτὸν αἰτιᾶσθαι τῶν κακῶν ἀλλὰ τύχην καὶ δαίμονα. . . .

70. See the interpreter's words in *Rep.* 617e and 619b. On warnings in the theodicy of early Greek thinkers, see *Solons Eunomie* 76.

71. *Rep.* 620a.

72. *Rep.* 620c.

73. *Rep.* 618b f.

74. *Rep.* 615a, 621d.

75. *Rep.* 621c5.

INDEX

The following Index refers primarily to the text (problems, authors, and works found therein). It does not include a list of the exact passages quoted in the footnotes, but it does include the notes in so far as they discuss problems.

A

Academy, of Plato, 83, 100, 177, 274, 305, 307, 309
Academy, Platonic, of Lorenzo dei Medici, 77
Aeschylus, 27, 62, 71, 213, 218, 335, 369
Agathon, poet, 176, 185
Alcibiades, 29, 49, 97, 196, 270
Alcoholism, 346
Alétheia, 39
Alexander the Great, 256
Ananke, 368, 431
Anaxagoras, 30
Anonymus Iamblichi, 201, 401
Anthropomorphism, 213
Antiphon the Sophist, 141, 377, 391
Antisthenes, 17, 21, 26, 55, 63
Aphrodite, 408
Aporia, 91, 169
Arché (principle of being), 287, 290
Archelaus, physicist, 28, 375
Archilochus, 133
Archytas, mathematician, 307, 420
Areopagus, 52, 378
Areté (perfection, excellence), 18, 38, 369
  of soul and body, 44, 405
  and happiness, 44f.
  of old Athens, 52, 375
  'lady areté' (Prodicus), 53
  'political' virtue, 61, 70, 97, 127, 388
  the four civic virtues, 61f.
  object of early dialectic, 62
  'virtue in itself,' 64, 116
  virtue as knowledge, 64f., 91, ch. 7 passim, 161, 381
  intellectualism, 66
  unity of virtues, 66f., 392
  no one errs willingly, 67
  problem of, in Plato's early dialogues, 89f
  separate virtues, see ch. 4 passim, 116f., 160f.
  teachability of, 113f., 123f., 266, 396
  and cosmos, 146, 375

Areté (Cont.)
  acquiring, ch. 7 passim, 172, 394
  essence of, 162, 170, 171, 387, 394
  and social recognition, 204f., 401
  misrepresentation of, by poets, 219f.
  pathology of, 242
  and wealth, 330 f.
  parts of, 381
  Aristotle's hymn to, 382
  of body, 395, 407
  rewards of, 401, 430
Aristippus of Cyrene, 52, 382
Aristocracy, 113, 137, 176, 247f., 319
  citizenship in, 409
Aristophanes, 30, 100, 176, 373
  in Plato's Symposium, 185
Aristotle, 22, 48, 61f., 77, 81, 86, 101f., 143, 164, 165, 166, 174, 182, 201, 210, 222, 227, 243, 253, 256, 286, 297, 300, 307, 321, 324, 329, 330, 335, 350, 404, 410, 420, 422f.
Arnim, Hans von, 383, 385, 391, 397
Arts, fine, 227, 228, 244, 245
  nakedness in, 408
Askésis, 47, 53, 173
Aspasia, 27, 36, 52
Até, 368
Athens, 238, 246, 274, 325, 424, see Socrates, Democracy
  after capitulation, 3f.
  the state, 4f.
  state education in after Chaeronea, 7
  middle class, 27
  society (kaloi kagathoi), 28
  and Spartan discipline, 52
  areté of old, 52, 375, 425
  regeneration of, 52
  power politics, 141
  danger of intellectualism, 137
  and eros, 181
  youth of, 204
  no state education, 210
Augustine, 77
Autarkeia, 55, 379

433

Mathematics, 47, 166, 167, 168, 201, 289f., 306, 419
  various branches of, 302f.
  proportion, 288
  as propaideia, 301f., 310, 311
  humanistic nature of, 301
Measure
  art of, 120f., 130, 142, 160, 286, 362, 387, 429
  the most exact, 286
Medicine, 231, 232, 233, 249, 306, 333, 392, 394, 398, 405, 425, see Socrates, Plato
  and natural philosophy, 32
  and philosophical hypotheses, 32
  as model of techné, 131, 145, 321f.
  and eros, 182f.
  and norm, 183
  and political science, 321
Melancholy, 346
Menander, pref., 9
Metabasis, 325f.
Method, see Dialectic, ch. 7 passim, 178, 290, see Knowledge
  the word method, 64
  empirical method in medicine, 32f.
  metaphor of the way, 381
Middle Ages, 77
Miltiades, 145, 148
Mimnermus, 220
Moira, see θεία μοῖρα, θ. τύχη, 218, 368f., 431
Morphology of culture, pref., 84
Music, 199, 224, 359, 404, 405, see Gymnastic
  musical instruments, 226
  ancient theory of, 225
  harmony of, and gymnastics, 409
  ethos in, 227f.
  importance for education, 229
  harmony of, and logos, 423
Mysteries, 151, 187, 206, 293, 377, 417
Myth, see Plato

N

Natorp, Paul, 395
Natural science, see Philosophy
Nature
  concept of physis, 43f., 407
  concept of human, 133
  naturalism, 134
  physis and nomos, 138, 391
  and norm, 183, 322, 390
  norm and degeneration, 321f.
  teleological concept of, 324, 375
  human, 352
  κατά and παρά φύσιν, 390, 407
Neo-Kantianism, 81
Neo-Platonism, 77

Nettleship, R. L., 400
Nietzsche, see Socrates
Norden, E., 403
Nous, 290

O

Oedipus complex, 343
Oligarchs, 390, 394, 425, 426
Oligarchy, 330f.
Orient, 42f., 53, 299
Orphism, 142, 151, 152, 368, 394
  and Socrates, 42
  religiosity of, 43
Οὐσία, 164, 166, 392

P

Paideia
  Athens as cultural center, 4
  dominating position of, 5f.
  struggle for, 9f.
  intellectual, and gymnasium, 34f.
  and God, 8, 376, see God
  subjects of sophistic, 47
  moral and intellectual, 48
  military, 50f., see Soldiers
  and Areopagus, 52
  must be 'political,' 49f., see Political, Politics
  education of leaders, 52, see Rulers
  liberal education, 55, 112
  as friendship, 58f., 111, see ch. 8 passim, 380
  Socrates doubts about, 59
  educational eros, see Eros, 60, 176, 177, 178, 180, 191, 400
  and talent, 60
  against cultural snobbery, 60
  and book learning, 61, 375
  and telos of life, 69
  Stilpo on, 70
  Menander on, pref. ix
  Plato and, 84f.
  and science, 85
  educational aspect of Plato's works, 105
  sophistic and technical, 109, 269f.
  average education, 109
  as political art, 112, 113, 154
  educational optimism, 113
  age of pedagogy, 114
  weakness of sophistic, 114
  Socratic and sophistic, see ch. 5 passim
  and knowledge, see ch. 5, 6, 7, passim
  and rhetoric, see ch. 6 passim
  by persuasion, by force, 424
  educator as statesman, 126, 200f.
  against power, 139f.